Adult male survivors of childhood sexual abuse

Other titles from Pitman include:

NSPCC: *Child Sexual Abuse: Listening, Hearing and Validating the Experience of Children* by Corinne Wattam, John Hughes and Harry Blagg
NSPCC: *Listening to Children: The Professional Response to Hearing the Abused Child* edited by Anne Bannister, Kevin Barrett and Eileen Shearer
NSPCC: *From Hearing to Healing: Working with the Aftermath of Child Sexual Abuse* edited by Anne Bannister
NSPCC: *Making a Case in Child Protection* by Corinne Wattam
NSPCC: *Key Issues in Child Protection for Health Visitors and Nurses* edited by Christopher Cloke and Jane Naish
NSPCC: *Child Speak: Children, Trauma and Social Work* by Ian Butler and Howard Williamson
NSPCC: *Participation and Empowerment in Child Protection* edited by Christopher Coke and Murray Davis
Making Sense of the Children Act (2nd edition) by Nick Allen
Female Sexual Abuse of Children: The Ultimate Taboo edited by Michele Elliott
Looking After Young People in the Care System by Pat Goodall, Tony Laughland, Simon Biggs and Fergus Smith
Getting Started with NVQ: Tackling the Integrated Care Awards by Barry Meteyard
Young People and Drugs: A Multi-Disciplinary Training Manual by Carr and Rosie Higgins
Answers: A Handbook for Residential and Foster Carers Looking After Young People Aged 11–13 Years by Ann Wheal and Anne Buchanan
Management and Delivery of Social Care by Max Taylor and Christine Vigars
Diversion from Custody for Mentally Disordered Offenders by Catherine Staite, Neill Martin, Michael Bingham and Rannoch Daly
Child Care Law for Practitioners in Social Work, Health and Education edited by Nick Allen
Competence in Youth Work for Part-Time Youth Workers by Mark Price and Rosemary Napper

Social Services Training Manuals

First Line Management: Staff by Kevin Ford and Sarah Hargreaves
Effective Use of Teambuilding by Alan Dearling
Manual on Elder Abuse by Chris Phillipson and Simon Biggs
Developing Training Skills by Tim Pickles and Howie Armstrong
Training for Mental Health by Thurstine Basset and Elaine Burrel
Monitoring and Evaluation in the Social Services by David and Suzanne Thorpe
Quest for Equality by Errol John and Barbara Deering
Care Sector Quality: A Training Manual Incorporating BS5750 by Steve Casson and Clive George

Adult male survivors of childhood sexual abuse

by

Kim Etherington

PITMAN PUBLISHING
128 Long Acre, London WC2E 9AN

A Division of Pearson Professional Limited

First published in Great Britain 1995

British Library Cataloguing in Publication Data
A CIP catalogue record for this book can be obtained from the British Library.

ISBN 0 273 61656 0

10 9 8 7 6 5 4 3 2 1

Typeset by Northern Phototypesetting Co Ltd, Bolton
Printed and bound in Great Britain by Bell and Bain Ltd, Glasgow

The Publishers' policy is to use paper manufactured from sustainable forests.

This book is dedicated to male survivors everywhere and especially the men who have allowed me to publish their stories.

Contents

Acknowledgements viii

PART 1

1 Introduction 3
2 Sexual abuse: definitions, prevalence and the abusers 13
3 Theories of sexual development 27
4 Male socialisation 32
5 Effects of childhood sexual abuse on male sexuality 43
6 Findings of research study 53

PART 2

7 The rent-boys' stories 95
8 The paedophiles' stories 120
9 The teacher/lover's boy 146
10 Abuse by mothers 156
11 Abuse by fathers 171
12 Abuse by sisters 194
13 Men raped as adults 213
14 Men abused by people known to them who were not family members 230
15 Abuse and patriarchal institutions 245

PART 3

16 Martin's story 273
17 Therapeutic journal: Kevin's story 293
18 Therapeutic work for sexually abused adult males 302

References 323

Acknowledgements

I would like to acknowledge the contributions made to this book by the men who have allowed me to tell their stories. Without their co-operation, courage and honesty this book would not have been possible and the shroud of silence that has cloaked acts of abuse would remain undisturbed: it is this silence that ensures the perpetuation of child abuse and upon which abusers depend. The men whose stories are told here are using their own negative experiences for the benefit of others and I thank them for that.

Many other people have contributed to my learning about this subject – not least my clients and students on courses I have taught. My personal learning and development has been supported and encouraged by numerous people over the last few years particularly Hazel Johns, Hazel Russell, Constance Nightingale (now deceased), Jane Mayers and Phyllida Parsloe. There are many others too numerous to name.

There have been times during the research, preparation and writing for this book when I have felt dispirited and angry and my belief in the goodness of mankind has been shaken; the love, kindness and care shown to me by my family has allowed me to balance these views and restore my faith. Lastly I wish to acknowledge the importance of my husband's belief in my ability to succeed in this work and his unstinting practical help with typing, printing and formating.

Part 1

1 Introduction

A personal perspective

All of my life I have been closely surrounded by males. I was born into a family of five boys and two more were born after me. 'The only girl' was so much a part of my identity that I soon developed a view of myself as different from the norm, special and even odd! I married at the age of 22 and by the age of 23 I had yet another male in my life – my first born son; three years later another son was born and nine years later, my third son was born. So it is perhaps understandable that males are important to me!

Both of my parents were Southern Irish Roman Catholics, so I was exposed to a double dose of cultural influences steeped in patriarchy. My mother taught me that, as a female, my role was to serve the males in the family. I was clearly inferior and my needs, if indeed I had any, were to come behind those of my father and my brothers; I was there to meet their needs and indeed, hers too. I grew up with a confusion of feelings of rage at the unfairness of it all and the feeling that in some way I was failing as a female if I were even to entertain such ideas. Another confusion was that, because I was 'special', I was treated, in some ways, as though I was superior to the boys. The local school was not good enough for me so I was sent to a private Convent Preparatory School where the emphasis was on sewing, elocution, prayer and ladylike behaviour. My brothers saw me as 'spoiled' by my father because I was clearly his favourite and I was given many of the material things they were deprived of, thus creating divisions between us and guilt in me because I knew this was not fair on them.

Much of my life has been spent trying to undo the negative influences of these and other early struggles within my family of origin, and as a mother I have worked hard to ensure that my sons will not be socialised into extreme gender roles that will cause them similar problems. Perhaps it has been easier for me than it was for my parents because of the societal changes in gender role expectations that have been slowly evolving since the impact of the women's movement started people thinking about the imbalance in the relationships between men and women. It may also have been easier because I have not had a daughter, and therefore, have not been 'tested' in that way!

The immersion in patriarchy in my first social environment, my family, is reflected in the wider society where patriarchy might be said to be everywhere and nowhere – like the air we breathe, so much part of our everyday existence that it is hard to identify in concrete terms, but we know it is there. So it was from this background that I set out to explore the experiences of males who have been sexually abused during childhood.

A professional perspective

My professional interest in the subject of this book has developed out of working as a counsellor/psychotherapist with, amongst others, adult survivors of childhood sexual abuse. As well as working therapeutically with women survivors, I have created courses which I have taught for the University of Bristol for other counsellors/therapists, whose case loads reflected a growing number of people wanting to work-through issues related to their childhood sexual abuse. Rarely do survivors present with sexual abuse as their problem; this is something that sometimes emerges painfully from behind depression, anxiety, addiction and other ways that people have used to cope with their pain. In almost every area of work there seem to be survivors of childhood sexual abuse; drug and alcohol services; social services; mental health clinics; AIDS and HIV treatment centres; and private counselling practices.

The growth of the women's movement allowed women to challenge their roles in relation to men and society in general. This in turn has caused men to examine their own roles; the inflexibility that patriarchy has imposed on them, particularly in terms of the societal stereotypes that have kept men from owning their vulnerability; and the possibility of sexual victimisation that may have been part of some males' experiences.

Men began to realise that some of what women were saying also applied to them and in recent years some of them have followed the example laid down by women and have begun to speak out about their childhood experiences of sexual abuse. What also became apparent was that little was known about male survivors and what was known seemed to be shrouded in mythology with few facts to base it on; so my research began. Much of what I read was contradictory and confusing, so I decided to find out for myself in the way that I work best; listening to the men who knew best, to the male survivors themselves; finding out what the experience of sexual abuse in childhood meant to them.

Historical perspective

It is a comparatively short time since professionals ceased to question the reality of childhood sexual abuse which is now acknowledged by most to be widespread. Masson (1984) found letters and documents indicating that Freud and others knew of such events even before the nineteenth century. When Freud presented a lecture entitled 'The Aetiology of Hysteria' to the Vienna Society for Psychiatry and Neurology on 21 April 1896, he spoke of his belief that childhood sexual abuse was at the root of psychological disturbances in some of his adult patients. He was treated with scepticism and professionally ostracised because of the unacceptability of his idea to the society of which he was a part; that sexual abuse was far more prevalent than had been previously realised. He wrote of his pain following the alienation from his colleagues:

> I am as isolated as you could wish me to be: the word has been given out to abandon me, and a void is forming around me, (quoted by Masson 1984, p.104).

The feelings expressed in this sentence seem to mirror so well the feelings of the child who tries to disclose sexual abuse and is not believed and because of this disbelief changes his statement. In response to these feelings of isolation Freud then changed *his* statement and created a theory that was more socially acceptable; he proposed that what he was hearing from his patients were the fantasies that were created in the minds of those who had an unfulfilled wish for a sexual relationship with their father, thus contributing to the denial and suppression of the reality of childhood sexual abuse for many years to follow. Paradoxically, had Freud insisted on his original theory he may never have been taken seriously in his subsequent work which has made an enormous contribution to the understanding of the psychological ego defence mechanisms and has been of great value to generations of victims of childhood abuse. It would seem that he was too soon with his realisations for them to be heard and accepted.

Miller (1984) describes the need for readiness when she says:

> People don't want to listen because they are not ready to bear what they hear. That is justifiable, for to achieve genuine insight is a slow process in which intellectual knowledge plays only a small part (p.304).

Nowadays we may be willing to concede that girls may be at risk of sexualisation by their fathers and other males, but resistance still exists to the claims that include victimisation of boys, women who are victimisers; and the bizarre ritualistic sexual abuse of boys and girls. However, research studies show that boys *and* girls are abused and that women abuse as well as men and that some therapists have reported finding ritual abuse in the childhood of about one fifth of their adult patients diagnosed as having 'multiple personality disorder' (Braun 1986); and that sex rings have been uncovered in Great Britain which involve boys and girls, separately or together, in bizarre ritualistic sexual abuse (Christopherson 1990). Since the spread of the AIDS virus an additional concern is felt for children involved in sex rings, which clearly increases their risk of them becoming infected (Bennetts, Brown and Sloan 1992).

Freud found several female perpetrators in his original research; of the eighteen victims he described, six were males. Freud himself wrote of his sexualisation by his nurse (Gay 1989) and Goldwert (1986) proposes that two of his disciples in the psycho-analytical circle, Jung and Rank, were themselves possibly victims of sexual abuse. The study of paedophiles establishes an overwhelming, often exclusive, preference of boys, leading Abel (1987) to believe that hidden boy victims must outnumber girl victims as paedophiles often engage in sexual activities with dozens of children over any period of time.

We will never know many people resist or deny the idea of sexual abuse because they have never come to grips with their own victimisation. Any group of which we are a part will probably include people who have been sexually abused as children; they might have been terrified, ecstatic or a confusion or mixture of these feelings; perhaps the fact that they cannot talk about it says something about our collective rejection of knowledge of the subject. Some people still react as if victims are abnormal or freaks; some close ranks against the discomfort of knowing the unknowable, not because we know enough about it already, but because what we already know sometimes feels like too much.

Not only victims are circulating unknown among us but also those who perpetrate such abuses. Paradoxically, they may be part of the body of people who are sitting in the ranks of the jury, judges, police officers, policy makers who make decisions for the protection of our society; they may protect the perpetrators, they may be judgemental and accusing of victims; they may appear dismissive of the problem in order to distance themselves from their own unacknowledged victimisation. The recent allegations made against Peter Righton, a man who reached the highest ranks of the social work educational system, highlight the fact that many paedophiles use their position of power and influence to create situations which allows them access to some of the most vulnerable children who are meant to be in the care of society.

Psychosocial perspectives

Generalisations about the effects of abuse on male survivors are difficult to make because largely they are unidentified, unknown and under-researched. Comparatively few studies have been made on the effects of childhood sexual abuse on males. It has been suggested that males are more reluctant than females to report abuse due to a cultural bias and negative connotations associated with homosexuality. Those studies that have been made indicate that one of the most powerful and damaging influences of sexual abuse on men has been the long-term effects on their sexuality.

Observation, clinical reports and the limited research findings available, suggests that most, if not, all male victims have some characteristics and behaviours in common, but may vary widely in others. In addition, men not known to have been sexually abused as children sometimes display behaviours associated with the effects of childhood sexual abuse. There are still many questions that have not been answered and little research that can be held up as methodologically unflawed. Children's lives are influenced by many variable factors; it is rarely possible to make definite causal attributions about adult behaviour based on childhood experiences. Maybe the best we can hope for is the awareness of possibilities.

When boys are sexually abused, gender and sexual issues include those related to fears about being homosexual; gender and sexual identity confusion; feelings of inadequacy as a male and fears about being effeminate; sexual compulsion, sexual addiction, and hypersexuality; and avoidance of sexual activity. Some male victims experience all of these outcomes, while others may experience few or none.

Although research carried out on known offenders identifies that some victims of childhood sexual abuse become rapists, child molesters and murderers, most do not. Although research has linked this range of outcomes to the effects of childhood sexual abuse, a significant number of such offenders are not known to have been sexually abused in childhood. However, these men may have experienced other forms of childhood abuse. Such findings suggest that psychological damage may underlie the effects of all forms of childhood maltreatment. Underlying psychological damage may be linked to a variety of outcomes, some of which are related to sexuality and some of which are not.

However, most of the research has been on samples of convicted sex offenders. The numbers of men in society at large who have been sexually abused as children and have never offended, either sexually or otherwise, are not known. The silent majority of victimised men are unlikely ever to tell their stories in public. In an effort to redress this inbalance it is my intention to give a few of these men a voice through my book – a small voice which added to those of others can, in time, be heard.

Focus

This book aims to bring together the data so far accumulated about the sexual abuse of males, the sexual development of male survivors and their perceptions of the effects of their abuse on their adult lives. I shall explore these issues in order to enhance the understanding of therapists, counsellors, social workers, probation officers, doctors and others who may be engaged in the process of dealing with or alleviating, the possible effects, as well as for the survivors themselves and their friends and families.

The book will provide an opportunity for an examination of differences and similarities between men who have been abused by males and men who have been abused by females, and the specific impact of the gender of the perpetrator on males who have been sexually abused.

The connection between childhood sexual abuse and the development of male sexuality is largely unexplored and male's experiences with these issues is under-represented in the literature. This book therefore hopes to add to this knowledge base by highlighting, through the personal histories of adult male survivors of childhood sexual abuse, the fears, struggles and misgivings they may be dealing with as an outcome of their experiences of abuse in childhood. The psychosocial and sexual development of males has been explored to provide a context within which to view how childhood sexual abuse might interfere with or change that development and to raise awareness of how the dynamics of abuse might be negatively exaggerated by the socialisation process and effects of male gender stereotyping.

Sexuality, for the purposes of this book, is conceptualised as the way a person defines himself as a sexual being; a personal definition and not one imposed by an external authority. The term denotes the person's view of their sexual identity, orientation, behaviours and emotional attachments. Sexual identity denotes an acceptance of oneself as a sexual being as congruent with the self-concept (Coleman 1987). If a person feels stigmatised by identification with a stigmatised group he may find this troubling and incongruent with his self-concept; for example a man with a disability may try to pass as non-disabled because he perceives the minority group as stigmatising. Homophobia is another type of stigma related to group membership. Sexual orientation is not a synonym for sexual identity. Sexual orientation describes an individual's erotic and affectional interests and attachments but does not imply an acceptance of those. Some people experience a lack of congruence between sexual orientation and self-concept and may experience sexual identity confusion. When the person accepts whatever orientation he experiences, then that person can be said to have assumed a sexual identity.

Men who have been sexually abused as children are sometimes confused about their sexual identity; sexual abuse may complicate the development of sexuality, depending on such factors as the age and stage of development of the child at the time of the abuse, the gender and relationship of the abuser to the child and the nature and duration of the abuse. Each individual has his own way of dealing with the abuse and therefore each case is likely to be different.

Silent suffering and homophobia have been identified in most cases studied and these may be seen to be the outcomes of the impact on males of societal taboos around male vulnerability, incest and homosexuality. This book therefore, will examine issues within the framework of patriarchy and homophobia; both likely to exacerbate the negative impact on males of disclosing, owning and working through their experiences of childhood sexual abuse. Increased research into male sexual abuse survivors might provide some answers to the questions concerning the possibility that child sexual abusers may have been themselves abused as children and that abuse lies at the root of the cycle of inter-generational abuse. This has ramifications for our understanding of how this cycle may be arrested and eventually prevented; the ultimate rationalisation and justification for research into this topic.

As a therapist my fundamental belief is that there is a need for more information about this subject so that counsellors and other helpers may inform their practice and provide access to suitable services; I share the idea put forward by Fraiberg, et al. (1975), that it is by creating an opportunity for men to feel and work through the pain of their own abuse in a supportive environment that we may have a chance to help them break the cycle of abuse. Perhaps we can help best when we have a good enough understanding of the dynamics and outcomes of the sexual abuse of male children and adolescents.

Finally, I shall outline the contents of the following chapters in order to provide the reader with a sense of what follows. I have divided the work into three parts and Part 1 consists of Chapters 1-6 which provide an overview of what has already been written by others with some comment and criticism from me and a presentation of my research findings.

Chapter 2 begins with a review of the literature concerning definitions, prevalence and the characteristics of the abusers, both male and female. Chapter 3 presents a review of the literature concerning theories of male sexual development. In Chapter 4 the literature concerning male socialisation is explored within the framework of patriarchy; and Chapter 5 examines the literature on the effects of childhood sexual abuse on the sexual development of males.

Chapter 6 presents the findings of my research study comprising in-depth interviews with twenty-five men who were sexually abused during childhood. None of these men would be included in any statistics on prevalence as their abuse was never reported to the statutory agencies at the time or since it happened. One man did inform a social worker who told him that females did not abuse and two others told parents who did not report it. I have formulated some tables to bring together some of the variables. The former part of this chapter deals with the factual demographic data which I have attempted to arrange in ways that might make some comparisons possible. The latter part of this chapter deals with the issues arising from male socialisation within a patriarchal society.

In Part 2, which contains Chapter 7–15, I have presented the interviews as a basis for the discussion of particular themes that have emerged out of the analysis of the research interviews. Chapter 7 deals with the stories of Harry and Mike who became rent-boys; two very different stories showing how adolescent boys become caught up in the twilight world of male prostitution, pimping, drugs and alcohol. Harry grows up to become a probation officer working the same patch in the West End with child prostitutes years after he started out there as a rent-boy. He tells of his flamboyant lifestyle and the development of his homosexual orientation. Mike tells of his progress from Borstal boy to drug addict and pimp. I have explored the application of two major theories of psychosocial and patriarchal explanations in relation to these cases.

In Chapter 8 I have presented the stories of George and Robert, two men who became paedophiles in adult life having been sexually abused in childhood by several people; one is a regressed paedophile and the other a fixated paedophile. Both men have abused their own child as well as others.

Chapter 9 presents Clem's story; a man abused during adolescence by his teacher's girlfriend. This story highlights the way in which sex-role stereotyping prevented him from acknowledging his abuse until his adult behaviour had caused him so much trouble – suicide attempts, a court martial, the breakdown of three marriages and the destruction of his business – that he had to face up to it.

In Chapter 10 we meet Harold, Paul and Roy, three men who were abused by their mothers. These stories highlight the difficulty in definition when the perpetrator is the person whose love is most needed. Harold had blocked all memory of his abuse; Roy tells of how his abuse was a continuation of his own mother's experience of having been abused by her stepfather. Paul tells of how he cannot admit to what happened as abuse but has to see it as 'over-loving'.

Chapter 11 presents the issue of abuse by fathers. Tim and Wayne tell two very different stories – one developed into a 'macho' man who has problems with his relationships with women – the other, a terrified person who was labelled as mentally ill, abused drugs and lived in a squat for years.

Chapter 12 concerns Sam and William men who were abused by sisters. Sam, aged 21, is in prison for his thirteenth offence of burglary. He shows how a young person, neglected and deprived of the right kind of caring, can seek comfort through drugs and sex in a children's home. William described how he uses an obsessive fantasy and the involvement of an animal in his self-abuse to cope with his childhood sexual abuse and the effect of that.

Chapter 13 examines the stories of two men who were raped as adults as well as during childhood. Both stories highlight some of the unhelpful attitudes that these men experienced in their contacts with helping professionals and how societal attitudes can re-victimise people.

Chapter 14 presents Jeremy and Justin, men who were abused by people known to them who were not family members. Both men used sexually based antisocial behaviour as a way of acting out their own abuse. Jeremy abused other children when he was a pre-pubertal child and became addicted to drugs; Justin became an adolescent flasher. Both stories demonstrate the deeply felt anger that an abused child carries into adulthood.

Chapter 15 focuses on the stories of Tony and Len, uncovering abuse by monks and priests and the contribution that patriarchal institutions make to perpetuating the damage. Tony who is an ex-priest and monk, had also been abused as a small child by his mother. Issues such as celibacy, homosexuality and secrecy are addressed here.

Part 3 presents issues relating to the recovery of males who have been sexually abused in childhood. Martin's story is presented in Chapter 16 and is followed by a discussion of the False Memory Syndrome and issues relating to disclosure. There will always be those people who read such first person accounts as I have presented and question their veracity. As a therapist I work with what the client brings; it is not my remit to judge the client's story or look for proof. As a researcher the veracity is in my presentation of the subject's story as true to his telling of his experience and this is what I have aimed for. The need for proof only arises when litigation is involved and it has been since survivors have started to seek retribution through the courts that such questions have become a burning issue.

Chapter 17 consists of part of a therapeutic journal kept by Kevin, a man who had repressed all knowledge of his mother's abuse until adulthood.

Chapter 18 identifies some of the pertinent issues related to working with males who have been sexually abused in childhood.

I hope that what I have presented in total will enable further understanding of a complex and difficult area. I now understand why comparatively little research has been done into this issue. The problems in finding subjects who were willing to come forward; the difficult ethical issues I faced on occasions; the pain and sadness of sharing such powerful stories, both as teller and receiver; the complexities of theories that ran parallel, intertwined and interwove and the decisions about how to present the material in ways that were true to the story teller's experience – all these have contributed what has been a difficult and rewarding experience.

Sometimes it has been hard to make the decision about whether or not to repeat exact details of the subject's experience when I have wondered if the language that has been used and the graphic portrayal of the events might cause some people offense. I have had to draw a fine line between voyeurism and the valuable presentation of stories which need to be told if the sexual abuse of male children is to be understood for the horror and evil it is. At no time has my intention been to offend or corrupt by the way I have presented the material. I leave the reader to be the judge of that.

2 Sexual abuse: definitions, prevalence and the abusers

Definitions of childhood sexual abuse

One definition used by the DHSS in their 1986 document *Child abuse – working together*, is that sexual abuse is:

> The involvement of dependent, developmentally immature children or adolescents in sexual activities they do not truly comprehend, and to which they are unable to give informed consent and that violate the sexual taboos of family roles.

Researchers usually define the age differences between abusers and victim as needing to be of five years or more. However, with recent concern about younger perpetrators, Johnson (1988; 1989) has advocated a two year age difference, along with other criteria, to define sexual activities that are clearly abusive.

Cantwell (1988) has advocated a definition for perpetrators of child sexual abuse focused entirely on the behavioural component and without specifying an age criterion. Thus subjecting a child to oral-genital contact or penetration of the vagina or anus with fingers or objects would be regarded as abusive whatever the age differential.

The term 'sexualized attention' has been used to describe the interface between clearly abusive and more appropriate interaction between adults and children, (Haynes-Seman and Krugman 1989). They suggest that this seems to depend on the affective state of the adult at the time (although this might be out of awareness) and whether they experience sexual arousal from such behaviour. Studies by Chasnoff et al.(1986) clearly indicate that there can be considerable impact on a very young infant, who may previously have been thought to have been unaffected by such behaviour, when a parent behaves in a sexualised manner. They describe three cases of maternal neonatal incest which took place during the first months of the child's life. Two of these children showed behavioural abnormalities at a later stage with excessive sexual aggression in their relationships with other children. Although this was a very small sample this view is supported by the work of Sroufe and Ward (1980) and Hewitt (1990) who suggest that seductive behaviour of mothers towards very small children can be associated with later behavioural difficulties.

Lawson (1993) proposes a model of maternal sexual abuse that I would agree with:

> subtle, seductive, perversive, overt and sadistic maternal sexual abuse (although these categories could be applied to parents of both sexes). Subtle abuse includes: behaviours that do not involve coercion; may or may not involve genital contact; are not intended by the mother to harm the child; may result from the mother's belief that the child needs such special attention; or may be the result of the mothers own unconscious need for sexual gratification. Subtle abuse is defined as behaviours that may not intentionally be sexual in nature but serve to meet the parent's emotional and/or sexual needs at the expense of the child's emotional and/or developmental needs (p.261)

Another category of abuse which has been excluded from previous studies may occur when a parent emasculates a child or humiliates him sexually. This may be seen more clearly as a form of emotional abuse and may or may not be in conjunction with physical abuse. A mother's rejection of a male child's sexuality may be an expression of her rejection of males in general or in particular when she may have been sexually abused herself.

None of the above definitions are in themselves adequate in my view, but taken jointly they may serve as a useful baseline which, as a therapist, I would use as filters for my understanding of what my client's experiences meant for them. I have always emphasised that it is the client's subjective experience of their life that decides whether or not it has been abusive but since working with adult males I have realised that definition from an external source can be a necessary part of their process of recovery. It is only in allowing themselves to acknowledge their childhood victimisation that they can work through and heal the abused child within. Men who have been taught to be tough and not to complain may need an outside observer to interpret what happened to them as abuse before they can allow themselves to see it in that way. In the same way that a person with a physical disability might need a diagnosis in order to be able to gain access to the right treatment, a victim of childhood sexual abuse may need to be able to define his experience before knowing how to gain access to help and understanding.

My own view echoes that of Urquiza and Keating (1990) who say that:

> given the wide range of sexual experiences (both appropriate and abusive) in which an individual may become involved during childhood and the many contexts and meanings for these experiences, it is doubtful that such a (clear) definition will ever be adopted, or if adopted, will provide any meaningful contribution to the field of family violence. Therefore, it is essential to note that problems of definition are a significant source of error in determining prevalence rates and that all stated rates are only an estimate (p.93)

If we acknowledge that prevalence rates are only estimates of the numbers of males that have been sexually abused, several uniquely male specific factors need to be addressed. The lack of definition of male sexual abuse is, I believe, related to factors associated with male socialisation within our society. Society's reluctance to view males, especially adolescent males as victims, must influence the definition of male sexual abuse. Finkelhor (1984) says that in general men view the impact of child sexual abuse to be less serious than women do. If that is the case then this view can be seen to influence the way they might interpret their own experiences as less serious. This position has been supported by research suggesting that boys rate their abusive experiences less negatively than do girls. Given these perceptions, it is less likely for men to view themselves as victims. It may be that only men who have irrefutable evidence through the involvement of others, such as social services and law enforcement agencies, or those whose abuse has been very severe, who define themselves as sexually abused.

Prevalence

In Britain there has been little research into childhood sexual abuse and our information is gained mostly through the literature published abroad. However, awareness has grown out of the publicity and media coverage of well-documented cases such as the Cleveland Enquiry (Butler-Sloss 1988) and the setting up of Childline in the United Kingdom. Hereward Harrison, the Director of ChildLine, writing in Elliot (1993), states that a child who rings ChildLine will not often refer directly to sexual abuse but will speak initially of general difficulties with parents and others. This leads him to believe that:

> the way children report, and talk about, sexual abuse may very well lead to an underestimate of the number of children who are sexually abused and an over-simplification of statistical information collected by the helpline (p.95)

Recent research figures (NSPCC,1990b) involving an interview survey of a 'nationally representative' sample of all adults over 15-years-of-age in Britain are that 12 per cent of females and 8 per cent of males were sexually abused in childhood. The NSPCC, on the basis of the number of children registered with them, estimate the national incidence in England and Wales of childhood sexual abuse for children under 14-years-of-age is 5,850 and 6,600 for children under 16 years. Of the registered cases 78 per cent involve female children and 22 per cent involve males.

The annual report from an organisation called Survivors (a charitable self-help organisation set up to offer counselling and support to any male victim of sexual abuse), gives a breakdown of clients seen by a sessional worker at St. Mary's Hospital in London during 1992 (Woollett 1993). Of the seventy men seen just under 75 per cent were abused before the age of 16. 10 per cent were abused by females; 14.28 per cent were under 5-years-old. Of the forty-nine or 70 per cent abused between the ages of 5 to 15 years the breakdown was as follows:

5/6	7/8	8/9	11/12	13/15
11.42%	21.42%	12.85%	10%	14.28%

The average time lapse between the abuse and seeking help for men in the 5/15 age group was twenty years. Over 59 per cent of these men had been abused by family members or close friends of the family.

A journalist writing in the *Guardian* newspaper, noted that the NSPCC stopped collecting its annual statistics in 1990, partly because the Department of Health had agreed to do the work, but she says 'the way the DH has collected data since has become a researcher's nightmare'. The department has failed to keep anything like the range of information kept by the NSPCC, making it impossible for researchers to draw conclusions about prevalent social factors in child abuse.

In the United States of America where the vast majority of research studies have been undertaken into childhood sexual abuse, a wide-ranging review of the prevalence of sexual abuse, comparing males and females in samples of volunteers, college students, and subjects from the community at large has been carried out. This research identified a wide variation in the figures, ranging from 6 to 62 per cent for girls and 3 to 31 per cent for boys (Bagley and Ramsay 1991; Finkelhor 1979; Fromuth and Burkhart 1989; Russell 1984; Wyatt and Powell 1988). Even the lower figures show this to be a considerable problem if those percentages are translated into actual numbers, especially since it has been recognised that many cases of sexual abuse go unreported, particularly those of males.

In a study by Risin and Koss (1987), 2,972 men in a representative national sample were asked about their childhood sexual experiences. Of this sample 7.3 per cent reported an abusive childhood experience before the age of 14 years. The vast majority (81.2 per cent) of these men had told no one about this abuse before. If this is representative of men's experiences there may be large numbers of adult males unconsciously responding to and reacting against the unacknowledged problems of their childhood victimisation.

Since males are socialised to be 'strong' and to 'take care of themselves', male victims may be more reluctant to report abuse. Finkelhor (1986) extends this hypothesis by suggesting that male victims have more to lose, such as their freedom and independence, in reporting. A strong argument can be made that men are probably more reluctant to talk about what might be perceived as their 'weaknesses', or vulnerability and/or past sexual experiences with members of the same sex. This has been used as an argument for anonymous data collection such as telephone research interviews. However, research suggests that the only truly accurate means of acquiring sensitive data is through the use of face to face interviews. Wyatt (1987) argues that many interpersonal characteristics between the subject and the researcher can influence the responses of the subjects when dealing with sensitive topics. Prevalence studies of mother–son sexual abuse must be specifically designed to address diversity of behaviours and associated affect surrounding the experience of maternal sexual abuse and that such abuse is more likely to be disclosed in long-term therapeutic treatment than from surveys.

Perpetrators

One overwhelming finding is that 91–97 per cent of abusers are male (Finkelhor 1984) and are known to their victims (Urquiza 1988;

Finkelhor 1979). The most recent figures in the UK suggest that 2 per cent of the perpetrators are female (NSPCC 1990b). Although the figure presented by survivors (Woollett 1993) show that 10 per cent of a sample of seventy men were abused by females. Again this may be influenced by the bias of under-reporting among female perpetrators themselves who are rarely prosecuted and therefore not available for research projects which are directed at known offenders or may be another reflection of the societal impact of male socialisation that confuses males about what is and is not abuse when a female perpetrator is involved.

Male perpetrators

Men who are sexually attracted to children have as wide a variety of individual differences as are found among men who are not sexually attracted to children. There is no personality profile or battery of psychological tests that differentiates sexual abusers from non-abusers. That is not to say that some sexual offenders do not have some personality traits in common. Many sexual offenders present with very low self-esteem, feelings of inadequacy or vulnerability, and difficulties in inter-personal relationships. Such features, however, are not unique or specific to sexual abusers. The same traits, for example, can be found among people who have been victims of sexual abuse.

There has been found to be a higher incidence of biological defects in clients for being treated for sexual disorders in the Johns Hopkins Hospital at Baltimore (USA). Chromosomal abnormalities, hormonal imbalances and genetic defects/variations are among those differences found between sexual abusers and those suffering from other psychological disorders (Berlin 1983). This indicates a predisposition towards sexually offending which of course does not mean 'predestination' – this interpretation concerns clinicians who are afraid that offenders might not take responsibility for their actions if they take the view that they are predestined biologically to offend in this way. It is important to bear in mind the view that no one factor is sufficient to produce a sexual orientation towards children.

From a developmental rather than a biological view Groth, et al. (1982) observed that many sexual abusers were themselves sexually victimised in childhood. This was usually repeated and ongoing trauma in a context in which the individual felt alone and abandoned with this problem. However, it would seem that abusers are formed and not born. Groth and Olivera (1989) say that:

> Biological flaws and childhood sexual traumas have been

> identified clinically as significant risk factors in such development. A risk factor is something that appears to contribute to a particular outcome but of itself may not be sufficient to produce the particular result. For example, if a person smokes, he is more at risk of developing lung cancer than if he does not smoke, but this does not mean that all or even most people who smoke develop lung cancer (p.317)

Relationships with male perpetrators

As many of the perpetrators are male and known to the victim, it can be expected that the relationship between the victim and the offender is best characterised as father or father-figure (stepfather), or other adult male such as uncle. There seems to be a scarcity of reports about father–son abuse even though fathers are cited as the most frequent abusers of boys, including sons (Pierce and Pierce 1986; Vander Mey 1988; Reinhart 1987; Faller 1989). Johnson (1988) found that 30 per cent of his study had been abused by fathers; stepfathers were found by these investigators to be the next most frequently cited perpetrators. A few studies seem to be slanted towards the view that abuse by strangers is more likely (Ellerstein and Canavan 1980; De Jong et al. 1982). Urquiza (1988) found only 2 per cent father or father-figure offenders, with about 30 per cent of the offenders being related to the victim. Rogers and Terry (1984) report that only 8 per cent of boys in their study were abused by a parent or parent figure. Data reported by Risin and Koss (1987) describe 22 per cent of offenders being related to the victims. Friedrich, Beilke and Urquiza (1988) identified 97 per cent being related to the victim. In all except this last study it would seem that a large number of offenders are not, therefore, father-figures or related to the victim. Although some cases of father–son incest have been described in the literature the incidence is not known, although Kempe and Kempe (1984) state that 'incest between father and son is not rare'. Pierce's revue of the literature in 1987 found fifty-two instances of reports of father/stepfather sexual abuse.

Abel and Harlow (1987) in a study of 561 self-reported non-incarcerated male sexual abusers, found an unexpectedly high proportion of sexual abuse perpetrated on boys away from home. These cases were the most frequently reported by this group compared with those who molested girls or those who molested boys in the home. This may indicate that there are greater numbers than previously realised of boys who maintain secrecy about events happening outside the home.

Types of male offenders

Wyre and Swift (1990) describe two types of child molesters: the fixated offender and the regressed offender. The fixated offender is one whose primary sexual orientation is towards children. He psychologically identifies with the child and he usually prefers male victims. This type of offender often has multiple victims. Many of these perpetrators convince themselves and their victims that there is nothing wrong in their behaviour and some use long patient periods of seduction to prepare their victims for their part in the sexual activity. Singer et al. (1992) have presented and analysed a letter written to a 16-year-old boy by a middle-aged man to entice the boy into sexual activity. They outline the strategies used to refute the usual reservations a boy may have about being sexual with a man, highlighting sophisticated grooming and seduction strategies used to victimise adolescents.

The regressed offender is one whose primary sexual orientation is to age-mates and sexual attraction to children is usually considered a temporary lack of self-control. He will elevate the child victim to adult status and may even court her. He usually prefers females.

Homosexual perpetrators

Are men who are sexually attracted to male children homosexual? The answer to this question depends to some extent on the definition of homosexuality. In the literal sense of the meaning of the word, homosexuality is described as sexual activity between same sex individuals. However, this generally refers to such activity between sexually mature adults who are attracted to other sexually mature adults of the same sex as themselves. The sexual orientation of men who involve themselves with boys is more accurately described as paedophilic. The exclusively fixated male has no significant adult sexual relationships and the non-exclusive and regressed group often have adult partners who are women. Groth and Olivera (1989) say that in over twenty years of work with more than three thousand perpetrators of child sexual abuse they have yet to encounter a single case in which a gay man regresses from sexual relationships with adult male partners to sexual relationships with pre-pubertal male children. On the contrary Groth and Birnbaum (1987) have found that men who have been identified as sexual molesters of boys have either been primarily sexually orientated towards boys or have regressed from adult relationships with women to contact with boys.

Many male sexual offenders are often homophobic and therefore require their boy victim to be sexually immature, lacking secondary sexual characteristics such as body hair. He does not regard his victims as gay or homosexual. He identifies with the boy and finds the prospect of sex with a mature male unappealing and the young boy erotically stimulating. Identifying with his boy victim he is able to return to a developmental stage of unfinished business or a point of arrested development. This relationship might be better described as narcissistic rather than homosexual.

The homophobia felt by the offender might be as a result of having been sexually abused by a male in his childhood. In this context adult sexuality may seem confusing or threatening and, therefore, to be avoided or they may have misidentified the abuser as a homosexual and carried over resentments for their victimisation onto gay men.

Female perpetrators

Why has the recognition of the sexual abuse of children by women been so slow to emerge? Allen (1990) proposes part of the answer may lie in the fact that it is seldom reported because of the unacceptability of such behaviour which deviates from cultural norms and deep-seated beliefs even more so than when males are the perpetrators. It would seem that females who sexually abuse may be seen as not only committing a crime against the law of the land but also a crime against nature.

Through the development of psychoanalytical theories, men were considered to be sexual predators and women docile recipients, qualities inherent in the psychogenic make-up of each sex. A breach of the incest taboo by a female is consequently considered to be a far greater deviation than incest committed by a male. These beliefs profoundly influenced professional attitudes in the decades that followed Freud's original formulations and as a consequence the sexual abuse of children by females was dismissed and treated, when acknowledged, as a rare occurrence which was taken as evidence of severe psychotic disturbance, mental retardation or organic brain damage.

Following the first conference held in this country in March 1992 which was organised by KIDSCAPE and focused on the issue of sexual abuse perpetrated by females, there was a morning TV programme which opened up a hotline for callers. In the course of a day they had over a 1000 calls and 90 per cent of the callers had never told anybody about their abuse before that. Of those who contacted Michele Elliott, the Director of KIDSCAPE, 33 per cent were men and 67 per cent were women (Elliot 1993).

Definitions of sexual abuse when the abuser is a female is complicated by the term 'penetration' which is often used as a definition of criminal sexual contact by a male perpetrator. Mathis (1972) dismissed the possibility that females could sexually abuse because it was unthinkable that a woman might seduce a helpless child into sex play and even if she did what harm can be done without a penis?

Unfortunately this attitude continued to exert a powerful influence. When the offender is female, it may be that the victim actually performs penetration. When an adult woman has intercourse with an adolescent male, she is the perpetrator even if he penetrated her. Definitions need to consider who has the power in the relationship, what the motivation is and whose needs are being met either covertly or overtly. A teenage boy might be very confused if the sexual contact is supposedly for his sexual education but in reality it is the female who is getting satisfaction from her abuse of power. The power in the relationship is an important consideration and is often far more relevant to the consequences of sexual abuse than the age differential.

Another barrier to the recognition of female sexual abusers may be seen to be the over-extension of the feminist explanation. In these perspectives childhood sexual abuse is considered to be caused entirely by the culturally based socialisation process which will lead to male domination and promote sexual exploitation of women and children. The over-extension of this theory promotes the view that women are only potential victims thereby seeming to dismiss the possibility of male abuse by females. Although the feminist view of the damaging effects of patriarchy is what underlies my view, it cannot be the *only* explanation. Patriarchy also betrays males who do not conform with the dominant stereotype e.g homosexuals.

The over-emphasis on this theory can only be upheld if we also believe that female abusers are so rare as to merit no theoretical understanding of them. However, it may be that the rarity is due more to the under-reporting or ignoring of the problem by those biased against believing in the occurrence. We need to acknowledge female perpetrators because they exist. Without knowledge and understanding we cannot help them or their victims. Russell (1984) claims that the problem of women as perpetrators has been overemphasised by men and those who are defensive about feminism but Kasl (1990) sees that it is Russell's defensiveness that might be preventing her from seeing something that might not be acceptable to her as a woman. She recognises that some women may fear 'incurring the anger of other women who may believe that by exploring sexual abuse by females we are apologists for men'.

Female abuse might be easier to disguise as inappropriate behaviour because of the greater access that females have naturally to children in their caring roles; another idea is that females are more likely to abuse boys but boys might be less likely than girls to report the abuse; still another suggestion is that female abuse might occur more often be incestuous and would therefore be less likely to be reported.

Conclusions about the rarity of sexual abuse of children by females have been made assuming that reports in the literature accurately reflects rates of female perpetration and that low rates of occurrence means low absolute numbers of instances. Authors writing in isolation from one another were reporting a few incidences conveying the impression that female sexual abuse of children was so rare that it was almost unique. The widespread acceptance of this empirically-based conclusion caused female child abuse to be ignored or discounted in the literature as something that only happened when one or both of the parties was severely disturbed or psychotic, (Sarles 1975). Freund et al (1984) assuming that only men were paedophiles excluded women from the study.

Women are stereotyped to be gentle, passive and nurturing and are, therefore, out of place in the criminal justice system; women may, therefore, be given more lenient treatment and special considerations than men if they are seen to conform to traditional expectations in their demeanour and meet the expectations of those in authority. If they do not meet these expectations they may be more harshly served for the same reasons. This is often seen in the sentencing of violent women offenders. Because of the belief that women do not sexually abuse children, it may be that informants will be less likely to report occurrences, investigators less diligent in pursuing reports, attorneys less likely to prosecute and judges to sentence.

Knopp and Lackey (1987) observe from data gathered from forty-four providers of treatment for female sex offenders that

> It is suspected, but yet to be determined scientifically, that the criminal justice process, reflective of society's double standards for males and females and low tolerance level for female deviant/aggressive behaviours, differentially apprehends, selects, convicts, and punishes female sexual abusers (p.3).

Marvasti (1986) observed that the mothers he studied in five cases of maternal incest had not been involved in the criminal justice system, were not psychotic nor was their abuse centred around themes of power and dominance. However, it is interesting that in these cases it was the mothers themselves who had reported the abuse, not their victims. He concluded that unless mothers and sons are psychotic and lack the necessary resources to keep the incest a secret, they may escape the attention of the professionals.

Johnson (1989) says it is impossible to understand the problem of female child perpetrators in Los Angeles County where she was doing her research into this subject because of the lack of response within the child protection system and the criminal justice system. In a study involving thirteen female child perpetrators she found that;

> None of the girls were filed on by the police, and therefore none were prosecuted. None of these girls ever spoke to a probation officer, and none of them were placed on probation. Child abuse reports were not filed. None of these children was mandated for treatment (p.571).

Denial of the seriousness of sexual offences perpetrated by young females has been noted in other states in the USA and the fact that parental rights are more frequently terminated in cases of women offending than in cases where men are the offenders. To assume therefore that the frequency with which cases of females sexually abusing children is reported in the literature is an indication of its occurrence may be questionable. This is particularly so when the possibility exists that attributions of traditional gender and sex-role behaviours may have prevented all but the most deviant cases to have been brought to the attention of the researchers.

Fromuth and Burkhart (1989) found some unusual aspects to their studies of prevalence among samples of college men in the United States comparing two separate regions; they found prevalence rates of 15 per cent in one sample and 13 per cent in the other. What was unusual however was the fact that the majority of perpetrators were reported as female; 78 per cent of female perpetrators in one sample and 72 per cent in the other. Their definitions of abuse included non-contact abuse and a high proportion described a single abuse encounter. These finding demonstrate how carefully attention must be paid to exact definitions of abuse used and the perpetrators involved. Fritz et al. (1981), in their report on a group of college men where abuse was described as 'physical contact of an overtly sexual nature', also found a high percentage (60 per cent) of female perpetrators.

A boy who has sexual contact with a female has probably been socialised into believing that he should enjoy it, whatever the circumstances; if the experience has created negative feelings he may be left with the anxiety that he is 'less than a man' or in some way abnormal. These stereotypes and socialisation messages serve to keep professionals and parents from identifying the warning signs of victimisation when they are present.

Carlson (1990) described four different categories of abuse by females; chargeable offences such as oral sex, intercourse, masturbation, fondling or sexual punishment; less flagrant offences such as voyeurism, exposure, sexualised hugs; invasions of privacy in the sexual areas of the body, including washing a child beyond a reasonable age, obsessive cleaning of the foreskin, intrusive questions about sexual matters; inappropriate relationships created by the adult such as substituting a son for an absent husband, sleeping with him, using him as a confidante about sexual matters. According to Carlson 31 per cent of men who completed a sex offenders programme had experienced the first of those four forms of abuse. When the second form was added the proportion of male perpetrators who were sexually abused by women rose to 50 per cent. Nearly all of the men had experienced some form of sexual intrusion included in the third and fourth criteria. However, to make causal statements about this would be impossible; most of these men had also experienced many other forms of abuse and neglect such as sexual abuse by males, physical abuse, exposure to pornography, the presence of incest in the home and alcoholism.

Information gained from men who have been identified as victim/perpetrators demonstrates that in a sample of forty-one rapists, 56 per cent were sexually abused in childhood; almost 40 per cent of the perpetrators were women (Burgess et al.1987). In a sample of one thousand adolescent patients in a medical clinic between 1982–1984, eleven male adolescents reported sexual abuse by females and fourteen reported abuse by males. This indicates a higher ratio of female perpetrators than previously found (Johnson and Shrier 1987). A sample of eighty-three men convicted of raping women, included 59 per cent who had been molested by women and 82 per cent of these cases involved intercourse (Petrovich and Templar 1984).

Groth and Burgess (1979) describe the victimisation history of 348 men who had been convicted of sexual assault. They found that 31 per cent of these men had been sexually victimised and that 41 per cent of their victimisers were female; 27 per cent were adult females and 14 per cent were peers. In this sample they found that of male rapists who had been sexually victimised, more of them had been victimised by females than by males and that more of the incidences were incestuous than not.

Why do females abuse?

Much has been written about the factors that lead men to abuse children in the previous section of this study and the two main theories, psychoanalytical and social learning theory will be described in a later chapter.

In the limited literature available on female perpetrators, one study found that among 26 mothers who had molested their children, 95 per cent had a history of physical or sexual abuse (McCarty

1986). The sample used by Knopp and Lackey (1987) and gathered from forty-four providers of treatment for sex offenders found that the incidence of abuse in the backgrounds of their clients varied by their age: Among girl child perpetrators below 11-years-of-age, 100 per cent had been sexually victimised; among the 11–17 year age group, 93 per cent had been sexually victimised; and female perpetrators over 18-years-of-age had been victimised in 93 per cent of cases.

The study by Johnson (1989) also indicates a strong correlation between female child perpetration and prior sexual victimisation; 100 per cent of the girls reported sexual victimisation in their past. Four of the thirteen girls were physically as well as sexually abused.

However, as in the case of males, victimisation cannot be the only factor accounting for females becoming perpetrators as there are many more females (reportedly) sexually abused than males and yet comparatively few (reported) female perpetrators. Several factors seem to appear significant: characteristics of the girls victimisation, the response to disclosure, the family history of the girls, characteristics of the parents, certain defence mechanisms employed by the girls, and pervasive feelings of anger, confusion, anxiety and shame. It is interesting to note that only one of the thirteen girls in Johnson's sample received therapy following disclosure of their sexual abuse. For eleven of these children their first experience of therapy came as a consequence of their perpetrator behaviour.

Because many women who have been abused tend to 'internalise' rather than 'externalise' their problems and therefore come to the attention of the mental health services with such symptoms as depression, anxiety, eating disorders, etc., they may be more likely to obtain supportive help than men. Men tend to externalise their behaviours in more socially unacceptable ways such as misusing alcohol, drugs or aggressively acting out. This might mean that they are less likely to receive support and more likely to receive punishment. This might be a factor which correlates to the fact that more men than women are being identified as adult perpetrators.

It does seem perfectly clear that the substantial evidence gathered from self-report studies indicates that rates of male perpetrators far outweigh those of females. However, barriers to the recognition of females as perpetrators need to be removed if those victims abused by females are not to feel stigmatised further.

3 Theories of sexual development

One way of viewing childhood development in general can be as a series of tasks that must be completed before moving on to the next stage of development; the successful completion of these tasks will bring with it a new virtue or strength. Erikson's model (1963) of psychosocial development describes the outcome of the first stage as ranging from the development of basic trust to basic mistrust; the outcome of the second stage from a strong sense of autonomy to a profound sense of shame and doubt.

During the first years of life infants learn to trust or mistrust the predictability of their environment, which includes the people within that environment. Through their experiences with the major care-givers and those they have a right to be able to trust, they learn whether or not they can depend on the world around them. The child learns about having faith, both in itself and in others within its world.

Erikson formulated his work upon the foundations laid down by Anna Freud's work (1937) and her elaboration of the workings of unconscious defence mechanisms of the ego and emphasised its healthy adaptive qualities. Another critically important contribution to the field of a child's cognitive development is that made by Jean Piaget (1929, 1952). His interactionist view – the child as an active agent engaged with its environment – is at the heart of his theory. He sees development hinging on the internal workings of maturation and the external forces of experience.

Development can be seen as an 'ideal' process, which is to be distinguished from the reality of what actually happens during the course of a life. Kaplan (1983) describes development as pertaining to a 'rarely, if ever, attained ideal, not to the actual'. With this in mind empirical studies can then furnish data concerning the extent to which individuals do or do not develop and may provide information concerning factors that facilitate or impede development. So we may need to see what is 'ideal' or 'normal' in sexual development before we can understand how sexuality can be determined by the factors that impinge either positively or negatively on that process.

The development of sexuality has received very little attention in research and literature, perhaps because until recently, the myth that children were basically asexual prior to adolescence prevailed (Waterman 1986).

According to one of the earliest theories of psychosexual development Freud proposed that children between the ages of 2 and 4 years are in the anal stage, where they struggle for bladder and bowel control; in fact, control is the general issue during this stage, with the child working to develop a sense of self and to exert control over aspects of their environment.

Between the ages of 4 and 6 years, children enter the phallic stage, during which they become increasingly aware of their genitals and of the differences between boys and girls. Masturbation and 'playing doctor' or other exploratory games with friends and siblings may be seen during this period. According to Freud, as children develop a clear sense of sex roles, they deal with their sexual feelings towards their parents through the Oedipal conflict. A child develops a romantic attachment to the parent of the opposite sex and is disappointed when the parent does not respond to his or her overtures. The child then identifies with the parent of the same sex in order to become more attractive to the desired parent. Children in this stage may show versions of stereotypical adult behaviour, such as strutting and teasing in little boys, and coy or flirtatious behaviour in little girls. The identification with the same sex parent helps children strengthen their own sexual image.

After the pre-school years, the latency period was postulated by Freud to occur between the ages of 6 and 12 years. He thought that interest in sexuality is less overt during this period, with a decrease in sex play, but with 'dirty' words and jokes holding considerable appeal. Although Freud's work undoubtedly was important in gaining an understanding of the development of sexuality in children, it may have been misleading when rigidly adhered to. Later research into sexual anatomy, physiology, behaviour and treatment of sexual disorders have placed some of these commonly held beliefs at issue (Masters and Johnson 1982). It had been believed that sexual arousal occurred only after the onset of puberty. In fact, with the exception of ejaculation, sexual arousal and responsiveness have been observed from infancy forward. The suggestion is that sexual responsiveness is an integral element of childhood development. It is not uncommon for pre-adolescent males to report first coital experiences long before ejaculation capacity has developed. Sexuality should not be equated with reproductive capability.

Another source of confusion is that of 'latency' periods of sexual development. Because this stage was considered to be one in which the child's interest in sexuality was abated, the child was then thought to be at less risk of sexual victimisation. In fact, sexual development continues unabated from infancy and throughout adulthood. Self-stimulation of the genital area begins, with apparent signs of pleasure, when motor co-ordination becomes sufficient. This pattern continues with pleasurable genital stimulation, increasing knowledge of body parts and reproduction, and direct questions about sexual behaviour which, unfortunately are often met with indirect answers, or behaviours which indicate to the child that this is a taboo subject which is to be ignored or hidden. Calderone (1985) suggests that this pattern may open the door to potential victimisation because children may be learning 'to keep silent and go underground' about their sexual feelings and behaviours.

Children during the latency stage are aware of the erotic and sensual nature of genital stimulation although they may not discuss it with adults. Sex play, exploration, curious and competitive (such as seeing how far the little boy can project his pee) contacts with peers of either gender occur during this time. This has been considered to be within normal bounds as long as coercive or aggressive behaviour is absent from it. However, the findings of Lamb and Coakley (1993) indicate that 'normal' sexual play in childhood includes bullying and manipulation when it is a cross-gender activity. When girls play with boys, they are more likely to feel that they have been persuaded, manipulated, or coerced into an activity that they are uncomfortable with. The researchers see another problem in rating these females experiences as 'normal' or not as being:

> whether boys, by nature of being boys (as gender is culturally constructed), have some status or power that is coercive even when children are of an equal age (p.524)

As the subjects of this research into 'normal' childhood sexual play were women, it may be that the findings would be different in same gender play. Same-gender sexual play in males where the less 'macho' boy might perceive the more 'macho' boy to have the status and power to coerce that a female child would feel, might mean that it is not so much the gender that influences the findings but rather where the power lies within the relationship.

As puberty approaches, sexuality becomes less of a game and more a deliberate activity. Physical changes no longer allow for dismissal of sexual feeling and partners are sought. Same sex partners are commonly a preliminary to cross gender activities. This selection of a partner will be dependent upon what the child has learned about his sexuality up to that point.

Another potentially damaging belief regarding the developing male is that they have a much larger sex drive than females – this belief seems to be based on the greater amount of testosterone present in the male. Hormonal studies have not been completely successful in predicting sexual behaviour. Testosterone is said to be 'the principal biologic determinant of the sex drive in both men and women' (Masters et al.1985). Women have been found to have lower levels but they also have greater sensitivity to smaller amounts. This would indicate the need to balance the view of the importance of gender-based sex drive levels.

Durden-Smith and de Simone (1983) quote Dr Gunter Donner, Director of the Institute for Experimental Endocrinology at the Humbolt University, who is a leading proponent of the argument that biology is responsible for male/female sex drive levels. For him, male and female sexual characteristics, including sexual identity and behaviour, are determined prior to birth. Essential to his theory are the sexual hormones which play a primary role in the differentiation of the sexes. Through their organisational effect these hormones ultimately influence the hypothalamus, producing either a male or a female brain, which in turn produces either male or female behaviour,(Moir and Jessel, 1989)

My own view is more in line with the theories of John Money (1972) at Johns Hopkins University who offers an interactional view in which biological and social/biographical factors participate together in the process of gender formation. For Money biology plays a significant role in the formation of gender, specifically in the differentiation of male/female morphology. In the end however, social/biographical factors predominate in the total process and can override the genetic and biological sex of an individual. He believed that through social transmission, the process of gender formation begins at birth, from the moment the infant is assigned a sex when the parents see its genitals. Those responsible for rearing the child will continue to confirm that a child is either male or female through their daily interaction with him or her.

It would appear that both genders share common sexual capabilities and both experience sexual development throughout childhood. Physiology cannot therefore completely account for the development of sexuality within the person. An equally critical variable is the learning that takes place within the child's first social setting, which is usually the family.

The 'stages' in sexual development might be broadly defined as childhood exploration and experimentation, adolescent transitions and adult sexuality. Each of these stages may be affected by the amount and type of information received, cultural expectations, parental socialization and peer relationships that occur. Distortions in these areas, such as those introduced through aberrant sexual interactions, may contribute to confusion, delays in development, or overt sexual dysfunctions.

Friedrich (1988) found that a group of sexually abused boys were significantly more sexualised than a comparative group of boys with conduct disorders who had not been sexually abused. The boys in the conduct disorder group were significantly more aggressive. Both these groups differed significantly from a 'normal' comparison group on all variables. Directly related to this finding of increased sexualisation in sexually abused children is a paper by Storms (1981) dealing with sexual orientation development. He writes that:

> erotic orientation results from an interaction between sex drive development and social development during early adolescence (p.436).

He also says that earlier sex drive maturation appears to encourage homoerotic development, a report that is supported by findings of research into latency age children who are sexually aggressive (Friedrich and Leucke 1988).

Little is known about what is appropriate at each stage of development. The Kinsey Institute has published a new report on sex (1990) which attempts to outline some of the more commonly found sexual behaviours among children and adults. There seems little certainty regarding facilitating or inhibiting factors in sexual development. It does seem defensible to suggest that inappropriate sexual contacts with adults or peers would interfere with and damage this developing sexuality.

4 Male socialisation

Gender and sex-roles

> Living through the development of male sexuality for me was like hitchhiking. It is more fun to talk about than it was to live through it (quoted in Bolton et al. 1989, p.11).

The above quotation may highlight one of the major difficulties of growing up male in our society; it is supposed to be easy, everyone talks about it as if it were easy and few males are willing to admit that it may be difficult.

Male children are socialised to be dominant, competitive, aggressive and tough. To be a normal male means to aspire to leadership, to be sexually active, knowledgeable, potent and a successful seducer. The burden inherent in these expectations is clear.

Some sense of gender-identity becomes established by the age of 3 years. The development of gender-based skills, solidification of gender identity, and the learning of sex-role attributes continues throughout childhood and into adulthood and what is expected of males and females is guided by these learned sex and gender roles (Maccoby and Jacklin 1974).

According to Metcalfe and Humphreys (1985), stereotyping is pervasive in the societal view of both male and female sexuality but perhaps more so for males. A 'real' man has frequent sexual interaction and is also seen as being continuously willing and able to engage in a sexual activity; the female is often believed to be more passive in her approach to sexuality. Stereotypical male sexuality is equated with successful and frequent performance. This could be seen to be linked with the view that masculinity is linked with compulsive male sexuality. Sexuality seems a crucial factor in the maintenance of masculine identity and may serve as part of the core self-definition of the male. To be successfully masculine is to be sexually potent, competitive with other males in sexual accomplishments, and dominant within sexual interactions. Failure in the area of sexuality may be linked with loss of masculinity and therefore of an important part of self-identity.

There are frequently some differences between parental expectations of a male child and a female child: there is for males a greater pressure for achievement and competitiveness, an expectation of greater control over feelings, more independence, greater assumption of personal responsibility, more authoritarianism towards the male and less acceptance of behaviours which deviate from the gender stereotype. Although this view may be changing slowly as the view of female roles is changing in response to the demands made by women, it is still in evidence today.

Often it appears as though male children depend more than female children upon the stereotypes to guide them; this is what Hartley (1959) has called 'overstraining to be masculine'. There is a pronounced avoidance of doing anything traditionally defined as feminine. A little boy who plays with dolls may be seen to be a 'sissy'; it seems that boys may be boys and nothing more. It is however, permissible for girls to be 'tomboys' without the same fear of being identified as at variance with their gender. There seems to be a short step between this attitude and the development of homophobia. Parents seem to define cross-sexed activities as likely to be more closely associated with homosexual activities in boys than in girls. If a girl dresses up in male clothing she can be assured of a very different reaction from that a boy might receive if he dressed up in girls' clothing or wore make-up.

This double standard spills over into sexual development. While Maccoby and Jacklin (1974) did not find different parental responses to expressions of sexuality in their male and female children, other researchers do. Masters et al (1985) describe a double standard in this area particularly at the time children enter school and again during adolescence. Females are cautioned against sex play but boys receive different messages; these messages are mixed. There seems to be some tacit permission for males to follow their sexual curiosity as long as it is strongly heterosexual; these parental attitudes are mirrored by peers. Since adolescents often acquire more sexual information from peers than from any other source this will be seen to have a great impact on the developing sexual attitudes and behaviours of young people.

It may be that differential sexual socialisation for males, affects the range of 'acceptable' sexual experiences. It may increase the presumption of pathological negativity of homosexual experiences and it may add to the confusion for males who are abused by older or adult females. If a 30-year-old male has sexual contact with a 12-year-old female it is usually viewed as sexual abuse. The same situation involving a young male and older woman may be seen as 'initiation' into manhood, negating any possibility of negative consequences on the young male and may even go so far as inducing jealousy from peers and older males – the 'you should be so lucky' response described by adult survivors who have attempted to disclose their abuse during childhood and particularly adolescence. Similarly, males exposing genitals to young females are prosecuted but if a female exposed herself to a young male, prosecution would be very unlikely. This double standard can be seen as one way of creating further difficulties in defining what is sexual abuse when applied to males.

Moir and Jessel (1989) share the view that masculine and feminine behaviour is determined biologically before birth:

> Infants are not blank slates, on whom we scrawl instructions for sexually appropriate behaviour. They are born with male and female minds of their own. They have, quite literally, made up their minds in the womb, safe from the legions of social engineers who impatiently await them ... six or seven weeks after conception, the unborn baby makes up its mind and the brain begins to take on a male or female pattern (p.20).

In some way this idea is more difficult to entertain because it seems to imply that we cannot change stereotypical behaviour when it is biologically based. There is some evidence that some of the violence men commit may be partially influenced by biological factors but the most that can be said as far as aggression is concerned is that some men may be physiologically more at risk than others to environments that stress their control mechanisms. It may be unhelpful to consider masculinity as a purely social construct with no physiologic basis. However, this idea falls far short of endorsing a view of an essential male propensity to violence. It would be necessary to demonstrate that violence was an inevitable outcome of feelings of aggression to support biologically based explanations of violence that men commit. Violent behaviour is learned and can be unlearned. It seems likely that propensities to violence are influenced by the way in which people are socialised rather than by their birth into a particular biological sex.

I prefer to believe that by changing the socialisation of boys we will be hopeful of creating a gentler, less aggressive and perhaps more nurturing environment for all. I do not doubt that biologically males are different from females; that they are naturally more dominant, aggressive, decisive and that females are more interested in inter-personal skills and more feeling orientated. What I believe needs to change is what society values in people; masculine and feminine characteristics are within all of us, both male and female. Patriarchy values masculine characteristics more highly than feminine ones – this is what needs to change. Until we can value equally the masculine and the feminine within each of us we will be perpetuating and supporting an environment in which males will not allow themselves to use the inherent strengths of their feminine.

Patriarchy

Apart from the parental and peer pressures to conform with male stereotypes there is a much broader pressure within which these attitudes operate; that of the larger sociopolitical context of patriarchy which I believe is a major factor in the issue of childhood abuse in general. My use of the term is in line with the definition used by Lerner (1986):

> Patriarchy in its wider definition means the manifestation and institutionalisation of male dominance over women and children in the family and the extension of male dominance over women (and children) in society in general. It implies that men hold power in all the important institutions of society and that women (and children) are deprived of access to such power. It does not imply that women (and children) are either totally powerless or totally deprived of rights, influence, and resources (p.239).

It should be added, however, that any person who fails to conform to the standards and norms set by patriarchy such as a homosexual man, is usually relegated to a subordinate status. In fact any man in a subordinate status to another man, perhaps in the workplace, may be subjected to patriarchal domination by the more senior man.

Patriarchy depends on the norms that underpin the sexual abuse of children. These have been described by Struve (1990) as chattel property, learned helplessness, sexual entitlement and the shroud of secrecy.

The norm of 'chattel property' is based on the concept that men have ownership of their wives and parents have ownership of their children; ownership implies the right to control. Women and children in our society are encouraged to be passive thereby conditioning them to accept the position of being controlled. Strong women are defined as 'aggressive' and strong children as 'rebellious' or 'defiant'.

Our society seems to overvalue control; therefore having a compliant child is seen as proof of being a good parent. It is easy to justify behaviour that might hurt a child in the name of discipline or as being good for the child. Alice Miller describes this as 'poisonous pedagogy' (Miller 1983). Struve (1990) sees teaching a child absolute obedience as grooming the child for victimisation. Within our culture the concept of chattel property is most readily employed as a male privilege. This is especially prevalent in the commonly held belief among men that they are guaranteed the right of sex on demand. These attitudes can be seen as underlying the remark made by a judge who freed and excused a child molester on the grounds that his pregnant wife's lack of sexual appetite had caused his three sexual assaults on his 12-year-old step-daughter.

The second norm, 'learned helplessness', is the ability to accept one's position of passivity in relationship to those who are defined as being more dominant, to such a degree that a person feels psychologically paralysed. These dynamics have been described by Seligman (1975) in his work on depression and elaborated on by Walker (1970), in her work with battered women. Children are economically, emotionally and physically dependent on their parents and other adults and can not survive without them. Therefore, most children feel powerless when harmed by a trusted adult.

The third dynamic, 'sexual entitlement', is the belief that sex is a privilege for the dominant person in any relationship and an obligation for the person who is non-dominant. The dominant status of adult males in our society or that of adults over children feeds into the felt helplessness of the child who is used by another for sexual gratification.

The last dynamic, 'the shroud of secrecy', operates from the underlying norm that sexual information is dangerous and corrupting, therefore considerable energy is spent in maintaining a shroud of secrecy over all things sexual; this contributes to a global anxiety about sexuality which discourages most people from discussing sexual matters openly. Such an atmosphere creates confusion, distortion and fear. Issues related to patriarchy are not only relevant to females, and to children; they are relevant in a particular way to male survivors of sexual abuse as well as men in general. There are numerous negative implications for men, including their greater social isolation and the cultural expectations that they must internalise or withhold emotions, which may account for the popularly held belief that men are likely to die earlier than women.

Male survivors are imprisoned by patriarchy by ignoring the realities of their sexual abuse. Too often male survivors deal with their abuse 'like a man' by conforming with patriarchal norms and deny their feelings in respect of their victimisation. The response of male survivors reflects the values and norms by which they have been socialised. Patriarchy grooms men to assume a privileged position of dominance and encourages them to perceive the position of victim as antithetical to maleness. The dissonance created by this often causes male victims to remain silent or identify with the oppressor and engage in sexually offending behaviours themselves.

The stereotype that sexual victimisation is less traumatic for males than females prevents many males from seeking help. An investigation by Logan (1980) into the attitudes of paediatricians, psychologists, teachers and social workers regarding physical and sexual abuse, who found that females rated abusive behaviours as more harmful than males did. She also reports a study by Fingleton (1989) of attitudes of male and female school psychologists regarding sexual abuse, which found that male school psychologists were likely to blame the mother of the abused child, and also believed that many of the girls fantasised the sexual abuse, whereas 51 per cent of female school psychologists felt that the patriarchal society and male power were responsible for sexual abuse. It seems to me that the person who is responsible for the abuse of a child is the abuser – society, mothers and male power may all contribute or re-inforce that abuse but 'responsibility', *per se*, rests with the perpetrator.

Eisenberg, Owens and Dewy (1987) reported that female participants in their research on attitudes of health professionals, believed the effects of incest to be more serious than male participants. If these attitudes are representative of what is generally found then these attitudes are being transmitted to our male children through their socialisation, along with other attitudes about power and responsibility.

Many male victims fear that their disclosure will be viewed as a 'rite of passage' and will be denied as a victimisation experience. When the teenage victim is a self-identified homosexual, the typical adult response is to assume that the experience was merely a result of his sexual preference which is stereotypically perceived as abnormal. The victim is then blamed for his homosexuality rather than the offender for the offence. Young males or 'rent-boys' who offer themselves for prostitution are frequently on the receiving end of sexual abuse. These boys are one of the most 'at risk' groups in our society. Rent-boys are often runaways, many from homes where abuse has been occurring for many years; many come from 'in-care' situations or institutions. Without legal means of getting money to survive these boys will either turn to prostitution or starve (McMullen 1990). The survival instinct is strong and often they turn to what they know best – the results of their 'education' through their earlier abuse.

A male victim may focus on feelings related to his inability to defend himself, and therefore his lack of 'manliness' and failure as a man. Having failed to protect himself from the abuse he may overcompensate for his anxiety by macho behaviour to re-establish his perception of himself in a strong male image. There may also be intensely strong homophobic reactions to the sexual victimisation experience which in turn may create problems in forming or maintaining intimate relationships with other men. Too often men assume emotional intimacy is female behaviour and this may make it difficult for men to align themselves with any attributes that appear to define them as 'sissy'. Fear of appearing weak, needy or frail (all considered female attributes stereotypically) contributes to avoidance of intimate self-disclosure.

Homophobia

West (1992) defines the word homophobia as:

> an intense, irrational fear of homosexuality, a pathological overreaction presumably caused by intra-psychic conflict. Its clearest manifestation is the state of homosexual panic that some men experience when another male suggests or attempts sexual contact (p.13).

The word has now passed into more common usage and is applied almost indiscriminately to any degree of dislike of homosexuality or homosexuals. West suggests that views such as these might be suppressed because of the popular theory that to show evidence of such dislike is a projection of suppressed homosexual inclinations and because a greater degree of tolerance seems to be growing in more liberal-minded people. However, disapproval, both overt and covert, remains pervasive and reveals itself in many forms in our society.

Condemnation of homosexual behaviour is deeply rooted in history and tradition. Orthodox Judeo-Christian teachings are unequivocally antagonistic. Hostility towards groups or minorities whose habits and ideas are different from one's own is an almost universal human characteristic; prejudice against gays is just one example. Their very existence challenges fundamental assumptions about life's purpose and the natural order of things.

Pronouncements by medical authorities in the past have been influential in promoting homophobia by equating homosexuality with psychopathology, degeneracy or moral turpitude. Although Freud challenged these assumptions and indeed saw it as part of normal sexual development, his followers were still insistent upon them many years later. It was only in 1980 after much protest and lobbying that the American Psychiatric Association voted to remove homosexuality, *per se*, from its diagnostic manual of psychiatric disorders.

There are many myths surrounding homosexuality which contribute to homophobia. Male homosexuals are regarded by some as child molesters, traitors, transvestites and effeminate; some are, as are some heterosexuals, but that is not to say that these are representative or typical.

The majority of homosexuals are not effeminate, even though Green's research (1987) demonstrates that boys identified as 'sissy' in their early years are more likely to develop a homosexual identity. However, using the label of 'effeminate' as a reason to despise men carries an underlying assumption that femininity is a despicable trait. This is insulting to women and a direct manifestation of the patriarchal attitude that elevates 'male' above 'female'.

Another myth is that homosexuals are dangerous to the young. This takes the form of them being child molesters and corrupters of youth. In this context, corruption presumably means introduction to the practice of homosexuality. However, the personal histories of adult homosexuals who have never been heterosexually aroused, suggests that their homosexual urges develop very early in life before social pressures or seduction experiences come into operation.

The realisation that boys as well as girls are victimised by sexual abuse increases the suspicion of a causal link between male homosexuality and child molestation. West (1992) sees the truth as:

> most men who have an erotic fixation on children and most of those who associate with children, because they cannot obtain or cope with an adult partner, are primarily interested in girls, although some will try to make contact with boys and girls. There is no evidence that homosexuals are more likely than heterosexuals to be attracted to pre-pubertal children, or of any association between homosexuality and paedophilia (p.17)

Homosexual paedophiles certainly exist and can be persistent offenders and able to argue in favour of their right to 'Greek love' so long as the boy is willing and benefits from the relationship. They see the payment of money as one such benefit.

The reality seems to be that homosexual men and boys are more likely to be victims of sexual assault than perpetrators. Groth and Burgess (1979) in an analysis of sixteen males who had raped males reported that 50 per cent of the offenders they studied were married and confined their consenting sexual activities to members of the opposite sex; 38 per cent were married and engaged in sex with both men and women, while only a small percentage were committed to sexual encounters exclusively with other men, none of whom were part of a permanent relationship.

McMullen (1990) sees the sexual assault of males as having little to do with sexual gratification and a great deal to do with power, anger and violence.

> Because the sexual element is essentially homosexual (male on male) in nature, the sexual identity of the aggressor is then wrongly thought to be gay. Gay males are then blamed and revenge attacks and rapes against other gay males sometimes result. One consequence of this is the furthering of already existing homophobic attitudes (p.52).

Far from standing for equal rights and non-discrimination, the law appears to encourage homophobic attitudes. Although female soliciting has been made a non-imprisonable offence, male opportuning still carries a maximum penalty of nearly two years' imprisonment. Women have to be given a police warning when first apprehended, not so men. Women only commit an offence if they are asking for money for sex, but men who are looking for a partner with no intention of payment are still liable to conviction. Female soliciting is a street offence but men can be prosecuted for importuning in gay bars or in any situation.

A heterosexual couple behaving 'indecently' where they can be seen or if they offend a member of the public, commit a minor common law offence. A male pair behaving in the same way commit a serious statutory crime of gross indecency with severe maximum penalties. Moreover 'in public' has a wider connotation where homosexual behaviour is involved and includes gay bars and other social scenes where gays normally meet together.

Although the status of homosexuals in British society remains somewhat ambiguous, this owes more to the adverse views of some vociferous sections of the public than to any legal provision. Persecution of homosexuals has no official backing in the United Kingdom although a former Metropolitan Police Officer (Burke 1993) recorded how policing gay cruising areas was seen as 'let's go and have a bit of fun with the poofs'. He also stated that many police officers were afraid to tell colleagues about their sexuality and how they lived in fear of being asked to leave on 'medical grounds'. There are, however, signs that attitudes are changing among certain sections of the establishment. A recent investigation into the murder of five homosexual men has drawn attention to the fact that gay policemen were publicly drafted on to the murder squad and that police and gays worked amiably together on this major inquiry. It is a measure of the change in the relationship between gays and police that there was such co-operation in this murder hunt and that a lesbian and gay police officers group has been given official blessing at a Hendon Police College conference, something that would have been unthinkable a few years ago.

However, as the law stands the age of consent for heterosexuals in the UK is 16 years but for homosexuals it is 21 (since writing this the law has changed and the age of consent is 18 years from April 1994); it is any age for lesbians. Criminal charges are often brought against men who are caught breaking that law. Between 1986 and 1991 there were over 2,000 prosecutions against gays in Britain. Even former communist states realise that a discriminatory age of consent is incompatible with democracy and human rights. In Poland the age of consent for gay relationships has been 15 since 1932. The Czechs equalised the age of consent within months of the overthrow of the old communist regime. Since 1990 Latvia, the Ukraine and Estonia have equalised the legislation. We still have a long way to go in establishing a fully tolerant and humane society that will afford people of minority sexual orientation the same respect that heterosexuals enjoy.

Struve suggests (1990) that dominant institutions within a patriarchal society invest considerable energy in cultivating homophobic fear, and those same institutions tacitly condone homophobic prejudice and discrimination. The implications of this for males who have been sexually abused by other males are clear. How can victims risk exposing themselves to questions about their sexual involvement with a member of the same sex whilst they and others have been indoctrinated within a homophobic society? Furthermore the attitudes of society which are introjected by the victim will increase the likelihood that, once victimised, the victim will not be able to form intimate relationships with non-abusive males which would provide him with an opportunity to mediate the effect of the abusive relationship and allow him an alternative learning experience out of which the seeds of his healing might emerge.

Homophobia can influence the parent's attitudes to the sexual abuse of their child; parents have been known to confess that they had 'worried that something like that was taking place' but were afraid to enquire for fears that their worst fears were true. When asked about their worst fears they admitted that it was that their son was homosexual and that they were relieved to learn that 'it had only been sexual abuse'. So their homophobia prevented them from taking action that would have protected and helped their son.

5 Effects of childhood sexual abuse on male sexuality

There are those who consider that sexual contact between children and adults is permissible. In the 1950s Raskovsky and Raskovsky suggested that sexual contact between an adult and child fostered psychosocial adjustment. More recently I heard a report of a question, propounded by a headmaster of a well-known public school, asking which of his pupils were more abused – the one whose housemaster had sex with him or the boy who had been 'neglected' by being excluded from this activity?

Beliefs such as these are held by such organisations as the North American Man–Boy Love Association (NAMBLA) and the Renee Guyon Society, organisations that live by the slogan 'Sex before eight (years of age) or it is too late'. They claim to represent thousands of parents eager to involve their children in 'gentle and loving sex' with adults. Some of these groups advocate homosexual and heterosexual contact. A recently published book entitled *Child-loving* written by a senior professor at an American University (Kinread 1993) has caused outraged reactions by British academics who have criticised Kinread's passionate championing of paedophiliacs and his expressed resentment against society's persecution of them.

An early Kinsey report (1953) stated that 80 per cent of the children in his sample had been 'emotionally upset or frightened' by their sexual contacts with adults. He saw this level of feeling as similar to that which children would show when they see spiders or insects or 'other objects against which they have been socially conditioned'. He went on to say that:

> If a child were not culturally conditioned, it is doubtful if it would be disturbed by sexual approaches of the sort which had been involved in these histories. It is difficult to understand why a child, except for its cultural conditioning, should be disturbed at having its genitalia touched or disturbed at seeing the genitalia of other persons, or disturbed at even more specific sexual contacts. (Kinsey et al. 1953, p.121).

He describes the 'current hysteria about sex offenders' as the possible *cause* of 'serious effects on the ability of many of these children to work out sexual adjustments some years later in their marriages'. Thereby, he removes the responsibility for these serious effects from the perpetrator of the sexual abuse of children and places it on the reactions of the adults surrounding the child.

Although I cannot agree with his view (and indeed question the motivation of any one who holds it) there is some evidence to suggest that the ways adults, both parents and professionals, respond to the child's victimisation can cause further damage which in some ways create another level of abuse (O'Hagan 1989). The unethical and unprofessional practices exposed by the Cleveland enquiry (Butler-Sloss 1988) have highlighted the need to provide an alternative to the traditional strictly punitive, child-centred, family-ignored responses, now so discredited. Assessing whether or not, and how to intervene is not only a matter of resource management but also of the appropriateness of the response for the crucial issue of child protection.

Finkelhor (1986) describes those who believe the negative effects of child sexual abuse to have been exaggerated as 'minimisation theorists'. Feminist writers are more strident and suggest these researchers to be members of a pro-incest group. Conte (1985) suggests that this research may be used politically to legitimate sexual abuse. He notes:

> there often appears to be an unspoken assumption that if sexual abuse turns out not to produce significant long-term trauma, that there is nothing wrong with it (p.117).

Conte (Conte and Schuerman 1987) noted that:

> Some children are profoundly traumatised by sexual abuse, some exhibit milder or transient problems, and some appear not to have been affected by the abuse (pp.201–211).

Child therapists C. Henry and Ruth Kempe (1984) provided the following prognostic insights to the child involved in an episode which takes place away from the home environment:

> A single molestation by a stranger, particularly a non-violent one, as an encounter with an exhibitionist, may cause transitory harm to normal children living with secure, reassuring parents (p.188).

However they did caution that the event:

> still needs to be talked out and explained at an age-appropriate level, and all questions must be answered (p.188).

Others in the field agree that sexual abuse produces emotional and behavioural problems, but disagree over their nature and severity. Many variables such as the age of the child, the relationship with the perpetrator, the type and duration of the abuse have been proposed as factors that influence the outcome. Much of the research has been criticised for its methodological flaws, such as size of sample group, lack of comparisons with control groups, the use of biased sample groups and the use of differing definitions of abuse (Hunter 1991). On balance however, it can be concluded that the majority of work in this area predicts that growing up in an environment which abuses a child's sexuality will be likely to result in some form of childhood, adolescent and/or adult problems (Bolton et al. 1989).

Urquiza (1988), seeing sexual abuse as a 'stressor', predicts from the literature concerning the physical and psychological consequences of stress on children in parallel traumatising situations, that boys will respond more adversely to stress than girls and will be more vulnerable to later psychological disturbance. Moreover, the externalised behavioural manifestations of trauma more usually employed by boys, (e.g. delinquency, aggression etc), may 'turn off' compassionate responses in others. Potentially supportive resources may then respond to the distress reactions in boys in negative or punitive ways thereby compounding the initial stressor and further increasing the vulnerability of the boy.

In the recent case of the murder of a 2-year-old child James Bolger, the outrage felt by the public at the behaviour of the two 10-year-old boy murderers made it difficult to keep sight of the perpetrators as being possibly traumatised children themselves.

There is then, a general agreement across the literature on child sexual abuse that the consequences of that experience can be both significant and enduring. Overall, male child sexual abuse victims suffer from psychological trauma at least commensurate in severity with that suffered by females, although few comparative investigations have been conducted.

Mediators

However, the effects of sexual abuse are undoubtedly variable and research has shown that there are factors that mediate and factors which protect some children from the more devastating effects that may be felt by others (Gilgun 1990). An emerging field of study, developmental psychopathology, brings attention to the study of resilience and protective mechanisms as well as the study of vulnerability, risk, coping and stress (Anthony and Cohler 1987; Cicchetti 1987; Masten and Garmezy 1985; Sroufe and Rutter 1984).

Social support may mediate in both short- and long-term effects of abuse. Researchers have found that the presence of someone in whom to confide and who is supportive appears to be important in helping individuals to overcome the effects of abuse and may be one factor which breaks the cycle of abuse, (Egeland, Jacobvitz and Sroufe 1988; Gilgun 1990; Wyatt and Mickey 1987). This finding has important implications for policy makers who need to provide services, perhaps through therapy or counselling, for this support to be available.

Accounting for the range of outcomes associated with the aftermath of sexual abuse of boys has other important practical, clinical and theoretical implications. Much of the literature bases its approach on understanding these outcomes from a psycho-analytical perspective (Osborne 1990; Freud in Masson 1984; Bowlby 1973). These theorists suggest that the use of psychological defence mechanisms, which protect the immature ego from disintegration in childhood and help the child to survive the abuse, can in themselves become problematic when carried into adulthood, preventing the adult from reclaiming memories, dissociating feeling and effect, causing automatic subconscious avoidance and aggressive behaviours which may prevent the adult from living in a way that feels satisfying and fulfilling. Much of the clinical work with adult survivors, who have refined these defences over many years, is to enable the survivor to feel safe enough to recognise and eliminate these defences when he is ready and able. Fraiberg, Adelson and Shapiro (1975) hypothesised that being in touch with the memories and pain of maltreatment in childhood provides a powerful deterrent against repeating abusive acts in adulthood. This is something I would wholeheartedly agree with and is often the focus of the work I do with adult survivors.

Summit (1983) describes the process through which the child sexual abuse victim 'accommodates' to the sexually abusive experience. Sepler (1990) comments on the fact that such accommodation is well documented in many female victims but:

> the depth of the accommodation and the intensity of the notion of mastery and control is a far more gender-specific response for male victims than female victims and should be expected ... neither powerlessness nor violence make any sense to a male victim who has accommodated the sexual abuse by adopting a pseudoconsensual posture or by reciprocating with aggressive acts (p.78).

He suggests that aggression and antisocial behaviour are the model choices of the male sexual abuse victim. Not being as tolerant of his helplessness as the female child, the male may rationalise that this dysfunctional sexual relationship is actually positive. The danger is not only that he will accept this relationship, but keep the power of it alive in his own adulthood through a series of similar relationships.

One useful way of viewing the potential for dysfunctional accommodation to sexually victimising experiences is offered by Finkelhor and Browne (1986). Although the Finkelhor and Browne model of four traumagenic dynamics was developed from analysis of literature dominated by accounts of female victimisation, it can be applied to male abuse. The four major areas of affective vulnerability are proposed by them to be betrayal, stigmatisation, powerlessness and traumatic sexualisation. It is this last dynamic, traumatic sexualisation, that I shall be focusing on for the purposes of this study.

Traumatic sexualisation

Traumatic sexualisation is described as the shaping of a child's sexual feelings and attitudes in a manner inappropriate for the child's level of development (Finkelhor and Browne 1986). For example traumatic sexualisation may produce concerns about a homosexual identity in a young male molested by an adult male; interpersonal relationship problems; sexual dysfunctions; and overall confusion about sexual matters.

An example of the possible response by sexually abused males to the traumatic dynamic of powerlessness is aggressive and delinquent behaviour, including re-enacting his own abuse. Men and boys in our society are brought up with an emphasis on mastery of self, environment and others; when confronted with a situation which is beyond their control, it is very unlikely that they will respond by acknowledging powerlessness (Goldstein 1987). It is also unlikely that they will view themselves as victims in the feminine sense of the word. Rather, many will respond by making and reinforcing the psychological, physical and social adjustments that lead them to emulate consent. These adaptations may then be reinforced by adaptive behaviour.

Males who feel traumatically betrayed by sexual abuse often develop angry feelings and may express these in forms of antisocial behaviour and other forms of delinquency. The traumatic dynamic concerning stigmatisation may cause a sexually abused male to develop homophobic responses and increase the risk of sexualised behaviour in order to 'prove' his masculinity.

Victimisation not only violates the masculine ethic of self-reliance, it also raises the stigma of homosexuality. When boys are sexually abused by other males, fears about homosexuality are common. The experience of a homosexual act contradicts the child's understanding of sexual relationships. A victim may worry that he is homosexual; that there must have been something about him that was recognisably homosexual for him to have been singled out by another male. In seeking an explanation for why he was selected, self-blame and guilt are common responses. A male may attribute his selection to a particular aspect of his appearance, his speech, his clothing or any other personal characteristic that might be perceived as effeminate and to have contributed to the assault. Through perceiving himself in this way the male victim may blame himself for having attracted the abuser. If he does not actively resist the molestation this may be taken as further proof of his lack of masculinity. He may be sexually aroused which creates further conflict in his sense of sexual identity and he may define himself as homosexual.

He may fear that the abuse experience will make him homosexual and that others will think he is homosexual. Not only do male victims worry about these issues but their parents and others related to the victim may also be affected by these fears. Parents of molested boys frequently asked about the possibility of this outcome.

The more closely the victim is psychologically identified with the perpetrator, the more intense and exacerbated are his sexual identity issues. Significant males, such as fathers and father-figures, play a large part in the formation of the psychosocial identity of young males and when sexual abuse occurs between a boy and a psychologically close male, the victim is likely to be left with a confusion about his sense of self-identity as related to his identity struggles with the offender. This struggle may be conscious, causing severe distress and confusion, or unconscious and therefore integrated into the self-identity; the victim becomes psychologically identified with the aggressor. Such internalised messages as 'Like father, like son' and 'I am my father's son' may contribute to these sexual identity confusions.

A distinction needs to be made between a fear of homosexuality and the development of a homosexual preference. An associated question is, does child sexual abuse contribute to the expression of a homosexual preference? Finkelhor (1984) thinks this belief is a myth, although his study of college students reported that boys victimised by older men were over four times more likely to be currently engaged in homosexual activity than were non-victims. Similarly Johnson and Shrier (1987), reported greater likelihood that boys molested by males would identify themselves as homosexual in contrast to those molested by females. Further the adolescents themselves often linked their homosexuality to their experience of sexual victimisation.

Fromuth and Burkhart (1989) looked closely at sexual adjustment and behaviour in their two large samples of college men and noted that sexually abused men were no more likely than non-abused men to report a homosexual experience occurring after the age of 12 years. However, they commented that the lack of relationship might be attributed to the majority of perpetrators in this study being female. Concerns about their sexual preferences were reported by a significant minority of adults in each of several clinical reports (Bruckner and Johnson 1987; Dimock 1988; Krug 1989; Singer 1989).

Of a group of 1001 adult homosexual or bisexual men attending a clinic for the treatment of sexually transmitted diseases 37 per cent reported that they had been encouraged or forced into sexual contact by an older or more powerful person before the age of 19 years; 97 per cent of these contacts had been with men. The median age of first contact was 10 years and 51 per cent had been forced and 33 per cent were involved in anal sex (Doll et al. 1992).

It is important to state that in general homosexuals do not report inappropriate sexual experiences in childhood and that only a tiny majority of homosexuals have any sexual interest in children (Finkelhor 1984). A male to male abusive act is not necessarily perpetrated by a homosexual.

In a group of hospitalised adolescents Sansonnet-Hayden et al. (1987) found histories of cross-dressing in five of their six boys in the sample. Correlation was not made with the identity of the perpetrator but it might be expected that in cases of father–son incest there might be greater sexual identity confusion (Watkin and Bentovim 1992). Society naïvely assumes that father–son incest is rare, however Pierce (1987) identified fifty-two separate reports of father–son incest in the literature and summarises these cases as indicating that a multi-dimensional explanation of father–son incest is likely to include three types of families in which father–son incest occurs; homosexual families, promiscuous families and violent families.

Myers (1989) found that all thirteen men in his sample had sustained varying degrees of damage to their subjective sense of maleness or masculinity as a consequence of their assault. Sometimes this gender identity shakiness was temporary and recovered in time; the others had long-standing difficulty. Many equated tarnished masculinity with loss of power, control, selfhood, confidence and independence.

Research into sexual compulsiveness or addiction described by Hunter (1990c) shows that 37.1 per cent of men and 65.2 per cent of women members of Sex Addicts Anonymous reported that they were sexually abused as children. Many other compulsions are also noted as well as sexual addiction; compulsive eating, drug and alcohol abuse are among those often noted.

The victim/perpetrator dynamic

A broad spectrum of theories on the issue of victims becoming offenders has been put forward that are based on clinical impressions to empirical data (O'Brien 1989; Freund, Watson & Dickey 1988; Hindman 1988). O'Brien's empirically derived theory suggests that a significant percentage of males who were sexually abused as children will become offenders. Moreover, he states that the gender of the perpetrator will affect the selection of the gender of the next generation of victims. However, Gerber (1990) extrapolates from his own experience when he says:

> As boys and men have a growing social permission to come forward and identify themselves as victims of sexual molestation and sexual assaults, we will see an increasing number of males referred who have not acted out sexually against others in response to their victimisation (p.153).

Most of the theories that support the 'victim becoming offender' view have come from studies of incarcerated known offenders which may have lent a great bias to this research, rendering it questionable in terms of generalising it to the wider public. It would seem more reasonable to acknowledge that according to research, it occurs with some frequency and causation is attributable to a number of variables. The transition from victim to offender is probably in direct proportion to a number of these variables which include the age of the victim at the onset of the abuse, duration of the abuse, and the level of trauma and arousal experienced by the victim.

The two main psychological theories that contribute to the understanding of how boys might move from the position of victim to that of victimiser are psychodynamic theory and social learning theory. In either of these theories the child will have come to know the passive side of the power dynamic.

Psychodynamic theory describes the dynamic of fixation which suggests that normal development is derailed and the child becomes stuck at one of the stages of ego development (Erikson 1963). For example somebody stuck in the anal stage might become highly conforming and rigid (anal retentive) or very sadistic and cruel (anal aggressive).

Anna Freud (1946) saw ego defences as operations the individual uses to deal with anxiety as a result of libidinal urges. Defence mechanisms have two common features, they distort reality and they operate unconsciously. Two of the commonly recognised defence mechanisms employed are those of denial and repression; victims may deny their victimisation or they may repress the memories of it. Identification with the aggressor is also seen as a way of defending against the recognition of the trauma of the abuse. A striking account of this defence was described in an article in the *Sunday Times* (Vincent 1992). A journalist reported a conversation between an offender and his therapist at the Gracewell Clinic, a rehabilitation centre for sex offenders in the UK:

> 'When did you start abusing?' Without hesitation, Ian replied, 'When I was four'. The therapist looked into Ian's bland small-boy-of-40 face and, keeping his voice level, asked 'And who did you abuse?' 'My father', said Ian.

It would seem that Ian's sense of self precludes a concept of himself as a victim. He can cope better by remembering himself as the 4-year old abuser of his father than confront the fact that he was a helpless abused child.

By a similar process, he cannot feel that the children he abused were victims; he identifies with them. He believes that both they and himself are sexually wanton creatures. This belief helps him to survive without fear of self-disintegration. The extreme anxiety unconsciously felt by the victim might be managed by compulsive re-enactment which is self-destructive or other-destructive as a way of gaining control and managing the unconscious feelings.

Social learning theory (Bandura 1977) also assumes that early experiences have a great potential to affect the child or adolescent developmentally. Social learning theory relies on the assumption that behaviour is largely acquired and such factors as reinforcement are sufficient to explain the maintenance and development of that behaviour. However, social learning theory also takes into account the social context of the behaviour and believes that modelling and learning from others is also important. Children learn from watching and copying the behaviour of adults or older individuals. Bandura describes a classic experiment (1977) demonstrating how children who observe aggressive behaviour are more likely to exhibit aggressive behaviour in a similar context.

In many cases the victim might experience pleasure and arousal in sexually abusive experiences; either same sex or opposite sex experiences. This response is more likely in young males who will frequently respond to their genitals being touched by becoming physically aroused. This might become sufficient reinforcement for that behaviour to be repeated with others as the child develops through adolescence and adulthood.

Social learning theory also provides some explanation for the fact that not all males who have been abused become abusers. Many relational factors may mitigate against re-enactment. If the child has other healthy relationships which counterbalance the abusive ones, they have more of a chance of learning that there is an alternative way to be in relationship with others and gain emotional satisfaction. Loving, balanced male role-models are helpful in this way and particularly among young male victims who are on the verge of adolescence.

6 Findings of research study

The sample group

Finding the subjects

In my preliminary discussions with colleagues and other interested people, the first question normally asked is 'Where are you going to find these men?' The question seems to indicate a collective understanding of the nature of the difficulty that men in our society have in coming forward to admit to childhood sexual abuse. This, of course, is the understanding which underlies my approach to this subject; that the socialisation of males in this culture creates an environment in which those who have been victimised in childhood or even in adulthood do not tell!

Although I set out with the expectation that there would be difficulties in finding such men, I now realise I was somewhat naïve in thinking that this was a problem that might be overcome easily with time, patience and dedication! So often along the way I have seen the subtle and not so subtle ways that my research has been hampered by negative expectations. From the start I became aware of what seemed like a reluctance to expose men to their pain. The warden of a university hall of residence said she would not approach her students because 'you never know what would be stirred up'; the leader of a survivors' group for men who had been abused as children said he would not ask his group if they would participate in the research 'in case it upset them'; a male counsellor said he would find it difficult to suggest to his clients that they might take part in the research as he felt their response would be hostile, although he said he would have no such problem if I wanted to talk to his female clients! I advertised for 'Adult males who were sexually abused during childhood' in a variety of places such as local trade papers, noticeboards in university departments, a religious magazine and a magazine for survivors; a local newspaper ran a small article about my research proposal asking for interviewees. The largest group of responses came from people who had some personal knowledge of my work either first or second hand.

Demographic details

The sample included men who were unemployed, students and people who were self-employed or employees. Two men are currently members of religious organisations. Eleven men are either in a helping professional/voluntary role. One man is in prison serving a sentence for burglary. Two men were retired early, one on the grounds of ill health. Twenty-three of the men were white Caucasian and the other two were of mixed race although they had been born in Britain. Other details can be found in Tables 6.1, 6.2, 6.3 and 6.4.

Parents' relationship

Ten men had parents who had separated; eight of those by divorce and one by death of mother, and one by separation (parents were not married). Five of these separations had occurred between the ages of 10 and 12 years; the other five were at the ages 6 months, 2-years-, 3-years-, 17-years- and 21-years-old. All of the men who had been separated from their fathers through divorce whilst still under the age of 16 years remained in the custody of their mothers; one was left with father for six months whilst mother arranged her life in order to take her child with her – this happened when the child was between 6- to 12-months old. One man whose mother died when he was 10-years-old stayed with father who re-married. Only one of the divorced mothers re-married during the childhood of the subject.

Only two men saw their parents' relationship as 'happy'; most mentioned some discord and several felt that their parents had not loved each other. Many men spoke of the almost constant fear of threatened abandonment by their mothers during the rows between their parents.

Table 6.1 Demographic details of subjects

Subject number	Name	Year of birth	Position in family		Marital status	Children	Sexual orientation
1	Jeremy	1974	Only	1st boy	Single	0	Bisexual
2	Sam	1971	4th child	1st boy	Single	0	Heterosexual
3	William	1969	2nd child	1st boy	Single	0	Heterosexual
4	Justin	1967	Eldest	1st boy	Single	0	Heterosexual
5	James	1967	3rd child	1st boy	Single	0	Bisexual
6	Mike	1966	Eldest		Single	0	Bisexual
7	Kevin	1964	Eldest	1st boy	Married	0	Heterosexual
8	Martin	1961	3rd child	1st boy	Single	0	Homosexual
9	Matthew	1960	Youngest		Male Partner	0	Homosexual
10	Clem	1960	Youngest		Divorced (3x)	0	Heterosexual
11	Tim	1959	3rd child		Single	0	Heterosexual
12	Wayne	1959	Eldest	1st boy	Single	0	Asexual
13	Pete	1956	Youngest		Single	0	Heterosexual
14	Roy	1954	Middle		Divorced	2	Heterosexual
15	Paul	1953	4th child	1st boy	Divorced	1	Heterosexual
16	Robert	1952	Eldest	1st boy	Divorced	2(1)	Heterosexual
17	Harold	1947	Eldest	1st boy	Divorced	0	Heterosexual
18	Denis	1945	Eldest	1st boy	Married (D)	2	Heterosexual
19	Jon	1944	Only	1st boy	Married	2	Heterosexual
20	Len	1944	3rd child		Married	0	Heterosexual
21	Charles	1944	Youngest		Divorced (2x)	1	Heterosexual
22	Harry	1942	Eldest	1st boy	Male Partner	0	Homosexual
23	Tony	1937	Only	1st boy	Single	0	Bisexual
24	George	1934	Only	1st boy	Married	1	Bisexual
25	Barney	1931	Youngest		Single	0	Homosexual

Table 6.2 Demographic details of subjects abused by females only

Subject number	Name	Year of birth	Position in family		Marital status	Children	Sexual orientation
2	Sam	1971	4th child	1st boy	Single	0	Heterosexual
3	William	1969	2nd child	1st boy	Single	0	Heterosexual
7	Kevin	1964	Eldest	1st boy	Married	0	Heterosexual
10	Clem	1960	Youngest		Divorced (3x)	0	Heterosexual
14	Roy	1954	Middle		Divorced	2	Heterosexual
17	Harold	1947	Eldest	1st boy	Divorced	0	Heterosexual
18	Denis	1945	Eldest	1st boy	Married (D)	2	Heterosexual
25	Barney	1931	Youngest		Single	0	Homosexual
Table 6.3 Demographic details of subjects abused by both males and females							
1	Jeremy	1974	Only	1st boy	Single	0	Bisexual
12	Wayne	1959	Eldest	1st boy	Single	0	Asexual
15	Paul	1953	4th child	1st boy	Divorced	1	Heterosexual
16	Robert	1952	Eldest	1st boy	Divorced	2 (1)	Heterosexual
23	Tony	1937	Only	1st boy	Single	0	Bisexual
Table 6.4 Demographic details of subjects abused by males only							
4	Justin	1967	Eldest	1st boy	Single	0	Heterosexual
5	James	1967	3rd child		Single	0	Bisexual
6	Mike	1966	Eldest	1st boy	Single	0	Bisexual
8	Martin	1961	3rd child	1st boy	Single	0	Homosexual
9	Matthew	1960	Youngest		Male Partner	0	Homosexual
11	Tim	1959	3rd child		Single	0	Heterosexual
13	Pete	1956	Youngest		Single	0	Heterosexual
19	Jon	1944	Only	1st boy	Married	2	Heterosexual
20	Len	1944	3rd child		Married	0	Heterosexual
21	Charles	1944	Youngest		Divorced (2x)	1	Heterosexual
22	Harry	1942	Eldest	1st boy	Male Partner	0	Homosexual
24	George	1934	Only	1st boy	Married	1	Bisexual

Relationship with father

None of the men had close relationships with their fathers after they had been divorced or separated from their mothers. One never saw his father again, another saw him four or five times throughout childhood and has recently met up with him again; another visited during school holidays intermittently. Others mentioned occasional visits. One men went to live with his father for a period when he was 12–14-years old.

Four men had been sexually abused by their fathers; one went on to be abused later by a neighbour; another was also abused by grandfather and mother; another was abused later by a stranger and thinks he may also have been abused by his grandfather. One of the four was sexually abused by his father in conjunction with his mother. This father set up the arrangement to include his son in his own sexual activity with his wife. This started when the child was 7. I see this as sexual abuse by the father as well as the mother. No men were sexually abused by a stepfather.

Nine men had fathers who were physically absent through marriage/relationship breakdown, prison or army service and thirteen men had fathers who were physically absent for much of the time through the demands of their work (a weekend father), and experienced as emotionally absent when they were there. The father who had sexually abused his 4-year-old son had attempted suicide when this boy was 6 – he then spent two years in a psychiatric hospital; this father was physically ill most of his life.

Eleven men used words to describe their fathers that indicated emotional absence; words like: distant, withdrawn, uninterested, unconnected, emotionally cold, stilted and remote. At the opposite extreme six fathers and one stepfather were physically violent and over-intrusive in their sons lives. One man who was sexually abused by his father said his father did not know 'when to let go' – he tickled beyond the point of pleasure and cuddled and held him when he wanted to be released.

Two men described a sense of being connected with their father that I would describe as 'symbiotic'; one believing as a child that he had been 'born out of his father's tummy' and the other believing that he and his father were the same person. Two men experienced their relationship with their father as healthy.

Relationships with mother

Thirteen men were abused by females and in seven of these cases the females were their mothers; one of these mothers was divorced during the childhood of the subject. Six men were sexually abused by a mother who was married (and living with a husband) at the time she was abusing her son, although one of them was temporarily separated for a year whilst her husband was in prison for sexually abusing children outside his family. He did not sexually abuse his own children although he did physically abuse them.

Five men were physically abused by their mothers; eight men were emotionally abused by their mothers; six men experienced their mothers as emotionally cold, absent or manipulative; one mother was mentally ill and hospitalised during the period of the abuse; another was constantly ill with polio and other illnesses and eventually died when the subject was 10-years-old; one mother was blind and separated from her husband, first by the war and then by his choice to live with another woman; four men felt they had positive experiences of mothering, although one of those, whose father was absent, felt that his mother was too permissive and did not give him enough guidance and another had a mother who had received head injuries just prior to his birth and had suffered depression and epilepsy during his childhood. One man had felt well cared for physically by his mother, but now realised that his emotional needs had not been met; his mother had been interned during the War in a camp in France before her marriage, something that he perceived as having affected her mothering.

One mother suffered post-natal depression following the subject's birth which occurred just after the death of her twin brother and another mother had suffered severe depression during the subject's early adolescence. Three men felt they had had positive experiences of mothering interspersed with very negative experiences. One man who felt he had a positive experience of mothering had been sexually abused by his mother for eight years. Four men said they suspected that their mothers may have been sexually abused in their childhood; one man knew that this was so.

Frequency of abuse

Six of the men had initially experienced a one-off sexually abusive episode; all but one of these men went on to become abused later. The one man who had a one-off abusive experience and had not been re-abused is a man I thought might have repressed an earlier memory. (Although this is speculation rather than a finding, I think it is necessary to point this out to avoid giving what might be a false picture.) Two of these men went on to be raped as adults by men known to them; one of them has been raped twice as an adult. Another had gone on to be further abused by an age-mate who was also being sexually abused by an older man. This is someone I have thought might have been abused at an earlier age but has repressed the memory. The others had recognised that the one-off incident had created for them a sense of victimisation which had led to further long-term abuses.

One man had been abused daily for about eighteen months from the age of 4 years; two men were frequently abused as rent-boys during adolescence; another, who described his frequency of abuse between the age of 4 and 12 as 'fairly regular', then went on to prostitute himself as an adolescent. One man was abused two or three times a week by both parents between the ages of 7 and 16; another was abused several times a week between the age of 12–17 years; another was abused 'quite a lot' from the age of 6 until he went into a care at the age of 12; those whose abuse happened during the first four years of life cannot remember the frequency but felt it to be fairly often; those whose abuse occurred whilst at boarding school described it as intermittent. One man has no memory of the frequency of the abuse by his father as a very small child but was further abused at the age of 8/9 by a neighbour during a two week period probably on a daily basis.

Types of sexual abuse

(a) Intrusive sexualised conversation e.g. Priest asks 'which way does your penis lie in your trousers – would you show me?' Teacher's girl friend asks about size of penis. Another perpetrator asks 'Do you see your cousin in the bath – what does she look like?'
(b) Abuse of sexuality e.g. sexual humiliation: 'My mother's behaviour ranged from hysterical mockery of my sexuality to abject horror of my genitals.'
(c) Oral sex e.g. subjects had been made to perform oral sex on both male and female perpetrators and had oral sex performed on them by both male and female perpetrators.
(d) Anal penetration attempted. e.g. subjects had been aware of perpetrator trying to push something in from behind them.
(e) Anal penetration performed e.g. subjects had experience of digital, penile and objects' penetration of their anal passage.
(f) Vaginal penetration. e.g. subject had performed intercourse on perpetrator. Another said 'She was putting my little hand inside her vagina.'
(g) Masturbation e.g. subject had performed masturbation on perpetrator or perpetrator had masturbated subject.
(h) Fondling e.g. sexualised touching of perpetrator's breasts, genitals, or of subject's body.

(i) Frottage e.g. hugging and rubbing up against body in sexualised manner.
(j) Deliberate arousal followed by punishment e.g. 'She in some way aroused me to erection and then slapped my penis telling me I was a naughty boy.'
(k) Sexualised beating e.g. headmaster would beat boy on buttocks with trousers down and before adjusting the trousers, he would insist on hugging to show there was no animosity.
(l) Sexualised kissing.
(m)Use of pornography. e.g. 'he would put a picture of a nude woman in front of my face whilst he was coming into me from behind'.
(n) Exhibitionism. e.g. 'she would make me crouch down and watch as she squatted over a mirror and defaecated'.

Some of the subjects were involved in one or several of the above types of abuse. Some overlap as in the case of one man who felt humiliated and disgusted by being forced to perform cunnilingus on his sister and oral sex whilst she was menstruating.

Contexts of abuse

Place abuse occurred are listed in Tables 6.5, 6.6, 6.7 and 6.8.

Although fourteen children experienced abuse in their own homes, it was more usual for the child to be outside the home when the abuse occurred (several children were abused both inside and outside the home, see table). Three boys were abused at boarding school which could be seen as the temporary home for a child. Abuse also occurred in temporary homes, such as a foster home and a hospital. Men who were abused by females were all abused in the home; one of these was a temporary foster home and one was the home of his abuser. The men who were abused by both males and females were abused in the home. All but one of the men abused by males were abused outside the home. One of them was abused at home as well as outside the home.

Age differentials

Seven men were abused by people who would have been categorised as children themselves when the abuse occurred. Five of these have also been abused by adults. In three of those cases the abuse by adults preceded the abuse by age mates.

Nine of the men had re-enacted their abuse experiences during their childhood with other children. Seven of these men reported that they now realised that their behaviour had been sexual abuse of age-mates. Two men identified themselves as abusers of children in their adult lives.

Relationship with abuser is described in Tables 6.5–6.8.

How the abuse was experienced at the time is described in Tables 9-11.

Thirteen of the men felt their first experience of abuse as negative at the time it was happening. Eight experienced it as positive (one of these was also in the previous group because he was later abused by his mother and experienced that as negative and positive on different occasions). Five had no feelings about it (neutral); four men 'got to like it' as the abuse continued.

Eight of those who experienced it as 'negative' had experienced pain or force of some degree, creating feelings of fear. Of the others who experienced it as negative, one felt shame and embarrassment and the other powerlessness and anger. These feelings were also described to some degree by the others who felt negative.

The three who felt it as 'positive' at the time had experienced the event as part of receiving love – two of them were lonely, isolated children who were deprived of attention and loving touch in their homes; the other was involved with sex with both parents which he interpreted as the way love was shown by parents to their children. One man who was constantly verbally abused by his older sister except when she was sexually abusing him found that this meant that the whole experience of abuse became associated with her 'being nice'. Another who felt positive described it as part of having 'fun' and 'messing around' – this included getting drunk at the age of 9. This was seen as part of normal 'working class life'.

One who felt neutral was at an all-male monastic boarding school where the culture was one of accepting that sexuality between males was 'normal' and part of everybody's experience. Two others who felt it as 'neutral' were also in an all-male environment – one in an all-male monastic boarding school and the other in an all male school for young offenders. One of these men had been sexually abused by his mother in early childhood and had no memory of his feelings about it at the time except that he was loved. Two who felt it as neutral at the time said they just didn't understand what was going on. Five who felt 'neutral' had been coerced either by money or the promise of some reward. All who experienced it as positive had been coerced by the promise of 'love' or affection.

How the abuse is viewed now

Twenty of the men now view their abuse as negative. They base this on the effect it has had on their lives. One man sees that it was not

Table 6.5 Abuse characteristics

Subject number	Age first abused	Age at disclosure	Year of	Gender	Relationship of abuser	Type of abuse	Place
1	4	12	1986	M&F	Babysitters and older girls	O A M Fo	Home and local
2	6	19	1990	F	Half sisters and sister	M F C VP	Home
3	4	23	1992	F	Sister	Ex	Home
4	4	14	1981	M	Neighbour	O M Fo K	Next door house
5	12	19	1986	M	Stranger and Father/G'F	O M Fo P	Railway tunnel and home
6	12	27	1993	M	Punters	O M F P	Rent-boy scene
7	0	29	1993	F	Mother	C F Fr	Home
8	10	29	1990	M	Father's friend and friend's older brother	M F Fo	River bank and Friend's home
9	14	23	1983	M	Peer	A M	Day school
10	11	31	1991	F	Teacher's girlfriend	M Fr	Teacher's home
11	4/5	33	1992	M	Father and Neighbour	A M	Home and neighbour's home
12	1/3	40	1991	M & F	Father, Grandfather and Mother	A Fo O M	Home
13	10	37	1993	M	Schoolmaster	Fr M	Boarding school
14	0	29	1983	F	Mother	AS	Home
15	7	40	1993	F & M	Mother and father	O M VP K	Home
16	83	5	1987	M & F	Soldiers and mother	O M Fo	Army bunker and home
17	0	31	1978	F	Mother	Ar & Pu	Home
18	4	44	1993	F	Carers (2)	AS	Foster-care
19	4	44	1988	M	Grandfather's employee	M O AP	Stable near home
20	12	17	1961	M	Peers, priest and chaplain	M SB & ST	Chaplaincy and boarding school
21	14	44	1988	M	Stranger	M O	Public lavatory
22	8	30	1972	M	Hospital patient, lodger and punters	A O K M	Hospital, home and rent-boy scene
23	0	56	1993	F & M	Mother and schoolmaster	Fr M	Home and boarding school
24	10	52	1986	M	Stranger and peer	M A O	Cinema, friend's home
25	7	62	1993	F	Sister	M O	Home

O= oral sex (where not stipulated if F or C), M = masturbation, Fo = fondling, Fr = frottage (sexualised rubbing against), F = Fellatio, C = Cunnilingus, K = kissing, AS = the abuse of sexuality (humiliating, mocking etc.), A = Anal sex, OP = penetration by objects, AP = attempted penetration, VP = Vaginal penetration, Ar&Pu = Arousal followed by punishment, ST = sexualised talk, SB = sexualised beating, Ex = Exhibitionism

Table 6.6 Abuse characteristics of men abused by males only

Subject number	Age first abused	Age at disclosure	Year of disclosure	Gender of abuser	Relationship of abuser	Type of abuse	Place
4	4	14	1981	M	Neighbour	O M Fo K	Next door house
5	12	19	1986	M	Stranger and Father/Grandfather	O M Fo P	Railway tunnel and home
6	12	27	1993	M	Punters	O M F P	Rent-boy scene
8	10	29	1990	M	Father's friend and friend's older brother	M F Fo	River bank and friend's home
9	14	23	1983	M	Peer	A M	Day school
11	4/5	33	1992	M	Father and neighbour	A M	Home and neighbour's home
13	10	37	1993	M	Schoolmaster	Fr M	Boarding school
19	4	44	1988	M	Grandfather's employee	M O AP	Stable near home
20	12	17	1961	M	Peers, priest and chaplain	M SB &	Chaplaincy and boarding school
21	14	44	1988	M	Stranger	M O	Public lavatory
22	8	30	1972	M	Hospital patient, lodger and punters	A O K M	Hospital, home and rent-boy scene
24	10	52	1986	M	Stranger and peer	M A O	Cinema, friend's home
Table 6.7 Abuse charactersistics of men abused by females only							
2	6	19	1990	F	Half sisters and sister	M F C VP	Home
3	4	23	1992	F	Sister	Ex	Home
7	0	29	1993	F	Mother	C F Fr	Home
10	11	31	1991	F	Teacher's girlfriend	M Fr	Teacher's home
14	0	29	1983	F	Mother	AS	Home
17	0	31	1978	F	Mother	Ar & Pu	Home
18	4	44	1993	F	Carers (2)	AS	Foster home
25	7	62	1993	F	Sister	M O	Home
Table 6.8 Abuse characteristics of men abused by both males and females							
1	4	12	1986	M&F	Babysitters and older girls	O A M Fo	Home and local
12	1/3	40	1991	M & F	Father, Grandfather and Mother	A Fo O M	Home
15	7	40	1993	F & M	Mother and father	O M VP K	Home
16	8	35	1987	M & F	Soldiers and mother	O M Fo	Army bunker and home
23	0	56	1993	F & M	Mother and school master	Fr M	Home and boarding school

O = oral sex (where not stipulated if F or C), M = masturbation, Fo = fondling, Fr = frottage (sexualised rubbing against), F = Fellatio, C = Cunnilingus, K = kissing, AS = the abuse of sexuality (humiliating, mocking etc.), A = Anal sex, OP = penetration by objects, AP = attempted penetration, VP = Vaginal penetration, Ar&Pu = Arousal followed by punishment, ST = sexualised talk, SB = sexualised beating, Ex = Exhibitionism

Table 6.9 Men abused by males

Subject number	How experienced		Relationship with father	Relationship with mother	Main self-identification
4	Neutral	(C)	Emotional neglect	Emotional neglect	Aggressor
5	Negative	(Force)	Sexual, physical and emotional abuse	Emotional and physical abuse	Victim
6	Neutral/Positive	(C)	Physically and emotionally absent	Emotionally and physically absent	Aggressor
8	Negative/Positive	(C)	Physical and emotional abuse	Emotional abuse	Victim/Aggressor
9	Negative	(Force)	Emotionally absent	Good but depressed	Victim
11	Positive	(C)	Emotionally absent and sexual abuse	Emotional neglect	Aggressor
13	Neutral	(C)	Absent/symbiotic	Good	Victim
19	Positive	(C)	Emotionally and physically absent	Emotionally and physically absent	Victim
20	Neutral	(C)	Good	Good	Aggressor
21	Negative	(Force)	Emotionally absent	Emotionally absent	Victim
22	Negative/Positive	(Fear, C)	Physically and emotionally absent	Emotionally absent, physical abuse	Victim
24	Positive	(C)	Physically and emotionally absent	Good but blind	Victim/Aggressor

Table 6.10 Men abused by females

Subject number	How experienced		Relationship with father	Relationship with mother	Main self-identification
2	Negative/Positive	(C)	Physically and emotionally absent	Physical abuse, emotionally absent	Victim/Aggressor
3	Positive	(C)	Physically and emotionally absent	Good	Aggressor
7	Negative	(Fear)	Symbiotic	Emotionally absent, sexual abuse	Victim
10	Positive	(C)	Emotionally and physically absent	Emotionally abuse	Aggressor
14	Negative	(Fear)	Emotionally and. physically absent	Physical abuse, sexual abuse	Victim
17	Negative	(Fear)	Emotically and physically abuse	Sexual abuse	Victim
18	Negative	(H)	Physical abuse	Good	Victim
25	Negative	(C)	Not known	Not known	Victim

Table 6.11 Men abused by both males and females

Subject number	How experienced		Relationship with father	Relationship with mother	Main self-identification
1	Positive	(C)	Physically and emotionally absent	Good but neglectful	Victim/Aggressor
12	Negative	(Fear)	Sexual abuse	Emotional, physical and sexual abuse	Victim
15	Positive	(C)	Sexual abuse	Sexual abuse	Victim/Aggressor
16	Negative/Positive	(Force,C)	Physical and emotional abuse	Sexual abuse	Aggressor
23	Neutral	(C)	Physically and emotionally absent	Sexual abuse	Victim/aggressor

(C) = coercion, (H) = humiliation

right for an 18-year-old to engage him in sexual activity as a 9-year-old but he does not know if it has had any effect on his life; however, he later said he thought it had caused him problems in forming relationships. This man has suffered premature ejaculation and has severe relationship problems with women. One man who felt it was 'OK' still sees it as 'what was' or 'fair enough' and does not think it has had a negative effect on his life. He feels more abused by the way his parents moved him from home to home without consultation during his childhood. This man experiences intermittent impotence, problems with monogamy, and ritualised sexual fantasies.

The other man who is not sure about whether it has been negative or not, feels that, when he is with a woman, he has been lucky to have been 'instructed' so well by his mother and father in sexual behaviour but when he is not with a woman he feels that his parents are to blame because 'they set such a high standard that I find it difficult to find anybody to match up to them'. This man is divorced and retired through ill-health at the age of 40, having had an ileostomy and five operations on his intestines. He recognises that this is a stress-related illness but does not connect the abuse with it. When he spoke to me it was the first time he had ever talked to anybody about it and he said he would probably never mention it again. He was included in his parents' sex life from the age of 7 up to the age of 16 when he left home. This involved his father setting up the situation for him to penetrate his mother as a small boy with his hand and later perform full intercourse with her and was fellated by his mother; it also involved performing cunnilingus on his mother and being digitally penetrated by her. He and his father never touched each other but father was part of the scenario whilst it was happening and set up the scene for action. His son described his father as generous, because he arranged for things to happen that other kids just talked about. (i.e. sex with his mother).

Whilst looking back over what had happened to them and seeing it as negative, many men also saw that what had happened to them had some positive aspects. This was particularly the case for men who were now working through their abuse and had arrived at the understanding of how the therapeutic work they had done on themselves had enhanced their lives and developed their ability to empathise, to understand and to be available to others. This view could fit with my earlier description of the concept of the wounded healer. Three men said that they felt that they had become a better lover through their experiences. Although this might seem contrary to expectations, it could be understood that people who have been sexually abused and have worked on that issue may become more comfortable with and more aware of their sexuality than people who have not needed to focus on this aspect of their development.

Problems defining abuse

Twenty of the men had difficulty defining what happened to them as abuse; this difficulty is connected with the use of the word 'abuse' as well as the activity involved. One had realised that he had been abused at the age of 4, when he had a flashback at the age of 14 during ejaculation but had felt too ashamed and guilty to disclose. Two others had realised that what had happened to them as 4-year-olds was sexual abuse on reaching the age of 12–14 and that was when they had become consciously distressed by it.

Repression

Repression of the memory of abuse had occurred in those who had been abused in their early childhood (0–4) and had been remembered approximately, 21, 27, 29, 31, 40 and 56 years later whilst in therapy. Four of them had been abused later; one by a stranger in a railway tunnel; one at boarding school by boys and staff. Two of them had been abused during their adulthood: one by his therapist, and one by a male nurse who had cared for him during a period of hospitalisation whilst having an emotional breakdown and who then engaged with him sexually following his discharge.

One man who had been abused at the age of 4/5 (and is in the second group) repressed the memory until he was 14-years-old and another (in the same group) until he was 12-years-old; neither of them were in therapy at the time the memories returned. Another man repressed the memory of his abuse at the age of 10 for nineteen years and remembered outside therapy. There were four men who I thought might still be repressing memories of earlier abuse whilst remembering abuse that happened later. My thinking is that there was a possibility of earlier abuse that had in some way created a situation in which they had been 'ripe' for the later abuse (this is explained more fully during the discussion). This word was one that was used by a young man who himself believed that he must have been abused earlier than his clearly remembered one-off abuse at the age of 12.

Repression of the memory of the abuse experience is only one reason why men are unable to define what happened to them in those terms. There were several other reasons for this difficulty which I have described below.

Pleasure and/or arousal

Twelve men who had experienced the abuse as sexually arousing and/or pleasurable either at the time it was happening or as it went on, found it hard to feel this as abuse, even when they intellectually knew it to be. The two men who became paedophiles, had both felt their abuse as loving and warm; one was abused by his mother and the other by a male stranger in a cinema (maybe repressed earlier memories).

For some, their need to be loved was so overwhelming that even as adults they had found it difficult or too painful to allow themselves to believe that it might have been abuse:

> I just remembered the feeling of him having love for me – I went through my childhood in a haze of sexual ecstasy. I didn't want to recognise it as abuse because that would make me feel even worse. I wanted to hold onto something, some little bit of warmth about my childhood – when you are young, anything to do with someone giving you pleasure, you think of as an act of love.

He described his abuser as the only person in his life to make him feel wanted and the only person who had shown interest in him as a person around the age of 4/5 years.

Sometimes the abuser was the person who was turned to for comfort during times of stress within the family, as in the case of one man whose neighbour abused him. He had felt frightened and confused about his parent's frequent rows and his mother's threats of abandonment during these times when his father was beating her. Most of the men who had experienced their abuse as pleasurable were emotionally deprived children who had experienced little warmth and closeness in their families. The man who had been abused by a stranger in a cinema said 'It was the warmest, most loving thing that ever happened to me before or since.'

When this warmth and love was part of the mother/father/child relationship, the confusion this creates can be considerable. The man who had been abused by his mother and father said:

> I didn't feel what was happening was abuse; it was very loving and part of giving affection (penetrating his mother and having her perform oral sex on him). When I was 16 and left home, I thought then that this was something I should have learned through my own experience and not from my parents. I think because it was my mother it was acceptable – if it had been a man then it wouldn't have been. Although I knew I shouldn't be getting it from Mum I thought of it as 'over-loving', not as 'abuse'.

He felt grateful and loving towards his parents so he could not allow himself to feel abused by them. He still has close contacts with his parents and their past sexual behaviour with him has never been referred to. He believes that his own abuse which started when his sisters left home when he was 7-years-old, had begun because his sisters were no longer available. He has never discussed this with his sisters.

A particular difficulty in recognising their experience as abusive was found with other men who had been abused by their mothers. Tony, whose father left his mother when he was 2-years-old, always remembers his childhood as being 'just the two of us and we were very close':

> I think it is difficult just linguistically. I'm very suspicious of this word 'abuse'. Abuse is used both for beating and physical assault and for sexual activity and in my case there is no question of assault of any kind. Sexual abuse now carries overtones of wickedness, prison and that kind of thing and I don't like to apply that for example to my mother.

One man who had been abused by his father and later by a neighbour had only started to realise he had been abused by his father when he heard that his sister had been abused by him. Then certain things started to come together and feeling memories returned. The other man who had been abused by his father had always hated being close to his father but had not realised why until his memories returned.

Degree of abuse

Most of the men said in some way that they weren't sure if they fitted with what I was looking for and when I asked them what made them unsure, they expressed the feeling that they had not been abused 'enough'; that it was 'only a one-off', or that no force or penetration had been involved or that it was not within the family. When I then asked if they thought it had affected their lives in any way all twenty-three men (even those who expressed doubt about the connection between the abuse and any of their present problems) said that it had probably affected them very negatively.

The use of language

The word 'abuse' was often referred to as being a difficult one to apply to their experience. As Tony previously stated, the word has so many negative connotations that might not be applied to individual experiences. I had not advertised for men who felt their abuse had been harmful but for 'male survivors of childhood sexual abuse'. Some felt that the word 'abuse' implied force and therefore could not be what had happened to them:

> I can see that in a way I was abused, but it was a different form of abuse compared with someone who had violent abuse inflicted on them or abuse within the family where it's awkward to say something. It's different from what is the main concept of abuse.

One of the men had been unable to identify his feelings until he read the book *Males at Risk* by Bolton et al. (1990) which used the term 'the abuse of sexuality' rather than 'sexual abuse'. He reported a tremendous feeling of relief at the insight this phrase allowed him in defining his experience of having been humiliated and derided about his maleness and his genitals throughout his childhood. His mother, who herself had been sexually abused in childhood by her stepfather, had developed an abhorrence of male genitalia and sexuality which she demonstrated towards her child.

Responsibility

Some men felt confused about whether or not they could allow themselves to apply the word 'abuse' to their experience because of feeling that they had some responsibility for what had happened. Sometimes this was the message the abuser had given the child:

> I thought I had done something wrong. He told us that what we had done was against the law; that I had broken the law.

For Mike who had become a rent-boy whilst absconding from a Borstal, it had been difficult to define his abuse as such because he had put himself in a position where the abuse could happen:

> That's why I say I haven't really been abused; because I went into it voluntary, quite voluntary, quite aware of what I was doing really, although when we got to his house he made me go up his arse and all that and I didn't really want to do that – I was only just 13 – I thought it would just be a wank.

When the children had been criticised as being effeminate or a 'sissy' they had assumed that it was this inherent fault in them that had caused them to be abused. Three men described the painful humiliation of their father's anger at them for not being sufficiently manly. Martin said:

> I remember as a child of 6 or 7, my father trying desperately to teach me to play football and I couldn't manage it. He began to refer to me as a pansy, a jessie, a queer because I couldn't play

> football and began to ridicule me; one day it all got too much and he physically beat me to the point where I had concussion.

Sometimes the child accommodates the experience by assuming the role of the 'bad' person; the 'bad' feelings the child experiences have to belong somewhere and as the child is so dependent on the adult, he needs to see the adult as the 'all good' care-giver; it then becomes impossible for the bad feelings to be put onto the abuser. In order to deal with the feelings the child must then take them into himself and thereby experience himself as 'bad'. This is even more likely to happen if the abuser is someone close to the child as it is easier to perceive a stranger as 'bad' than a parent or close friend of the family. Martin coped by believing that he must have been to blame for his abuse because of his badness:

> It must have been my fault … I must have been a bad person who caused these good people to do these things to me and particularly when it happened the second time – there was definitely something strange about me that had caused this.

This coping mechanism allows the child to hold on to a sense of self-mastery; this avoids the need for the child to face up to or deal with the feelings of powerlessness and vulnerability which might be an anathema to the self-concept:

> I thought, there's something wrong with me – that I had got myself into this situation – it was my responsibility. I felt as if there was something inherently wrong with me that had made him do it.

Responsibility for the abuse is often imposed on the child by the abuser who might use all sorts of ways to coerce the child into the activity. This is often part of the grooming process used by paedophiles who become skilled at a range of techniques which are designed to leave the child feeling responsible. This ensures the child will keep the secret and allows the perpetrator to continue with the abuse:

> I felt it was my fault because I had allowed myself to be coerced. Part of it was money – he offered us hundreds of pounds. It was more subtle than that – sort of hinting at what he might want or he wanted us to do and what he was going to do but not being explicit or direct about it. He said 'it is something we all do – all your friends are doing this'. Persuading us it was totally natural – that it was right not wrong.

This form of persuasion relies on the socialisation of boys into believing that all 'real men' want sex in any form, that this behaviour is 'natural' or normal among males.

One man had been told by his abuser that the abuse was a form of 'practice' for what he would do with women; his abuser encouraged his 9-year-old victim to find a girl friend. Another abuser bribed his victim with the promise that he would find a woman for him to have sex with in return for his co-operation in the abuse in a public lavatory and yet another man had been abused by an older boy who promised his victim the 'use' of his own girl friend if the abuse was complied with.

Fear of disclosure

Those who had disclosed their abuse after it had ended and whilst they were still children had experienced either disbelief or their parent's need to keep the disclosure away from the statutory agencies for fear of the further distress that might be experienced by the system:

> I told my mother and father about my abuse when I was 14 and they believed me and comforted me obviously because I was crying. But the abuse was never reported to the police because the person who abused me was mentally ill and was institutionalised. He sometimes came back and visited his parents' home next door to me; he was on heavy sedation and my mother and father didn't think it was worth raking it up because it would be his word against mine and it would be more likely that he would not be prosecuted. I think they thought it would do me more harm than good.

One mother accused the abuser of her 7-year-old child in a face-to-face confrontation but did not report him to the police or social services. The child was no longer abused by that perpetrator but continued to be abused by others. Had she reported it to the statutory agencies the child might have been given the help he needed and the protection from the abuse perpetrated by others or he might have suffered further from the way the system works. Although he could rationally understand his mother's wish to protect him from the exposure of Court proceedings, he had also felt anger towards her for her decision which left him exposed to further abuse.

Fear of judgement, especially amongst those children who had been criticised as effeminate, played a major part in non-disclosure:

> Mostly I didn't tell because I was scared. What did it say about me? Who did it say I was ? Would my parents believe me? What would happen to the people who had abused me? I

couldn't face the publicity and being at the centre of something so awful. I wanted to live on the edge; life was so precarious as it was. I couldn't bear any further exposure.

This last sentence highlights how the child might feel the 'exposure' to investigation as a reflection of the physical exposure they have undergone during the abuse.

Prevalence related to definition

Prevalence can only be measured if abuse is defined, acknowledged and reported. From the above section it can be seen that problems males have in defining abuse will make it unlikely that they will acknowledge or report what has happened in those terms. Prevalence figures in the literature have been gleaned from sources that make it unlikely that such men as those I have interviewed would be included. Although this is a comparatively small sample, it seems reasonable to expect that there may be many more incidences of male abuse than are reported.

Problems with definition can be explained by psychodynamic theory (repression) and by the socialisation of males; it can also be seen to be influenced by the attitudes engendered by that socialisation being within a patriarchal society which makes it difficult for males to acknowledge their vulnerability.

Disclosure of abuse

Only one of these episodes of abuse had ever been reported to a member of the statutory agencies, and that one was disbelieved (females don't abuse males) by the social worker to whom it was reported in 1986 – only seven years ago. This man did not attempt to disclose again until approximately six years later. One had told his parents when he was 12-years-old at the time it had occurred and had not been believed (priests don't abuse); he went on to be further abused by other people and did not attempt to disclose again until he was 17-years-old. This is the man who finds it hard to accept that his abuse has damaged him.

Another man had disclosed to his parents at the age of 14 that he had been abused by their neighbour from 4–12 years of age. Five of the men had told nobody about their abuse before being interviewed by me. Two men had first disclosed to their wives; nine had disclosed to close friends as adults; three had disclosed to psychiatrists during treatment; one of these men was being treated for 'homosexuality', one for violent behaviour and one for depression and admitted at this time to abusing behaviour (although this was not reported); none of them felt they had been listened to. Three had first disclosed whilst in therapy and had felt helped.

It is interesting to note that of the thirteen men who disclosed during the 1990s, nine had been abused by females and five of these had disclosed for the first time in 1993. The first ever conference on the subject of females abusers was held by KIDSCAPE in March 1992, thus opening the door for this type of abuse to be acknowledged and discussed publicly.

Disclosure had occurred between one year and fifty-six years after the event; the average being just over twenty-eight years. One man had told his mother when he was 7 that he had been abused since the age of 4 (it just slipped out in conversation) but he did not disclose that he was also being abused by others and this abuse continued.

The main reasons for non-disclosure were fear, shame and guilt; inability to define what happened as abuse; and repression. Only three of the men had disclosed their abuse to a parent as an adult. One of these received the message that he had been 'equally to blame' for his sisters abusing him from the age of 6; the others had not felt helped by the disclosure. Most did not think of telling their parents because they felt they would not want to know. Others felt it would be too painful for their parents who were now elderly and they would feel responsible for causing them hurt. One man said he would not tell his mother because he had read in a book that someone who had done this had been caused 'aggro' and he felt he had had enough of that in his life. Others felt that they now had a reasonable relationship with their parents and which they did not want to jeopardise. The underlying theme was that parents really did not want to know!

Male socialisation

As well as the messages about the need for males to be perceived as strong and 'in charge', the messages about the roles and expectations of males and females in sexual relationships have added to the difficulty in recognising their experience as abuse:

> I couldn't see it as her abusing me because I was the man of the house as well as being an emerging man in my own right and apart from being my mother, she was a woman. I'd been educated by my father that women were there for cooking, cleaning and sex. They were put on earth for our benefit and every man should have several. They were not abusers, they were victims and abused upon. So how could she abuse me

when I'm the man?.

The above quotation highlights the double difficulty in accepting firstly that his mother was capable of abuse and secondly that a woman could be the aggressor in sexual relationships.

All of the men presented themselves for the interview as men who had been abused – even the one who thought his abuse was 'OK' In fact it was because he had heard me saying that I thought all abuse was harmful that he decided to put himself forward for interview – in order to put the opposite view. At the age of 15 he had woken during the night whilst staying at the Chaplaincy to find a priest in his bed. This man was a trusted family friend.

> I'd performed a service for him and as long as everybody kept quiet about it then it wasn't going to be a problem. I felt sorry for the guy. I liked him, I loved him and still do. I'm fond of him. He had a good war record and came from a landed family; he'd espoused celibacy for Christ – with a plonker like that it was a bit of a shame really. He should have been making himself and some partner happy. So it was kind of 'out of the way' but as long as it doesn't become 'dirty' then it was no problem. If he'd done it to a girl, that would feel quite bad. Taking advantage of a weaker person – that would have been abuse. My morality says in that case it wouldn't have been right for him to go to bed with someone who was staying in his house, and he just slipped in during the night. He ought to have negotiated it ... in male company it's alright – like playing rugby.

This quotation contains so many reasons why this man could not allow himself to feel what happened to him negatively. Male socialisation messages about what is OK between males and how this is different for females; the difficulty of feeling abused by someone who is loved, admired and in a position of trust and authority; the feeling of needing to keep quiet if it is not to become 'dirty'; and the sense of self-mastery and being in control which is expressed by him needing to keep quiet in order for everything to stay OK. None of the responsibility is being put onto the abuser and all is being taken by the abused, even though he can see that the behaviour would not have been acceptable with a female who he perceives as a 'weaker person'. Holding onto a sense of responsibility allows him to avoid feeling 'weak' – something that is often more painful for males to acknowledge than it is for females.

Tim had difficulty in accepting that he had been abused as this might then mean that he had to identify himself as a victim. He could accept that his sister who had also been abused by their father was a victim but that was acceptable because she was a woman. Several men said in some way that they were not comfortable with applying the word 'victim' to themselves.

The need for the male to see himself as the one with the sexual power created confusion for Clem who was abused from the age of 13 by his teacher's 23-year-old girlfriend:

> Diane was something good that I had messed up; it wasn't abuse as such. But this is where it clicked. When the social worker said: 'Well OK, you are saying that you were just as responsible as she was. If you do to a 13-year-old girl what Diane did to you – do you think that is on?
>
> I said: 'Of course not – that's a form of abuse isn't it?'; then she said: 'well that is what happened to you'. But the trouble is I don't feel abused – this is the trouble. All I know is that I just feel quite worthless. My business has gone; I've lost three wives. I don't think the harm she did me was sexual – I think it was that I didn't have a normal development. She didn't take me to bed.

Outcomes of abuse

Traumatic sexualisation

This is a man who masturbates six or seven times a day even now as a 49-year-old man, who never experiences orgasm when with a woman and who engages in sexual activity with women much older than him and frequently changes his sexual partners. He is never fulfilled or satisfied with his sexual behaviour. It is only during the last six months that he has begun to realise he was abused and has started to work on that. He has spent the last twenty-six years re-enacting his abuse unconsciously in a desperate attempt to make sense of his experience and gain control of his life. Yet he does not see that the abuse has damaged him sexually.

Twenty-three of the men reported sexual problems either currently or in the past (see Table 6.12). Twenty-one men expressed fear of intimate relationships. Eighteen men referred to compulsivity and one to 'difficulty with monogamy'. Eight men have engaged in compulsive masturbation to the extent that it had interfered with their lives to a great degree and felt self-abusive; four men also had sado-masochistic fantasies whilst masturbating which caused anxiety and distress and one man said they felt it was 'sick' and another 'out of balance'. One man felt a compulsion to dress up in his sister's clothes and masturbate; he also engaged in compulsive sexual

Table 6.12 Negative sexual experiences

Subject number	1	2	3	4	5	6	7	8	9	10	11	12	13	14	15	16	17	18	19	20	21	22	23	24	25	Total
Sexual dissatisfaction	+		+	+	+	+	+	+	+	+	+	+	+	+	+	+	+		+	+	+	+	+	+	+	23
Excessive masturbation			+	+	+	+	+			+				+											+	8
Flashing					+	+																				2
Sexual compulsivity	+	+	+	+	+	+	+	+		+	+			+	+	+				+	+	+		+	+	18
Lack sexual confidence	+	+	+	+	+			+	+	+	+	+	+	+		+	+		+		+			+	+	18
Abuse self sexually	+		+		+	+	+			+	+											+		+		9
Intimacy problems	+	+	+	+	+	+	+	+	+	+	+	+		+	+	+	+	+			+		+	+	+	21
S&M fantasies			+	+			+													+						23
Fear of women		+	+	+					+		+	+		+	+		+	+								10
Fear of men				+				+	+			+		+							+					6
Paedophilia																+								+		2
Gender confusion	+		+		+	+		+	+			+				+								+		9
Orientation	+			+		+		+			+	+								+		+	+		+	10

activity with a dog and fantasised about sex with other animals. Two men suffered premature ejaculation and three suffered intermittent impotence and difficulty with arousal.

Five of the men have been convicted of sex offences; two men admitted to 'flashing'; one of them had been charged for this behaviour when he was 13-years-old; the other had never been caught whilst flashing and masturbating in public between the ages of 16–18. This man was arrested recently for shouting and screaming obscenities in a public park. He had been shouting at his abuser who is now dead. Another man had been charged at the age of 15 with 'gross indecency' for having sex with his 14-year-old girl friend on a grave in a cemetery. One man had been charged with 'gross indecency' for picking men up in public lavatories for sex. Another man had been charged with gross indecency for abusing his daughter and her 11-year-old friend. Another self-identified paedophile, has never been charged with any of his offences on at least seven children, including his own son (recently imprisoned).

Two men reported using prostitutes currently and one of these men admitted to abusing them. Pornography was used by six men. Neither of these issues, the use of prostitutes or the use of pornography, was specifically raised during the interview. It would be useful perhaps to include questions on these issues in any later study.

Two men had become rent-boys; one of these had engaged in this behaviour whilst absconding from Borstal; the other had lived at home during this period but had never been supervised by his parents. The first of these men had become a pimp for his girl-friend who had also been sexually abused in childhood. Another one later prostituted himself in a relationship with an older man.

Anti-social behaviour

Apart from the five men convicted of sexual offences, seven men had been convicted of other offences – making the overall number of convicted offenders twelve. The most up-to-date figures available from the Home Office (1993) describe a cohort study of men born in 1953 which showed that 36 per cent had been convicted of serious offences by the age of 35 (excluding traffic offences). The number of men who had been convicted of sex offences was 0.6 per cent This indicates a higher percentage of the men in my study (50 per cent) than the average population have convictions and particularly convictions for sex offences (20 per cent) which (although taken from a small sample) seems significant (see Table 6.13).

One man had been court martialled for having sex with an officer's wife whilst in the armed forces and also for assaulting a guard and taking and driving away a vehicle whilst he was being

Table 6.13 Problems experienced by research subjects at some stage

Subject number	1	2	3	4	5	6	7	8	9	10	11	12	13	14	15	16	17	18	19	20	21	22	23	24	25	Total
Depression	+	+	+	+	+	+	+	+	+	+	+	+	+	+	+	+	+	+	+	+	+	+	+	+	+	23
Suicidal feelings	+	+	+	+	+		+	+	+	+		+		+	+	+			+	+	+	+		+		18
Behaviour problems	+	+		+	+	+				+	+	+				+				+	+	+				12
Criminal record	+	+		+	+	+		+		+	+					+					+					10
Sex problem	+	+	+	+	+	+	+	+	+	+	+	+	+	+	+	+			+	+	+	+	+	+	+	23
Drugs	+	+		+		+						+				+										6
Alcohol	+	+		+		+				+	+	+				+					+	+				10
Fear or anxiety	+	+	+	+	+		+	+	+	+	+	+	+	+	+		+	+	+		+	+			+	20
Illness			+								+	+			+				+			+			+	7
Hyperactive		+						+		+					+	+						+				6
Relationship problems	+	+	+	+	+	+					+	+	+	+	+	+	+	+		+	+			+	+	18
Confidence loss	+	+	+	+	+	+	+	+	+	+	+	+	+	+	+	+	+		+		+	+	+	+	+	23
Concentration loss	+	+	+	+	+	+	+	+	+	+	+	+	+			+	+		+							16
Schoolwork suffered	+	+		+	+	+			+	+						+			+							9
Isolation	+	+	+	+	+	+	+	+	+			+	+			+	+		+		+	+		+	+	18
Revictimised	+			+					+	+		+	+	+				+		+	+	+				11
Perpetrator	+	+				+		+			+					+				+			+	+		8
Passivity or aggression	+	+	+	+	+	+	+	+	+	+	+	+	+	+	+	+	+	+	+		+	+		+	+	23

held in custody. Another has been convicted for being drunk and disorderly and on another occasion for 'threatening behaviour'. Another was fined for aggressive behaviour, which involved him throwing a bottle at a passing car in which a child was injured; another young man had been convicted of shoplifting; one man has been convicted thirteen times for burglary; another has been imprisoned twice for deception and attempted burglary; two more men admitted to stealing but had never been charged; three men admitted to drug dealing but had never been charged; one of these men had also engaged in gun-running after leaving the Army. Six men had used drugs and four of them had been addicted. Ten men had used alcohol to excess.

Depression and suicidal ideation

All of the subjects had described some degree of depressive feelings and all but two, severely. Those who had suffered from severe depression spoke of feeling suicidal and nine had made serious suicide attempts. One man had taken an overdose on three separate occasions, another on two occasions; another described his attempts as 'frequent' and 'twice in one week' during one period; one had taken an overdose and been hospitalised at the age of 6 years, just after his abuse started. He acknowledged that this might have been a 'copy-cat' as his sister (who had abused him) had been admitted to hospital having taken an overdose the day before he took one.

Several men spoke of their depression as 'constant', 'every day', 'always present' and one likened it to 'a great pool of heaviness' that was with him from the moment he became conscious at the start of each new day.

Martin had felt suicidal the day after telling his parents he was a homosexual and felt their rejection of him:

> It was the day after I had told them I was gay and they had reacted so badly. I relived in those few hours all the pain of childhood, of being and feeling unwanted, of not being what they had hoped me to be.

He had walked out under a bus which had swerved and missed him. Using the same method, Matthew had walked out under buses and trucks frequently between the ages of 15 and 16. He realised he was ambivalent about what he was doing as his religion taught him that it was a mortal sin to commit suicide and he was fearful of dying with a mortal sin on his soul. He wanted someone else to take the responsibility for whether he lived or died, so he played a kind of Russian roulette with the trucks and buses.

Wayne threw himself under cars hoping that if he behaved

sufficiently dangerously then sooner or later he would succeed in killing himself. He said he had a constant 'death wish' during this period of his life.

William's depression was with him from his first moment of consciousness each day and he described how he would hold a gun to his face or a knife to his throat 'to cheer myself up'; he did not want to kill himself but knowing he had the choice made him feel better.

Justin has slashed his wrists when he has felt suicidal and engaged in other self-destructive behaviours. Several men acknowledged that their suicidal attempts had been a way of trying to draw attention to the fact that there was something seriously wrong in their lives and they knew no other way of admitting to it. Jon had decided to kill himself in his car, making it look like a road accident, when he came to the point in his life that he felt he could not carry on. Robert had made up his mind that he would not reach the age of 40 and identified in retrospect the ways he had courted danger; joining the motorbike display team, engaging in drug running and gun running; living dangerously. Sam was run over by a lorry at about the age of 10. It is interesting to note how frequently men used motorised vehicles as a way of attempting to kill themselves.

> I didn't want to live until I was 40. I wanted to kill myself but I didn't have the balls to do it in cold blood so I tried to drink myself to death, smoke myself to death, fuck myself to death. It was just manic activity to stop myself from thinking.

Mike saw his drug abuse and careless, promiscuous, sexual behaviour as a way of living dangerously – especially since the awareness of AIDS.

Coping mechanisms

The depressive feelings often led to isolation, loneliness, withdrawal from contact with others, and stemmed from fear, shame, suppressed anger, self-hatred, low self-esteem and distorted body image. Many men mentioned how their school work suffered as their concentration deteriorated or was taken up with deceit, anxiety, relationship problems or excessive masturbation. During adolescence sexuality became the focus of attention for most of the men and frequent masturbation meant that they were distracted from doing other things that they needed to be engaged with, such as school work or examinations. Several spoke of 'shutting down', 'going onto automatic pilot' and drug-taking to eliminate the emotional pain that always lay just beneath the surface.

Sam describes this when he says:

> I just wanted to smoke and be in oblivion all the time – to get away from the hassle in my everyday life; just to hide it all away and be Jack-the-lad. At the end of the day I became the hardest kid in the school.

Three men used their school work as a way of coping with the other areas of their lives and threw themselves into it as a way of avoiding the necessity to socialise or deal with their feelings. Paul described his over-activity which he saw as a way of preventing himself from feeling 'Every time I started to think about what was happening I would make myself busy and do something.'

Martin described this as 'workaholism':

> I measure my worth, my sense of self by productivity, constantly producing new work, new documents, new packaging, new ideas, constantly proving myself. It's left me guilty about taking days off, about being good to myself.

William had coped by having 'something that I was very good at'. He had always been interested in chemistry and at times when he felt suicidal he would engage in a project that gave him a reason to live. William also used his obsessive fantasy of a girl with whom he had a close relationship during primary school as a coping mechanism during his most difficult period. This fantasy relationship was so real to him that his schoolfriends believed in it as well as William.

Eleven men identified that they had coped by using religion, meditation or some expression of spirituality; one man spent most of his time in art galleries as an adolescent, losing himself in the pictures and connecting with the world of fantasy. Harry immersed himself in the world of ballet and opera, living in a fantastic world of which he became a recognised part. Another used music as a way of escaping from the painful world he lived in. Jon became the clown; always laughing and entertaining others as a way of never taking anything seriously and hiding his true self from others. Others used sex, alcohol and drug addiction as a way of coping and, as previously mentioned, others tried to cope by re-enacting their abuse or through the other anti-social behaviours previously identified.

Denial had been a favoured way of dealing with the abuse for some men. Denying that it was abuse; denying the seriousness of the abuse and normalising the events in their lives that had clearly been most abnormal. One man was still in denial and had been operated on for intestinal disorders five times. He identified that his illness was stress-related but did not acknowledge that he had been harmed by the abuse both his parents had perpetrated on him between the age of 7 and 16 years. Another man had developed a speech disorder at the time his abuse started and still suffers from this as an adult. Another developed asthma at the time his abuse started and this stayed with him throughout his life. He also suffered from obesity.

Dissociation was another identifiable coping mechanism used by many of the men who remembered the events but dissociated any feeling from them. Harry felt nothing about his first episode of abuse when he was 8-years-old. He had been in hospital between the ages of 7 and 9 years and had been taken by a 16-year-old patient into the lift which was then stopped between floors. Harry was thrown to the floor and anally raped; it was all over in a few minutes and no words were spoken; Harry was then taken back to the ward and left there. He did not refer to this as his first experience of abuse; he saw his first abuse as that which happened on his return from hospital when his parents allowed their lodger to take him away to Margate for a fortnight's holiday; this man abused him every night for those two weeks and continued to abuse him when they returned home. He said the lift episode had not affected him in any way so he did not think of it as his first experience of sexual abuse.

Two men who had 'numbed out' during the episode of their early abuse recognised how this behaviour had been re-enacted during their rape as adults. It was the recognition of this process as a defence mechanism that had allowed them to associate it with their earlier experience and had enabled them to re-connect with feelings attached to their childhood abuse.

Re-enactment of the victim role was identified by several men as a coping mechanism which was experienced as unhealthy. George re-enacts his victim behaviour as a 59-year-old by allowing and even seeking out older men to abuse him; he has also repeated the behaviour that was enacted upon him by abusing other children.

Jeremy allowed himself to be used sexually by an older man in return for his board and lodgings, he said 'It used to bring back memories of when I was little – it was almost as bad; that's what excited me sometimes – the sordidness of it was a turn on.'

Wayne had stayed in an abusive relationship with a male nurse for eighteen months until he finally 'ran away'. Low self-esteem was evident in the way most of the men spoke of themselves. Several referred to the fact that they never expected to be sexually attractive to anybody and that they chose women who had a slight defect as they could not expect to be liked by someone who was not 'imperfect'. Many spoke of the way in which they constantly strove to please others; they feared rejection and had to ensure that they did nothing to deserve it but expected it whether or not it was deserved.

Wayne was one of several men who spoke of hypervigilance – an ever present sense of imminent danger. He never looks at anybody in the face in case he sees rejection or something else to fear; his demeanour is that of a totally non-assertive person.

Men who experienced their abuse in childhood as, in part, positive were inclined to revictimise themselves. William's sexual abuse by his sister was re-enacted by himself on himself, each level of self-abuse worse than the last as he needed more and more extreme methods to satisfy his craving for sexual excitement. Because of the geographical isolation of his home and the self-imposed isolation because of wanting to keep his two separate worlds apart, he had no companionship with boys or girls during his adolescent years. Entirely cut-off from others, he turned to the family dog for sexual activity; something that added to his belief that he was indeed 'a monster' and reinforcing his need to shut himself away from other people.

The two men who went on to become child abusers had both experienced their abuse as positive at the time it was happening and one even now found the memory pleasurable whilst at the same time acknowledging how it had negatively affected his life.

Men who experienced the event as totally negative had not re-enacted the role of abuser but all of them identified themselves in the victim role though not always as a sexual victim.

Denis feels that he is always victimised by women; something that has caused him difficulty in his work place. Wayne had been verbally abused and physically threatened by his 'boss' for two years before he finally involved the union and put a stop to this. Others have seen themselves as the victim in other personal relationship disputes. One man who has been been beaten up at least five times in his life does not see this as exceptional in a 'working class' environment.

Several men recognised how they had become identified with the aggressor as a way of dealing with their victimisation. Sam who had been a scared and 'wimpish' child became the 'hardest kid in the school' as he grew into adolescence. Robert became the aggressor whilst in the army; Jeremy tried to become more 'macho' as a way of proving to himself that he wasn't a 'poof'. Matthew, a man who identifies himself as a homosexual, said quite sadly 'I would love to be Mr Macho man but I'm not; life's a lot easier for Mr Macho man.'

Patriarchal socialisation

Power

Patriarchal attitudes were described in terms of the interviewees perception of who held the power in their homes and lives. Four men had perceived that their mothers had the power in their households – this power was demonstrated through manipulation; the threat of walking out; or the withholding of sex and in five other cases the mother's violent behaviour had given her the power. Interestingly in one of these cases the man felt that his father still had the power to prevent his mother from behaving violently even though his son saw him as 'weak'; his father did not use that power for fear of causing his wife to be angry with him.

One man described a household where his two grandmothers held the power and neither of his parents had been treated as adults by the older generation of women. The men who saw the females in the house as having the power were either the children of absent fathers or who perceived their fathers as weak and pathetic men. Most of these men also recognised that ultimately the males had the power as the women were mostly dependent financially on the males. Mothers were sometimes perceived as having the power within the home but the power outside the home was perceived as being male.

Male power was demonstrated in the homes of ten of the men through the violent and abusive behaviour of their fathers either towards themselves or towards their mothers. Those who attended all-male schools also identified that physical control through punishment and beatings was the norm in this all-male environment. Three of these schools were under the auspices of the Catholic Church – an institution that does not permit females to have the equal right of ordination and sees women's role within the Church as a support for the males in authority.

The influence of fathers on their son's behaviour was evident throughout, especially in terms of talking about the painful feelings experienced after having been abused. Jeremy said he couldn't tell people how he felt because he did not want to be judged; when asked whose judgement he feared most he answered:

> This is what messed me up about my Dad for a long time; my Dad says he doesn't like losers; he wants to be on the winning team not the losing team.

Another man spoke of his father's influence on him:

> I feared he could see into me and judge me and that I wasn't good enough for him. He wasn't like me, he was far superior to me. I always felt I wasn't as male as he was. I wanted to be but I knew I wasn't. I just somehow felt he didn't feel like me inside.

Harold's father was a schoolteacher and he feared his disapproval:

> My father was constantly putting me down, my school work

> was not good enough; always picking on me every day 'straighten your back'. He bought me pair of chest expanders.

Wayne said his father was 'unpleasable' and a 'perfectionist' but sometimes he felt driven to try yet again to do something that would please him, and never succeeded. Even though he hated his father he never stopped seeking his approval.

When James tried to tell his father, the first time he had ever tried to disclose his abuse to anybody, he had received the message that he was 'making a fuss about nothing' and that he should 'stop being silly'; he had felt angry with his father but had not been able to express that anger:

> I immediately took on the view 'Oh, it's not important, it's irrelevant' and I ignored it for the next few years.

Patriarchal attitudes, which are closely linked with homophobic attitudes within the family and society, created an environment for some of the men that made it difficult to disclose their abuse for fear of being thought of as less than a man. One man whose junior school headmaster had complained to his father about his lack of manliness because he preferred to play with the girls at school, recognised that he had a reputation for being 'a wimp' and was disliked by the other boys and teachers on that account. When he was assaulted and anally raped by a class mate in the school lavatory at the age of 14, he felt that he must protect his reputation by keeping silent:

> If you keep your mouth shut then nobody is going to accuse you of wanting it; nobody is going to accuse you of causing it, especially as I was a bit of a wimp. I was a prime candidate for that accusation.

The all-male environment of his school heightened the need for him to make sure that his rape remained a secret:

> It was a very aggressive, masculine boys' school and I had to be very careful about my reputation. Where you've got mainly male teachers setting a very aggressive male standard, you can't speak, you can't risk it coming out ... I didn't trust my father not to turn round and blame me (which is exactly what he did when told 14 years later, following a second rape).

Homophobia

Eleven men mentioned during the interviews that they had felt a degree of homophobia at some time during their adolescence or adult life. Three men had parents who had expressed extremely homophobic views in relation to their perception of their child's lack of machismo. One man spoke of the time when he told his parents he was a homosexual:

> When I told my parents I was homosexual, my mother screamed repetitively 'I wanted a boy'. To this day when she refers to the make-up of our family she says 'we have two girls, Martin and two boys'.

Two of the men had parents who were accepting of homosexuality in others outside the family. James's mother worked in a gay bar and he grew up to feel that a homosexual orientation did not denote inequality. Tony's mother was friendly and accepting towards several of the well-known men he would read about in the newspaper reports about homosexuality (this was during the period of time that homosexuality was still illegal) yet even as an adult he felt he could not talk to his mother about his own homosexuality:

> There was a whole spate of homosexual prosecutions while I was at school – many of them were famous people; one or two had been friendly with my mother in her younger days. As a result of the publicity I was very fascinated by all that. When I was at university and thinking about becoming a priest, I put it to myself that there was a good chance that I may be homosexual ... becoming a priest was a way of finding a positive sublimation of it; something that would be creative...in that I couldn't marry, I couldn't make a woman happy or be happy living with a woman. I suppose I thought that I could sublimate my sexuality and make it a positive thing by being a priest and teaching in a school run by my congregation.

Although Matthew's father's best friend was an 'effeminate grand dame of an old queen', who was well liked by all of the family, his father found it very hard to accept his son's homosexuality:

> When I first told him about my rape and that I was living with a man, he said I could come home for dinner but I couldn't stay – not even on my own and certainly not with my partner.

Several men recalled their own attitudes towards homosexuality during their adolescence. Tony said he didn't like gay people generally, although he was fascinated and avidly interested to read anything that appeared in the newspapers; he found the sexual details 'quite titillating'. Len, who attended a monastic boarding school, said he knew it was a sin because masturbation was a sin; therefore to do that with another male was equally a sin. He had been told by an older boy at school that he should go to confession when he described to him his first experience of masturbation to ejaculation.

Others recognised that there was a taboo against sex with other men without realising exactly where that message had come from. For others the strongly negative feelings had arisen from their experience of sexual abuse on them by another male. Mike, who had become a rent-boy after absconding from Borstal said:

> When I was young I used to think 'am I a queer' but I always hid that. People who knew me when I was 17 or 18 and had just come out of Borstal, have told me that I used to go on about queers all the time – that I would say 'let's get them, let's beat them up'. I can't remember being like that but my mates tell me I was. I knew the men who wanted sex with me were queer; I'd think 'they want sex with me they're obviously queer'.

Charles who was raped at the age of 14 by a male stranger in a public lavatory said:

> I've always thought it was entirely wrong, disgusting. I've always called those sort of people queers rather than gays because I think gay is too good a name for them. I still get scared off by strange men.

On his way to meet me for the interview Charles had been approached by a man with a bible tract who asked him if he would like to go back to his flat to explore it. The coincidence seemed striking that this should happen on this particular occasion. Charles spoke agitatedly about this meeting 'I'm thinking that he was queer and he just wanted to get me back to his flat and do something to me.'

This had re-awakened the fear he had been left with from thirty-five years ago. Once again he asked himself if there was something about him that attracted these type of men to him. Charles is quite clear that he is heterosexual. There seems to be a basic assumption that men who assault other men and children are homosexual.

Jeremy interpreted the gender of his male abusers as an indication of their homosexuality 'I used to say "oh, queers, stay away from me", but then I found out that two of my step-uncles are gay. It made me feel a bit uneasy.'

Some men felt that their experience of being abused had shaken their self-concept as being a normal male even when they had been seen by others as lacking in stereotypical masculinity.

> I thought I was like anybody else until Christopher assaulted me. My confidence went because I wasn't a macho kid and people called me poof; whereas before that happened I had a fair amount of bravado and refused to take it to heart.

Attitudes to maleness

It saddened me to hear from so many of the men their negative attitudes to their gender. This was not something I had sought during the interviews but time and again men referred to their gender in derogatory ways; some expressed the wish to have been born female and one man wanted to have a sex change.

> There have been times when I have looked at silky underwear, soft sensuous stuff and I have wondered how it feels to wear it so I have tried it on. There have been times when I am in the company of women that I would like a sex-change. I believe in re-incarnation and I hope I come back next time as a woman.

Several other men spoke of trying on women's clothes and enjoying the sensuous feeling that aroused in them. None of these men identified themselves as homosexual.

Some men had felt confused and distressed when they had recognised that their abuser had a shared gender with them. They saw this as part of a maleness that they wished to dissociate themselves from. Martin said:

> It was such a set of confused ideas; my father did not work for me as a role model; if this is what it was like to be a man then I didn't want to be a man. To be abused by other men meant that I didn't know what it was really like to be a man. I did not know what men were, what they were like and if these three persons were indicative of the adult male then I did not want to be a man.

It is interesting to note that twenty of the men said in some way that as children they had not experienced themselves as strongly masculine; four men used the word 'wimp' when describing themselves and nine men saw themselves as 'feminine' or 'effeminate'. However, none of them had seen this as evidence of their developing homosexuality, including the men who now identify themselves in that way but rather that they did not fit the stereotypical picture of maleness.

James said: 'I never really identified with the rugby playing shitheads at school.'

Descriptions included: more in line with the feminine; gentle, soft, effeminate, timid, frightened, unmasculine, passive, inward looking, frail, blob-like, didn't fit the normal boy type, mummy's boy, wimp, timid, feminine, not hard enough for father, I liked the soft things, gentle, sensitive, meek, mild, scared, male with a good streak of the feminine, masculine but not macho.

Other self-descriptions included: totally angelic altar-boy, tolerant, warm, affectionate, mixed up, nutty, out of control, fearful, lying, hypochondriacal. Only three men saw themselves as 'a typical boy' and one of these said he did not like macho boys or games such as football; the other said he liked the boys' games on bikes in the woods and seemed to see himself as what is generally thought of as 'a normal little boy'.

However, when the men who described themselves as non-macho were asked if they had felt it was OK to be that kind of little boy, most felt that they had been criticised and made to feel abnormal. Martin described the pain of feeling that it was not OK to be himself in his family:

> It definitely wasn't OK for me to be that kind of little boy. My father had been a PE instructor in the RAF. My mother had played professional netball for her country – sport was everything in our house and to have one child out of five who was not participating was not OK. To have a boy who was sensitive, who preferred to play with girls, and who preferred knitting and gentle things and playing the piano – all these things meant it was not OK to be me in my family.

Matthew's father had been called up to the school because the headmaster thought he spent too much time playing with the girls. Interestingly his father had responded that he saw this as good evidence that his son was a 'normal healthy male' who was taking more interest in females than in males. It would seem that the headmaster interpreted his preference for playing with the girls in quite the opposite way.

Socialisation messages about what it meant to be male covered a wide range and nearly always meant that feelings could not be expressed:

> Being Mummy's little man meant not hurting. It was alright to cry if I got grazed when I fell down, but it meant recovering from those things – it probably meant not being hurt by other people's taunts as well.

Sam's understanding was that being a man meant 'facing up to things' in a macho kind of way or to say 'that doesn't bother me' and to just get on with life.

Martin's father taught him that 'real men played football very well, were hard and had no emotional closeness with other males'.

George's understanding was that:

> Being a real man meant being like my dad; easy going, stern, a likeable womaniser, a drinker and unfaithful. Being a man means being sick, driving when you are drunk, getting VD –

which is what my father did!

Roy remembered that 'I was not allowed to show my feelings, especially fear or sorrow or to cry; they were prepared to spend money on my education.'

Sam, who is at present in prison for the thirteenth time remembered thinking as a child that 'Being a real man meant being a policeman!'

Robert took his impression of manliness from how his father presented himself:

> Being a male meant being the sort of person my father was – all barrel-chest and bollocks! He would push his way in anywhere, he took up a lot of space; he struts around the place, and huffs and puffs; he's got an awful lot of power.

Peer pressure was identified as a important influencer especially during adolescence. Being seen to be macho was harder for those who had not identified themselves in that way as younger children. Mike regretted the way he had allowed peer pressure to influence his relationship with the first girl he felt emotionally involved with:

> I finished with her two days later; it was only because I was with my mates in the park and she came round with her two mates and sent a message to say she wanted to see me; but I felt stupid in front of my mates so I said 'just give her a message to say I've finished with her'. I was a bit disappointed afterwards that I had done that but it had been said. It was stupid but I didn't want to lose face in front of my mates.

Clem spoke of how good he felt when his teacher's girl friend, who abused him, came to chat to him in the playground in front of his friends 'I would feel quite big in front of the other boys.'

Messages from the media were also identified as having an important impact on the developing adolescent male; sometimes these messages were not in tune with those received in the home and served as further cause for confusion about what was right and what was wrong:

> There was the idea that proper men should be seducers like James Bond, yet my father's message was that I shouldn't be giving in to all that temptation – 'control yourself!

Family scripts can be recognised as influences in some cases. Jon was told that his mother had wanted a little girl and how his given name had been a derivative of that which would have been given to a daughter; he has changed his name as an adult from this one. Harry was named after his mother's twin brother who was much loved and had died about three months before Harry was born. This man was a homosexual as is Harry now and, as a little boy, Harry had believed for some time that he was the re-incarnation of his mother's twin.

Mike's father had called him 'the golden boy' and wanted his son's life to be better than his own. The message to Mike was 'you are going to be something special'. Tony's mother had obviously adored her father and held him up as a model for her son who was born shortly after her father's death and was named after him.

Wayne's script had been like tapes playing in his head which caused a noise like 'static':

> Every time I had a decision to make or things to accomplish I would get a noise in my head like static; like thinking through treacle. I couldn't get my thoughts through.

A friend suggested he listened to the snatches of words he heard on the 'tapes' and when he did he heard a constant stream of verbal abuse – that which he had been subjected to by his parents all through his childhood and had introjected.

Family attitudes to sex

Family attitudes to sex were universally negative or non-existent. Robert described his home as one in which 'sex was always in the air'; not talked about but always there as an oppressive force; his father was convicted of sexually abusing six young girls in his neighbourhood when Robert was 11-years-old. He described his father's attitude and how it had rubbed off onto him for a long time into his own adulthood:

> His attitude was that any woman around was there for the taking and to be sure a lot of that attitude stuck with me. My wife was the sixty-third woman I had sex with. I kept a little black book of conquests.

George's mother saw herself as liberal-minded and with an open attitude to sex. Her message to him that 'it was better to do it to a hanky than to a woman' had given him the message that masturbation was OK but sex with a female was not; although it cannot be seen to be causal it is interesting to note that George cannot have satisfying sexual relationships with adult women. Len had felt his parents' attitude to be liberal, accepting but 'closed' as sex was not openly talked about in the family.

Jeremy had seen his mother having sex with several different men when he was a child and he was aware that his father had sex with several women. He and his age mates were brought up in an 'open world' 'All our eyes were open to everything; we saw everything at a young age.'

Five men said that sex was 'ignored' although in many cases there was an awareness, such as the fact that an older sister was obviously having sex with her boyfriend. Five men had overt messages from their mothers that sex was 'dirty' and several men mentioned that their mother had been 'uptight' about sex; one man heard from his father that sex was bad and had to be denied and controlled. Sex was something described as taboo, dirty, bad, ignored, that school would take care of, to be controlled or saved for marriage. None felt that their sexuality had been an acceptable part of them or something they felt would have been easy to openly discuss within the family. When Tim was 15 he asked his mother about the best form of contraception and was told that 'the best contraception is to wait until you don't need it'.

There seemed to be a clearly understood difference between the 'normal' childhood experiences of sexuality, such as playing and exploration between friends and peers, and abusive behaviours which were enacted with peers/younger children, both from the subjects' active and passive roles. Ten men reported that they had engaged sexually with other children in ways that they now saw as abusive and in which they had been the initiator. Several men were reluctant to admit that their re-enactment of their abuse on their peers/younger children had been abusive. George described his behaviour with his 14-year-old peer who had also been abused by an adult male as:

> ... definitely abnormal. It was abuse; we abused each other; it was not the sort of normal activity that adolescent boys engage in. I experienced sexual activity with other boys during that period which felt quite different and was not abusive.

Sam had engaged in frequent sex in a children's home from the age of 14 with his peers; he thought that about half the girls in the home had been previously sexually abused as he had; he felt that staff knew about the sexual activity but they did not interfere. He referred to this as his 'first proper sex' by which he meant that it was not with his sisters.

Jeremy used the interview to unload the guilt he had carried for five years since realising that at the age of 9 he had abused other children; he had forced one 7-year-old child into anal intercourse with him. He still mixes with this boy who is now about 17-years-old:

> ... that is the one I feel really guilty about. I can see it in his eyes sometimes when he looks at me; that is when I feel I have corrupted him.

Part 2

In Part 2 I will present some of the first person stories of the men I have interviewed. Spoken interviews come across very differently from written life stories – they are natural, alive and give a sense of presence which allows the reader to tune in to the experience in a way that enhances understanding. I have been most grateful to the men who have shared their painful stories with me. All of them wanted to be heard, although, at the same time some were afraid of being heard. I hope I have made a safe hearing possible for them in my presentation of their stories. Names and other identifying details have been changed in order to ensure confidentiality.

The stories have been shortened due to the constraints of the book but I have tried to leave out nothing that seemed crucial or immediately relevant to the focus. Along with the presentation of the story I have endeavoured to discuss some of the pertinent issues that are particularly demonstrated. Because the stories contain numerous overlapping issues, I have limited myself to a few for each story; this will enable me to present a greater variety of stories without becoming repetitive. My concern has been that I do not betray the trust the men have shown in me by misrepresenting them. If that should happen I can only say that it was never my intention. I deeply honour and respect the openness, courage and enthusiasm these men have shown. Their sharing, often at a deep and personal level has encouraged me to feel that, contrary to popular belief, there are men out there who can take emotional risks, who can value intimacy – for that is what I have seen and felt in our meetings. At times the pain of the stories has evoked the need in me to 'mother' and comfort – none of which was appropriate to my role – it has been hard at times to walk away and know that we will probably never meet again and yet I have known, also, that it is precisely this fact that has allowed some of the men to share with me so deeply. There have been no necessary repercussions for them and, having tested out the 'water', some men have gone on to find somebody with whom they can share their story in a therapeutic environment. This knowledge has been the greatest reward for me at this point.

7 The rent-boys' stories

Mike's story starts with a view of a 'normal' childhood, an almost ideal picture of family life. Hints of a different reality creep in as he goes on to describe the breakdown of his parent's marriage, followed by the breakdown of his mother's mental health. Just on the verge of puberty, Mike's home and school life disintegrates and he turns his anger outwards into sexual crime and theft. I have asked myself why Mike's anti-social behaviour was of such a sexual nature and wondered if there may have been earlier sexual abuse which is not yet conscious for him and which might have traumatised him to re-enact it in this particular way. Sgroi et al. (1988) make the same speculation in similar cases. Mike is the only man I interviewed who has assaulted adults sexually as an adolescent. It is appropriate for a young adolescent boy to be interested in exploring intimacy with his peers or even with older people but it is not appropriate for him to use force or intimidation to gain access to the body of a stranger. It has been identified that in one study 62 per cent of children who sexually abuse others had themselves been sexually abused; 82 per cent had been emotionally abused (Holder 1993).

Ten of the twenty-five men I interviewed admitted to sexually abusive behaviours with other children which they had initiated during their own childhood or adolescence. Home Office figures for 1993 identified that 32 per cent of convicted sex offenders were under 21 and 17 per cent were under 16. Another study showed that 59 per cent of offenders admitted to becoming sexually abusive while teenagers (Taylor, the *Guardian* 25.4.94). Four of the five men I interviewed who were convicted of sex offences committed these offences before the age of 16. This excludes men who admitted engaging in sexually abusive behaviour with other children during their own childhood. Young abusers are being identified in ever-increasing numbers and the first programme in Britain for assessment and treatment of young sexual abusers was set up in January 1994 at the Tavistock Clinic. So far, the results have been 'distressing but predictable', in that all young abusers have themselves suffered some combination of sexual, physical or emotional abuse (Holder 1993).

Mike's case demonstrates the way a child becomes involved in the rent-boy scene, linking him with the world of drugs, homosexuality and pimping. The Children's Society reports that one in seven teenagers in Leeds (the focus City of their study) runs away from home for at least one night. Many of these children run away from homes in which they are abused by parents (Children's Society, 1993). Ironically Mike was running away because he wanted to go back to the home he had known as a small child; a home in which there were two parents and everything was 'normal', a home which no longer existed in reality. Children who run away need to find shelter and rarely turn to professionals for help. Mike describes how his need to find a place to 'hang out' had led him into a very unsafe twilight world of drug dealers, addicts and rent-boys.

Mike's story

Mike was born in 1966; the oldest son with a brother four years younger and a sister four years after that. He saw his childhood as 'normal', with a father on shift work and mother working part-time so she would be there when the children came home from school. He realises now that things had not always been ideal, and that at times his father may have hit his mother during arguments. When Mike was 12-years-old his parents' marriage broke up and his father left to live with another woman. Mike remembers blaming his mother for his father leaving home. His mother attempted suicide and was hospitalised. It was at this time that he started to sexually assault women. Mike is single and unemeployed; he has no children.

Mike told me:

A couple of weeks after dad left I started going into subways indecently exposing myself to women, grabbing their breasts and running away. I suppose I was imagining my dad with this other woman and that was like the fuse that lit it. I was 12, going into adolescence; I was becoming aware of my body but I hadn't discovered masturbation. I thought that was what I should do to get sex but I didn't really know what sex was. When I got caught, I started going to see this child guidance officer; he asked 'do you rub your penis and does white stuff come out'. I didn't know what he was on about. My mum was very uptight about sex; sex was a dirty word.

I got caught one day when I went to the football match and a woman there recognised me. They arrested me there and then in the football ground. When my dad heard about it he came down and whacked me. He had always been a disciplinarian but he wouldn't normally beat you with his fists; he did that day. Normally, he'd give me a good few open-handed whacks, it wasn't like a cruel continuous beating, although it was sometimes a bit harsh for the crime. My dad was either someone to be afraid of or a really nice bloke.

It was like a 'force' was happening and life was being changed around me, but mentally you are not with it – like looking at yourself from the outside. Indecent exposure was only one part of it; I was blaming mum and I was angry with her. One week I pinched her whole wage packet; it was all she had to bring us up on and I bought big platform shoes and bought all my mates chips.

I had to go to see the child guidance bloke but I thought he was slimy – asking all these sexual questions because he was preparing the court report, not because he wanted to help me. When I went to court they asked me whether I wanted to live with my mum or my dad but I said I couldn't choose; so they said 'we'll put you into care then'. It was just one of those things.

I went into Borstal with 200 boys, all quite a lot older than me. I was tall for my age and physically well developed. Within a few days there were boys messing about with each other and I discovered masturbation. It was done secretly and it didn't feel OK. There were no women there at all. There was one kid I had a close relationship with and it was different with him because we had a deeper friendship. We always used to do it secretly. I remember that time as happy. I had good friends, lots of laughs; the staff were quite easy going. Within three months of going there I had dots on my fingers (that stood for 'all coppers are bastards') and a tattoo on my arm. A classic tattoo in these places is a cross, MUM and LOVE and the devil's fork with DAD over the top. All the kids in there had these tattoos. The cross was for the death of love and the dots were a secret sign – all the kids have been taken away from their homes by the police.

I was assigned a social worker; they are the ones who decide after a couple of years whether you'll go back into a normal school or what. I never saw my brother when I was in there; I didn't see mum because she was in and out of hospital; she had a breakdown. A couple of neighbours looked after the other two kids. I just had to settle down into the life there but after 3 months I ran away and that was when all the prostitution started.

I ran away to go to the football match with my mate. We got split up after the football and I was walking down town and some kids were going to beat me up because I was a Rovers supporter. I told them I was on the run and so they took me down Anchor Road. This bloke pulled up in his car and a skinhead of about 17 spoke to him and then said to me 'go for a drive with that bloke and make some money'.

That's why I said I haven't really been abused because I went into that voluntary, quite aware of what I was doing really; although when we got to his house he made me do anal sex on him and I didn't really want to do that. I thought I would just have to touch his cock and he would wank me off and that would be it, but it wasn't like that at all. I had to lay down and he got on top of me, he did all kinds of things. I didn't want to do it but I just let him.

Well, it is abuse isn't it, because if that was now, I could say 'don't do that', there'd be some choice, but because I was 13 and he was in his thirties, you don't know how to say 'no'; but he wasn't horrible to me; he didn't try going up *my* arse; that would have been pure abuse – or trying to put it in my mouth – so he wasn't that bad. So I let him carry on – it was over in about fifteen minutes and I got two quid, in today's money that would be about a fiver. Afterwards I felt a bit strange, quite empty, a bit of a weird feeling, and he dropped me back at Anchor Road. The other blokes had a bit of money too and they said 'now were going to take you to a club'; this was at 2 o'clock in the morning and I was 13. It was a gay bar – there was some stupid bloke behind the bar and he started stroking my arm but I realised what was happening so I just sat there drinking.

It's interesting about that business of saying 'no' because after we left the club, we slept in this van that they had parked outside (I think they did business in there) and one of these kids said 'if you tell anyone about this I'll slit your throat'. I realised he was just bull-shitting, but I was a bit scared too because he was older and a skin-head and he said 'OK then, give us a blow job' and I said 'no chance'; he didn't force me, it was left at that. I woke up a couple of hours later and they were still asleep and I went back to the home. I told one of my mates I'd made some money, so when we ran away any time after that and I didn't have any where to go we'd do that. Some-times I didn't charge because by then I had got it into my head. Not because I really wanted to but because I had nowhere to go and I needed the money and I was just hanging around and bored and when you're a kid, you get sexually excited easily – it just went on and on. I kept running away and committing other crimes as well, stealing purses from hospitals, schools, wherever you could find a handbag. So I went right through the system; a series of Borstals, detention centres – rent-boying now and then when I'm on the run. I didn't really know what was going on; I was drifting in a timelessness; there was nothing to aim for.

I didn't think I was a homosexual but I did wonder. Obviously when you are that young you wonder if you are queer but I always hid that. My mates tell me that when I was 17–18 I was always going on about queers; saying 'let's beat them up!' I knew the men who picked me up were queer. I'd think if they wanted sex with me they're obviously queer. It did sexually excite me; I'd get a hard on easy. I did have an interest but I had no female friends until after I'd come out of Borstal. I'd done quite a lot of rent-boying here and there but it had always been just oral sex and masturbation except for that first guy – that was a one off. I never did that again. I would do oral sex for money.

After I'd come out of Borstal I fell in love. After we made love I thought 'is that all?'; I didn't have an orgasm. It was better than with men, sleeping with her all night. I finished with her two days later. She came round with her two mates but I felt stupid in front of my mates so I sent a message back to say I'd finished with her. Afterwards I was a bit disappointed that I had done that; I was afraid of losing face.

I got engaged to the girl that I fell in love with after that. We did have sex but I didn't really know what I was doing; whether I was satisfying her sexually is very doubtful. I wasn't really satisfied either. It was better than rent-boying because it was a woman – but it wasn't anything spectacular.

But all the time I was hiding all this stuff inside myself. My mates on the inside were playing about with each other; there was never any of that messing around with my mates on the outside. When I was home at the weekends or on home leave we went out to pubs, parties. I had to keep that part of my life a secret; even keeping it from friends on the inside who didn't do that.

In the meantime my girl friend was pregnant. Her mum said she had to have an abortion – looking back on it perhaps it was for the best, but who's to say? I admit that I was 17 and I was a joker but I was quite looking forward to being a dad. Then the relationship started breaking up because her mum was keeping her away from me so I just went out one night and drank loads and loads of beer; everyone went home and then about midnight I went out again and started smashing shop windows, car windows – totally senseless. I was put back in Borstal for that. She didn't write to me and when I came out I rang her up and her mum said 'You are finished as far as we are concerned.'

When I was 18 I left Borstal again. I'd go up to the Downs just walking about; sometimes prostituting, sometimes just going up to have a look – occasionally I might do something for nothing. I didn't really want to do it but I didn't know how to do anything else. Then I started smoking dope and it was a revelation to me – a whole new life opened up before me. I just started seeing deeper inside myself. Cannabis resin – it's such a good laugh, giggling all the time, going out to nightclubs. It was a totally different mental perspective. I had no need to do all that other sex stuff; for the next year I started dropping acid, speed. I wasn't even thinking about all this rent-boy stuff. The drugs buried that, cut me off from that. The experiences I was getting from LSD were so strong, everything was so colourful – it was a whole new world.

When I was 19 I met Jenny who had been sexually abused by her foster-father from the age of 6–9. Sex was good with her straight away; she hadn't smoked before so I just gave her a couple of joints. Her mum and dad didn't want to know me. I had a reputation. Even when I first met her I was still on the edges of the rent-boy scene and I was doing speed. My mum didn't want me at home because she could see I was on drugs so I decided to go away to Europe. First of all Jenny was dead keen to come with me but she changed her mind at the last minute and I made her feel guilty saying 'what am I going to do if you let me down?' So we went abroad but after a few weeks we had run out of money. But now I had control of Jenny.

Just before I met Jenny I used to hang about with one of my mates who had a girl on the game. When I met Jenny I had no thoughts about it ... well maybe I did have a few little thought about it; I did have an awareness of what could happen. I asked her how she would feel about going on the game and she said 'Oh, no!'; but by this time I had no money at all, no work and my mate was coming in with £500 from London, with his girl. He went abroad; then I went abroad with Jenny and I said 'either you go and make some money or I am leaving'. I made a big game of pretending to leave her stuck in the middle of Europe on her own – not very nice at all. So she did it.

So for the next couple of years we went all over Europe and England; she was a prostitute by now but she was like me – she wasn't any good at it because basically she was a nice person. We were still having a sexual relationship and we were doing drugs as well – she became better at sex, she was learning how to do sex for money.

This is the sick thing now. Sometimes I would spy on her doing it and I would get off on that. I felt guilty about it and guilty about her being on the game but the money was so good. This went on until 1986. We both knew it couldn't go on. At this time we were getting to the stage of her going out and getting a punter and bringing him back and I'd tell her to say she would do loads more than she really would, just to get him to pay £40 or £50; as he was handing over his money and getting undressed, I'd appear. It was sick but it worked.

It was doing our heads in because she wasn't the hard type. She'd give really good sex and half the time she wouldn't even be using Durex. Sometimes she'd pick up a bloke and drive off with him; when they'd get where they were going another bloke would jump out of the boot or there would be three other guys there waiting.

Then it all went bad. We split up and she went to Jersey for a year and I went right off my head. She'd got a proper job in a hotel and she'd send me money to go and waste on drugs and to pay prostitutes for sex. I was jacking up speed, then going up the Downs – not selling myself any more and not even really getting into sex, but I had nowhere else to go and I just wandered about; sometimes there was a couple up there and I might just watch or sometimes join in. I wasn't attracted to men at all but I was if there was a couple together.

After a year of her being in Jersey, Jenny's real dad died. So she came over to bury him and she rang me up and we got back together but it was chaos. She was going out to work and I couldn't find a job or I wasn't getting a job and we were doing speed to have good sex. But it wasn't good sex; it was just pure hard core abusive sex. That's how we'd spark off one another. Afterwards I used to feel just pure emptiness, like everything had been drawn out of me, my whole life, every little sense. At this time, with the speed, I wanted a bigger buzz. I wanted to get off with other couples. You want the sex because it feels so good but once it's over you feel just shit. All the perverted thoughts inside your head make you feel so bad. All the time we knew it was wrong so we split up again.

I think your experiences are what you are and I don't believe you can change that. If you have a family or a career, maybe you can begin to change some of that a little bit. But once you've had these experiences they are imprinted on your mind, on your character and they almost *are* you.

I can see that in a way I was abused, but it was different from the main concept of abuse compared with somebody who had violent abuse inflicted on them or abuse within the family where it's awkward to say something. I had put myself out there looking for something but that wasn't what I was looking for – I think that's where the abuse came in. When I used to hang about up on the Downs and all those other places – those guys could have said 'hey it doesn't look right you being on the streets at your age – get yourself home'. Instead they decided to take my vulnerability and use it for their own satisfaction. But I was aware of what I was there for as well – so it's just a different kind of abuse. What I was really looking for was to get back home, to my normal life as I was before it all happened. But I couldn't go back home.

Up to three months ago I used to pick up prostitutes all the time and sometimes I'd play tricks on them to avoid paying. I know that's totally wrong. The form of lovemaking or closeness is just a game, a release and I want to take that game further and further and it's got to the point where it is now quite dangerous; dangerous thoughts for me to be thinking about. Not in the sense of killing anybody but in the sense that I just pick a woman up now and I could have what I want without paying her and drive off. I've got the power, not just physically, but mentally. But I've never been a very nasty person so I can't play that game and that's half the problem. All my experiences have made me that person and sometimes I want to be that person. I feel bad just about ripping them off, but at the same time I want the sex; especially when I can be in control.

I've been living with my mum for the last couple of weeks. I had a really bad acid trip – it wasn't like acid because I know what acid is like, it was just like having all this stuff that I've been talking to you about, presented before me in an image; you don't see that image – you feel it; it was just like God putting you right down to nothing. Since that bad trip it's been hard to believe in myself. It's like a cross between fantasising about and wishing I could have a normal life but in reality – is it really possible? All the thoughts and feelings you get are far from normality – plus now, half the things that are normal, I don't want anyway.

Harry's story

Harry was born during the war in 1942 at a hospital just outside London. His mother's twin brother was killed in the war a month before Harry's birth and he was named after him; his mother became profoundly depressed after the death of her twin brother from whom she had felt 'inseparable'. Both grandmothers had been bombed out and lived with his mother. His father was away at war and although he must have returned at some stage, as Harry had a sister one year younger, he remembers his first meeting with his father at the age of 5. Another brother was born after his father's return from war. Harry is a social worker and lives with a man with whom he has had a homosexual relationship for twenty-five years. He has no children.

Harry told his story:

Everybody told me that I was very like my mother's twin and it was fairly obvious to me from what I heard that he was a homosexual. He was idolised and canonised as being a friendly, cultured and beautiful person who never lost his temper. There was a time in my life when I believed that I was literally his reincarnation and I was fascinated by this idea. I thought if he died the month before I was born, the time schedule would allow me to be his reincarnated soul. So it bothered me because I didn't know if I was myself. It made it very hard to get a sense of identity.

There was a lot of laughter in my home. These three women (and my sister as a baby) got on terribly well together. My paternal grandmother (who was 100 when she died) ruled with a rod of iron; she was a fantastic woman; she had a tremendous personality. Even in her late 90s, she would never sit in an easy chair, she thought that was bad, so she always sat upright. So what I remember is laughter and a kind of stoicism that Cockneys and Londoners have. We were evacuated to Wales for three weeks but my mother said she would rather be bombed in her own house than live in lodgings.

They used to say: 'Oh, Harry was a wonderful little boy. We stuck him in his own room when he was a year old and he slept the night through and never cried.' The counterpane in that room was a silk one which was given to my mother's twin; it had a kind of symbolism and I had terrible nightmares as a child. Although this sounds fanciful, I know my earliest thoughts as an infant were, 'What is the meaning of this existence, what is life?' I grappled with very strong feelings about 'what am I, who am I, if I were to be dead, what would I then be?'

I didn't meet my father until I was 5. I've got a sister exactly one year younger than myself so he must have come back, but I don't remember him. I've got a brother who was born when my father returned home after the war in 1947. From the moment he came back he was absent because he wasn't cut out for marriage; he was an alcoholic and a gambler so he came home at midnight to guzzle down a dinner that had been kept in the oven. He never touched us, never played with us, never showed any interest. If he had been a bit more friendly he would have been just like an older sibling because he was treated by the two grandmothers as a grown-up earner. My mother was passionately in love with him and she was very unassertive; they never argued. She just accepted his drinking and gambling. He was terribly good looking, very clever and very funny. He was a con artist really.

I was the only male in the household until my father came back in 1947, but I didn't have any sense of masculinity or femininity. I wasn't aware of bodies at all, because the ethos in our house was that nobody touched anybody else. I was never touched kindly by my mother. She slapped us a lot until I was about 10 or 11; she had a cane on the mantelpiece which she used. The ethos in our house was that children should be seen and not heard and although they didn't have a religion, we were sent to the Baptist Church three times on Sundays. We joined very much in the life of the Church, Boys' Brigade and Sunday School and it was a wonderful place to be.

Children didn't have any value or opinions. My sister (who is in America and has been in analysis for about fifteen years) has been in and out of drug and alcohol treatment units and once she asked my mother why she brought us up like that. My mother said it was because she didn't know how to be affectionate; she thought it would spoil children. Adults around us actually said 'spare the rod and spoil the child'.

When I was 7, I got scarlet fever which became a serious kidney infection which was later diagnosed as glandular tuberculosis. I think the earliest conscious recollection of my developing sexuality is while I was in hospital when I was 7. I was entirely deceived by my parents and the hospital who used to say: 'Oh you'll be out next week', or 'you'll go to a sanatorium on the Isle of Wight'; but it never happened. I was very, very frightened in hospital because the treatment in 1949 was horrible and I didn't have any education. I now realise the reason I later joined the BBC, is that all I did was listen to the radio. So I became fascinated by words and music. I used to read voraciously.

I became very institutionalised. I was in a ward of chronically ill adults. I saw naked men for the first time; I'd never seen my father naked. In those days men wore nightshirts in hospital. So I used to see men, with what seemed to be huge animal-like genitalia, shuffling around the wards. I was terribly preoccupied with my own inner world. Relationships didn't feel very important. I didn't feel I was part of the human race and I stoically accepted that. It was just a sense of isolation really.

My first experience of being sexually abused was when I was 8. It didn't make an impact on me. I was kept in bed in hospital for two years with fever for most of that time. I could get into a wheelchair and push myself around. A 16-year-old youth who was in the same ward said he would push me around. He took me into a service lift which he stopped between floors, threw me on the floor and had anal intercourse with me. It took about three minutes. I was so abused by the entire hospital experience of not being treated like a child, seeing lots of people die in that ward, I simply assumed it was just a matter of time before I died. I was feeling terribly frail, ill, having injections, drips and stuff; I was entirely stoic. Whenever the doctors or the nurses came I froze; I let things happen to me; it was the only way to cope. I was told I was a brave little boy. So when this youth threw me to the floor and screwed me I had no idea what he was doing. I remember looking back and thinking, 'I wonder why he did that?'; I didn't know anything about sex or homosexuality and it hurt when he penetrated me. I remember the dirty floor of the lift, feeling very dirty (not spiritually contaminated). I didn't know why he was lying on top of me and why he was thrusting into me and I didn't know how long it would last; it didn't last very long. He just dusted me down and put me back in the wheelchair and pushed me back to the ward. It was an entirely isolated event. It didn't seem anything at all. I thought, 'Why don't the nurses wonder why I am dirty?', (my clothes were dirty from the floor), but nobody did. It didn't occur to me to tell anybody. I didn't speak to anybody about anything at all. I suppose he had sussed out that here was a blob-like passive child; I just lay there like you see a bull servicing cows; it was as primitive as that. I didn't shout out or remonstrate with him, I don't suppose a word was exchanged; no threats. It doesn't have any conscious meaning at all. It wasn't as frightening as what was likely to happen to me in hospital.

But my history of sexual abuse started when I was 9. I came out of hospital and found that my parents had taken in a man my father had met in the services who had come to live with us. My parents allowed him to take me on holiday to Margate for two weeks and he sexually abused me for the next three years. He never physically hurt me; he never tried anal intercourse. I remember the first night very clearly. I didn't have any pyjamas on and he started to touch my cock; I was absolutely petrified, terrified into silence. I couldn't understand why he was doing it. He started to become very excited and he ejaculated and I thought he was bleeding or pissing. For a while he made attempts to disguise what it was. It was absolutely horrifying having this man kissing me, breathing heavily and getting terribly excited. I didn't know what the excitement was but just that energy. So having learnt stoicism in the hospital, I let him do that for the 14 consecutive nights while we were in Margate. So that was the beginning.

I came back to London and I tried to tell my mother for about two weeks afterwards. I picked my time, around five o' clock while she was getting the tea ready but I had no language to use. Trying to explain in everyday words what had happened to me just defeated me. Also, I felt she would have blamed me and held me responsible. So after two weeks had passed, I remember thinking, 'Well the boat has sailed; I can't go back on that now'.

He had a couch-bed in our front room where there was this ghastly old piano and one of the treats for me on coming out of hospital was to learn to play it. If I look back with gratitude on anything my mother ever did, it would be her opening the world of music to me; she couldn't afford these lessons. The piano was in this man's room and I was locked in there for thirty minutes a day to practice.

So going in there, smelling his smell and seeing his stuff. After the two weeks of not telling her, I was playing the piano and the Mantra going through my head was, 'Well I can't tell her, it's too late now'. I decided in that moment to embrace, (what a horrible expression), the abuse. As he wasn't going to leave the house, and as I couldn't tell anybody, and as he was still doing it, there was only one alternative, which was to give in to it, and so from that moment I did.

If I got up early he would call me into his bed and my mother saw me in there, (not my father, because he would be recovering from a hangover everyday), but nobody questioned it. Then I got to like it and he started off the process of me enjoying being touched. I reached puberty when I was 10 and I remember very clearly ejaculating in his bed and he explained what that was; then I knew that he'd been 'coming' and it really opened a furnace of feelings. Then I desired it very much and two years later when he moved into his flat at Streatham I went there voluntarily. It was terribly exciting and I couldn't do without it. It went on for three years.

In the meantime I had got into prostitution in the West End. When I was 12 I got a bike and when I wasn't in school, I would spend my time cycling up to the West End. I was picked up by a man who was much better looking and younger than the man who was abusing me. As I was finding more excitement in the West End, I weaned myself off my abuser.

The man who picked me up was desperate to have sex with me and I was very anxious to have sex with him. The only place we could go without anyone asking questions was in the lavatory in a hospital. It escalated a process of meeting lots of men in the West End. Don't forget this was in 1953/54, when homosexuality was illegal and there weren't any boys on the 'Dilly' – before the meat rack started. I used to go and sit in the reception area of the Strand Palace Hotel and you didn't have to be there very long before somebody came up and said: 'Would you like to come to my room?'; it was terribly exciting.

I remember going with somebody who gave me a fiver and I said: 'What's that for?', and he said: 'That's what you charge isn't it?' It had never occurred to me but I was willing to be flexible; if somebody wanted to pay me that was fine but I didn't stipulate it or contract it. I very quickly absorbed the West End lifestyle; I spent so much time there and at a very precociously early age I knew the right place to get your hair cut and where to buy clothes.

I was passionate about ballet and opera and I used to queue up at the Royal Opera House to see anything I could. I used to say to my parents, 'I am going to queue up for tickets for Fonteyn so I won't be back tonight'. I had a best friend who didn't know my lifestyle and I used to say, 'I'm staying with my friend tonight'. I never had to be in and was completely unsupervised; I kept all my clothes at my friend's house.

Two standards existed; the strict regime operated when you were present in the house but they didn't give a damn about when you were outside and because I was well-behaved and an accomplished liar, (being forced into a twilight world at the age of 9), and I was a 'good child' – I didn't arouse anyone's suspicions.

I had failed my 11-plus, because I hadn't had any education for two years while in hospital and I went to one of the first comprehensive schools with 1,500 kids divided into streams. I was in the Grammar stream because they saw I was bright enough, so from the age of 12 I was bunking off. I only went to three lessons and I was the first kid in my school to get 'A' levels. I used to go in for the register at 9.30 am and I could be in the West End in ten minutes. Although I came from a poor Cockney family, I lost my accent very quickly because I was so often in a different milieu.

I didn't have a friend in the world until I met this boy called Andrew. I assumed that I would be utterly lonely all my life. I was very lonely and very, very sad and I thought, 'this is the way of life'.

When I was 14 we moved to another district which was an even longer journey to school and Andrew, who was in my class at school, got on the bus and, to my amazement, he threw himself into the seat next to me and sat close. I couldn't believe it; I thought, 'this kid actually wants to sit next to me and wants to talk to me' and we became inseparable until we were 18. I was passionately in love with him although we never had a sexual relationship. We slept together sometimes but I didn't dare declare my love. He didn't know about my activities in the West End.

I had got into crime by this time and was stealing enormous sums of money. When my parents moved they opened one of the first corner shops, open seven days a week for twelve hours a day and it was like Coronation Street. People would come in, sit down and stay for three hours talking to my mother. My mother had a great genius, warmth and commonality for being with people, even though she never showed this towards us as children. She liked running the shop although it was hard work and because my father used to go greyhound racing on Tuesdays, Thursdays and Saturdays, I had to work in the shop, evenings and all day Saturday and Sunday. They paid me quite a lot of money but I started stealing from the till. In fact they went bankrupt and I'm sure I contributed to that.

And then my sister and I took up shop-lifting in the West End. We really enjoyed planning it; it was so easy. There was a film in those days called *Trouble in Store* with Norman Wisdom and Margaret Rutherford and we modelled ourselves on that. We both wore school uniforms and looked angelic and we could argue the hind leg off a donkey. We were never caught. We stole things to order sometimes and things to sell to people in the neighbourhood. I didn't make this a secret from my friends at school. It didn't actually seem wrong. My bedroom above the shop was like Aladdin's Cave. Because the supervision was so non-existent, I started bringing back clothes from Andrew's. I had a tail suit made to measure by the time I was 14 – talk about Little Lord Fauntleroy! I used to go to first night at Covent Garden. I used to get a tremendous thrill out of washing and laundering the waistcoat and learning how to tie the bow tie and putting the studs in.

I used to get dressed at home and then scuttle to the tube station in a mac covering this tail suit; I'd come out of the tube at Covent Garden and up the lift like Phantom of the Opera. I'd throw off the mac and there was this tall, skinny 'little boy' wearing this outfit. I knew the general administrator of the Opera House and I knew a lot of singers and dancers. They thought I was a rich kid; they didn't know I lived in this horrible little street.

I make it sound fun; it was terribly exciting and very colourful. I did things beyond my peer group's wildest dreams. I was in three worlds; I was in the world of fundamentalist religion going to this Baptist Church which caused a great deal of grief because I'd never had a personal relationship with Jesus. The issue was that I wouldn't go to heaven – you were a sinner even if you were good; I thought 'if only they knew what I was up to'. I was also a Corporal in the Boys' Brigade; I just thought 'if they had the slightest inkling that this evening I'd been up the 'Dilly screwing'; it was inconceivable. The other life was so wildly separate – it's amazing that I didn't go into juvenile schizophrenia. I didn't have a sense of badness because intuitively I was doing something that was natural to me; I wasn't doing anything abnormal. I was also enjoying, in a different way, love. I didn't call what I was doing 'homosexuality' because I thought it was a phase that I was going through and I assumed and hoped that I was heterosexual and that I would marry a nice girl and have children.

I never had a bad experience with the men I had sex with. I made friends with some of them; everybody was kind, nobody hurt me. I started to have anal intercourse very early on with a ballet dancer which I liked very much. In some ways I saw it as an initiation rite into the world of ballet and opera. I knew a lot of people very quickly and going to Covent Garden five nights a week provided me with a family. I was desperately ashamed of my own family.

When I was 14, I did fall in love with a girl called Margaret who was the same age as me; we went to the same school. I remember sitting next to her in Church, being terribly physically excited and walking around with her after evening prayers until it was dark and taking her home, wanting to have sex with her. Her mother must have intuited this because it threw her into a complete panic and she locked this girl up. I'm not anti-women, none of my homosexuality has to do with the rejection of women. Some of my closest friendships are with women. I sound like Godfrey Wynn or Beverly Nichols don't I?

I had had a colossal amount of imprinting; the other Mecca for my activities was the Savoy Turkish Baths in Jermyn St. I used to stay the night. I was the perfect man about town; the manly thing to do was to have a Turkish Bath and I always had the same masseur. There were some times when I used to go into the steam room and I would lay down on my tummy and I would be screwed by any member there. I wouldn't even turn round to see who it was. It was sexually very exciting to be desired and fucked.

I'm a recovering alcoholic. It's part of the scenario of alcoholism – you have to do something to its ultimate. I am also very hardworking. For the last seven years I've done a fourteen-hour day. I drank all my life; my bedtime drink as a child was a very large tumbler of black rum with sugar and milk in it to help us sleep. My mother was a heavy drinker and my father was an alcoholic; so I've always drunk.

The lifestyle was fantastic but the inner voice within me said: 'This is wrong and you are going to have to stop this' and when I was 16 I thought, 'Oh God I'm finding it harder and harder to imagine giving up homosexuality'. So I went to our GP (who was very nice and had been our family doctor all our lives) and said: 'I think I'm gay'; and he said: 'Nonsense, it's a phase you're going through but I think I'd better refer you to the Maudsley Hospital.'

So I went to the Maudsley where I was abused by the notion that they could cure me. I used to have to bunk off school two afternoons a week and lie on the couch and do Rorschach tests, word association and voyeuristic questions into my lifestyle by a psychiatrist. He is now well known and I think he used me as a case study, as frequently happens, which was abuse. I went through that for a year and I hated it. It had no meaning for me whatever except that occasionally I tried to stop my promiscuity. I thought the only way I would get better was if I didn't screw around but I wanted to; the treatment wasn't doing anything to stop me wanting that. So that created even more anxiety and tension in me. Then my parents bought a farm in Sussex and I stayed with some friends in London and again when I was 17 I thought: 'This is wrong; I must cure myself'.

So without too much embarrassment I went back to the Maudsley Hospital and they said: 'O.K. You can have group therapy' and that was even worse. I remember sitting in this room, (again for about a year), with two abusive psychiatrists, a woman who was frigid, a lesbian, people with the most peculiar sexual problems. There were microphones hanging from the ceiling and a glass screen where presumably thousands of psychiatric students were. I don't suppose I said a word. I was definitely not cured – in fact I stopped going.

I don't believe homosexuality is really part of my identity; I think it is something that has been created by the lifestyle. I've lived with a man now for twenty years and we have a very loving and very friendly, trusting relationship.

I suppose really the major effect the abuse has had on my life, in a word, is depression. For years and years I thought I'd blown everything; you see I desperately wanted children and there's a strange phenomenon that I attract women. I've had a lot of women passionate for a relationship with me. When I went into the BBC I became friends with a girl and we went everywhere together for three years; she didn't know about the other part of my life. She was a fabulous girl and I loved her really and she kept wanting to go to bed and I kept saying: 'Let's wait until we get engaged'; I didn't deliberately string her along. I didn't want to have sex with any woman. I wanted the friendship. I'm afraid I did use her – I hadn't thought of that. When I went into the BBC when I was 18 I'd have died rather than them know; it was my darkest secret. Although people think everybody in the BBC is gay, it wasn't the case at all. It was a good cover to have a girl friend and I used her by flaunting her around various places and my parents thought I was straight. There was an unsaid expectation that we would get engaged and get married. I thought: 'Oh, God what about sex?' We had sex once and I just hated it.

We didn't talk about it. I felt a failure and she clearly didn't enjoy it. Because I liked her so much I decided to tell her I was gay. It was a horribly difficult experience because she couldn't believe it. Three days later she got engaged to a boy and married him very quickly. Now I tell people at the start of a relationship that I'm gay so that either we can have a relationship or we can't. But why should I have to do this? In the organic development of a relationship people don't suddenly blurt out something like that, but I was so terrified after that experience with my girl friend.

Just after I had told her, again I thought: 'This is unbearable.' I was 21 by this time. So I went to the Institute of Psychiatry and I saw somebody there who said: 'Spend a day with us and we'll ask four or five psychiatrists to talk to you.' I don't know what they were practising but it was certainly humanistic and it wasn't clinical and they were loving. They said: 'Well, we think you are gay and we think you should enjoy it!' I almost somersaulted around the room with relief. Finally they had put the seal of approval on it and they said: 'If you want any help adjusting...' and I said: 'Oh no, I don't need any help with that!'

I haven't ever actually worked on my abuse; I've read some of the books. I've tried but I cannot do it. I view it as a part of the journey that has made me as I am. Because I was ill as a child and because I was abused, I have a tremendous feeling for victims which makes me extremely successful in my work as a social worker. I know that I've healed a lot of people just by the quality of the relationship and the acceptance of their pain that, in some transmutatory way, has been healing for them. I suppose it wasn't by accident that I became a social worker twenty years ago and started to do a lot of reading and identifying with the issues of abused children. The first job I got was in the West End. I contracted TB again from working with dossers and itinerants, and I was in hospital again for a year in 1978, very, very close to death.

From an early age I've been aware of healing. I had a very healing experience at a Spiritual Community. I was doing a workshop there and for the first time in my life I cried. I'd never cried before, certainly never in front of somebody else. Religion means nothing to me but spirituality does. I feel that I have been blessed all my life with beautiful friendships; I attract a lot of loving relationships. I've had some very loving sexual friendships and in fact I still sleep with a man occasionally that I met when I was 18.

I identify very much with what it is to be a child and what it is to be a child in the people I work with and, although I don't do it consciously I know that, on a spiritual level, I often talk to the child in those people. It sounds ludicrous when you think that some of them are mass murderers. I don't have to explain it. I just go straight into it and somehow they know where it is coming from and their own intuition tells them it's OK.

I never thought of myself as sexually abused until within the last ten years. I suppose it's because of the stoicism. For years and years I prided myself on being impervious to pleasure and impervious to pain.

I have worked with cases of 12-year-old rent boys who have been picked up by punters and I can see *that* as sexual abuse. It can't be by chance that I was the social worker in the West End working with boy and girl prostitutes. So I suppose in parallel, albeit years later, I was vicariously dealing with my own abuse. I've dealt with it in other people's lives and I very quickly worked out for myself a very ethical approach, a spiritual approach of using, transmuting, that love energy into something useful for the client. That is a great gift that I know I have given to a lot of people.

How could my parents have let this happen to me? I blame them entirely for throwing me into this man's arms, for throwing me into hospital and not rescuing me from that experience. My father died two years ago. I hadn't seen him for five years by choice and I saw him three weeks before he died because I knew he was going to die. I didn't hate him, there was no feeling at all. I only went to the funeral because my brother asked me to go. It was nothing. I was glad he had died. I'm glad he's out of my life.

An understanding of Harry's story

I shall attempt to help the reader understand through Harry's story the way a child can become exposed to such a destructive lifestyle. The reader might identify ways in which both Mike's story and Harry's are similar. Harry's story begins before he is born; something that is true for all of us but not acknowledged by most. The influences of our time in history, our environment and our family all play an important part in how we live our lives. As children the attitudes our family holds may be absorbed from the atmosphere around us; nothing is necessarily named, written down or acknowledged but somehow we know how we are expected to live our lives to satisfy the needs of others.

When a close family member dies just prior to the birth of a child there is sometimes a superstitious or supernatural sense of that person being replaced by the new baby; a life for a life. In Harry's case the man who dies was a very special person – his mother's twin; someone she closely identified with as one part of her self. When a young person dies heroically he is often idealised – 'only the good die young', or 'he was too good to live'. Death had separated Harry's mother from her twin in a painful, sudden way and she was overwhelmed with her grief and sank into what he called a 'profound depression'. So Harry was born into this situation: a grieving, withdrawn mother, an absent father, a war-torn city and the hardship that people suffer through the deprivation that war inevitably brings in its wake.

We know from the work of Bowlby and his colleagues (1973) that one of the most distressing things that can happen to a young child is the lack of attachment to, the loss of, or separation from, his mother. The development of the child's basic ability to trust is impaired, and the child doubts its ability to elicit care and affection – a term Bowlby named 'anxious attachment'. The child might deal with this by the defence of 'detachment' from others, becoming self-absorbed and compulsively self-reliant.

A child who abandons hope of achieving the emotional satisfaction of the early attachment to his mother may turn inwards and create a symbolic world which then has equal value. Harry tells us something of this internal world when he says:

> I was terribly preoccupied with my own inner world. Relationships didn't feel very important. I didn't feel I was part of the human race and I stoically accepted that.

The early bonding that a child needs with the mother during those first crucial weeks of life cannot occur when the mother herself is profoundly depressed. The evidence of this can be seen in the studies on post-natal depression. Bowlby describes the stages a child goes through when its attachment needs are not met. The first stage is one of protest; the child cries and searches for its mother. If there is still no response the child might progress to a stage of despair; he becomes quiet and withdrawn. The third stage is when a child becomes detached, he may appear to be quite happy on the surface and appear to have got over his despair; he may even begin to relate to others. However, it may be that he has given up on his need and love for his mother rather than have to feel the pain of it. A substitute mother may provide the necessary conditions to ameliorate the effects of the absent mother. In Harry's case there were other women who may have substituted the maternal role for him; both grandmothers lived in his home. However, one of those women was the mother of the young man who had been killed and so maybe she too was not able to fill that gap for Harry, perhaps being more concerned with her own loss. His paternal grandmother was described by Harry as one who 'ruled with a rod of iron'; a woman who seemed to model for Harry the stoicism he came to value highly and to emulate as a way of coping with adversity.

Harry had no male role-model during this period of his life and indeed even on the return of his father who was inadequate as a father and as an adult male. It may be that his grandmother carried the 'masculine' role for him with which he could identify. In his description of this woman it is clear that he held her in high esteem, valuing the aspects of her that might be stereotypically considered 'masculine'.

The cultural influence of the 'cockney' way of life taught Harry the importance of laughing at life than acknowledging vulnerability, fear and the need sometimes to admit to feeling weak or overwhelmed. All of these cultural values can be seen as stereotypically 'masculine' values; which once again are elevated over the stereotypically 'feminine' values.

I have dwelt at some length on these early conditions in Harry's life because I think they may have created a situation which laid down the foundations for his later sexual abuse. The pain of the early emotional deprivation felt by Harry was probably defended against by the mechanism of dissociation; splitting off that part of his experience into his unconscious. The additional separation during his hospitalisation between the ages of 7 and 9 is likely to have triggered those dissociated feelings; all his unresolved anxieties may have arisen and overwhelmed him and been added to by the extra trauma of his illness and renewed separation.

The early defence mechanism of dissociation, which may have been utilised to protect Harry's fragile developing ego, may be one that he used again and again during the repeated traumas of his life. He indicates this when he says:

> Whenever the doctors and nurses came I froze – I let things happen to me – it was the only way to cope. I was told I was a brave little boy.

Dissociation is often described as 'freezing', 'numbing', or 'spacing out' and is an excellent coping mechanism which helps a person to survive when faced with intolerably painful experiences which are inevitable. Harry was seriously and dangerously ill and in order to survive (quite literally) he had to undergo painful and invasive treatments. He had no emotional support; he felt abandoned by his parents and was unsuitably placed in an adult ward where there was no contact with other children who might have supported him through play. He had no teaching or contact with any adult who seemed to care about his emotional welfare.

His first experience of sexual abuse is remembered in an entirely dissociated way; he did not allow himself to feel 'spiritually contaminated' at the time and has kept the feelings out of consciousness ever since 'so it doesn't have any conscious meaning at all' to the extent that he describes his later abuse as his first, 'my history of sexual abuse started when I was 9'.

The abuse that occurred when he was 9 is described with feeling details such as 'terrified', 'distressing' and 'horrifying'. He dealt with this 'stoically' as he had dealt with all his experiences in hospital; he had been socialised into believing that this was an acceptable way of dealing with frightening and inevitable experiences.

On his return from holiday and having allowed himself to experience those feelings at some level, Harry attempted to tell his mother what had happened. He feared being held responsible and he did not have the language to describe the events.

A cognitive explanation

The sense the child makes of the events and the defensive strategies used will depend, not only the level of ego development, but also on the level of cognitive functioning as described by Piaget's theory (Osborn, 1990). This theory is based on the idea that a child is born with a few intrinsic strategies with which to cope and interact with the world, which Piaget calls 'schemas'. Schemas can be defined as:

> core beliefs or expectations about self and others.(Mc Cann et al. 1988, p.558)

Schemas represent and direct the way the child make sense of and interacts with his world. As the child grows and develops the few intrinsic schemas are added to and adapted by the process of 'assimilation' and 'accommodation'. Assimilation is the process by which a child takes in and adapts the new experience to fit with his existing schemas of the world. Accommodation is a process of adapting, modifying and extending existing schemas in order to integrate the new experience (Osborn 1990).

When Harry tried to tell his mother about his abuse and failed to do it, he realised that he would have to find a way to cope:

> As he wasn't going to leave the house and as I couldn't tell anybody and as he was still going to do it, there was only one alternative which was to give into it and so in that moment I decided to embrace (what a horrible expression) – to embrace the abuse.

What Harry seems to be describing here is the moment he assimilated the abuse to fit with the existing schema which he had formed in the hospital, 'I am powerless and helpless to change the bad things that happen to me.'

Beck (1967) sees schemas as developing and changing with continuing interaction with the environment. Schemas affect how we understand and interpret events and influence our emotional responses. Latent schemas become re-activated by conditions similar to those in which they were first developed and the new experiences matches up to them. If there is a good match between schema and new input, then the schema will be reinforced. If the new experience is discrepant with the existing schema, then conflict ensues and a need to reduce the state of arousal that conflict induces. This conflict can be avoided or reduced by adaptation or assimilation.

Mc Cann et al. (1988) propose a model for understanding sexual abuse victimisation in which they describe five core areas of schemas which may be particularly affected: trust, safety, power, esteem and intimacy. Victimisation will affect schemas relating to self and others in each of these five key domains.

Attribution theory is also relevant here. When we try to make sense of our experiences, we usually look for the causes of events, our behaviour and the behaviour of others. When we try to integrate events into our schemas we may interpret the events as being caused by ourselves (internal attribution) or caused by the situation (external attribution). This causal attribution will have serious consequences for how our resulting schemas will feed back into our view of ourselves. This helps us to understand how different people may view the same event in different ways. This will depend on their level of development and how their environment has influenced the formation of their schemas.

Trust

Erikson (1968) believes that a child develops a healthy positive sense of trust through the response of the caretakers in his early life which he is then able to internalise. As previously stated Harry's early caretaking was probably not sufficient to meet this need.

When the responsible adults in a child's life repeatedly contradict the child's own feelings and judgements the child's ability to trust itself will be damaged. When Harry's parents and doctors lied to him about going home soon or going to the Isle of Wight they were invalidating his feelings of anxiety and horror. This would probably have affected his ability to trust others.

If the child has a basic sense of trust, which has previously developed before the abusive experience, then they may be able to limit their distrust to only 'some people'. However, damaged trust can work both ways. The child who has not been able to learn the rules of discernment (by which we usually decide a person's trustworthiness/untrustworthiness) might be unable to trust or he might misplace his trust, thereby putting himself at risk of further abuse.

Harry lived very dangerously in the twilight world of the West End, putting his trust inappropriately in complete strangers in ways that risked his health and welfare. His parents, by sending him on holiday with a man who sexually abused him, and who they invited into their home, may have confused his ability to discern how to trust. He had trusted his parents to keep him safe and they had failed; he had trusted the hospital staff who were 'in loco parentis' to keep him safe and they too had betrayed him. A child who does not react with suspicion and mistrust might react in an opposite extreme by trusting anybody and everybody, constantly seeking the 'good parent' by whom he can safely be 'held'. Neither of these extremes is useful as they are both manifestations of an unconscious reaction to feelings outside the person's awareness. It is by making these feelings conscious that the person can take control of them and use them to make a free choice of response.

Safety

Safety can be seen to be a basic human need. When a child finds himself in an uncontrollable situation, which is experienced negatively, he will be likely to develop a negative self-safety schema. Harry's hospitalisation experience will almost certainly have produced a negative self-safety schema for him. A child who comes from a stable home environment in which his emotional needs are met, will be less likely to develop such a strong negative schema in the face of a one-off traumatic event.

Peterson and Seligman (1983) describe how the attributions a person gives to an event may interact with his general thesis. If the child experiences the trauma in a place he expected to be safe (such as his home), he is more likely to give this an internal attribution, (I must have done something to make this happen); if this happens outside the home, he is more likely to give it an external attribution because he was in a situation that could be considered less safe, (this is something to do with the situation). However, as Harry had been in the hospital for two years, it could be seen as a temporary home for him and a place he should expect to be safe. He also had a right to expect to be safe in his own home and with the person his parents trusted to take him on holiday.

Power

Harry's first experience of sexual abuse in the hospital involved his personal sense of space being invaded against his will which is described by Finkelhor and Brown (1986) as a central 'traumagenic dynamic'. However, his experiences of medical treatment could equally be seen to have been experienced by him as an uninvited invasion into his body space; he felt powerless against these invasions both in relation to himself and in relation to others. This trauma may result in 'learned helplessness', a state in which the child becomes extremely passive, depressed or even suicidal, or to a situation in which he attempts over-control and regain power by constricting feelings of vulnerability and powerlessness and splitting them off.

Learned helplessness was described by Seligman (1975) who conducted experiments with dogs who were subjected to continuous and uncontrollable electric shocks. The dogs seemed to learn that the shocks were uncontrollable and gave up looking for ways to escape even when it was possible for them to do so. These studies have been applied to human victims who are exposed to continuous trauma over a long period of time and go on to develop a generalised belief about future uncontrollability (Osborn 1990). The attributions that the person makes about the events will affect their view of its controllability.

It may be that Harry developed 'learned helplessness' as a child in hospital and responded to this by reacting against his dissociated feelings of vulnerability by taking control of the situation; choosing to put himself into situations in which he felt in control in an effort to master unconscious feelings by re-enactment of his abuse. His description of himself in the Turkish Baths when he lay face down and was anally penetrated by any man who chose to use him that way (much the same as his initial abuse experience in the hospital lift), without him even seeing the face of the person who was using him, could be seen in that way.

Esteem

The basic need to be accepted, valued and understood by another human being is at the root of the development of our self-esteem; a child needs to be taken seriously by its caretakers. A very young child who is abused by a trusted caretaker has too much invested in preserving the image of his caretakers as 'good' and is therefore unlikely to develop a negative esteem schema towards others – he is more likely to turn that into a negative self-esteem schema, taking the negative feelings onto himself. Negative self-esteem schemas can result in depression and self-destructive behaviours whereas negative esteem schema relating to others may cause chronic bitterness and anger towards people.

Harry describes the major effect of his abuse as being 'depression'; an almost permanent state that he has struggled with all of his life. This feeling has been graphically described by most of the men in this study as a powerful accompaniment throughout their lives and can be seen over and over again in the interviews. Several men referred to how they went to bed at night almost afraid of waking the following day because they knew they would feel this depression.

Intimacy

A positive self-intimacy schema is necessary if we are to be able to feel good when alone or to be able to soothe ourselves when distressed. This is usually derived from having internalised a sense of a good loving parent figure. Children who are sexually abused by a trusted adult may develop negative or unstable self-intimacy schemas. This may develop into a need to look to external sources for comfort such as food, alcohol, drugs which mask feelings of neediness.

Harry described himself as an alcoholic and a compulsive

worker; both could be seen to be ways of looking to external sources for comfort. The same could be said of his sexual compulsiveness which he saw as a way of feeling loved. Typically when a child has been sexualised through abuse they may confuse sex with love and indeed might only be able to feel love in connection with sex which might also be connected with pain if the abuse has been forced. It may also be that a child becomes addicted to the adrenalin that is released through fear associated with a sexual experience.

Erikson suggests that a healthy feeling of intimacy and connectedness with others is necessary for psychosocial development. Fear of intimacy will result in problems with interpersonal relationships and feelings of isolation. Harry didn't have any friends in the early part of his life:

> I assumed that I would be lonely all my life ... I was very lonely and very, very sad and I thought 'this is the way of life'.

Some of the isolation experienced by children who are abused is caused by the need to keep that part of their lives separate and secret. Harry kept the secret of his life in the West End from Faust, the only real friend he had during adolescence who was described as his 'other half' and 'inseparable'. Harry realises that the necessity to split off parts of himself risked the development of a psychotic state. The psychic energy this kind of living requires ensures that the child constantly needs some relief from the anxiety this causes. Harry's early addiction to alcohol and his involvement with the fantastic world of the ballet and opera may have helped him cope with this anxiety.

Another area of his life which could be seen as a way of coping, his Church activity, also caused him additional anxiety. The fear that his Church friends would find out about his 'twilight world' in the West End fed into his anxiety and depression, disallowing him from a relationship with God that seemed to be the necessary way for salvation. The strength that his Church gave him in his early years (as well as during his adolescence) seems to have been like a double edged sword. The nurturing of his spiritual aspect seems to be one of the few positive experiences in his childhood and one that he has drawn upon in his adult years throughout his healing process.

8 The paedophiles' stories

In this chapter I shall present the stories of two men who have been convicted of committing sexual offences against children. At the time of George's interview he was molesting children but was not admitting to it directly; shortly after the interview he was arrested when a child he abused reported him to his mother. He has now been imprisoned for fifteen months. Robert was awaiting trial when the interview was conducted and has since been put on probation.

George might be classed as a fixated paedophile and Robert as a regressed paedophile. These were the only two men out of twenty-five I interviewed who abused children during adulthood. Several others had abused during childhood or adolescence but had not continued with this behaviour.

George's story

George was born in 1934. He has been married for over thirty years and has a son in his 20s. He is a retired senior manager in the City. He was an only child and his parents split up when he was 10-years-old. His father had another woman during his marriage and he married her after the divorce.

George said:

I was about 3 when I realised my dad was a womaniser; my first memory of him was of him drunk as a lord, his pyjama trousers around his ankles, and my mother trying to get him off the loo. I was 10 when my parents separated, the most vulnerable time (which was when the abuse happened), and that was devastating.

I don't remember much of him before I was 5. I have developed a tremendous liking for motor cars because he would sit me behind the steering wheel when I was very little and drive along. I didn't see a lot of him, he was working and, I suppose, out with this other woman; then the war came and he joined up. Mum was a professional musician; an extrovert character and we always had terrible rows about everything but we both had a sense of humour. I was the man of the house; I did miss my dad, (that thought still brings tears to my eyes). I saw him two or three times a year at the most. I felt a tremendous vulnerability. He went off to the war and just didn't bother to come back.

Mum wasn't really affectionate but neither was she unaffectionate; not cloying or anything like that. I'd have hated that. She cuddled me sometimes but not overly. She was born nearly blind and could only see about four inches in one eye. She had struggled through life and, oddly enough, she wasn't over-protective. I had a tremendous amount of independence. She let rooms in the house and that kept us comfortably.

The worst period of my life was when I was about 15; it hit me that my father wasn't there. I still have a fantasy that breaks me up. Well it's nothing really – just about him discovering me in the boot of his car wrapped up in an eiderdown.

When a man has been brought up by a woman I think you develop an awful lot of characteristics of the woman but it doesn't make you effeminate. I was quite a masculine boy. I used to play chess, climb trees, and play on the swings; I liked the museums and art galleries. Maleness definitely wasn't a particularly attractive thing to me as a child. Being a man meant being sick; driving when you're drunk; getting VD – my father did! I've always eschewed the macho image. I don't give a damn about a football, or a golf ball or cricket ball really. I found them quite unintellectual pursuits. Not one of them could play chess. That's what used to get me.

I always went off by myself. I went to the cinema one day during the summer holidays when I was 10; it was an 'A' film and children were only allowed in accompanied by an adult but when a man or woman came along we would say 'will you take me in please'. This chap in his early 20s came along and I asked him if he would take me in. I offered him my money but he paid for me. He offered me a shilling before the film started and when the light went down he put his arm round me and pulled me towards him. I was only very little, wearing short trousers, a shirt and sandals. He undid my flies and put his hand down and fondled my genitals; he pressed his finger onto my anus. This went on throughout the afternoon. When the lights went up during the interval I said I wanted to go to the toilet. He replied so quickly 'I'll come with you', that warning bells must have sounded, because I said I would go later and sat tight. He asked me to meet him there again the next week and I agreed but I never went back. If he had not responded so quickly and with such vehemence, I should have probably have met him a week later. He became a bit too intense for my liking and he frightened me off, although I wanted to be there with him. It was almost as if I was in control of it. It was absolutely wonderful. Even today that is the most gentle and caring thing that has ever happened to me. (*Since I wrote this, George has contacted me to say he has now connected with the negative feelings about this abuse and realises that he had blocked it out.*)

As soon as I got home I said to my mother: 'A man gave me two shillings in the cinema.' She immediately said: 'Did he touch you – did he do anything to you?' I said: 'Good Lord, no; I'd never allow that.' You see I'd had such a wonderful time, I didn't want to get him or myself into trouble. Maybe if she had approached it slightly differently I might have told her. I realised it was wrong from the way she reacted. I'd never experienced it from anyone else except my peers. I still don't feel there was anything wrong. Not at all; it's terrible, I'd go back now. I have never progressed beyond the age of 10; that's why it's wrong.

Just before this episode our house had been requisitioned and we stayed with some friends who had two daughters of 11 and 8; I was 10. The 11-year-old girl was the more sexual of the two. We spent every waking hour stark naked on the bed, simulating sexual intercourse, investigating each other's genitals. I was fully aware of the sexual needs of a young lady of 11! I tried my first go at sexual intercourse with a girl of 6 and she was as hot for this as I was. I probably coerced her because she was only 6 and I was 10 but she really liked it.

In 1947 when we moved to Battersea I would spend hours at the Tate Gallery, the Science Museum and the Natural History Museum. Only once did a man approach me on a bus – I asked a lady next to me if the next stop was the one I wanted. This man leaped across and said 'I'll show you where it is young man'; and I thought, 'I know your sort.' Immediately I saw it was the same intensity as the man in the cinema. He didn't use the right approach. When you sexually abuse children you must groom them. You mustn't frighten them.

When I was 12 I used to go to the park with my mother and she and her friends would sit and natter. I would gather all the little children around me and tell them stories. This was when I realised that I could captivate children. Maybe I drag them up to adult level or maybe I go down to their level; I think the latter is more true. I have more of an affinity with children than with adults; I have very few adult friends. I'm nearly 60-years-old and I love pop and heavy rock music; I listen to music that none of my contemporaries has the slightest interest in. I'd love to have a relationship with women but if I don't know them already by the age of 11, I can't start a relationship with them, male or female.

There are two little girls near where I live and when I appear they both leap up at me; it's cuddles and kisses. Oh God! I get on so well with them. They are smashing kids. In another house there are three of them. Sally is 12 now – she is a super kid – they comes in and I have to do their homework with them. Her young brother is 8 and he loves to be with me. There's a little one who is 5 – I don't like him very much. Because of what I now know, I appreciate that they are in grave danger. As long as I keep appreciating that, it's a help for them and me.

There is something else that has happened and I don't know what to do about it – nothing I suppose. There is a little girl down the road who is 10 and she has fallen in love with me – hard to imagine. We have talked about it and I have said: 'This can't happen – you realise this can't happen'; she's got a crush. I cuddled her and I gave her a kiss and I said: 'We can't do this; we just cannot have a relationship.'

And this goes on I think 'Why me, why has fate picked me for this?' I don't want to be nasty to these children and tell them to keep away, but at the same time I don't want them with me because there's a possibility of the danger; so far I've managed to control it. My past history ... it goes a long way back. My son is 25 so I'm working on him as the time factor.

I have read a great deal about what happens in incest cases between fathers and sons and mine in no way comes up to ... or down to, that sort of level. The activity with him was brief and I think on three occasions before he was 10 probably. I don't go into the bedroom and chase around after him when we are alone; nothing of that sort. Casual ... very casual things. That's why it is so dreadful because it has buggered his life up. I'm not a predator. I slept with him once at my mother's house and I touched him. I don't remember but he tells me I did and I take his word. There was once – it was only two minutes – I don't remember another occasion but he does. We have talked about it. I blocked these things out. Even more so now that I realise the damage that it does.

I would tend to suggest that 99 per cent of all men who have children touch them up at some time or another. The more mealy-mouthed and righteous and upright they are, the more I distrust them.

Realising what happened to me in the cinema was sexual abuse implies enlightenment and that can only have come about 7 years ago.

I joined Scouts when I was 11 and we went away for camp and it was appalling weather and food was awful because the Scout master was never around. I once asked one of the other boys where he was. He said 'In his tent training'- I always wanted to go in his tent because every day there was a different boy in there but not me and I thought there must be something wrong with me. I went with one of the boys to phone his mum and dad; he was in tears and wanted to go home and they came and took him home. The camp broke up – we all went home. Shortly after that Jack was arrested for sexually abusing children.

I used to think I might be a homosexual because of the feeling of wanting a man to touch me. I had a friend when we moved to London, he was 13 and I was 12 and he introduced me to oral sex. He had a man friend whom he saw regularly and he didn't want to introduce me to him. We stuck things up each other's bottoms and this went on for years – between 12 and 15. We spent hours and hours on this huge double bed experimenting. Despite the fact that he was only one year older than me, it was abuse; I wanted to be abused and he did it; in the same way he wanted to be abused and I did it. I am pretty sure it had a tremendous effect on me. I don't think the sort of activity we had was normal sexual activity between two boys of the same age. It was mutual abuse. I went out with another boy who masturbated me and that was OK; that wasn't abuse.

From the ages of 11–16 I had the same girl friend who was the same age as me. We had a sexual relationship and we had intercourse only once but she wanted it more. My mother once said to me, 'It's better to do it into a handkerchief than into a woman' and I've never forgotten that – so masturbation became the OK thing to do but sex with women was not OK, because of venereal disease. That's always been one of my things (my father had VD); in the end it became very obvious that I am not very adequate at sexual intercourse. I probably am, I don't know, but I feel I'm not, so I don't do it. I haven't had intercourse for about 8 years.

I fantasised about my girl friend for years. No fantasies with males oddly enough. My girl friend found someone else by the age of 16 and I had a whole string of girl friends after that. Lots of petting and oral sex. I began to hate these girls; I wanted to hurt them – not physically. I would just take my pleasure and I wasn't the least bit interested in them; then I would drop them and take another one on. A lot of people think that is just natural male behaviour but I think that's a load of codswallop. It's just the male way of asserting power and being a bloody nuisance and a beast. I would take a girl home in the taxi and then go back to the party and carry on with someone else. I was engaged five times.

One particular day after I was married, about 26, something happened that brought out the abuser in me. It had been totally dormant in me until then. I took the two children from the neighbourhood to the seaside on a bank holiday. I took one of the children back to the car to change into his trunks and I just had this overwhelming feeling, a real 'high' – as if you have had a shot of a powerful drug that lifts your adrenalin. I said: 'Would you mind taking your trunks off and letting me have a look?'. He said: 'What will you give me for it? He lived next door and he would stand at his bedroom window naked and I shone my torch up there on him.

Some years ago I tried to find out if I was homosexual or not by actively seeking an older man. I found one very quickly through an advert; a photographer looking for male models. He is gay and considerably older than me. I got quite a kick out of it and he liked me, there was no sexual intercourse; we engaged in mutual fondling, masturbation. He has introduced me to other people, most of whom I wouldn't have anything to do with to save my life. The odd one or two I haven't minded have been in their 70s.

I then went away to a gay guest house for a holiday. I had a lovely time. It was run by two gay men. They were lovely people, highly intelligent, creative, human; I was no more attracted to them than fly in the air, nor them to me. I was very interested to see older men with younger men; some had been together for many years. I've never ever had a prejudice against gay people – my mother had. I would say I was bi-sexual but I don't fancy men. I see myself in an abusive situation with men. That is what I like best. I'm absolutely 100 per cent certain that I'm not gay. So how can I be bisexual? I couldn't kiss a man. I think I am heterosexual by nature but have been sexualised to enjoying abusive relationships with men, but only older men. I like children and I like young girls and some young boys; that would be me wanting to abuse them. Then there's a gap from 15 right up to 70 or 60 that doesn't interest me. At the top end of the age range – I want to be abused by them.

I love pornography. I adore nude bodies of any age. I've seen photo essays of little boys which are no more pornographic than fly to the moon. They are beautiful productions for paedophilic men and the photo essays are not in the least pornographic; they are photos following a nude little boy from the time he gets up in the morning to the time he goes back to bed, perhaps at summer camp, none of them in a lewd pose or anyone doing anything to them. I've seen the magazine *Arab Boy* which is not really hard core or anything like that. But there are usually two boys – one is usually a teenager with a small boy of about 8 or 9. Very satisfying for me to look at because the older boy is doing what I would like to do and the younger boy is getting done what I would like to be done to me. If I had just one of those magazines I think that would be all I would need.

(This interview was given by George in August 1993; in October 1993 he was arrested for the indecent assault of two children. He is currently serving a fifteen month prison sentence. In November 1993 George contacted the overwhelming negative feelings about his own abuse experiences both by the man in the cinema and the boy who abused him during adolescence, a boy who was re-enacting his own abuse by an adult male 'friend'.

The making of a fixated paedophile

George classifies himself as a paedophile. Wyre and Swift (1990) use a classification of the 'fixated paedophile' which would fit George:

> The fixated paedophile is not usually sexually aroused by adults, may only really be comfortable in the presence of children and have no enduring relationships with people of his own age. What friends he has are likely to be other paedophiles. Many men in this category have been sexually abused as children and have incorporated their experience of abuse into their own sexuality (p.39).

Fixated paedophiles are sexually attracted to children based on their identification with children and their desire to remain childlike. George recognises this in himself when he says: 'I have more of an affinity with children than with adults; I have very few adult friends.'

When George talks about his relationship with the child who imagines herself to be in love with him, it would be easy to forget for a moment that he is talking about a 10-year-old:

> We have talked about it and I have said: 'This can't happen, you realise this can't happen'; she's got a crush. I cuddled her and I gave her a kiss and I said: 'We can't do this; we just cannot have a relationship.'

Paedophiles are expert at identifying vulnerable children; they tend to target the lonely or neglected child. They know how to talk to them and to assume the paternal role. As the victim of a paedophile, George described himself as solitary, vulnerable and missing his father when his abuse occurred just after the divorce of his parents.

George seems to be saying that he started to educate himself as a paedophile when he told stories to the children in the park and realised that he could 'captivate' them. He started to develop his sexual interest in other children at a very early age; something that caused myself and (he told me) professionals who have counselled him to question whether the abuse at the age of 10 was indeed the first time he was abused. It may be that he had been abused at an earlier age but had no conscious memory of that.

Many children engage in 'normal' sex play with peers which is age-appropriate except in cases when one or more of the children has been sexually abused. George describes sex-play with other children before the age of 10 which does not seem age-appropriate. The 11-year-old daughter of friends he stayed with, seems to have been very sexualised and engaged in more adult sexual behaviours. George himself wondered in retrospect if she had been abused by her father; a man he could look back on now, with the eyes of an abuser, and see in that light. It may be that George was already sexualised by her before his meeting in the cinema.

George experienced sexual orientation confusion because he knew that he wanted a man to touch him; as an adult when he had attempted to discover whether or not he was gay, he realised that he didn't 'fancy' men. His story clearly demonstrates how a heterosexual male who is sexualised by another male can suffer from a distortion in his understanding of his sexuality in a way that makes it impossible for him to gain sexual satisfaction as either heterosexually or homosexually orientated person.

An important message was conveyed to me by George concerning peer abuse. He had become very clear in his own mind that the sexualised behaviour he and his male friend engaged in during their early adolescence was abusive and damaging. All too frequently males are socialised into believing that same sex juvenile activities are harmless and 'just part of growing up'. This normalising of abnormal events adds to the difficulty in dealing with abuse. George was able to differentiate clearly between 'normal' adolescent sexual exploratory activity (which involved mutual masturbation and fondling) and the abusive, intense, compulsive, penetrative sexual behaviour that he engaged in with his peer who was being sexually abused by an older man. This was happening during the same period that George was in a relationship with his girl friend, from 12–16, and may account for some of the distress and sexual anxiety he experienced during those years. It might also account for his aggressive sexual behaviour from the age of 16; reclaiming his power by treating women badly, sexually and emotionally, whilst at the same time trying to convince himself of his heterosexuality.

Nowadays pornography seems to meet part of his need to experience himself sexually. His entrapment in the role of both victim and perpetrator is summed up when he says of his favourite pictures in pornographic magazines:

> There are usually two boys – one is usually a teenager and the other a small boy of about 8 or 9. That is very satisfying for me to look at because the older boy is doing what I would like to do and the younger boy is getting done what I would like to have done to me.

Although he has been working on these issues for six years George still seems confused and distressed by his attraction to children. I believe that until he feels safe enough to dispense with his defence mechanisms and to reveal to himself and others the negativity of his own abuse, he will not be free. George's sadness and his confusion between love and sexual abuse can be summed up in his final question: 'Do you know what it feels like to wake up every day and wish that you hadn't? And all this because someone showed me love.'

Defence mechanisms

Freud believed that the ego arose from the need to cope with unconscious processes which sought expression without regard to external reality, (primary process). When the ego is immature, not yet differentiated from these powerful and chaotic impulses, they are defended against by what he called 'splitting'. Unacceptable thoughts or impulses would be split off with whatever part of the self that has been contaminated by them. In this way the integrity of the remaining part of the self would be preserved even though depleted. If splitting continues this can result in the fragmentation of the self.

These split off parts are then projected out onto others and experienced as coming from them. George disowns the negative aspects of his sexual abuse and his abuser but speaks with vehemence of 'mealy mouthed self-righteous men' whom he suspects of abusing their children, something he minimises when speaking of his own abuse of his son: 'I have read about what happens in incest cases between fathers and sons and mine in no way comes up to that sort ... or down to that sort of level.'

George displays another defence mechanism – 'identification with the aggressor' which was described by Anna Freud (1946) as one of the most natural and widespread defences used by the primitive ego. When the anxiety felt during abuse has been disowned, split off or repressed into the unconscious, only the positive feelings remain conscious; contact with the negative feelings may be too threatening to the immature ego.

George admits to feeling threatened by the man in the cinema and that was why he didn't go to the lavatory with him or go back to meet him again the following week; he also recognised the same type of man on the bus and although, on the one hand, he says he would go back there any time, when given what might be the opportunity, he does not take it. He has not contacted those feelings in any real way; he defends against them by only allowing himself to remember the warmth and closeness. George was able to identify with the abuser as the person who left him feeling 'absolutely wonderful'; this allows him to re-enact the abuse with other children without having to accept the responsibility for any negativity at an emotional level although he does at an intellectual level. At the same time George splits off his feelings of victimisation which he cannot accept as part of his self-concept, perhaps because of his social conditioning. This split-off part is therefore not accessible to be worked through and the pain of victimisation is buried.

These psychological wounds when denied or buried, constantly press for attention. George's need to recreate his victimisation by seeking older men to abuse him may be his psyche's way of trying to draw attention to the split off part; to free himself from the trap of feeling his abuse as only positive. This conflict is evident when he says: 'I still don't feel there was anything wrong. Not at all; it's so terrible. I'd go back now. I have never progressed beyond the age of 10; that is why it is so wrong.'

In order to assimilate the anxiety of the experience he has undergone, he may have introjected some of the characteristics of the anxiety object (his abuser) and by identifying with the abuser he transforms himself from the person who was abused to the person who abuses. This can be understood when he says: 'I wanted to be there with him. It was almost as if I was in control of it.'

This need to see oneself as 'in control' may be another way of defending against the overwhelming anxiety of being out of control. In reality George may have realised that he was not as powerful as the adult male who abused him; it would have been intolerable for him to feel the degree of his powerlessness and vulnerability, especially as he also felt he had put himself in the position where it had happened.

When a child is embattled with an adult whom they know to be more powerful, he might cope by accommodating the experience into being something that he had sought and is therefore in control of. This defence can be seen in more everyday terms when a child who is told that he cannot have pudding until he has eaten his vegetables responds with, 'I didn't want it anyway, I don't like that pudding!' This allows him to maintain control without having to acknowledge his powerlessness.

Robert's story

Robert was born in Hong Kong in 1952 where his father was a soldier. A brother was born on their return to England two years later; a stillborn boy was born two years later and then another boy six years later. Being a military family they were always on the move; Robert went to seven schools in eleven years. Robert has two children, a son and a daughter. He is divorced and unemployed.

He told his story:

My father was always strutting around the house like some huge, rampant bull; pushing us out of the way like we were a threat. He always had to be physical to prove he was strongest; he was very dominant towards my mother but as we got older and stronger he would have to resort to subduing us with 'nerve holds'; he used to teach unarmed combat. We used to see him hitting our mother. We tried to stop him and we would get beaten to the floor. One day when I was 8 he was beating me and my 6-year-old brother came in kicking and scratching at his ankles and he picked him up, took him into the next room and tried to throw him into the open fire. I rushed in and grabbed my father on the back. My mother came in from the shops with my youngest brother in the push chair and she managed to get the two of us out. We lived in bungalows above the drill hall – about thirty feet off the ground; we got down the concrete fire escape only to see him hanging over the parapet holding my little brother by the ankles, dangling him upside down from this flat roof saying, 'If you don't come back I'll drop the bastard; he's not mine anyway.'

We never actually saw sexual gropings but it was always in the air. My father was convicted of sexual assault on six young girls when I was 11 and he was sent to Nettley where he spent a year or so. When I was 10 I stumbled in on an indecent assault that he was perpetrating on two girls who were about 8 or 9. He was the manager of this rolling skating rink at the weekends while he was in the army.

I ran away and joined the army when I was 17 – straight into what he wanted anyway. His daily litany was 'You are not man enough; not good enough; not big enough and you never will be'; it sunk in and I lived my early adult life believing it, so every time I got somewhere that looked like I might succeed, there was this voice inside my head saying 'You are not good enough' or 'You can't do that because you are not big enough' – so I lived my life by getting close to the top and then shooting myself in the foot and failing.

I got him back when I was 21 and my brother was 18; we had a joint birthday party and my mother was dancing with a black guy; my father is a racist too and he couldn't handle it. That night at home he went for my mother and she defended herself by grabbing a poker, he disarmed her with ease and went to strike her with the poker. By now I had learned unarmed combat and I came from behind him and disarmed him; I put the poker into the point just below his voice box and I held him against the hot Rayburn while she packed her bags and left and she never went back. My brother and I left at the same time.

She was a really good mother. When my dad was thrown out of the army we were evicted and we had nothing; no home, no blankets, no plates, knives or forks because it all belonged to the army. My father also left huge debts and she had to pay them too. She worked night and day as a cleaner. She was hard working and very loving; I can only remember one incident when she raised her fist at me; it wasn't very hard or well-directed but the fact that I had upset her enough for her to want to do that hurt me a lot. We wanted to champion her; she was the one who always worked hard and she was kicked for it. She did as well as she could for us boys; I loved her and still do; we all do. I am in touch with her on a weekly basis. Whatever else happened later she earned our love; without her we wouldn't have survived.

As a little boy, and even now, I like soft things, cleanliness, nice fabrics, plants. I don't like an overly oppressive masculine room. I enjoy the arts, creativity. I also prefer female company; I feel more at ease with women than with men, unless the man is the sort that can express feelings and talk. I was quite happy to be that kind of boy but my father wouldn't allow it – he wanted me to be hard all the time. He would drag us off to the firing range. I quite enjoyed just having a gun and firing it but it was the constant pressure to achieve and if you didn't achieve, you were pushed down for it. Later I became a good soldier. Today I am a male and I have no trouble. So I don't feel weakened by my softness.

My father would march us to the barbers every fortnight for a close back and sides; he would march us everywhere we went; he wanted us to be superhard, superfit. He succeeded in driving us away from that mentality; I have no time for it.

Being a male meant being the sort of person my father was; all barrel-chest and bollocks. He would push his way in anywhere – he was a huge man between 15 and 20 stones; he struts around the place and huffs and puffs. He barrels his way into everything; when he walks into a room everyone feels crowded; he takes up a lot of space. He's got an awful lot of power; he is a very intelligent man but he misuses it. He gets himself into a position of trust but then he tries to pull a fast one to earn a quick buck or he steps on somebody's toes. That is one of the reasons we were always moving in the army – no officer wanted to have him in their unit; with him it was just 'post him on'.

I was 7 or 8 when I was coerced into sex with 11- or 12-year-old girls by some 18–19-year-old soldiers; they were big men to me. We were in our den which we had created. The girls weren't normally part of our gang. They came in with some boys of their own age; the soldiers followed them in. The den was in a subterranean bunker in a disused part of an army camp. We had kitted it out with old horse-hair mattresses, blankets and stubs of candles to light it.

It started off with us titting up the girls and taking our trousers off; showing our willies and things. One girl, who was about 12, was coerced into giving me a blow job and she didn't know what she was doing and I didn't know what she was doing and she bit me. It hurt and I pulled her hair and shouted; she was shocked and started crying and I started crying and felt horrible. She was pulled one way and I was pushed the other way, into the far corner of this place. I was full of tears and my other friend was crying too, he didn't like it either and we both wanted to go home. I felt so angry, so dirty and I took this candle and I flashed it to this horse hair mattress. I was really surprised at the speed it caught fire and it just went 'whoosh'. Thick black smoke and flames filled the whole place.

We were furthest from the door and everyone else got out but me and this boy were trapped, blindly blundering around. We were pulled out by a sergeant who was a friend of my father's and he took me to one side and made me promise never tell anyone else about what had happened in there. I kept that secret until I was about 38. I did remember it and I didn't. I knew something was there but I didn't remember the details. It was very traumatic when I did remember it after 28 years during an acupuncture session. I had gone to this acupuncturist (who was a trusted friend) after I had abused a little girl. She had agreed to try and do what she could and worked on all the points that worked on dissociation. Floods of stuff came out then. It was like a huge zit. That was when I started remembering some of the abuse but I was only able to go so far but I wasn't able to go back to it – just shadowy things until a few months ago.

I think the next abuse happened after my father was put away and they evicted us from the army. My mother needed someone to lean on; she took me to one side and said 'You are now the man of the house' and I took it to heart. I got a job working on a pig farm every evening, weekend, school holidays. Social Security wasn't brilliant and I was able to bring home enough vegetables to feed the family for a week. Also, we used to share her bed so she could sleep, because she was quite tearful sometimes. There was no groping as such, nothing like that, she never fondled me around the genitals but I remember one night in particular when she cuddled me from behind and I could feel this incredible heat and I became really aroused. I sensed there was arousal there for her too – I could feel this energy and I didn't know what to do with it; it really frightened me. I asked if I could sleep in my own bed and she was a bit shocked, hurt and surprised by that. I don't know if she was aware of what she was putting out or that I could feel it, but I did. I never slept with her again.

When I was 12 or 13 she would often say how handsome I was and if she was younger how she might fancy me, which used to make me feel on one level quite nice but, on another level, I didn't really want that. Then, when I was about 13, there was a period when she started wearing pyjamas right up to midday if my father wasn't about. The top had buttons missing and she was at that time still a very attractive woman and childbirth hadn't ruined her figure at all. Then there was a time when we had a little cuddle and she leaned against the back of the sofa bed and we had a little hug; then we started kissing and I found that her leg went between mine and then mine went between hers and I had an erection; she was highly aroused and so was I. She stopped it and went away and I didn't see her for a couple of hours; I had to go and masturbate. If she hadn't stopped it, I would have made love to her then and there – I really wanted to.

The next morning I came down wondering what the situation would be and she didn't address it. She was sitting at the kitchen table again wearing the same pyjama top and I went over and put my hand down inside her top and fondled her breast. She said 'No, no, you mustn't' – she stopped it after that. It never happened again. She never wore loose clothing around the house again and she was very careful. She had become aware that not only I was aroused but she was too. In her eyes I had become the man of the house; my mother had almost become my lover.

It took a while to get over that – it wasn't until I started having girlfriends with whom I was having sexual intercourse that it changed. I became a father at the age of 15. I had a girl friend who was nearly 16 and she was my first lover and she became pregnant. She became a ward of court; we were kept separate and the family moved, but I know I have a little girl somewhere who must be about 24 now.

By the time I was 13, my father's behaviour towards us changed slowly and about the age of 15 he stopped hitting us at all. I had stopped being bullied at school, and at about 13 I became a tyrant myself; if I saw a big boy beating up a little boy I would just walk in and floor the big one. I wouldn't ask questions, I'd just walk in and stop it. They made me a prefect; the teachers used me to sort out the fights at school. I had learned that was the best way to stop it.

There were a couple of other instances of definitely coerced sexual behaviour. There was this older boy who was about 15 when I was about 12 and he had a niece who was 10 and we all went across the fields one day. He was quite an aggressive bully and he started putting pressure on the girl to show what she had and then he put pressure on me saying 'how does that make you feel'. He took his own prick out and compared it to ours saying how big and hard it was – he coerced us into masturbating the girl while he watched. I found out later that this was the beginning of his long-term assault on her which went into full sex and I understand that by the time she was 16 she was a heroin addict and she is dead now. That makes me feel really angry.

Then there was Smithie – the boy who finally broke the bullying for me at school. He was the hard boy and one day he picked on me and I faced up to him and didn't let him get the better of me. We knocked each other insensible. But eventually he said 'no more' – that's when I suddenly realised I didn't need to win and I didn't need to lose; I just have to be. So we became great friends and one day I was invited to stay at his home. He was from a military family too. (If you want to investigate sexual abuse even today I think you should go to the army camps; you'll find a lot of it and you won't have to look very far.)

Anyway I went to his house and we were sitting watching TV and his father was in the armchair at the other side of the room. Smithie's sister, who was about 14, had come in with a tray of tea and biscuits and gave them to her father. Smithie started nudging me saying 'look at that'. His father had his hand up his daughter's skirt and the mother was in the kitchen through an open door and in full view. He was another man like my father.

It both attracted and repulsed me at the same time and I became erect. The next day was Saturday and we were left alone with his sister when the parents went out. We started teasing her, sexual teasing and she lay down on the floor in the living room with her knickers off and her legs open. I was really excited and was about to enter her and there was this kind of deadness in her, like a wooden object, she had just 'gone'; her eyes were dead, she was just laying there – uuggh something happened – I don't know what it was but my erection disappeared. I felt horrible and I never touched her after that.

My father's attitude to sex was as the bull male; that any woman around was his for the taking and a lot of that attitude had stuck with me. I like to think that is very different now. I have many close women friends now that I don't have sex with. I used to have a reputation when I was married for being a man who dipped in everywhere. The fact that I never had another woman during the eleven years I was married didn't seem to matter. I carried that sexual energy in the presence of women that I had from my father.

Before I was married I was horrendous. I had a little black book of conquests which was how I viewed it – it was a sexual pursuit. Even now I have a very strong sexual energy but I am learning to divert it and channel it in other area in order to cope better. My wife was the sixty-third woman I'd slept with. It was how I measured my manhood. Notches on my gun. It was an addiction. Even now I would say I am a sex addict. I think I was becoming a sex addict by the time I was 15. In a way it was a sense of power.

After I left the army I was just drifting, supposedly selling insurance during the day, but I was actually a drug-runner and I was involved with anarchists who were gun-running, stock piling for the big revolution that never actually happened. I wasn't into robbery, theft, mugging and stuff like that. To me if I was going to do something it had to have a cavalier attitude as part of it. Actually walking through police cordons with a briefcase full of drugs, dressed in a suit and being called 'sir' by this policeman did the trick.

I was anti-society. When I joined the army I rode for a motorcycle display team. There was an element of danger. I have broken almost every bone in my body. I lived close to the edge. My last years in the army I was in the SAS and out in the Kenyan/Ugandan border and that was very dodgy. I always had to put myself on the edge. When I left the army I had to find something else to do that. I was a very heavy drinker. I didn't want to grow old, to live to 40; I wanted to kill myself but I never had the balls to do it coldly so I tried to drink myself to death; tried to smoke myself to death; to fuck myself to death. It was manic activity without thinking about it.

I hated myself. I changed my name because I didn't want to be that person but now I've changed it back to the name I was christened. I'm actually 41 now as well! I'm living life now in the way I want to. It's as if I really have died; I'm a different person. I still drink, but to enjoy myself not to kill myself.

I've often wished, when I am in the company of women, that I could have a sex-change. There have been times when I have looked at silky underwear, soft sensuous stuff and I have wondered how it feels and I have tried them on. There have been many a time when I thought 'wouldn't it be lovely if men could walk around in colourful clothes, silk kaftans and things'. I couldn't walk down the street wearing coloured slacks without being propositioned by every homosexual in the neighbourhood. I believe in re-incarnation and I hope that I come back as a woman next time. I much prefer the female life-style even though there are terrible thing like sex-attacks that women have to cope with and violence; it's the last legs of patriarchy and they are digging in and being vicious; I don't like it at all.

I know I have been an abuser of children myself but none of the abuse has ever been violent, coercive or threatening. I am a paedophile; attracted to girls of about 11–14. I have been convicted of indecent assault. I abused my daughter. I would fantasise about sex with my daughter when she was coming into puberty. I also had fantasies about the other two other girls that I assaulted who were precocious sexually – my daughter was not precocious. I think there was an unconscious voice inside my head saying 'it's OK to do it to these two because they are used to it'; but the other part of me rebelled against it.

It was only during counselling for being an abuser that I began to see that what happened with my mother was sexual abuse and I started to look at it from that angle. I couldn't see her as abusing me because I was the man of the house as well as being an emerging man in my own right and apart from being my mother, she was a woman. I'd been educated that women were there for cooking, cleaning and sex. They were put on earth for our benefit and every man should have several. They were not abusers; they were victims and abused upon. So how could she abuse me when I'm the man?

It's getting easier to talk and think about it as abuse. At some point in the future my mother and I are going to talk about this together and that will be difficult. There will be no anger or recrimination – I don't feel at all angry with her; I can see the position she was in.

The only negativity at the time it happened was that I was left feeling horney; at the same time I felt like my manhood had been inflated. It wasn't just genital; I felt big and strong. I felt I could take on the world. The first instance in the bed when I was 11 felt 'iffy' but not the later episode when I was more mature. I was confused by it the second time and excited the third time.

The abuse I perpetrated on my daughter was something that came from being close, intimate and cuddling, which came from a point of deep love. I still do love her. I don't know how she feels about me now. At the time she loved me. It was love; there was no coercion, no aggression, no force, no violence. My daughter had come into our bed in the morning when I found myself with an erection, which I then placed between her legs as I cuddled her to my front. I came to myself and I thought 'No this is wrong' and I stopped it. I had hoped it went over her head. I stroked her head and gave her a peck and rolled over facing away from her. It was never addressed – she never said anything about it until recently when it all came out. There were other times when I touched her breasts.

It has affected my whole life completely until I had my breakdown when I was 37–39; between 39–40 I was slowly coming out of it and 40–41 is where I am now. I had so many opportunities that I screwed up. I wrote songs with a friend who took them and used them and is now a multi-millionaire living in California. I could have made a career out of the Army but I shot myself in the foot. There have been times when I have started my own businesses and I've got them to a certain point where I could start making money, right on the point of breakthrough, and I screwed up every time, because I haven't felt like I deserved it. I wasn't good enough; I had no right to success.

The making of a regressed paedophile

Psychoanalysis also provides us with an understanding of how a man who has been sexually abused by his mother might become involved in sexual activity with his own and other people's children. Social learning theory is also used to examine how Robert's father may have influenced his development. His story is also examined within the theory of patriarchy.

Paedophilia

Robert describes himself as a paedophile. He has recently been convicted of sexually abusing his daughter and some of her friends. The similarities between his description of his abuse of his daughter and that of his own abuse by his mother are clear in his interview; at times he uses the same phrases and words and insists that it was 'through love'. He minimises the seriousness of his abuse of his daughter by comparing it to perpetrators who use force or coercion, in much the same way he minimises the effects of his mother's abuse on him.

Robert fits the description of a regressed paedophile used by Wyre and Swift (1990) who say:

> The regressed paedophile is someone who may have a stable relationship with a woman or be sexually attracted to women, though he may also be insecure about his sexuality and be immature in his relationship with them. He is said to be most likely to molest a child impulsively after or during a crisis. He may have a drink problem, or have lost his job, or be suffering from depression. He may 'pseudo-mature' a child – treating or

thinking about her as an adult – or regress, seeking comfort and support from the child.

Although it has been said that women are not paedophiles it can be seen that this description would suit Robert's mother as well as Robert himself.

Research has indicated that people who sexually abuse others have themselves often been sexually abused in childhood. That is not to say that people who have been sexually abused in childhood will become abusers – only two of the twenty-five men I spoke to had molested children during their adulthood. Research has also shown that women and men who have been abused in childhood sometimes re-victimise themselves by forming relationships with abusers, who, in turn, may also have been victims of abuse in their own childhood.

The eldest son is probably the first intimate contact a woman has with a totally dependent male; maybe allowing her to feel more powerful and dominant with a vulnerable male than ever before; perhaps presenting her with the first opportunity to re-enact her own abuse unconsciously.

Psychoanalytical theory

In Robert's case we see a male child whose father is unacceptable as a role model; a man who emotionally and physically abuses his son; a man Robert is theoretically supposed to connect with in order to separate from mother as part of his gender identity formation. At the 'genital' stage Robert has two options; he can identify with his role model and become like his father and separate from his mother or he can remain attached to his mother and identify with her, the victim, whichever is the more acceptable model for him to imitate – this choice will probably be guided by his positive or negative experience of these people.

This creates a twofold problem for the little boy. If he adopts the behaviours of his preferred role model (his mother), and identifies himself as a victim in his relationship with others, he thereby reinforces negatively his experiences in the wider world. He describes himself as a victim in every school that he moved to; the frequency of these moves also meant that he was always the outsider, never staying long enough in any place to develop supportive friendships which might have helped him undo some of the damage of his father's behaviour towards him.

The other problem is that of being left with a confusion about his gender identity; something Robert describes in his interview. He feels himself to be masculine but is confused by his preferences which seem to be of a 'feminine' nature. Children who experience themselves in this way during the latency period are often under much greater peer pressure to conform to stereotypically male behaviour during adolescence. This can clearly be seen in Robert's changed behaviour during his adolescence; he becomes the 'tyrant'; behaviour that is rewarded by his teachers who approve of his toughness and aggression, repeating the messages from his father.

During adolescence sexuality becomes a powerful drive, with new energy and interest through the input of powerful hormonal changes. Sexuality seems to be more closely related to self-identity in males than in females and in Robert's case this period of renewed sexual energy and interest was closely related to the time that his father left the scene, leaving the stage open for him to step out onto. At this important stage of his sexual development his mother began to engage with him sexually. His mother was everything his father was not; caring, loving, and hard-working. She was also a woman who emotionally and sexually abused her son.

Mothers who themselves have problems with boundaries (perhaps because their own have been transgressed during childhood), may predispose their sons to later difficulty with boundary keeping. A child and his mother need appropriate levels of closeness and distance at different stages of his development. At each stage the mother needs to take care that the boundaries neither merge with, invade or deprive the child. No matter how close and loving the bond between the mother and the child, the child's psychological health is compromised to the degree that his mother does not see him as a separate being.

A child needs to believe in the goodness of its parents; when one parent is overtly a 'bad' parent, the other parent might carry all the 'good'; they may become the idealised parent; they can do no wrong. When his mother adultified him by depending on him as 'the man of the house', as the provider and as the one to meet her emotional and sexual needs, Robert may have defended his fragile ego from feeling the pain of this by the defence of denial. He construed his mother's sexual behaviour as love; sex is therefore confused with love. His father's physical abuse and the sexual abuse by the soldiers would almost certainly have damaged his self-esteem; he was a vulnerable, needy child; his total dependence on his mother is now recognised when he says: 'Without her we wouldn't have survived.'

In replacing father's role, Robert took on his new identity as 'man of the house'. Robert has learned from his father what it means to be a man. It is noticeable that it is at this time that Robert lets go of his identity as 'victim' and becomes the aggressor. As he grows into manhood he adopts much of his father's behaviour, he impregnates his under-age girl friend and becomes involved with the

Courts on that account; he becomes addicted to sex; he keeps a little black book of sexual conquests as a way of measuring his manhood. Later he joins the army and involves himself in the illegal use of drugs and other anti-social behaviours.

Robert used the phrase 'like father-like son' several times during his interview, indicating the power of the socialisation messages that he may have unconsciously introjected even whilst expressing his disgust at his father's behaviour and his attempts to be a different kind of person. It was almost as if he could not help himself following the pattern laid down before him.

So in spite of his wish to dis-identify with his father the boy cannot entirely disentangle himself from his role model. He introjects the 'bad' of his father and is full of self-loathing and self-hatred. These feelings follow Robert throughout his life; his deep-rooted self-disgust causing him depression as he turns all the negative feeling in on himself; always feeling that he is not good enough to live, to be loved or to have any positive expectations for himself. He lives dangerously, believing that he does not deserve a good life but never sure enough to end it. When the child turns its aggression inward because of his inability to turn it on the 'love' object (his mother) he may become driven by the wish to destroy himself. Hate, as a polarity to love, points the way to self-mutilation or destruction.

Incest taboo

The deep-rooted incest taboo within our culture and indeed in that of all cultures, that mothers and fathers are forbidden objects of sexual desire to their children, is usually concerned with forbidding sexual activity between fathers and daughters although equally the incest taboo is against sexual relations between mothers and sons. Indeed Freud was first theoretically concerned with mother–son incest prior to father–daughter incest (Freud 1912–13).

Freud's theorising of Oedipal feelings is that the direction of feelings runs from the child to the parent, not as in the British version of incest, from parents (nearly always considered to be fathers/father-figures not mothers) to child (nearly always considered to be daughters, not sons).

Robert clearly felt sexual desire towards his mother and wished that she should become his lover. Freud postulated this desire of the child toward the parent in his theory of childhood sexual development. Society, which at that time could not cope with the idea of childhood sexual abuse, chose to interpret that as meaning that the child was responsible for the abuse and indeed desired it. Freud was at that time attempting to present the notion that children have sexual feelings and that these can be met appropriately through cuddling, stroking and being held but not through what is considered sexual behaviour from an adult perspective.

By denying the whole theory we are in danger of 'throwing out the baby with the bath water'. We need to recognise that children are sexual beings if we are to help the child to identify, own and control those feelings in ways that do not expose them to the risk of being abused by adults who are ultimately responsible for holding the taboo. The fault does not lie with the child for having those feelings, but with the adult who does not hold the boundary. When the parent holds the taboo and does not respond to the child's sexual feelings inappropriately, then the child will be free in the future to experience those sexual feeling with an appropriate adult at an appropriate time in their development.

The child whose parents (or other significant adults) do not hold the taboo will seriously damage the child's ability to form healthy sexual relationships in their adulthood. The feelings of guilt and 'badness' the child experiences cannot be directed at the parent who is gratifying the deep feeling within the child. The child must take the guilt and shame and internalise it as if it belongs to them rather than the responsible adult. The child's anger may be turned inward and directed against the self, manifested through depression and self-mutilation. In the male child it may be more usually turned outward; such behaviour is perhaps considered more 'normal' among males according to the rules of gender stereotyping.

When Robert eventually turns his feeling outwards he turns them against the society which seems to represent all that his father holds dear and all that he despises in this man. He has not learned the language of feelings from his role-model or from the other males in society; he has learned the behaviour that males use to act out their distress; aggression, anarchy, and addiction.

Sex-roles

Psychoanalytical theory also defines men and women as having very strictly laid down sex-roles; men are sexual predators and women are passive recipients of sex. The confusion that Robert felt about perceiving what his mother did as 'sexual abuse' is therefore compounded; he cannot allow himself to think of himself as her victim; neither can he allow himself to think of a woman as the initiator of sexual activity.

Having remembered the abuse in the bunker during which he was frightened, overpowered, traumatised and forced by male aggressors, he can clearly see himself as a victim. He has no problem with that. He does not re-enact that abuse, having allowed himself to experience it as abuse and as fearful. The trauma attached to that episode, which must have been considerable, involving the fire and fear of entrapment on top of the sexual abuse, all of which was compounded by the sergeant's injunction for secrecy, was dealt with by repression.

Anna Freud (1946) describes repression as a defence mechanism which is capable of mastering powerful instinctual impulses in the face of which other defensive mechanisms are quite ineffectual. However, as well as being the most powerful defence mechanism, it might also be seen as the most damaging. When the child undergoes powerful trauma, it might deal with this by dissociating the effect and memory from the ego which is then defended from the necessity to deal with such intense feelings.

The dissociation from the ego, entailing the withdrawal of consciousness from whole tracts of instinctual and affective life, may destroy the integrity of the personality for good. The child who represses powerful feelings can become controlled by those feelings; reacting to situations which might trigger those unconscious feelings without ever becoming conscious of the source and thereby remaining stuck at the developmental level at which the trauma occurred. Such people might act out their anger, their fear, their aggression, their sexuality, using whichever part of their person contains the traumatised and cut-off aspects of themselves. This might be seen as addictions, compulsions and re-enactments.

Robert says he was addicted to sex by the age of 15. It was only when he became sexually active with female age-mates that he no longer wished to have sex with his mother. In talking about his abuse by his mother, Robert was still reluctant to allow himself to contact the negative feelings about it or to direct them towards his mother. He expressed compassion and understanding for her as behaving in the only way she could have done at the time. He denies her full responsibility for the act; to place the responsibility for her behaviour on to her may require him to feel anger towards her, something that still feels too threatening and contrary to his sense of needing to be her protector, her champion. He cannot allow her to 'fall from grace'. This fall from grace is a necessary part of the separation of the child from the adult, a healthy necessity which, providing it is not too sudden or too traumatic, can be seen as part of growing up.

In order to defend himself from the threat of abandonment by his mother, a boy who has been sexually abused by her may repress any negative feelings he may have towards her; to make doubly sure these feelings don't escape, he may use the defence of repression combined with reaction formation. Reaction formation is when the repressed feelings are controlled by superseding them with the opposite and unthreatening feeling. Thus a child who feels anger at his abusing mother but cannot bear the threat of her abandonment, may repress the feeling and put in its place one of idealisation; an extreme feeling of love and warmth and a belief that she can do no wrong. In reality most parents, and indeed most people, have within them the capacity for both 'good' and 'bad' – neither one aspect negating the presence of the other.

However, because the repressed negative feelings will call for attention they may emerge in situations that trigger them but are not associated with the person; such as when Robert allowed himself to abuse his daughter and other little girls.

Social learning theory

This theory is based on the belief that children learn through observation, imitation and reinforcement (Bandura 1969). A child observes adult behaviour, tries to imitate that behaviour and is either punished or rewarded. Children's behaviour is shaped by parents and other significant people so that rewarded behaviours are repeated and sought and non-rewarded or punished behaviours are avoided or feared. Behaviours that are gender-based which are unacceptable to a parent, such as a boy wearing his sister's dress, will be rejected by the child who will be influenced in future choices by the attitude of the parent from whom it seeks approval or love.

This seems to be based on the assumption that an individual has the propensity to adopt either/both 'masculine' or 'feminine' behaviours and whether they do or not depends to a great extent on the acceptability of those behaviours to the significant adults who are responsible for their socialisation. My belief is that each individual has within them the contrasexual opposite which will need to be acknowledged if the person is to develop into a fully integrated individual. In Robert's case the early messages he received from his father were that his behaviour was not acceptable to standards of masculinity, a message that was imposed, reinforced and introjected to the degree that Robert grew up believing that he did not deserve or want to succeed as a male. As the most dominant person in Robert's life his father's messages would be most influential, especially as his model of maleness and therefore the 'same' as him.

This authoritarian father's over-control has been reacted against in Robert's case: 'He succeeded in driving us away from that mentality; I have no time for it.'

One reaction to this type of fathering is that the man does not know how to be a father. Over-permissiveness has been one of the more unfortunate reactions: in effect the autocratic father has annulled his son's strength (Pirani 1988). Although now that Robert has understood the effects of his fathering and does not therefore need to react, his reaction against maleness as contained within his father may have led him to devalue his masculinity and elevate the value of his 'feminine' aspect. Although Robert seems to feel a revulsion against masculine values, ironically in attempting to abandon them altogether he became their victim and therefore controlled by them as demonstrated by his behaviour during late adolescence and early adulthood. The suppressed side inevitably becomes voracious.

The formation of the self-concept is based on the messages we receive from the significant people in our early lives. The messages Robert received from his father during his formative years were that he was not good enough and that he would never succeed. When we behave in ways that are out of keeping with our self-concept we experience 'cognitive dissonance' (Festinger 1957). This dissonance creates anxiety and discomfort which can only be relieved by changing our self-concept to include the new information or by changing the external experience to match the self-concept. For Robert, whose self-esteem had been badly damaged by his father's physical and emotional abuse of him, this meant that whenever he came close to success he experienced such a strong feeling of dissonance that he 'shot himself in the foot' thereby ensuring his failure and relieving the dissonance; in other words changing the outer experience to match his inner reality.

Patriarchy

Our culture has elevated the value of the masculine over the feminine through patriarchy and male children who adopt stereotypically female characteristics are often criticised or devalued as males. The fact that females who adopt more stereotypically masculine behaviours, such as a little girl who dresses in boys' clothes, will not be devalued in terms of her femaleness, seems to indicate that maleness is the preferred norm. There seems to be more pressure on males to conform to stereotypes. This study has identified that the majority of the subjects did not perceive themselves to be high on the scale of stereotypical 'maleness'; they describe themselves in terms that indicate the more stereotypically feminine aspects of personality. For most of these little boys this felt like a way of being that was acceptable to themselves but certainly not acceptable to one or other of their parents or other significant persons. Their version of being a boy was not compatible with the world's view of how boys should be (Phillips 1993). Because such qualities as gentleness, sensitivity or traits that may be seen as more stereotypically feminine are not labelled as masculine behaviour, it may be that they are not included when surveys are conducted into gender even though they are there. It may be that there is no model of masculinity for these boys and they are therefore being forced into a 'hole' that is the wrong shape and which they cannot possibly fit without feeling distorted or pressured. It may be that these boys are not 'misshapen' and that it is the shape society has made the 'hole' that is wrong.

Robert describes this phenomenon clearly in his interview: 'I was quite happy to be that kind of boy but my father wouldn't allow it – he wanted me to be hard all the time.'

His father is described almost as a caricature of the dominant male, even to the point that he is not seen as acceptable to other males; this resulted in him being moved on from posting to posting, causing disruption for all of his family. This man's power to disrupt his family seems endless; they were moved on from home to home, school to school; Robert always finding himself the new boy and the object of victimisation maybe because of being an outsider and on account of his adoption of the victim role through his father's physical abuse of him. His father was imprisoned for sexually abusing children; his family are evicted from their home, losing even the contents; losing their livelihood, their friends and the respect of the community.

Robert, like the majority of the men in the study, was the first son. Because of the elevation of the male in our society the birth of a son is often seen as the way a man has proved his manhood. The importance of the eldest son has been recognised throughout history in matters of inheritance of titles, wealth and land. With this role comes an expectation of responsibility, success and a worthiness to carry the family name forward into the future generations. The pressures engendered by this responsibility are inevitably powerful.

9 The teacher/lover's boy

One of the rules taught by a patriarchal society is that there are strict sex-roles which usually require the male to be seen as the active sexual predator and the female as the passive recipient of the male's advances. Although this rule has also to some extent been laid down by psychoanalytical theorists, it is usually taught by the overt messages that are instilled in children of both genders and is largely responsible, in my view, for the perpetuation of the mentality that denies the possibility of thinking of a male as a victim and a female as an aggressor, especially in reference to sexual behaviours.

Clem's story

Clem was born in 1960, the youngest child with two sisters and one brother. When he was 11 his parents divorced and lived separately in the same house for a few years until Clem and his mother moved out. Clem is awaiting his third divorce and is about to lose his business. He has no children.

He talked of his early life:

When I was little I loved my dad but my mum said he was a sexual abuser but he never touched me in any way except in normal fatherly ways – smacking me if I was late in, sitting me on his knee to tell me a story or ruffling my hair – to me he was a good dad. The way he brought me up, his attitudes to things and his values, made me wish I'd had more time with him. But all the time mum was telling me evil things about him; how he'd touched my sisters; he'd squashed the neighbour's cats with the back of a shovel; he'd done wicked things during the war.

The conflict was always there because I loved him, but my mum was saying he was evil and I loved my mum as well and she wouldn't tell me lies. So I ended up spying on my father for her. She had a baby alarm concealed behind one of the kitchen units and she used to sit up in her bedroom and listen to him talking to whoever came in. I used to stand guard over this thing and she would say 'if your father says anything you come and tell me'. He was supposed to be an alcoholic but I only saw him drunk on one occasion. I had this picture of this evil dad that I didn't know. I ended up disappearing into the Air Force because I couldn't cope with any of this.

I treated my father rather badly. I didn't go home and see him before he died. I was upset because I hadn't told him I loved him and when I went round to say thank you for all the cards that people had sent, I found out that he was a well-liked chap. I did see my sisters at his funeral and I questioned them about this touching and they didn't know what I was talking about. I then realised that my mother had lied about so many things. I ended up disliking my mother intensely over that and there were several years when I didn't contact her – in fact until about Christmas last year.

For most of my life (up until the last six months really) I don't think I've been a very nice person to know. I am an expert liar, I'm a bit of a con-merchant without the intelligence to do myself any good. Since I've had the therapy recently, I've decided that at 33 it is time for a fresh start; I should have done it years ago. I've been married three times – my third divorce will come through next year. I've managed to just about lose my business.

The only time sex was discussed in our family was when my brother left home – he was the last to leave home. He and his girl friend (who later became his wife) had sex in his bedroom when I was outside playing – and when my mother found out that they had been doing this 'dirty thing' upstairs, out goes all his stuff and 'I never want to see you again – I disown you;' a very dramatic scenario.

When I was in the first year at secondary school my woodwork teacher took a shine to me because I was keen and he would let me stay behind after school. He was going out with a very attractive laboratory technician in the physics department. She would have been 21, ten years older than me. She had long reddish blonde hair and tight teeshirts with a gap and a lot of us boys used to have smutty, schoolboy fantasies and talks about her. One evening after school she came to talk to me in the woodwork room. She had this ability to make me feel quite good about myself; she was always very complimentary; never any sex talk or anything. This went on for quite a long time – I called her Diane. I masturbated to fantasies about her. By now I was looking at magazines and sex was becoming much more defined.

I used to live to see her. She used to ask me about girls and she would give me her opinions about sex and they would be exactly the opposite of what I had heard from my mother. She would say it was something beautiful, deep and caring. When I look back on it a lot of what she said was quite true but she shouldn't really have been discussing it with an 11- or 12-year-old; she treated me like an adult.

It turned physical one day when I was cutting a bit of wood on a workbench and she came and sat on the bench behind me with each of her legs on either side of the leg that I had out behind me. I was all mixed up because I could feel the warmth of her thighs and one side of me felt grown up with her and the other side of me was quite confused, scared and I didn't know what to do next. I remember being aroused and getting an erection and being scared at the same time, and when the teacher came back in I was quite relieved that she moved away. When I was in the playground with a group of my friends she would come over and talk to me and I would feel quite big in front of them.

When I was about 13 my teacher came in late one day because he had something wrong with his car and he said 'If I give you the next two periods off will you go round and put this part in my car'. So I said yes and it was only a minor job and it was done very quickly.

Diane was living with him by now and she brought me coffee when I was working on the car. I felt quite manly and in my little brain I was in this fantasy role. I was playing the husband and she was the wife bringing me the coffee (all very sexist) and I was working on the car and really this was my home. When I had finished the job I had oil all up my arms and I went inside to wash. Diane came up behind me to pull my sleeves up for me; while she did it she was pressing against me and I liked this – I loved it; we ended up having a cuddle. That was all that happened for a long time. I used to go round to her house when I knew she would be alone and we would go into the hall and we'd press our bodies together; sometimes there would be a moving of the groin. As it progressed there would be talking about sex and fantasising. She'd discuss my penis and she would talk about herself physically but we never actually saw anything – that went on for a considerable length of time. She was just part of my life, going round there, cuddling, rubbing – I always felt like a man.

But then I started to feel a bit inadequate, quite jealous of my teacher. They had a house, a car, a caravan. I just thought about the material things. I wanted to buy a house, a car and to be able to take her on holiday so she would leave him and move in with me because she had told me she loved me and how much she wanted to go to bed with me. In my head all we needed was the house, the car and the holidays abroad. I felt empty and sad because I couldn't do what I needed to do to get her.

I used to masturbate maybe about six or seven times a day. Sometimes I would do it on the way home from her because I couldn't wait. That started to worry me because I thought I was a pervert and I started to think about stealing her underwear. Because I couldn't have her I wanted something that smelt of her; that probably sounds a bit crude. I became totally infatuated with her. When I got to 14 or 15 it got a bit more physical and we would start to rub using hands.

Then I went into the Air Force. I was very homesick during the first six weeks and I used to write to her every day, how much I wanted her, loved her, missed her and she would write back the same things. Then I decided in my childish way to test how much she loved me and I said, 'Diane, I am 17 now and I think it's time I found someone. You are married and you have a home and a husband and this isn't right, so I think I should separate from you and go my own way' and what I wanted her to do, what I expected her to do, was throw her arms around me and tell me how much she loved me and needed me and beg me to stay but what she actually said was, 'OK if that's what you think, that's fine.'

It was the summer season and the lads would go down to Newquay and they all started going out with these girls who were on holiday. I wasn't really interested; none of them came up to Diane; they were all silly giggly girls and Diane was this beautiful, intelligent woman who made me feel good about myself. These girls just wanted to go to discos.

I missed Diane so much and I felt so bad – everything crumbled. I went off and promptly took a load of tablets because life without Diane wasn't bearable. One Friday evening after I had written to Diane and she hadn't replied, I locked the door knowing my mates wouldn't be back until the Sunday night or Monday morning and I took as many aspirins as I could. But it had started raining and my room-mate, who had a motorcycle, changed his mind about going home and decided to come back because he was getting wet and cold. He called the medics and they put me in hospital and sent for my mother because they weren't sure what was going to happen. Then they sent me to a neuro-psychiatric centre and I saw a psychiatrist and I went through things.

After about a week he said, 'I think all you need is rest.' While I was there I met this lady called Betty, I was 18 and she was 39 – she was a squadron leader's wife. I was still missing Diane very much but Betty was lovely. I started fantasising all the time about Betty; she had a similar coloured hair to Diane but she had travelled the world with her husband and again I was extremely flattered that this worldly wise woman was paying me attention. I was actually quite astounded that she found me attractive.

I'm very, very grateful to her, because she was a lovely woman and she used to say things like 'If you don't want to do this you don't have to'. I lost my virginity to this 39-year-old woman – and I was 18 but she was so kind and gentle and I was all edgy like a rabbit and she slowed me down. She made me feel so good about myself and I really felt warm and close to her.

Then I was discharged and I went back to Cornwall but I couldn't live without Betty so I nicked a mini-bus and I spent three days driving around, sleeping rough in the van. I ended up being arrested by civilian police. I was charged for being absent without leave and taking a mini-bus and I was thrown into the guard room. I tried to escape; I'm not proud of anything I've done but this was quite wicked but I just had to get out. The duty officer was bending over the safe and I hit him over the head. They caught me as I left the Guard House and threw me into my cell again and I just flipped. By that time I'd switched off – I'd become a very aggressive, nasty person. I didn't care a damn about anybody else. I was court marshalled.

The result of all this is that I still think I've got pretty warped ideas about sex – I don't mean deviance – but I don't seem to have normal healthy attitudes to sex. Whether I orgasm or not is really not that important to me but if the woman does, I feel good. I don't generally have an orgasm; I take far too long. I masturbate a lot six, seven, or eight times a day and at the weekend it can be a lot more than that.

When I make love to a woman I take far too long. They've finished, packed their bags and gone away and I'm still doing it. One of the things that my last wife said was 'Just once I would love you to do it because *you* want to – don't do it for me; do it for yourself', I tried again and again and failed. So every relationship I get into is great for a while but I get in from work and we can't just make love for the fun of it but it becomes something I almost dread. I never seem to do it right. I always feel I'm conning them. I have affairs. I used to love my last wife until it ached but that didn't stop me from going to bed with my boss's secretary on the night before our wedding. I knew exactly what I was doing but I didn't think about Lynn at all. At the wedding – I didn't feel guilty – I had switched it all off. I am very capable of lying, deceiving, having affairs left right and centre. I can come out with the most amazing excuses and people seem to believe it. The last time I took tablets was Christmas last year. I couldn't see the point of anything. I'm a pointless piece of shit.

I had thought that Diane and I was a beautiful thing that had happened; I can see now that what happened has all the hallmarks of abuse because I was an 11-year-old boy when it started. It all clicked when the social worker said: 'Well OK you're saying that you were just as responsible as she was; if I go out of the room and bring an 11-year-old girl in here and you start doing to her what Diane did to you – do you think that's on?' I said, 'No, of course not.' She said: 'Why not?' and I said: 'That's a form of abuse isn't it?' She said: 'Yes, and that is what happened to you.'

But the trouble is I don't feel abused. All I know is that I actually feel quite worthless. My business has gone, I've lost three wives. I've got a relationship at the moment with my cousin. I met her six months ago. Having seen the social worker and having sorted it all out, I am now having a sexual relationship with my cousin who is that much older than me. I'm not saying there is anything wrong in having a relationship with an older person – all I know is that I seem to have done it again – I've gone straight into it.

I find masturbation more satisfactory than real sex. I'd like to think that we are going to bed to give pleasure to each other and also to get pleasure for ourselves. In other words we get pleasure by giving pleasure and we take the pleasure that is being given. But what I feel is that if I go to bed with a woman I have to give all the time; I don't feel right about taking. If she is satisfied then I've accomplished what I need to do, but having said that, when we come out of the bedroom I feel quite smug. I'm one of these men that women hate. It's another score on the score board. When I'm doing it I think my intentions are genuine – I want to give this girl pleasure but when I've done it I'm all bloody smug. I'm cocky – I've done it – I've given her pleasure – she must think I'm great.

I don't think the harm Diane did me was sexual. I think the harm she did me was that I didn't have a normal development. I don't think that did too much harm to the sex side – if any. But I wish she had allowed me to develop normally; to make a fool of myself with girls; to have great times with girls. I wish I could develop normally. I suppose I'm beginning to feel anti-Diane a bit.

Discussion

Sex-role stereotyping

Clem's story highlights the damaging effects of sex-role stereotyping. He was brought up to believe that males are the sexual predators and females are the passive recipients of sex. His mother presented herself as his father's victim and his father as someone who was an abuser; she accused his father of having abused his sisters sexually, of abusing animals and there were vague, dark hints of his abusive behaviour during his career in the army.

All of this invalidated Clem's feelings and beliefs about his father based on his actual experience of him. This probably created confusion and an inability to trust his own feelings or experience. Clem was dependent on his mother as the main caretaker and therefore if he took sides it would need to be with her against his father. Her powerfully negative messages about sexuality, as being something that resulted in excommunication from the family home, was demonstrated in her reaction to his older brother when he was discovered having sex with his girlfriend.

All of these messages can be seen in terms of social learning theory to have had a strong influence in the shaping of Clem's attitudes to himself, the world and others. Our attitudes are formed within our first social group which is usually the family and those attitudes influence our feelings and behaviours towards or away from a person, idea, object or event (Allport 1937). Clem was rewarded by his mother for spying on his father; she taught him to believe that men were not to be trusted, men were sexual predators, and that sex was something that deserved punishment and rejection.

When a boy is indoctrinated with these negative messages of maleness by his mother, he may understand a woman's need for a loving sexuality which is non-aggressive, but he may feel confused by the conflicting feelings within himself to be sexually 'proactive' which he may have internalised as 'aggressive'. This notion might be both exciting and repellent in a boy who has been socialised in this way. So when Clem was approached during his early puberty by a 21-year-old woman, he was surprised and encouraged to hear different messages about himself and sex; that sex was beautiful, that he was attractive sexually as a male; and that it was acceptable for him to relate to her in that way. He did not need to deny his sexuality as something dangerous or negative. For a boy on the verge of the strong hormonal changes of puberty this must have been welcome news indeed!

Most boys during this stage in their adolescent development learn about their sexuality by tentative exploration with people of the same age. They make mistakes and learn from them; they struggle mutually with strange, powerful and unfamiliar feelings. Each new relationship carries its own learning and that learning is then taken forward into successive relationships; an experiential process that builds upon itself and creates a firm and healthy foundation for long-term adult relationships.

Clem had been so indoctrinated in sex-role stereotyping that he could not allow himself to feel anything but flattered by the attentions his teacher's girl friend showed him. He felt like a man; she made him feel adult and, at the same time, confused and afraid:

> I remember being aroused and getting an erection and being scared at the same time, and when the teacher came back in I was quite relieved because she moved away.

Kinsey et al. (1948) found that in the age group 15 and younger, any slight physical stimulation of the genitals, general body tensions and generalised emotional situations may bring immediate erection, even when there is no specifically sexual situation. Bancroft (1980) cites human studies in which anxiety provoking situations can lead to a genital response. The release of adrenalin as a fear reaction can of itself cause a male to have an erection. However, most young males who experience an erection have been socialised to believe that this is linked with arousal and sexual pleasure eventually leading to ejaculation. This may lead them to believe that the fact that they have an erection means that they have some responsibility for the event and that sexual satisfaction is the only outcome for an aroused male.

In a situation where an older woman engages a boy in sex, society generally takes the view that this is sexual initiation; the 'you should be so lucky' response that victims are often met with. This is a view that is often reinforced by portrayal of such relationships in the media or films as comedy. When an 11-year-old girl is approached sexually by a 21-year-old man the situation is usually seen as abusive. Clem perceived himself as fortunate to have been selected by his teacher's girl friend; a sign that he was 'a man' – something that evoked the envy of his peer group. Clem says at the end of his interview that he now wishes that he had been left to develop normally, to make mistakes with girls of his own age. At the same time he cannot see that this early inappropriate sexualisation may have largely contributed to the sexual problems that he has experienced in the past and still experiences.

This type of female offender has been categorised as the 'teacher/lover' (Matthews, Matthews and Speltz 1990) and is probably one of the most under-recognised forms of sexual abuse of adolescent males. This type of offender usually become involved with young vulnerable males during adolescence and their relationship is seen as a 'love affair'; they often have difficulty in understanding the negative impact on their victims. The victims (usually between 11 and 16) are often a step- or foster son, a friend of one of her own children, a neighbour, a resident in a treatment centre or pupil. Initially she befriends the naïve or troubled boy and discusses her own problems with him. Her involvement may escalate and become a welcome escape from her own troubled relationships. She loses perspective and sees the boy more and more as peer and herself as 'in love'. These women often find it difficult to acknowledge flaws in their own character and behaviour. They may be very angry but may act out that anger rather than express it assertively.

Because the young victim is so needy for adult attention, approval and closeness, he may welcome the relationship and seek to initiate the contact once the adult has given their approval of it. He may begin to think of the relationship as something he has established and is therefore responsible for.

Approaching adult relationships from the standpoint of that first sexualised relationship can be disastrous. All three of Clems's marriages have ended in divorce; he has probably tried to recreate that fantasy-like relationship within his marriage and failed. Relationship problems that have caused him, at times, to try to end his life, can be seen to stem from his childhood abuse but he still needs to deny the harm of that to defend himself from the pain of realisation.

The sexual relationship between himself and Diane was clearly to meet her needs and was inappropriate to his own sexual needs and desires which would have been more appropriately met by his peer relationships. As the older woman she had the power in the relationship. It would seem that Clem still relates unconsciously to women sexually in a way that has to meet their needs at the expense of meeting his own – he rarely experiences orgasm. His own need is to feel like a sexual 'man' – and a man is someone who meets a woman's sexual needs. He sees every conquest as a 'notch on his gun' – he is smug when he has given a woman sexual satisfaction.

Clem knows what a healthy sexual relationship should be like – a mutual giving and receiving, but until he accepts, at an emotional level, the inequality of that first sexualised experience he will probably remain stuck with that belief. His need to hold onto himself as the one in control denies him the possibility of experiencing himself as a vulnerable victim. By turning the situation around to show him how his sexist indoctrination is disallowing him from seeing what happened to him as abuse, the social worker has helped him to understand that if he had been a girl and Diane had been a man, it would have been entirely different; he is just beginning to feel 'a bit anti-Diane'! The difficulty is that he still meets with Diane and in trying to discuss this with her she has told him that if he should reveal her as a child abuser she would lose her job. His fondness for her and his need to meet her needs before his own continues to impede his progress.

This case highlights the problem of definition when the person has been socialised into polarised sex roles. Until he experiences his abuse at a feeling level, Clem will probably be unconsciously driven to re-enact it in other relationships. He does not feel abused – he only sees the outcome of it and judges himself negatively because of his failures in relationships; his obsessive masturbation which distracts him from concentrating on business and other everyday activities; his lying and deceiving – something that he needed to do in order to cope with living between two worlds as an adolescent and continues to do when he becomes involved in relationships with more than one person at a time. He is beginning to understand his behaviour and feel more compassion for himself.

His obsessive relationship with Diane during his adolescent years denied him the normal open peer relationships which would probably have been part of a richer developmental process of socialisation and perhaps without such a focus on sex. Clem clearly describes the dissatisfaction he felt when in the company of peers he calls 'silly giggly girls' – he had been used to the company of a mature woman and nothing else felt satisfying.

In Clem's story it is possible to see the importance of abuse being defined from an external source before it can be owned internally. The 'non-abuse' has been internalised in the societal indoctrination when a young male is abused by a female and therefore perhaps the same external force needs to be applied to reconstruct and re-evaluate that experience. It can be seen that, in this instance, an alternative perspective was required before Clem could begin to break free from the trap in which he had been caught.

I have heard time and again that it was an external influence that helped the boy or man to realise that he had been sexually abused. Sometimes that source was a book or an article in a newspaper; sometimes a television programme; others realised when hearing another abused person relate their story (usually a woman). Most of us have been socialised initially within a family and this can prevent us from seeing our experiences for what they are. A dysfunctional family, in which physical, emotional and sexual abuse is the 'norm', is often the child's only experience and one which they internalise as 'the way life should be'. It is only when moving out into the world that the person can begin to measure their reality against the rest of society. When the dysfunction is within society – as I believe it is (especially in the messages of patriarchy) – then the process is much harder and can take much longer.

10 Abuse by mothers

In this section I shall present some of the interviews by men who were abused by their mothers. Just over half the men I interviewed were abused by females (thirteen out of twenty-five) and seven of those females were their mothers and in four of those cases, the subject was also abused by others. One of these mothers abused her son in the presence and with the co-operation of his father. The seven men who were abused by their mothers were first born sons. A study conducted by Elliott (1993) in the UK identified that out of thirty-two abused men, twenty-two were abused by mothers and another four by mothers with another person. In recent years it has become more obvious that some mothers do sexually abuse their sons (and daughters) and in spite of the natural revulsion that most people feel when such an idea is put forward, we must not deny the evidence. The mother–child relationship has been idealised and expectations that females are less sexually aggressive than males have lent credibility to the idea that such abuse is impossible.

Other female abusers in this study were sisters, half-sisters, two teenage carers, two adolescent girls and a teacher's girlfriend. All of these females were in the role of care-giver (or mother-substitute) except for the two adolescent girls and the teacher's girl friend. It would seem that females who have the opportunity to handle children intimately, may have opportunities for abuse that may have been overlooked previously. The socialisation messages children are given, that males are the sexual predators, may contribute to the child's inability to interpret his experience as abuse when he is approached sexually by a female. None of these female abusers was coerced by a male, although one mother was helped in the abuse by her husband.

I have dealt previously with the case of Clem who was abused by his teacher's girlfriend in the role of the older woman initiating a young boy into sexual activity – the teacher/lover role and one that is often dismissed and smirked over if it is acknowledged at all. I have dealt previously with the case of Robert whose abuse by his mother was seen as part of her close and loving relationship with him and a fulfilment of his role as 'man of the house'. In chapter 12 I have presented Tony's story, a man who was sexualised by his mother at a very early age and went on to be abused by males later in his school life; these cases will not be included in this chapter but should be held in mind.

I will focus firstly on Paul who was abused by his mother with help from his father. The confusion between love and sex is apparent in his story, as is the way his mother's over-intrusive behaviour has interferred with his ability to develop a satisfactory long-term loving relationship as an adult. He also demonstrates how a man who has been sexually abused by his mother finds it impossible to blame her or judge her behaviour as wrong. He still wants to be loved by her and cannot risk the possible loss of her love that might be entailed if he was to identify her behaviour as abuse rather than 'over-loving'. Paul had never spoken to anyone about these matters before his interview with me and he states that he probably never will speak of it again. His body pays the price through illness.

I shall present some of Kevin's poems and a diary of his therapy in Chapter 16 so will not include him here. Kevin was abused as a small child by his mother and repressed all memory of his abuse until he was in therapy at the age of 29. The description of how these memories were reclaimed in a therapeutic setting will also link with the discussion on repression and 'The False Memory' debate which can be seen at the end of Martin's story in Chapter 15.

The second story in this section is told by Harold, who as a toddler, was abused by his mother who died just before he was 10-years-old. He had repressed all memory of the abuse until he was 31. His mother had responded to his childish spontaneity by becoming sexually aroused and by stimulating him to sexual arousal for which she then punished him. He quickly learned that spontaneity must be removed from his repertoire of behaviours as the cost was confusion, rejection and fear. He describes how this fear has affected his ability to trust life and particularly the development of his self-confidence in intimate and sexual relationships.

The last story in this section is told by Roy whose mother had been sexually abused as a child by her step-father. She physically abused all her children and demonstrated a profound disgust and horror towards Roy's genitals as a child – presumably as an unconscious response to her own abuse. It may be as a consequence that Roy had grown up with a deeply held belief that his sexuality contained 'badness' but because there had been no direct sexual contact between himself and his mother, he had not been able to understand his feelings; when he recently discovered the term 'the abuse of sexuality' (Bolton et al.1989), he began to understand.

When the abuser is the mother, the child is deprived of the most fundamental bonding relationship that is essential to us as dependent human beings. The mother is the first person in the child's life and the attachment the child has to her occurs, not so much by learning, as by instinct. Mothers and children do not need to learn to love one another because they are innately programmed to do it from birth. These attachment bonds are proposed by Bowlby (1973) to be a direct expression of the genetic heritage of our species. Stevens (1990) proposes that our capacity to form a durable bond with a member of the opposite sex in later life is largely dependent on the success (or failure) of this primal bond.

The mother's relationship with her son may reflect the image of her relationship with her father/father-figure which might shadow their encounters if that relationship has been a negative experience for her (Leonard 1982). Her sense of powerlessness in a previously abusive relationship might be reacted against when she finds herself in a position of ultimate power with a small dependent male for the first time. All of the men in my study who were abused by their mothers were first-born sons.

A consistent experience of appropriate mothering confers upon the child the priceless gift of 'basic trust' (Erikson 1968), the secure feeling that mother, life and the world can be relied upon. These stories illustrate the damage that is done when this trust is betrayed.

Paul's story

Paul was born in 1953. He had three older sisters who all left home by the time he was 7. At the age of 40 he has retired from his work as a computer operator because of ill-health. He has had five intestinal operations and is awaiting another. He was married for seventeen years and has one daughter who is 14.

He told his story:

When I was 7 my parents involved me in sexual activity with them – it was a threesome. It would happen in the bathroom. They would put my little hand inside my mother's vagina and my mother would put my penis in a warm place, her mouth. While she was doing that my father would be putting his penis into her from behind. When I was older and bigger I used to insert my penis into my mother's anus and vagina. When she would get me excited she would sit on my penis and sometimes I would be frightened that she would hurt me because she was a big woman. I used to worry sometimes when I saw the fluid coming out of her mouth because I thought I was making her sick. I didn't know about ejaculate then.

I was quite a tolerant, outgoing and affectionate little boy. I would play rough games with other boys but only if I knew there were girls around to see me winning – if there weren't any girls watching then it wasn't worth it. When the other boys used to say it would be nice to see what was inside girls' knickers I thought they were a bit backward; I would think – why are they talking about it surely they must know?

My mother used to say that I was doing what all the boys would like to do. She was always generous, warm and affectionate and always there. She met all my needs and I felt very loved. If I did something wrong she would punish me by stopping me having sex with her. My father was generous in that he arranged things that my mates just talked about. He was very placid – he had no power, except that he earned the money but my mother had all the power through sex. She would give or withhold it according to whether you deserved it. She showed me affection by kissing, cuddling and sex.

I never felt confused about my gender; I learned that what I was doing with my mother meant that I was definitely a man. I don't have any feeling about homosexuality. My father never touched me himself and I never touched him – it was the two of us doing things together to my mother. So homosexuality hasn't been an issue and it doesn't bother me if other people want to do it.

Sex as a subject was taboo when my sisters were at home – they were told it was something you saved for marriage but I have a feeling that it started for me after they left home because maybe they were having it before that. I don't know – it's just a feeling. One of my sisters has been married four times and one three times and the other one has been married once. I am divorced now. My wife didn't like to do the things I had got used to being able to do with my mother and when I was making love to her it was boring; I would compare my wife with my mother and I would feel lonely and deprived. About an hour after I had sex I would want it again. I wanted it much more than my wife. If I bought her a bunch of flowers I would expect her to want to give me kisses and other signs of affection for days afterwards. It got to the stage that when I kissed her she would wipe it away with the back of her hand and turn away from me. Because I didn't get enough sex from her I had affairs outside my marriage. I needed a lot of closeness and affection. I have a girl friend now who seems to like doing the things I want to do.

I didn't feel what was happening was abuse. When I was 16 I left home to do an apprenticeship – then I thought that this was something I should have learned through my own experience and not from my parents. I think because it was my mother it was acceptable – if it had been a man then it wouldn't have been. Although I knew I shouldn't be getting it from mum I thought it was because she was over-loving – not as abuse. Now when I am with a female and having sex I think I was lucky that they did that with me – if I am not with a female then I blame them because they set a standard that was very hard to live up to.

I have suffered a lot from depression and I am a very nervous, tense and hyper-active person. Whenever I would think about the abuse I would do something, get busy, to stop me thinking about it – so I had to be always doing. The depression is because of the ill-health; post-operative depression. I know this bowel condition can be caused by stress but I was never anally abused so I don't think it is connected. Sometimes I have thought seriously about suicide but I've never attempted it. I think this is when I feel as if I am wanting more than I am getting and feeling lonely. I take pills for it. I've never talked to my GP – it's all put down to the operations. I don't sleep very well – I wake up sometimes dreaming about the things that my mother and I did. Sometimes I remember the way I thought I would suffocate when I ran out of breath doing oral sex on my mother and sometimes I wake up thinking about the scene in the bathroom when I used to worry that I had made her sick. Maybe now that I've talked about it I won't have those dreams any more. I've never told anybody else about it – mainly because I liked it. My parents are both still alive and we still have a close relationship and I am fairly close to my sisters. I've never thought about having sex with children myself. It has been helpful to talk but I probably will never mention it again.

Harold's story

Harold was born in 1947 and he has a brother five years younger. His mother suffered from polio and died when he was coming up for 10-years-old. His father remarried and had another son and daughter. Harold is divorced and has no children. He works as a computer programmer although he is a highly qualified engineer.

He looked back over his life:

I don't have many memories of my mother. I remember her being ill – something wrong with her leg; she was in and out of hospital. I remember her standing at the top of the stairs with her crutches. My whole childhood, up to the time she died, is almost a complete blank. When she was ill and after she died my brother and I were farmed out to friends of the family for the summer holidays.

I was very shy as a child. At the age of 7 or 8, I began to realise that I didn't fit the normal boy type. I suppose I generally felt fragile. I didn't like to play the rough and tumble games. I was wary of people, wary of other boys. I tended to go off on my own and dream a bit. I had no memory of being abused at all up to the age of 31. There probably were little hints at times that I could have picked up on had other therapists been able to recognise them. I had been in therapy as a student and a teenager in the sixties and at university because I could not have relationships with women at all. The whole deep emotional shock of being abused was buried completely and the only time it would remotely get triggered was when I tried to initiate a relationship with a woman. I couldn't evoke those memories; I didn't even know they were there, I just knew there was something wrong. When I approached a woman I would begin to blank out, to feel dizzy and sick. I would tell myself 'well now I am 20-years-old, I can meet a girl, invite her out' and that would just about go alright but the following night, leading up to the next date, I'd get so nervous and so shaky that I'd call it off.

So when I was 31, I met a woman who I was really attracted to and I thought I'm just going to push myself through this. Fortunately I was in therapy at the time. I literally walked in to my therapy session one day and without any prompting I just started screaming 'Don't play with me, don't play with me.' All sorts of stuff just fell out.

All the therapy I had done up to then had been with a man; those few sessions were with a woman. The bubble burst at that point. I did a lot of further work with my sexuality because it was just a non-event. I managed to establish a relationship with this woman – we lived together and we got married. I dropped therapy then; I thought I needed a rest from it, but there was still stuff niggling away. I still couldn't cope with the outside world. I am divorced now and in therapy again; the feelings are emerging now, the traumatic shock, a sense of loss, fear of … perhaps I should say what precisely seemed to have occurred.

When I was a toddler, with the natural exuberance of a small child, I would be jumping up and down and something about that would excite her and she would invade me. She was sexually arousing me somehow, (if that is feasible in a 2-year-old child), and then smacking me immediately. So there was pleasure and attraction; 'this is nice' and then 'you are a naughty boy' – fear and pain. These are not conscious, definitive memories – it is like awarenesses coming back that I had to quell the act of being happy in the presence of a woman and the only place I could go was into sadness. I couldn't risk being aggressive – there was a very strong fear of my father.

I can only assume that it was my mother, it seems most likely. There was no other female around. It also fits with what she might have been going through; the first born male she's got around with no clothes on that she can smack and do ... so as a result of that trauma (you realise how deep sexual abuse trauma goes?), I just ceased being a spontaneous child. When you turn all that energy in as a little boy, where can it go except into daydreams or into avoiding. I became a passive, frightened, easily hurt, little boy and I've been stuck with that virtually all of my adult life.

My father doesn't come into it at all. The family was growing, the war was over, things were settling down a bit. We moved into a new house and he was very keen on gardening, on DIY, on doing things. He didn't actively play with me. We'd go for short walks, with my tricycle, to the shops and things like that. He never liked other children on his patch. He was never a sociable man, he had no friends, he wasn't a patient man, he never went out to the pub; he did go off to the rugby matches very early in my childhood. I've learned since his death that he had been a sportsman before the war; he'd won awards for sporting achievement at school and college but he never talked about himself. He would never say what he did in the war or before that.

As a teenager I couldn't talk to girls; I was terribly shy. My classmates were dating girls; I always wondered what relationships were all about. It seemed so unfair – the man had to make all the moves and the woman had this power to say 'yes, yes', and then 'go away, piss off' – even when they fancied you. I didn't connect. Why did I have this terrible fear that this would happen? When this huge rage and crying came out in therapy I kept shouting, 'Don't play with me.' There was this memory and feeling of enticement, this pull in to be aroused or to be seduced or played with or encouraged; then there is this smack on the penis, chastisement for becoming aroused.

I felt terrible about my body as I was developing. I was very thin, not very strong, not very co-ordinated, I couldn't play sport. I was more and more aware during adolescence that something was desperately wrong. There were times when I felt totally out of touch with things. I was having to crush my breathing to such an extent to hold in the emotions, not to fall apart, I was getting a bent back. My father would say 'straighten up' and he got me a pair of chest expanders. I started to improve in the 70s when I was in therapy groups and doing Alexander work. It transformed everything; it changed my breathing so much.

I wrote a pleading 'O' level essay when I was in the fourth form, entitled 'Friendship: how I can't make friends'. The ironic thing was that I got full marks for it. The teacher read the marks out in class when he handed out the books and everybody wondered what on earth I had written to get such a high mark. My friend told me the girls would read it after school and cry about it. Still there was no response from anywhere. This pleading boy, desperately wanting help.

I decided when I was 14 that I wanted to go out to youth clubs like everybody else. My father was very strict, he said 'No, you get on with your schoolwork, (he was a schoolteacher), the big boys will knock you around'; and that was my greatest fear. By the time I was 15 or 16 I didn't want to go out any more. I buried myself in college, managed to get to university and got a degree. My father had tremendous power over me. I didn't have the strength to stand up to him; whereas my younger brother and even my younger half-brother, at 6-years-old, could stand up to him. There was me at 18- or 19-years-old and I would just dash off to my room and cry.

Sex was obviously never talked about with father in the family at all. However, being a teacher he did have, tucked away deep in his desk, some very old pamphlets about 'the growth of a boy' and 'the growth of a girl'; I got hold of these and started reading them covertly. I thought he wasn't around but he was and he looked in on me and said, 'Oh yes, you should read those' and then went away again!

My wife is the only sexual partner I've ever had. I had to go to a men's sexuality workshop to overcome the enormous blockages I had. I revelled in finding someone who wanted to be with me and I was able to enjoy it. There had been a lot of unused sexual energy which had built up. It was very exciting but it ran its natural course. She had one child from a previous marriage. I never felt that family life or having children was for me. I put my energy into working on my relationships with men and women after I finished university. There was also another issue about what work I really wanted to do and why I wasn't really as good an engineer as I should have been for someone with my qualifications. I didn't feel at home with it. I gave up work in the mid 80s – I couldn't do it any more, I was just overwhelmed. I was a designer of electronic equipment and it just became too much for me and we moved out of London. I have taken more menial jobs. I come home depressed. I don't like doing the job I have at the moment but it is all I feel I can do.

My wife was growing in all directions. She had been a craftswoman; she went on to become an astrologer – she had done counselling work many years before. She trained as a marriage guidance counsellor. She persuaded me to give up therapy and then she kind of stole right the way round the back and crept up on me 'I've done all this counselling training – I'm now a counsellor!' I was aware that she had occasional relationships with other men when she went away. It didn't really worry me. If that's what she needs to do then well – people need to explore these things to find out. Sex died and she said she didn't want a relationship with me any more. Quite a large part of me was fairly relieved. I suppose I'd always had this idea that a marriage had to be for life and two people would work through these things together but relationships seem to be collapsing everywhere. I've always had this sense of solitariness. Now sex is very anxiety provoking again and I prefer to be on my own rather than try and start another relationship.

I have never spoken to any of my family about the abuse. It triggers off emotions, even tears. I don't quite know what their reactions are likely to be – so I have chosen to keep it to myself. I've never told anyone except therapists about the abuse, although I do seem to remember trying to tell my wife on one occasion but she was very sceptical. I think I'm always afraid of another person saying they don't believe me.

The fact that the perpetrator was my mother meant that I had to grow up alone – the natural child/mother bond was severed and I suspect that I've been trying to recover this bond ever since. The one person I needed to turn to for comfort, caring, and love, was the very person I had to avoid to stop the abuse. I have grown up frightened of other people and by intimate sexual relations.

Throughout my childhood years, and I suppose up to the age of 14 or so, I did not know what the difference was between boys and girls. I sometimes fantasised that I was a girl being brought up as a boy for the purpose of a scientific experiment – to see what would happen – I didn't like being a boy as I hated what most boys were like.

Roy's story

Roy was born in 1954; he has a sister four years older and a sister four years younger. He is divorced and has a son and a daughter. He is a mature psychology student.

He started his story with a view of his parent's life before he was born:

My father was away at the war without home leave for four years shortly after they were married and my mother didn't know where he was. She had a stillborn child during the blitz. Life was based on the notion that 'everything was alright'. I can see that was a reasonable response from a generation whose lives had been ripped to shreds but it tied in very closely with my mother's attitude to herself and life in general. My mother was quite ferocious, irrational and physically quite violent to us as children; we could never quite tell when she was going to strike. When my father came home that would stop. I still hear the sound of a key in a yale lock and feel myself relax.

Mother punished physically; father punished very subtly with disapproval. He was quite remote. I think he was aware of what was going on but he turned a blind eye. I think he was a coward. I always longed for a male rescuer. When I was very little he used to play with me a lot – well, probably not very often really; he was very nice and gentle but quite unapproachable and very withdrawn, but somehow he seemed to exert this influence with my mother who went into a completely different mode – like a clockwork doll. After my older sister went to school – most of my young childhood – there were never any other children in the house; we weren't allowed to go out and play with other children – they weren't good enough.

I went through a period of absolutely loathing and detesting my mother. I had even fallen for thinking my father was a wonderful man; it has taken a long while to revise that and to realise the appalling pressures on her. The fact that she was sexually abused as a child was an enormous blockage for her. It still is and it led to a great deal of self-distrust and self-loathing and an inability to love us; an inability to cope with us being three alive children. She had a need to contain us and destroy us in some way and a very infantile view of our father as being her 'wonderful daddy'. In her eyes he wasn't importantly my daddy but he was her daddy; she was good enough for him, but I wasn't. I don't communicate with my older sister very much but I've had long, tearful, very good conversations with my younger sister about it and we can both remember being beaten and our mother screaming at us that we didn't deserve to have such a good father. That was obviously a very important theme.

As a little boy I was acquiescent, frightened and very, very timid, desperate to please; sycophantically polite and I had very, very long antennae that could sort out what was required in order to avoid a beating. I was very nauseatingly placatory and never succeeding. I was brought up by my mother to believe that being male was disgusting and I had to be pure and strong, hard working, uncomplaining. I felt from my father that even if things were happening with my mother, then I shouldn't complain. Physically I was totally unco-ordinated, totally unmasculine.

Going back to watching her as a child, during those years before going to school – there was a curious intimacy between us. As long as I stayed the other side of the room, where I could see her, it might just possibly be alright, but if she was close I would feel very frightened. After lunch she would have a rest and I would listen to 'Listen with mother.' I would sit on my own, often in another room because we had an extension speaker, and she would go to sleep. After she woke up, she would go upstairs to her dressing table and make herself up and do her hair in preparation for my father coming home. I was fascinated watching her becoming this other person for him.

I found out rather darkly from my older sister about my mother being abused by her stepfather. I remember her being completely jelly-like terrified when he called unannounced at the house. He was a pathetic, little round man, quite hearty and jolly and both my parents were very tense when he called. He was always known as Mr Brown – never by his first name.

I went to France with my mother's younger sister seven years ago and I let slip something about my mother's behaviour towards us. Her jaw dropped and she said 'I thought you were such a happy family!' She said that was exactly the way my mother was to her as an older sister. Then she told me about the abuse between my mother and stepfather and how he wasn't interested in her because my mother was the beautiful one and she was the plain one. Obviously she had been quite jealous about the rewards my mother got – she now realises this was for sexual favours.

My mother suddenly told me her about her stepfather abusing her. She said 'I've never done anything about it because it didn't affect me', and I just felt like saying, 'well it affected me actually and if I hadn't sought some help it would have affected my children', and to some extent it still does. The point at which I became aware of the way the abuse had directly affected her relationship with me was when some friends were telling me about a TV play they had seen about incest; an incest survivor had said how she found it very difficult to bath her sons, to actually touch their genitals. I found myself crying almost uncontrollably and I thought, 'that must be it!' My mother had vacillated between hysterical mockery and abject horror of my maleness and I had internalised that there was something quite revolting about my body. That realisation was a relief and a terrible sadness.

I can remember my father bathing me very much at arms' length and him being incredibly anxious about touching my genitals, and me sort of mildly surprised by the sensation of being touched but also realising there was something terribly disturbing going on for him. When my daughter was in puberty and he came to say goodnight to her in bed, he started touching her breasts; she told me it was as if it could have been done accidently and I thought 'well what on earth is going on with him – what is his story?' Why was he so terrified of sexuality? It was a terrible taboo.

As far back as I can remember I have known I was different from the girls; I was certainly not allowed to show fear, sorrow, to cry – some of that happened to my sisters too – my mother was cruel to us in different ways. My mother would say 'you are a disgusting little boy', saying things about my genitals – but also saying things to my sisters like 'no man will ever want you!' I was treated differently in that they were prepared to spend money on my education. It was clear that it was important to educate males but not so for females. We were all expected to do domestic chores – I remember being beaten for not dusting behind the TV. She used to beat us around the head with her hand and she would sometimes use objects like the mop handle. Once when I was about 7, I was expected to clean out the cupboard under the stairs and she became furious and shut me into the cupboard but I didn't know what I was supposed to do. It was dark and there were things that I didn't recognise. She hit me across the back until the handle broke and I think then she came to her senses. For years she kept that mop and kept using it – nothing was ever said about it and in my teens I used to look at it and think 'I didn't imagine that'. If I had done that I would at least have wanted to get rid of the evidence.

I have been a bit reluctant to name my experience as sexual abuse. I do think my view of my sexuality was very distorted by that (my younger sister would say the same) and I'm very relieved to have found out what the root cause was – not that it makes it alright but it gives me a way of unloading some of it; it's not just me and it's not entirely her fault. It is good to have a way of starting to exonerate her as a very pressured and damaged person.

In my teens sexuality was unutterably guilt ridden. It even got to the point that when I was masturbating I got to a moment of panic-stricken guilt which would happen so close to orgasm, I would physically suppress ejaculation. This was physical, tangible proof that there was a badness in me. A terrible badness that I couldn't control but I ought to control.

I received my information about sex from a book given by my father. I had a lot of sexual information and misinformation from peers. The book said nothing about masturbation which was my sex life and it didn't say it was pleasurable. It was at secondary school that I started masturbating to orgasm. Earlier there had been some sex play with the girls next door and some cousins who were highly sexualised.

And then when I started having sexual relationships with girls I felt as if I was despoiling, besmirching them in some way until suddenly in 1967, when I was a student, the pill was available. There was this tremendous liberation among young middle-class women and stuff being written like the *Female Eunuch* and I thought 'Oh I don't have to do these awful things'. It was as if I no longer had to be a seducer or a perverter. I guess it was literature and the media that gave me the idea that proper men should be seducers; James Bond films and things like that – and yet my father's message was that I shouldn't be giving into all that terrible temptation. I did play all these games about not going all the way; I was technically a virgin until I was 20 which didn't stop me having a rich sexual experience by then and I did feel terribly guilty about that. I guess I was feeling the pressure to be a sexually competent male from women as well as from other young men; the bravado about being a young male, sharing sexual exploits etc., but I always had these feelings that I shouldn't. Certainly a socialising pressure that is a fairly common male experience.

When I was 29 I was going through relationships at a rate of knots. I was on this hope/disillusion cycle – always hoping that the next one would be the one that changed me, the one that is the magic wand that would make me OK. I became quite suicidal, depressed and I went to a good GP who put me in touch with a woman therapist. I worked through a good deal of that with some very good bits of gestalt (very loud sigh) and then the relationship developed into something else and I ended up having sex with her. She became pregnant and we married.

So that set up a pressure that was an echo of my childhood; pretending it was alright and of course it wasn't. I keep on understanding more as I do more training as a psychologist; understanding the power in that relationship, the abuse of that power and yet at the time I thought it was quite the opposite; that I was somehow being saved and that this woman, to whom I had showed my worst fears and my feelings of being worthless and my sense of my own evil, should want me sexually, was massively and extraordinarily wonderful. As soon as that started going wrong, it was potentially, wholly destructive. If the therapy with her hadn't been as good as it was I'm sure I would have ended up committing suicide. I was within a whisker of it. Our sex life deteriorated very early on and she refused to have counselling because she was saying 'I'm a therapist – we can't admit anything is going wrong!' so we went through years of that but then she was pregnant again and we hadn't had intercourse at all. Suddenly she was taking a lot of interest in me sexually again. I decided to leave at that point because there was no trust between us and I've since discovered that she had been having an affair with somebody else but I had negotiated the end of that marriage believing that I was abandoning a woman who was pregnant with my child. I was strong enough to come through that somehow and whether that strength had come from what I had come through in childhood or from the strength I found in therapy – I came through it and have just not stopped since then.

It was immensely powerful to find myself wanted by my children and able to give in such a strong, non-sexual, positive way. I've been through this stuff with my older daughter who has a strong sexuality. She will say 'kiss my ear dad' and she'll wriggle and say 'my bum tickles'; she's absolutely brilliant! My children live with their mother. I lived quite close to them until recently. It was quite interesting when I had them to stay on my own after we had split up. I was glad I had worked through some of this stuff because it could be quite worrying. I can see why some men become very afraid, especially if they have become very lonely, hurt and are in need of affection and touch. Actually hugging my children is wonderful, especially after not touching anybody for a couple of weeks. I'm very clear about the absolute line. That's great that she feels a strong sexuality, but it's nothing to do with my sexuality. I am able to permit her sexuality because I have clarified some things for myself.

There were the usual homosexual experiences as an adolescent. Nothing since I was aware of the concept of orientation, but certainly a lot of fantasising and it's interesting how the steam has gone out of that now. I think it's like a cloud moving across the landscape. The guilt and fear about sexuality has been dispelled now by knowing what it means to hold a man and actually being able to ask when I want a hug from a man friend when I haven't had one for a couple of days and that dispels the fear of sexual crossed wires.

I guess that it's no accident that I have fears about men and fears of what I feel for a man; fears of my sexuality because I am a man – fears that have evaporated since my father died. I felt he could see into me, judge me and that I was not good enough for him. I always felt I wasn't as male as he was. I wasn't alright like him. It's funny how I didn't identify myself as being the same as him; I wanted to be but I knew I wasn't. I just somehow felt he didn't feel like me inside. It's only since he has died that I realised I am quite like him really. I look like him and my voice is like his was and some of my ways of laughing, some of the things I do with my children, he used to do with them. I could deal with him when he was like that but my mother didn't really allow him to do that. I felt she was jealous because we liked him more than we liked her, but it suddenly came to me that she thought if he liked us then he wouldn't like her.

It was only when I read *Males at Risk* that I thought about it as abuse. If someone comes away from an experience feeling confused, dirty, involved, then something has occurred whether or not you touched them. I do feel it was echoes of the abuse that was done to her that was being carried on. I wouldn't have thought of myself as being sexually abused. I am wary of getting into the victim role and saying 'Oh look poor me – aren't I wonderful because I managed to survive!'; I don't want to falsely claim something. It's like I'm saying I wasn't abused enough! I certainly admit that my sexuality was abused. I came away from my childhood sexually 'wrong', thinking that I was wrong, that I was bad and my sexuality carried that wrong.

Now I am very involved with somebody who is at the end of a marriage – it's not clandestine in any way. In sexual terms it is getting better and better; the terribly over-heightened unreal, drug-like excitement when all the sounds go funny has gone now. I always knew at the top of that peak, there was a tremendous plummet. What happens now is that there is a physical climax and then I feel more excited, not sexually but emotionally; it's almost like sometimes I can't wait to get the orgasm over because I know I am going to feel even better. I am waking up to what people have been writing about – a tremendous closeness. Previously the climax was a shattering disappointment; a confirmation of emptiness really. Very like coming down from a drug.

I used religion as a coping mechanism during adolescence – as a way of getting away from all of it. I thought after I had been confirmed then I would stop being sexual – it lasted for ten days! Around early adolescence I fantasised about sex with my older sister. I sometimes identified that women I have relationships with have reminded me of my sister. For some time I hankered after the innocent sexuality of childhood; wanting to think myself back into that time, for what I missed.

11 Abuse by fathers

I have commented earlier in this book on the fact that there seem to be a dearth of examples in the literature of father–son abuse although it is said that fathers are most commonly the abusers of boys as well as girls. At the point of having completed twenty-one of my twenty-five interviews I had not found a single example of a father acting independently as an abuser of his son. There had been one case of a father arranging for a sexual threesome involving himself, his wife and his son, although no direct sexual contact occurred between father and son. There was also the case of James who had been abused by a stranger when he was 12-years-old who was beginning to wonder if he had been abused by his father or mother at an earlier age (later he became more certain of this). However, there were no men who had told me directly of abuse by their fathers alone and I had begun to think I might complete the interviews without having such an example to offer. Interview subjects 22 (Tim) and 23 (Wayne), were both men who had been abused by their fathers (and abused later by others) and I have presented them below; James' story has been presented in Chapter 12.

Tim did not refer to his abuse by his father until the interview was nearing completion; he had focused on his abuse by a neighbour when he was 9-years-old and had made a passing reference to the fact that this was the abuse he remembered clearly, indicating that there might be something else that was less clear. Later in the interview he acknowledged that about six years ago he had begun to remember that he had been abused by his father when he was about 4-years-old. The reclaiming of these memories had come about as a response to his sister remembering her abuse by their father whilst she was in therapy. It is interesting to note that male children are often only brought to the attention of the statutory agencies 'second hand' – often as a by-product of a female child's identification as a victim of child sexual abuse.

Wayne's father had sexually abused him as a small child and his mother had physically and emotionally abused him throughout his childhood. There were also some unclear memories of sexual abuse by his mother and by his paternal grandfather and grandmother. This ties in with the notion that men who abuse, may themselves have been abused and it would seem possible that Wayne's paternal grandparents were also abusers, reflecting the concept of the chain of abuse when one generation passes their own abuse on to their own offspring. There is some hint also of Wayne's mother extreme dislike of her father; she did not want a male child and she links this with her anger towards her father. Wayne however, describes his close, connected relationship with his maternal grandfather.

Since completing the interviews I have been contacted by James who has now remembered that he had been abused by his father but is confused because his mother seems to think it impossible as he was never left alone with his father. It seems surprising that a mother could say that with such conviction. When a child lives with his father, as James did, between the ages of 1 and 17 years when his parents were divorced (his father was in prison during the first year of James' life), it would seem feasible to think he had spent time alone with him; and if not, why not? His mother is more inclined to think that James may have been sexually abused by his paternal grandfather with whom he spent a lot of time as a small child. However, James mother's denial of his father's abuse may be more to do with her inability to face such an idea than a fact. Sometimes one parent may wish to deny the abuse by the other parent because of their own guilt at not protecting the child. Denial can range from refusing that anything at all took place, refusing to accept the details of the abuse, or refusing to think that the abuse had any impact on the child. Sometimes the non-offending parent might have unacknowledged sexual abuse in their own childhood; admitting their own child's abuse may be too painful because of the memories or emotions it may trigger off and their denial may be necessary to suppress their own unconscious feelings. Once again the cycle of abuse seems to be a possible factor. He may, of course, have been abused by both his father and his grandfather.

In a dysfunctional family such as James', abuse may become the norm and the negative consequences are then denied. The first person James told about his abuse by a stranger was his father. His father dismissed this as 'making a fuss about nothing' – an expected response from an abuser!

In Tim's case he talks to his brothers about his abuse and they believe him, but it is discussed no further; he does not want to tell his mother. His sister's abuse is alternately denied and acknowledged by his mother. Tim does not want to tell his sister of his abuse even though he realises that it might help to validate her feelings – he knows his sister will pass the information on to his mother, if only to strengthen her own accusation, and his need to remain close to his mother and protect her (and maybe his fear of her rejection) is greater than his need to help his sister, a fellow victim.

Tim, Wayne and James have all experienced being anally penetrated – something that has left them fearful of intimacy within relationships. Anal penetration is usually connected with pain and force; for Tim who was abused in this way when he was 9-years-old, (if not earlier by his father), this was also connected with the pleasure of closeness he experienced with his 18-year-old abuser. Tim's main problem seems to be one of difficulty sustaining intimate relationships with women. It seems that when he becomes close enough to consider a long-term relationship, he fears loss of control and withdraws. He does not consciously remember his abuse as negative or painful, either emotionally or physically, although intellectually he is beginning to question this. Tim demonstrates the frequent use of denial in his interview; he minimises and normalises his experiences by such phrases as 'that's very common' or 'a lot of people feel that'. I perceived this to be a defence mechanism which he is beginning to dismantle. He is now realising that his abuse may be at the root of some of his problems.

Tim has quite a severe stammer, the origin of which he connects with the commencement of his abuse. One way of understanding the possible link between his stammer and the abuse can be found in the work of a contemporary of Freud, Georg Groddeck (1923), who in his major contribution to psychosomatic medicine proposed that the unconscious expression of emotions is manifested through the body in many ways. Though this theory was very controversial in his time, his work has become the basis for the psychoanalytical approach to psychosomatic medicine. The psychosomatic approach holds that repressed emotions are directly related to symptoms such as high blood pressure, sexual dysfunction, depression and other disorders. In 1933 Reich published work which he developed more recently (1972) which was more directly related to the work of Freud although he was aware of Groddeck's theories. He held a belief that the musculature of the body allows for emotional expression or withholding. This emotional withholding creates chronic muscle tension which requires direct manipulation to facilitate expression of the withheld or repressed feelings. Timms and Connors (1990) believe that strong emotional events leave lasting memory traces in the musculature and neural pathways between the brain and the muscles. When seen from this perspective, it may be that Tim's psyche repressed the memory and the feelings connected with his abuse and his body has 'acted out' the problem which is struggling for recognition. Tim's stutter could be interpreted as a manifestation of his internal conflict between the need to 'tell' and the need to remain silent; it hinders him from 'telling'! I wonder if his early abuse by his father was associated with oral abuse. The function normally associated with the part of the body that is mis-used in the abuse is often the part that carries the disconnected feeling. For women this might be manifested as vaginismus or other sexual dysfunctions – when the body refuses to accept the activity that unconsciously triggers the abuse.

Wayne also describes the way his body 'acts out' his feelings as they surface; other men have identified ways they believe their body had carried the memory of their abuse which they have not understood until their memories have been retrieved. Harold identified the value of body work using the Alexander Technique in helping his recovery from his abuse by his mother and Robert's first memories of abuse occurred during a session of acupuncture. Psychotherapy with men might prove less successful than body work as many men tend to intellectualise and rationalise as a way of defending themselves against their emotions. Timms and Connors (1990) suggest that body work combined with psychotherapy might be a more useful approach. Waynes's psychologist indicates his understanding of the psychophysical approach when he suggests that massage might help.

Wayne describes how his body carries the memories of his abuse. He feels a pressure or pain in his rectum and a choking sensation in his throat. His arms and legs flail as though fighting off an attacker. These descriptions are common among survivors of childhood sexual abuse. Braun (1988a, 1988b) explains this phenomenon in his description of his model of dissociation which is conceptualised along four dimensions of experience: behaviour, affect (emotion), sensation (body feelings) and knowledge. For example when a client talks about a brutal rape in a very calm way the dimension that is lacking is affect (emotion). Sometimes a client will describe with strong emotion an assault which must have been physically painful but he will describe himself as feeling 'numb'; hence missing sensation or body feelings. When the event is forgotten then the dimension that is missing is knowledge. Behavioural components can often intrude into the client's present life and become frightening. Wayne describes this when he talks about lying on the floor and his body convulses (behavioural). Sometimes this behaviour is accompanied by sensations (a feeling of choking or pain in the rectum). These combinations of sensory and body clues occur without cognitive experience (knowledge) and are referred to as 'body memories'.

Wayne is constantly on the alert for danger. He both wants and fears closeness and intimacy. Some of his fear is likely to be connected with his mother's violence towards him, but he also recognises the fear he has felt when he has been close to his father. After his father's death, Wayne was able to remember the abuse; it would appear that he no longer had to fear his father as a real threat to him. Because his father's abuse had sometimes been connected with feeling loved, Wayne is confused. Love and fear seem to be tied up together, making it impossible for him to experience one without the other.

This confusion is also experienced by James who is terrified of men and women and his sado-masochistic fantasies connect pain with love and fear. Both James and Wayne have been re-abused as adults – I have described James' rape in Chapter 13. Wayne was sexually abused by a man who had nursed him through a period of hospitalisation – he now says that he was seeking 'the good father' – a man who would love and care for him in the way for which he longed. His boundaries, which had been trangressed by the most important man in his life, were unclear and were trangressed again by someone he sought to relate to as a 'father-figure'.

Unclear boundaries may be the result when a child has had the experience of their physical boundaries being transgressed by someone in a position of trust. Establishment of physical boundaries is probably an important step in developing psychological boundaries. A very young child needs to learn where his body begins and ends as part of identity formation, a recognition of 'self' as being separate from 'other'. When a child has been sexually abused at a very early age, he may feel as though he is symbiotically attached to his abuser, especially if that abuser is a parent. If the abuser is the same gender as the child or if the child is abused by parents, it may be that they will have a greater problem with self-differentation and the establishment of a personal identity. Wayne felt that his parents gave him the message that they could do what they liked with his body, and indeed they did; his sense of autonomy was seriously damaged. Tim also speaks of his problem with autonomy – always needing to be reassured that what he did was acceptable. When a child's sense of autonomy is damaged they are full of self-doubt. If this damage is related to their sexual development then it may be that it is their sexual identity formation that is affected.

Children who have difficulty creating a sense of their own identity, might respond by feeling fearful of being controlled by others. It is interesting to note that both Tim and Wayne have begun to acknowledge their abuse by their fathers after the death of these men; they were no longer under their control or in a position to hurt them. Both acknowledge their need to remain tightly in control in relationships, something that can contribute to problems with intimacy which usually requires the sharing or release of control, particularly at moments of deep intimacy such as during orgasm.

For the men who had been abused by their father, this had begun during the very early years of their lives and it is important to note that they had all repressed the memories of the abuse until they could allow themselves to remember in adulthood. There is a great dispute about the validity of such memories which I have discussed after Martin's story. No one likes to think that sexual abuse occurs during infancy – Wayne struggles with accepting this during his interview. It had been thought that very young children could not possibly be affected by such early abuse and that no one remembers events which occur at such an early stage. However, Hewitt (1990) reports studies which have shown incidences where a child has been eroticised at a very young age, perhaps by a mother fondling the child's penis, and this has resulted in the child re-enacting and re-stimulating itself and others in the same way. A child who has not yet developed language skills has a 'second language' consisting of a behavioural repertoire which communicates to an aware adult that something is happening to the child which causes it distress or anxiety. Clinicians have found that children who have been abused as young as 7 to 15 months will act out or describe their abuse at a later stage. When a child displays behaviours which indicate abuse, such as sexualised acting out with themselves or other children in an aggressive way, it may be that they are seeking a way to express their experience.

It is important to note that adults in therapy, who are struggling to recall what they think are past abusive experiences, may only recall fragments of information. Wayne describes this process very clearly, along with all his doubts and misgivings. It is quite possible that the recall comes from a memory store that was created during a very early developmental level. Looking back across the gap of time, the quality of the perception and storage gives these fragments a dreamlike quality. Sometimes misperceptions can occur as to who the perpetrator was – especially if it was someone related who may have resembled someone else, such as a father or grandfather.

Experienced therapists will usually be able to identify this struggle for what it is; the details may be out of sequence or peripheral, such as the details of a room, and they may be accompanied by a physical response as described by both Tim and Wayne. Dr Eileen Vizard of the Tavistock Clinic says (CROSS Newsletter) that, as psychotherapy continues the picture becomes clearer:

> Bad interviewing techniques can induce misleading disclosures but not to the extent of the victim giving a very complicated, elaborate story with idiosyncratic details.

In my own experience of working with clients, it is the nature of the self-doubt and frequent need to slide back into denial that adds to my conviction about the validity of this process. I have yet to meet a client who remembers early repressed memories who has been clear and convinced of their veracity from the start. That conviction grows for the client when they are patiently accompanied through the confusion of images, feelings and memories, and are allowed, in their own time, to answer their doubts and questions from the store of knowledge that lies deep within themselves.

Relationship problems

In this section I shall focus on the relationship difficulties that may be the outcome of childhood sexual abuse. Finkelhor and Brown (1986) propose a framework for understanding childhood sexual abuse trauma that attempts to look more specifically at the impact based on the dynamics present in the traumatic event. These impacts are categorised according to the type of trauma that occurred: sexualisation, betrayal, powerlessness, or stigmatisation. It would seem that all of these areas of trauma might impact on the formation of relationships for the adult who is dealing with the after effects of such abuse. In this discussion I shall attempt to examine the different kind of relationship problems that subjects have spoken about in their interviews.

Sexual relationships

When a child has been inappropriately sexualised they may develop into an adult who is afraid of or uninterested in sexual relationships. This in turn may lead to difficulties with sexual arousal and in responding to the sexual advances of a partner. He may suffer from lack of motivation, impotence, lack of sexual satisfaction or a variety of sexual dysfunctions. At the other extreme the person might sexualise all their relationships, confusing sex with love and mixing sex with affection, anger, power and violence. He may become addicted to sex and engage in abusive and promiscuous activities such as prostitution, which may connect with drug and alcohol addiction and pornography.

All of the men I interviewed were sexually dissatisfied and the majority lacked sexual confidence. Most of the men described problems with intimacy, created by fear of closeness and/or fear of men or women, fear of losing control and/or a lack of assertiveness resulting in passivity, aggressive or manipulative behaviour. Many of the men identified with the victim role and saw themselves as being re-victimised through their intimate adult relationships, some choosing abusive partners repeatedly. Some men identified with the aggressor role and became sexually, physically or verbally abusive when upset.

Betrayal

When a person's trust has been betrayed during childhood he may not have been able to develop an ability to trust appropriately; he may trust without discernment and put himself into situations which are dangerous, thus exposing himself to the risk of re-abuse. Wayne's story demonstrates both extremes, when problems with trust are manifested by an inability to trust anyone; they may be constantly on the alert for danger, even when there is none.

The constant 'testing out' of others in relationships may cause the very rejection they fear as their friends and colleagues become impatient with their evident inability to trust them. Friendships require a degree of mutual trust and the acceptance of the other person's goodwill. The presence of post-traumatic stress disorder may add to the problems especially where the person uses dissociation as a mechanism of defence which results in an inability to respond emotionally in intimate relationships.

Powerlessness

People who have been abused in childhood may present themselves in relationships as a victim and this, in turn, might evoke the persecutor in the other person, who may well have been attracted to someone available for them to victimise. In the victim/perpetrator dyadic relationship each partner may maintain the other's position by the acceptance of the preferred role, which might switch from the one extreme to the other as the situation requires (Berne 1961). Powerlessness is a particularly difficult feeling for a male to come to terms with, having been socialised within a patriarchal society which portrays power as a measure of masculinity.

The development of the victim mentality usually occurs when a child has been repeatedly abused and is then left to cope with it alone. This attitude may become one of the most crippling aspects in the formation of adult relationships. The world is not seen as safe, predictable or controllable. The abused person has learned that what he feels, thinks and does has no impact on his life and that he is powerless to control difficult situations. Everything that then happens is seen through this perspective and may become a habitual response and add to the deeply felt belief about himself, the world and the other people in it. These beliefs may cause the person to disregard any evidence that contradicts them. Most of these beliefs are self-defeating in adulthood; underneath, the person may be defending himself from having to face up to the mistaken idea that what happened might have been in some way his own fault or that he had some choice.

Although the victim mentality might be seen as a coping mechanism during childhood, it can become problematic if it is carried into adulthood. The adult might go through life giving other people the idea that it is acceptable for them to treat him badly, (as Wayne did in his relationships with the nurse who abused him as an adult), by being passive and not standing up for himself. Because the abuse was a 'normal' part of his life as a child, he may go on to expect it from others – putting up with harassment from employers or other authority figures.

Stigmatisation and touch

Fundamental to all close relationships is the issue of touch. Some people who have been abused have difficulty tolerating being touched physically; this may cause the person to avoid social situations in which he fears crowds or coming into contact with others whilst dancing or partaking in sport. This may severely limit his opportunities for meeting people with whom he may develop an intimate relationship. Having once overcome this problem, he may then find that normal contact such as hand shaking or touch during greeting or parting from others may become difficult. He may refuse to allow people to touch him in a comforting way when distressed or ill; some abused people fear that if someone touches them, they might contaminate that person through that touch. Many normal aspects of the person's life may be affected by this problem; a visit to the dentist, medical examinations or hospital procedures may be avoided through fear of contact, resulting in long term health problems. All of this avoidance behaviour may be interpreted as 'odd' by those who have no way of understanding it and the person may be ostracised by people who become fearful of his 'oddity' and withdraw. Many victims of childhood abuse complain of feelings of loneliness which might be accounted for by self-imposed isolation.

Other men (see Harry and William's story) have spoken of the need to keep separate the several different parts of their lives, something that often causes the person to become 'split' – almost to the degree of becoming psychotic, when the person creates another 'world' to balance the unacceptable reality of his present one.

Orientation confusion

A man who is confused about his sexual orientation will experience extra difficulties in his formation of intimate relationships as the confusion sometimes makes it impossible for him to enjoy either homosexual or heterosexual relationships (see George's and James' stories). This might create difficulties within a marriage/partnership or contribute to the reason why the person avoids forming relationships.

Half the men I spoke to who had been abused by males were confused about their sexual orientation as well as almost half the men abused by both males and females. This did not seem to be such an issue for those abused by females; cross gender sexual activity being line with the 'norm'. Those men who defined themselves as homosexual and had been abused by males only, were clear about their orientation, although one of them said he did not think he would have been homosexual had he not been abused. It would appear that when a boy is sexually abused by a male, this distorts his perception of 'normal' sexual relationships. His self-concept as a sexual person, in line with the 'norm' of male-female sexual contact, is contradicted by the event and causes him to become uncertain about whether he is homosexual or not. Most of the men who had been abused by males had thought of their abusers as 'homosexual' rather than paedophile. This caused them to ask themselves such questions as 'who does this say I am?' – seeking a self-definition in terms of the sexual behaviour of their abusers.

Men who defined themselves as bi-sexual were confused about their sexuality. Two of them had been abused by males only and the other three had been abused by both males and females. The man who described himself as 'asexual' had been abused by males and a female.

Gender confusion

Of the men who were abused by both males and females 60 per cent were confused about their gender at some stage; 33 per cent of those who had been abused by men were also confused. Strikingly, only one of the men abused by females was confused about this. It would seem that when a boy has been sexually 'used' they see themselves as having adopted the passive role which they equate with the female role, perhaps in response to socialisation messages. Several men spoke of their inability to see themselves as sexually proactive in a relationship and several fantasised about being a woman whilst having sex. Some who had been anally penetrated likened this to the female role.

Parenting

One of the most striking findings during my interviews was that so few men were parents. There were several men who would be considered too young to be parents in a modern society in which many young people are postponing parenthood until their late twenties and thirties; none of the men below the age of 27 were parents. However out of the remaining twenty men, only seven had parented children. Most of these men had not had their emotional needs met as children. Sexual abuse in childhood often goes hand in hand with emotional abuse and physical abuse. When a person has not been adequately parented themselves, they may not have learned the skills of parenting; they may not wish to take on the commitment of a child of their own. This was an issue for several of the men I spoke to, although as the majority were not in a committed partnership, the idea of having children was not one that seemed sensible or even possible. Sometimes men expressed a fear that they would be inadequate parents in that they may over-protect children or that they may inadvertently abuse them.

Tim expressed anger towards the woman who assumed that because he had been abused he might become an abuser and therefore would avoid having children. In fact most of the men I interviewed were very vehement about the horror they felt at such an idea and they felt certain that it would be more likely that they would over-protect a child rather than abuse them. Only two of the twenty-five men men are still married to the mothers of their children. Both men who abused children as adults, have abused their own child as well as other people's children. However, it is important to note that only two out of twenty-five men I interviewed (by far the smallest proportion) abused children as adults. Two of the homosexual men expressed a desire to father a child; one has donated his sperm to a lesbian woman.

Family relationships

Most of the men I talked to came from 'dysfunctional' families in which physical, emotional or sexual abuse was happening (see Tables 6.11, 6.12 and 6.13). This is not an environment which is conducive to the development of close loving family relationships which support and maintain people in their childhood and adult lives. Many men felt angry towards their parents for abusing them or not protecting them from the abuser. Only six men have spoken about their abuse to one or the other of their parents. Those who had some level of satisfaction of their present relationships with their parents, seemed to resist the idea of talking about the abuse as it might cause trouble. This usually meant that there were large areas of their lives that needed to be excluded within those relationships. Most feared rejection by their parents if they were to know of the abuse or that they simply would not understand. None of the men who had been abused by their mother had confronted her, although two plan to do so in the near future. Two abusing mothers are now dead. One other man knows his mother was abused herself and feels he cannot blame her; another 'does not want the aggro' that might ensue and the other does not want to jeopardise the good relationship he feels he has with her.

Of the four men who were abused by their fathers, two fathers are now dead; one does not want to upset the good relationship he feels he has and the other has told his mother but she denies the possibility of father abusing him.

When sisters had been the abusers, the men usually believed that their sisters must have been abused and therefore were not responsible for their abusing behaviour; there was also a need to avoid being seen as the cause of disruption within the family unit. When this kind of abuse is recognised as the probable result of a sister's own abuse, it may create further difficulties for the adult male in working through his own victimisation. It may also be more difficult to talk about it within the family, particularly as the girl's perpetrator might also be a family member.

Tim's story

Tim was born in 1959. He had an older brother and sister and a younger brother; there is about two years between each of them. His father died about eight years ago. He is a higher degree student, unmarried and he has no children.

When Tim was 8-years-old his family home was compulsorily purchased and they moved on to a council estate. At that time his father had been in a psychiatric hospital for two years since he tried to commit suicide. His father had had asthma from when he was about 3-years-old and had TB after the birth of his first child.

Tim's mother had been an au pair/teacher in France when the Germans invaded and she spent four years in an internment camp. While she was there she became a Catholic. Tim believed the years she spent there had a very big influence her later behaviour in that she is a great hoarder and consequently his home was 'a real mess'.

Tim remembers that he was quite aggressive at primary school and the older boys on the estate would goad him to attack other boys of his own age. He became frightened at the age of 10 because he was beaten up by two lads of about 12 while their 16-year-old brother looked on. He remembers himself as 'a macho little boy' who was also a day-dreamer; good at sport. He modelled himself on football heroes and not on his sickly father.

He experienced his mother as undemonstrative and realises she still finds it difficult to give him a hug although that is better than when he was a child. He remembers envying other children who had broken their arm because they received attention but excuses his mother's inability to give him what he needed on the grounds that he was one of four children and so it was unrealistic to expect individual attention. His mother showed her affection by washing and cooking for them but she gave her children very little instruction about what they should do; consequently he managed to avoid going to the dentist for nine years and suffered from unattended flat feet for years. He grew up thinking he had a lot of freedom but looking back, he realised that it was because his parents were not able make a decision or say 'no'. As he grew older he was allowed to attend football games alone at a great distance from his home. He now sees this not so much as 'freedom' but lack of a normal degree of care and attention by his parents. Sex was never talked about in the home.

He recalled his sexual abuse:

The sexual abuse I know of occurred when I was 8/9 and that was by an 18-year-old neighbour. He was probably a bit backward but I think he works now – he never got married. I went with him and his father to my first football match. There was another boy about a year older but the rest were up to four years older and we used to go round together. I was quite tall for my age.

The part I remember clearly was when I was just turning 9 and this bloke's parents went away on holiday for about two weeks and he had the house to himself. We used to go round there and he would buy cider and we would get drunk. I used to go round in the morning when I woke up and get into bed with him. I don't remember how it happened the first time. I was downstairs on his knee on one occasion and the others were there too; he had my penis out. I don't know if I had an erection – I don't think I knew what it was to have one. He had anal penetrative sex with me. I remember masturbating, holding him – there was no oral sex. It felt a bit of a mixture of pain and it was OK too. I don't know if I was arousable at that age. I remember, not that many years later, seeing what it was like to put a toilet brush up my anus. At the time it happened he couched it in terms of it being 'practice' for when we went with women; he said we should go to this pub where we could pick up women. I was 9!

That's why I never saw it as a particularly abusive thing. It was as I got older I started to question the fact that I was only 9 – I didn't know what was going on and he took advantage of that. I don't remember being hurt. I felt jealous of other people if they went with him. Once after we got drunk, and one of the other boys was on his knee, I pretended to be unconscious until he dropped him. I wanted the attention. I liked him. What I got from him was 'fun', messing around; we used to accidentally destroy things in his house. It always happened in his house so, even though it seems to have been a longish period of time, it can only have been during those two weeks.

I had no reason to tell anybody about this because it is only in the last few years that I have thought there might be anything wrong with it. It has changed from me thinking it was 'just an experience', to thinking 'perhaps there was something wrong about it'. I suppose I have been influenced by the increased interest in sexual abuse; I'm influenced by the fact that I behave in certain ways towards people and I'm interested to know why; I've become more academically enlightened. Looking back I see myself as this 9-year-old boy and I can't help seeing him as this 18-year-old and I think 'what's he doing?' I couldn't say if it has had any effect on me – it's hard to say. Maybe it hasn't.

I remember the first time I masturbated; I was 9 or 10, after this incident with this bloke. It was quite an unpleasant feeling, a bit of a shock. I had found a magazine called *OZ* in my father's drawer and I read it while I masturbated. Around the same time I remember going into a shed and lying on top of a boy who was lying on his front; he was a year younger than me. I suppose I was doing what had been done to me.

I think from when I was 11 I regularly masturbated – maybe three times a week. I was into girl friends when I was 14–16. It was very serious – we were getting engaged, getting married. She didn't want to have sex until we were married and although it started out with us physically experimenting, she became less and less interested. She would say I shouldn't want to do it, that we should wait. After her, I met a girl on holiday and we had sexual intercourse – she made all the running and she was very keen. I had quite a few girl friends after that but I was always very nervous. I didn't feel very attractive.

When I was 18 I had an ongoing relationship but at the same time, whenever I had the chance to sleep with someone else, I would. On a few occasions I had three relationships going at the same time. I had a problem (I think lots of people do), with premature ejaculation.

My friends and I would go out in a group; other nights you saw your girl friend but on Fridays and Saturdays you went looking. This is a very male working class thing. Being a 'right on' bloke meant having lots of conquests, that you wouldn't back down from a fight, that you would drink. The lads who wouldn't do those things were wimps.

I've never been interested in homosexuality. I used to hitch hike a lot and on numerous occasions I've been propositioned. I've never been interested in having sex with a man. I never thought of the activity with that bloke as homosexual. When I was an apprentice we would talk about homosexuals as 'bum boys' – I remember going into a public lavatory once when I was in town and I saw two pairs of feet under one of the doors and I kicked the door and shouted 'you dirty bastards'. But it was part of the language to be anti-gays when I was an apprentice.

When I was younger I'd have had sex with anyone who would have sex with me. There were a lot of one-night stands. Usually I would be drunk because I thought I would never be able to meet anyone when I was sober because I wouldn't have the confidence. I think that is very common. I never approached attractive women because I thought they wouldn't be interested in me. I still don't think I'm attractive sexually. If I look back I have always lacked confidence. At school and when I was an apprentice I would always have to ask if this was OK or that was OK.

I believe I was first abused by my father was when I was 4 or 5 years old. It is a process of putting things together and having tactile memories – feeling memories. Occasionally I have images of shapes in the dark and my feeling memories of something very big and hard; it goes back before remembering holding this man's penis when I was 9. It's something to do with the dark.

Six years ago I discovered that my sister had been abused by my father. She had remembered this when she was in therapy and I never doubted her. Nobody in the family doubted her. My mother didn't doubt her at first, then she did and then she didn't. I don't know where she stands at present. We don't talk about it now. It has become unmentionable. She would have been about 5 or 6 – I would have been about 4. We shared a room. I found out recently that for a long time after my third brother was born, he slept in the same room as my mother and my father was in a different room. I haven't told my sister I was abused too. She blames me for being there; I don't know what he did to her. I don't really want to – it's of no consequence to me. It is and it isn't. I don't think I'd be any more … whatever for knowing. I feel very sad for my father. I'm sure he had a loveless life and marriage. At first they were probably reasonably close. I suppose I see them both as losers.

I developed my speech problem (which I still have) around the time I was abused by my father. That was one of the things that has made it easier for me to think it really did happen. I don't think of myself as a victim. If I was my sister I would definitely see that I was a victim. The difference is that she had been through bulimia, teenage pregnancy, she's got a child that she doesn't have/won't have through her own choice – she can't deal with it. She's had a lot of crap relationships and no fixed job – she went to university a couple of times and just managed to scrape a 2:2. I look at my life and I suppose I've had a lot of success with certain things.

The difference is – it might sound very reductionist – she's a woman. Her boy friend is four years older and has taken over her life. I don't know how old they were when they first had sex, but I think it was probably about 14; that's when she began to drink for the first time. When I was 16–20 drink played a big part in my life but I never needed it. I was working – I used to go out at weekends and drink – it was the thing to do – it wasn't the alcohol. I've never been interested in drugs. I've tried cannabis a few times but I don't like the effect it has on me.

I have behaved aggressively occasionally. I've put my fist through glass windows and hit walls – that's quite common. I was taking out frustration. In the aftermath it was painful but at the time the drink would anaesthetise me. I have been convicted twice but nothing very serious – drink related offences. One was 'drunk and disorderly' and the other was a football match when I was accused of 'threatening behaviour' which I denied completely. I wasn't a very violent youth. I got beaten up by groups of people more often than I did it.

I'm still not very confident. I often think I'm boring, that I've got nothing to say; I have a great need to please people. I have problems because of having several relationships at the same time. I don't finish relationships because I don't want the hurt that would be involved. I can't really handle a proper relationship because of the sexual abuse. I feel unable to attach myself sufficiently to someone. I don't want them around all the time. I don't think it's that I haven't met the right person; I just can't do it. For the first time in my life I was having a relationship with someone and I didn't want to be sexual – although at the same time I was seeing someone else who I did want to have sex with – and by then I just didn't want it – it didn't feel good.

I have had close relationships that look like they could be permanent; I'm sure had I wished to, I could have been married a few times. I've had a series of relationships where it's all going well and then suddenly, I withdraw. I think it's when I'm losing control; I've got to try to get control back again. In the past I've always tried to avoid conflict to the extent of actually hoping that something would happen to the girl so I wouldn't have to do anything about ending it.

When I have sex I like to be in control and the prime thing is that I take responsibility for them enjoying it. I want to feel that I can please them and they'll like me more for that. I am very conscious of wanting to be liked by everyone; of not really knowing about sexual signals.

I disclosed about the abuse at 9 after about twenty years; it was last year that I disclosed that I had been abused by my father when I was much younger. The first time it started to sink in seriously was after my sister disclosed she had been abused. I was writing to someone else who had been abused at the time and there was something that I felt connected by; the more I explored it in my own mind, the more it seemed to fit. I have asked myself 'was I trying to make it fit' or 'do I want to be a victim' and I don't really – not now. I have told my brothers and neither of them seemed surprised, but neither of them said a lot more about it; I have told a number of my friends who have been very supportive. I told a woman I had an affair with. She suggested that the reason I didn't have children was that I thought I would do the same thing to them. I was very angry. I know people say that all men are potential rapists but I've never believed I am and nobody will ever convince me that I would touch a child. I don't want the responsibility or commitment of a child; it's not that I've ever been attracted to children. Afterwards she did apologise.

At the time it was happening, the abuse was of no real consequence; it was a harmless thing. I never told my parents anything about anything – so I wouldn't have told them about that. I wouldn't tell my mum now because she's 73; she's a strong Catholic; she doesn't have an awful lot of good things going on in her life; she doesn't have a lot of friends. It's to protect her really. Maybe she did neglect us when we were kids; maybe she did know what my father was doing. If she did know, I'm sure she has suffered an awful lot because she is a caring person. It's hard to believe but maybe she did know. As a Catholic, divorce is not on the cards and when you have got four kids it's a major problem. If we were both twenty years younger, and if her life was different, I might tell her. I wouldn't tell my sister because I know that she would throw it at my mum. I suppose she would in order to strengthen her own position – maybe it's selfish of me but it would hurt my mother immensely. I know that of all her children, I am the one who has stayed in touch, the one she likes most. I suppose I love her – I don't know. I think I know what it is to love a woman, I think I know what it is to love a friend; I'm not sure what it is to love a mother. There's no reason not to love her – she's done a lot for me. I don't love my sister.

Wayne's story

Wayne was born in 1959 and his sister was born four and a half years later. His mother was obsessional about cleaning the house and did not go out to work. His father died four years ago and his sister is married with her own family. Wayne lives at home with his mother now since starting a nursery nursing course. Since refusing to allow his mother to continue to put him down, the relationship between them has improved and she has begun to show him more care and respect.

He has managed to connect with his blocked childhood memories in the last four years; his memories initially returned in the form of words and then pictures formed of a very abused childhood.

He recalled the words he remembered his mother saying:

She used to say she hated me, that she'd kill me, that she'd give me away. I have some memories of her saying that she didn't want a boy and of her making comments about her father. There's memories I've been into and run away from and pretended didn't happen and then had to go back to. I'm very good at disbelieving them.

All my panic attacks are linked with physical violence and sexual abuse. My deepest fears are of being attacked/killed. I can feel it in my body and it's bad. I have just gone through a difficult patch where I couldn't work in a room without being wary of the door. It's always the same – this shadow person that comes in, goes over to an area by the wall, picks me up and carries me out. I have to try and fight against it. As I am getting memories with feelings attached and it all gets very real, I'm starting to feel very, very ashamed. Sometimes it's good to tell somebody, but I don't like to think about it and yet I've got to look at what I'm frightened of because I can't do my work.

It's difficult to believe that a child's body can be entered by an adult without breaking. I have gradually accepted intellectually that it obviously does (watching the news lately) happen with children over 5. I suppose I have at least three problems when it comes to thinking about children younger than that; one is in accepting that it can happen, i.e. that it did happen (to me); secondly reconciling with reality some strange misconceptions/fears/dreams/memories about the size of an adult penis. (I think an inappropriate view of an erect penis in my childhood has caused me to belittle my own penis most of my life); and thirdly, accepting that a child can ever accommodate that. I think it happened to me – somewhere between the age of 1 and 3 to 4 ; before my sister was born and before I went to school.

Although I've fought it off, tried to deny it and pretend it doesn't happen, the fear of something really terrible happening is with me every day; I'm not able to relate to people very well because of that.

I am absolutely sure that anal penetration did happen; I have just felt the fear of being raped so strongly that to try and sort myself out, I have lain down on the floor or on my bed and, if I link with my body, I move in a really spasmodic way – it just seems to take over.

My fear of women is stronger than my fear of men. My mother treated me so badly all the time and she never showed me any affection. I think my father must have sometimes showed me affection; at the age of 7, my father went to cuddle me and I absolutely refused. Even up to the day he died four years ago, I would never voluntarily stand next to him. I just need to see a picture of him for it to bring up feelings of hatred. I belong to a church and people talk about forgiveness but I'm afraid I haven't forgiven him – yet. I'm working on forgiving my mother. I haven't told her about my sexual abuse. I took a hint from a book about a man who told his parents and he got a lot of aggro. so I've worked through things on my own mainly, using books. I've sensed that people don't want to talk about it, so apart from the odd close friend, I haven't.

Mum has always put the house first and never took me into account at all. In the last year she can't do enough for me; she cooks me meals, sews for me and the last few weeks has been really quite strange. She's getting older – she's 64 – dad's not there and I am. I've grown up a lot since dad went and I feel a big change of roles has gradually occurred. It could be that she has read something that I've left in the drawer in my room – it's always in there and I trust her not to read it but if she does then that's her choice really.

I had dreams as a child of wooden figures going backwards and forwards and there's a cave behind them. I know that there is someone in the cave but the wooden people won't listen to me. I am desperate and then I see that there is a shelf (which could have been a sofa or similar) in the cave and on the shelf is a broken doll. The back room of our house is where my father's parents stayed for eighteen months – I started to realise that that room was different at one time. Then I had a growing awareness that, in my home when I was a child, there was a place like a cave in which terrible things happened but which I couldn't find afterwards. So I always had that fear that it was somewhere but I didn't know where. Memories that have come back about that room have been very confused, but I've been a small baby and my father and his parents were in this mental picture and I feel something going inside my anus and my mouth; I choke and choke. These are isolated incidents that come in fragments, so I'm not sure if there is more than one incident. I want to be absolutely sure, but on the other hand I don't want to believe it at all.

I also have a memory of my mother pulling me into her vagina. That hasn't come back full force yet; it's just pictures and words but the feelings and the senses haven't all come back – it's still coming.

I struggle with all sorts of memories of physical and verbal abuse; the sexual abuse memories are harder to get into. I don't feel any attraction to women in the sexual sense. I've never been keen on the vaginal area. I feel a deep attraction to the male body.

I have terrible confusions about men. A few years ago I decided I was gay and got very upset about it. I was very sexually repressed. Sex talk in our house was taboo and intercourse was a dirty disgusting thing that animals did because they didn't know any better.

My dad died four years ago and I bought my first book of male nudes no more than three years ago. I knew I was attracted to good looking men but I didn't know in what way so I got a couple of books and I thought I would actually get some feelings which would be great, but when I saw the pictures of naked men with an erection, I had a really deep horrible feeling inside. This was before I had started remembering and that was why it was so confusing. It was like being thumped in the stomach from the inside. A few days later, because the fear hadn't completely worn off, I covered up the genitals on the pictures and they became very attractive again. It was obviously the genitals that caused the fear. That was confusing because if you have just decided that you are gay it doesn't make sense.

When I was at school, when I woke up I used to get a massive panic attack and I used to masturbate purely as a release of tension. I have never felt a sexual need to masturbate and pictures of men don't excite me to masturbate – they are separate. I seem to expect love and kindness from good looking men but I don't actually have any relationships with men in real life. People in real life are just too dodgy. It's actually better for me to keep that part of myself for books.

The main problem is that people can control me too easily. I have got terrible compulsions to keep people happy because I get frightened that I am going to get hurt. My psychologist says that maybe a massage would get me over the fear of being touched but I've decided that people are so hard to control and so threatening to me that I don't want to bother. People don't touch me a lot – I notice sometimes that I overreact when people do.

I was a very frightened little boy, very quiet. I think I always used to wonder what I had done that was so bad. I started to go out with other children but I wasn't allowed to get dirty. I joined my first gang and that was brilliant because I never thought the others would want to play with me. That was only for one day and when I got home my mother was mad and she wouldn't let me play with these children again. Gangs were all about belonging to a family. I didn't feel wanted at home.

My father was a perfectionist. All my life I had this compulsion to try to please the unpleasable father; nothing was ever quite right for him. My father didn't know when to let children go; that was very obvious when my sister's children were born; one of the first things she taught them was that they didn't have to be cuddled by anyone if they didn't want to.

My biggest problem at the moment is that I look for danger everywhere. I get quite suicidal sometimes. I attempted suicide for the first time when I was 19; I have limited sight in one eye from the barbiturate overdose which caused damage to the optic nerve. I took two overdoses in a week; I just went crazy. I think I had gone past the idea of doing myself in; I thought if I just kept on taking risks, it would happen anyway.

I was very, very anxious coming up to 'O' levels and I had panic attacks coming up to 'A' levels. I think I felt much worse than anyone (including myself) ever believed. My mother always belittled any illness I had; my parents never believed me but ridiculed me instead. I lasted nine months at college before I took an overdose. My school work was always very good but I was very anxious about doing it.

After I took the overdose I was sent to a psychiatric hospital. Then I was sent home; I was told that I was suffering from depression (which I wasn't – I was suffering from memories) and I was pushed by my parents to go and work in a wild life park. I made a succession of mistakes and I fell apart. I was made to go sick and they closed the job down on me. I ended up being a porter in a college. I have 9 'O' levels and 2 'A' levels and I can't do anything with it because I can't cope with the choices. I am doing a nursery nurses' course now but I don't know what I want to do next. I discovered that I like children about four years ago when I was persuaded to help in a nursery. I have barriers with adults but I let children straight in. I have been working with this problem family who have three children all under the age of three. I have spent so much time cuddling these children that I am beginning to see myself as a father. I've never really felt that I needed to have my own child and I don't think I'm ever likely to make a close enough relationship for that to happen.

Judging that things can change, I would say I am asexual. I have certainly operated asexually for years. I never feel aroused by people. I have never had a sexual appetite. I can meet blokes in the gym who have fantastic bodies and I can become excited by that but it causes no genital reaction.

I was abused by an older man during my 20s. This chap was a nurse – he was a nice, good looking bloke really. I had met him in church and I had liked him very much. I was lost and lonely and looking for a dad. And then he stopped nursing me and started sexual activity. I stayed with him for eighteen months but then I literally ran away. I was frightened that if I took my stuff and said I was leaving he would hurt me. It started with him getting into my bed on the pretext that, because we were both Christians, we could trust each other. First he fondled me and I responded; then he sucked me off. After that he said I *had* to return the favour. During that time, even though I was upset about it, he insisted on anal penetration twice a week and sometimes more often. I was the passive partner. He wanted me to penetrate him so that I would feel better about intercourse and I tried but I couldn't do it. I haven't made any other relationships that were that close.

For six years I was very badly bullied and threatened with violence by my boss. He's got a character problem. He would give me a shove on the edge of the stairs to make me fall off. In the end I got the union in.

That time when I had the breakdown after leaving the wild life park I acted very irresponsibly; I was just crazy. At the wild life park I used to get drugs from a friend. When I was younger, after my first overdose, I had a crazy time then too. I wasn't too bad when I was sober but if I had a drink I would throw myself in front of cars – the fact that they always missed me is amazing – perhaps I wasn't very accurate. I had a terrible death wish at the time. In the 70s I used to get very drunk. After that I had my breakdown and then I went home. I got upset at my parents, walked out and I was out on the streets for a day or two; then I collapsed and a voluntary organisation took me to a squat and I lived in squats for three years. I was smoking dope most of that time. Dope and lots and lots of downers – people were giving them to me free – I was passing it on. Most of my most dangerous drugs were given to me by my doctor. I used to get barbiturates from other people.

It would have been about two and a half years ago when it really came home to me that I had been physically abused. It was a big shock; I have memories of being shaken and thrown about, of me crawling and my mother hitting my hand with a hot poker. I kept making the wrong choice and I kept getting hurt. I didn't understand why my hand was hurting me. I remember being held in the air, in the garden and having my legs smacked red raw and mum saying:

> Go away I don't love you; I've never wanted you, I hate you. You don't care about anybody but yourself. I wish I had never had you. You should have been a girl; you were a mistake. I don't know how to put up with you.

She was determined to break me, again and again and again. She terrorised me. I remember having the clumpy legs of a toddler and I would have to run away but they wouldn't take me far.

My father was a fussy, small bald person, and he used to move with short quick steps;there was a lack of masculinity rather than effeminate gestures. My father's father was an abuser so maybe my father was abused by him; otherwise why did he do it to me? I have a memory of my father in the bath with me playing boats and harbours and I remember him putting a finger in my anus and pushing me forwards and backwards and telling me he loved me. I felt hot, crushed, trapped and frightened.

My mother's father always took me to the zoo; he was lovely to me. He didn't take much interest in my sister. I was ill a few months after he died when I was 13; I was taken to hospital and they couldn't find anything. I became so terribly insecure that I felt sick. Until quite recently I used to go to Grandad's grave and cry. It's the only place in the world where I feel safe, peaceful and secure.

I have felt confused about my gender. There's something in me that wants men to take over – I imagine them much bigger than I am; I seem to want someone that size to take over – sexually. I can't actually imagine myself in the male sex-role; I can imagine myself in the female role, being cared for by a man who is obviously larger than me because I am a child, but to imagine that is to imagine being sexually abused. I seem to imagine it right up to the point of that happening but there is a cut-off point; after that point we are in a horror story.

So the overall effect on me I think, is that being handled by a man like a man handles a woman would arouse me, but men want power and I want the power for myself. I am frightened of adult males and females. I am turned on by male bodies but rarely by the whole person. I have developed a complex clamp down on thoughts and feelings; attraction makes me vulnerable. However, I do not think I could ever perform a dominant assertive role in sexual activity with either sex. Really I still just want a father who will cuddle but not screw me; someone to believe in and to be an anchor. Sexual activity may never play a part in my life; control of self and having my own power take precedence. However, if I ever do become emotionally involved, it will be with a man, not a woman. I have a big female side to my character. I like holding people (physically or spiritually) and cuddling, encouraging, enabling and protecting children and making them feel secure. In daily life I repeatedly play the rescuer; I wish I could rescue myself!

12 Abuse by sisters

Adolescent female offenders tend to fall into the category of the experimenter/exploiter and this description fits the adolescent perpetrator of William's abuse as well as that of the others who were abused by sisters (Jeremy and Barney) and those abused by other adolescent female offenders (Jeremy and Denis). The experimenter/exploiter is described as being usually under 16-years-of-age and they generally choose a male child. The abuse usually takes place when the offender is in a position of responsibility such as babysitting the child, a role often ascribed to older sisters. Often the female will caress the child, have oral contact with his penis, or have the child touch her breasts or vagina or suck on her breasts and attempt intercourse. This may be a one-off event and is characterised by detachment and lack of feeling, and the offender denies or is not aware of any sexual arousal. These girls are usually fearful of sexuality and express disgust at their own bodies. Within the confines of the babysitting relationship they have authority, power and control over their young male victims whom they view as safe.

William and Sam's sisters all had control and power over their brothers when they were left in charge of them. Both Sam and William surmise that their sisters were acting out their own abuse thus making it difficult for the men to allow themselves to feel anger towards them. Almost half the adolescent offenders in one treatment programme in the USA (Matthews, Matthews and Speltz 1990) have themselves been sexually abused prior to them abusing younger males and the type of abuse they perpetrate is a reflection of what they have suffered. The abuse is either a re-enactment of their own abuse or the result of learned deviant arousal patterns, boundary confusion and/or thinking errors.

When this kind of abuse is recognised as the probable result of a sister's own abuse, it may create further difficulties for the adult male in working through his own victimisation. It may also be more difficult to talk about it within the family, particularly as the girl's perpetrator might also be a family member. When Sam told his mother about his sister's abuse of him she accused him of being 'equally to blame' although he had been 6-years-old when it began. By blaming the child she was able to avoid attaching any blame to herself for not protecting him or for her own neglect and physical abuse of him.

Sam tells a story of a childhood lacking in food, comfort, warmth and good parenting. He was physically abused by his mother and his stepfather; he was separated from his natural father and he was sexually abused by three of his sisters from the age of 6. His story tells of the way a young person, deprived of the right kind of love and attention, seeks what he intuitively knows he needs. He was not listened to, there was no emotional warmth in his family and he learned to seek his comfort through sex in a children's home and drugs in the outside world. Sam has had several convictions for burglary, he has been convicted of indecent assault on his under-age girl friend, he was given a 'place of safety' order after committing arson. He now sees some of his early anti-social behaviour was a way of asking society to help by removing him from the very unhealthy environment of his home. A society that values 'the family' above the individual needs of the child, can be one which further abuses the child by insisting on keeping the family together. His behaviour might also be seen as a way of acting out the anger that he felt towards his sisters, his parents and society for not noticing his pain.

William's story is unusual in that he has spent a lot of time and effort analysing his behaviours and his coping mechanisms. I have included it in this section as a demonstration of how an obsessive phantasy relationship can be used to protect the person's ego until such time as they are strong enough to face reality. Obsessive relationships can be the result of a deep need for love and affection; in view of the number of men in the study who experienced emotional neglect and abuse it might be expected that such obsessive relationships might not be rare. When both partners share this obsessive love they might become co-dependent; with each partner maintaining the position of the other, resulting in painful, destructive and unsatisfying relationships.

William's story

William was born in 1970. He is a higher degree student, single and he has no children. His Victorian father was brought up 'with a silver spoon in his mouth' and his mother came from a working class background. His father, as a small child, suffered from a severe twitch and even now goes through 'familiarisation patterns', such as repeated taps and shrugs. His father is very possessive and over-protective and is still exerting a large amount of pressure on William to go back and and live at home. He remembers his father as 'unusual' and 'stilted with affection' but kindly. William remembers his mother and aunt (who also lived with the family) as 'very good'.

William's sister became obsessed with jealousy when her baby brother was born when she was 8-years-old. He remembers how she tormented him as a small child; making him eat soil and generally treating him in a punishing way. Their home was a large isolated farmhouse on a large estate and William was entirely dependent on his sister for company. He badly needed and wanted her to like him. She would criticise everything he said or did; neither her mother nor her aunt could prevent her behaviour and her father's frequent absence meant she was virtually uncontrollable.

William idolised his sister and continually made an effort to be nice to her even though she treated him so badly. Being an extremely intelligent child William developed a great attachment to nature, animals, plants and anything scientific. They kept horses and other animals on the estate and up to the age of 12 he kept his spirit alive.

William takes up the story:
I think I was a normal little boy up until I was 5. When I started infant school (which was about the time my sister started doings that were more than nasty); I was very isolated. I didn't have any real friends until I was about 7 when I met my best friend Sue and we just clicked. I always went home for lunch because my parents were a little bit over-protective so I didn't have time with friends in the lunch break when I was in the infants school.

I think it's fair to say that I don't have a clear image of myself as a child. I was shy and I wanted to be the leader of the gang. I've always been physically strong; emotionally and intellectually I was probably more than half way towards the female end of the continuum. When I was a teenager I was completely submissive. My sister called me an 'obnoxious brat' but that wasn't what I thought about myself. Looking back I was a 'know-it-all'. I was lonely sometimes, but I wasn't unhappy. Everything interested me. The teacher was excellent: she would move us around to find who we worked best with and I sat next to Sue. She was the most confident, individual person I had ever known and I really admired her. She was top in everything and we invented our own games and played together in the playground. We attracted others who wanted play with us. She used to spend a lot of time slagging the boys off, saying they were only interested in playing football and that was very shallow – pretty good for a 7-year-old. I didn't play football. When we went up to the next level we stayed friends but it changed. On the last day of term she said 'I'll miss you'; I didn't know what she meant at the time, but it was never the same after that.

I was about 5 when the abuse started (if you could call it that). It coincided with when I started school and when I was beginning to have health problems and possibly failing to eat properly.

My sister could be a nightmare but sometimes, when my parents were out of the way, she would start being really nice to me. One time she got in bed with me – it sounds quite innocent but with hindsight ... she wanted to play this game; I would have to tell her if her finger was on her foot or in her bum and of course it would be in her bum. She was a teenager so basically she was masturbating and getting me to smell her finger. Now a 5-year-old doesn't know this, I stress that, I didn't have a clue.

At one point my mum came in the bedroom when my sister had dressed me up in her clothes and she said she was modelling but there was more to it than that. I enjoyed it – I got a buzz out of it. I got to look forward to these things because she was nice to me and it was something I associated with 'nice'. I have this image of her when she was about 13 or 14 with tight black leggings and being very strong, very dominant and I'd be enjoying little subtle things that I can't quite remember – there was quite a lot of it.

Then she did a couple of things that were very dodgy in the extreme. One time she sent me downstairs to get a book to read while she was on the loo. When I brought it she locked the door behind me. She squatted over a mirror and made me look into it. In my language of that time, she then 'did a poo' and I was very surprised and shocked by this. And then she'd be horrible to me afterwards.

Another time I wanted to go up into the attic but she said 'don't go up there because there are ghosts and green-eyed dogs up there'; then she got me to go out into the garden instead and made me watch her relieving herself, which is quite bizarre. I would be very interested to know what would make somebody do that ... unless she'd seen somebody else do it? Until I was 16, I didn't regard it as anything unusual – I just thought it was normal.

When I was about 6 I started copying what she did. I would put my finger up my backside and I very aggressively, sadistically, forced a female stuffed toy dog's nose hard against my anus; I would dress up in my sister's underwear. My dad came into the room and saw me putting her tights on and he thought I was just dressing up, but I had an erection and I was getting a real buzz out of it.

At the age of 11, I had 'controlled breakdowns' lasting about an hour during which I would hysterically cry and laugh alternately. One happened spontaneously during a lesson at school and the teacher asked me if I was OK (obviously aware that I wasn't) and I broke off manic crying, looked up and said in a coherent, calm voice that I was fine and then burst out laughing again. The teacher asked me if there was anything wrong at home. I replied (in a coherent pause) that everything was fine at home. At that point I honestly believed what my dad continually told me – that I was very lucky indeed, very privileged and happy.

From the time I was 12 onwards I went to an archaic all boys' private day school and then I really started abusing myself very badly. I always assumed it was coming from me until I made the link one day when I was in the sixth form. My sister was going up into the attic and I said jokingly 'don't go up there; there are green-eyed dogs and ghosts up there' and she looked horrified and said 'What?' I told her that she had said that to me once and she said 'No I didn't, no I didn't!' She really reacted out of context and that got my mind working. Without her reaction to my words 'ghosts and green-eyed dogs' I might never have realised; until then I had assumed that all the filth came from me.

I had no contact with girls at all. I went from an environment where I was well known at school and had lots of friends, to where I didn't have any; to where the idea was to take the piss out of everyone, at every opportunity, because if you don't, they'll take it out of you. Like being fat, I blamed school for all my other problems, but it really wasn't what I needed at the time. I went downhill very rapidly within six months. I was academically towards the top of the class.

I wanted school to be kept separate from home; I hated school obsessively. Some months ago I went back to visit this school with an old school friend. If I go back to middle school, I get really nostalgic; but at this school, I felt as if I had never been there, although I knew the place well. Effectively, I've cut four years out of my life – the time during which I was completely in a fantasy world. My childhood ended at 12 when I left middle school; adolescence started at nearly 17 when I started the sixth form. This gives me an emotional age of 20, which is about how old I feel now.

The time at this school seems nightmarishly long. From 12–16 I felt utterly filthy and I got very, very depressed. I would wake up in the morning and I'd have to think of suicide before I could get out of bed. I'd be frightened to go to sleep because I'd know I'd wake up again; it was like that for three and a half years. At weekends and holidays I would often stay in bed until mid- or even late-afternoon. After my university finals (aged 21) I woke up one morning and thought 'Oh good. I can get up!', which was the first time I had felt like that in the morning since I was 12.

I didn't actually try to commit suicide because I wanted to end this misery but not my life; so I used it as a reassurance – it was there if I wanted it. We'd got a shotgun at home and I loaded it once and sat and looked at it to cheer myself up; another time I held a pen knife over my heart. The depression gradually died away, and, about once every couple of months even now I get brief bouts of depression (during which I cannot imagine what it is like not to be depressed). I told my mum I was depressed and she said I didn't know what depression was. Which was fine – she didn't understand. She was depressed herself so I have no qualms there. I wouldn't have cried for help; I'm not like that.

My sister had gone off to university for three years and I'd come home from school, undress down to my underpants, (she had left behind a few select items of clothes that I would put on) and I'd masturbate. My back passage came in for rough treatment. I was just trying to gain sexual satisfaction; I was completely isolated from females, I was terrified of them so I was just using my imagination. I used hair brush handles, marbles, and all sorts of things to abuse myself. I started copying what she had done over the bathroom mirror.

I was very scrupulous about making sure people didn't find out. It was a completely different reality and the two didn't touch at all. It was a continuation of the reality of when it happened with my sister. I can't remember how often it went on with my sister. I think there were a lot of minor things I don't remember.

The thing I found most difficult to come to terms with was the dog. We had this big male labrador dog and my sister had trained the dog to hate me. At every opportunity she would tell it to bite me. Then one day when I was watching TV on my own I took my trousers down and I thought the dog would just come and have a sniff but it licked me and I didn't expect that. That became a really regular thing. I really hated this dog and treated it very badly most of the time, but was nicer to it when I wanted it to lick me. Does that sound familiar? It was the same as my sister did to me. Also, I was tempted to do things sexually with other animals but consciously decided not to. Eventually I started feeling really bad about it. I thought that I would never have a relationship with a woman. I felt like a monster. It got to be like an addiction. I couldn't fight it. I really hated myself.

When this was going on from 12–16 I didn't have any contact with females so I created one for myself. I started thinking about Sue quite innocently at first but it grew into an obsession. So apart from the sordid world where she never ever trod, the real world consisted of talking to the imaginary Sue for 24 hours a day; a real false consciousness. I saw her twice from a distance during this time but I didn't talk to her. I got a lot of power/strength from this imaginary relationship and to this day, a lot of my schoolfriends still think that I was going out with somebody then. When this was happening I would brainwash myself by using double think into making it all true – I knew it wasn't really true but by the end of four years I really believed it. It was a 24 hour a day obsession. Then in the sixth form I thought that if I started going out with Sue again, everything would be alright. I had to believe there was a quick way out of the mess I was in.

I knew I would be coming into contact with two or three girls in the sixth form. I was a compulsive eater. I was the class fat boy. I would come home from school and stuff my face to take my mind off it. So I had to do something about my weight before I got to the sixth form. I had not made the connection by this time – I hated myself but I didn't know it was wrong or abnormal. It was normal but it was abnormal. I pinned all my problems on being overweight (there were a fair few problems) – so I put myself on a strict diet during the summer before I went into the sixth form and slimmed down to a reasonable weight. I started running, I was asthmatic so exercise was difficult, but I stuck to it. I go through with things once I decide them. I lost faith in just about everything I had except that. Everybody remarked on my weight loss. That's when the fun really started because depression just hit me over the head.

I really felt very, very different from other people. I thought girls were for others and what was happening to me was for me. During my teen years I regarded girls as Godesses of 'Clean', and it took years before I saw them as merely other people. I felt smelly; I had a very low self-image. I made a concerted effort to stop the dog business. I went on holiday to my uncle's house and I got on great with his dog and from then on I regarded dogs as dogs.

I had fantasies. Some of them were me being abused by women. When I was about 9 I had to have physiotherapy for bad posture, I was very hunched; I also had a funny voice – I didn't speak clearly at all – I just sort of shuffled. Both of these were manifestations of fear of expressing myself in case I was slammed down. I used to have fantasies about being forced to do physiotherapy in the nude and bondage and stuff. When I was abusing myself I used to imagine there was somebody forcing me to do it.

On entry into the sixth form, my only previous experience of girls was with my sister so I expected to be exploited and treated badly, but at the same time I revered them. Because there were girls about, I didn't get satisfaction from those things any more. I tried some of my sister's clothes on after I went into the sixth form and I just felt stupid.

I had a female friend in the first term of the sixth form – we got on OK at the time but I hadn't got the confidence to ask her out or anything but that contact was very good to have. But I got very very depressed because I felt so different. I was nearest to suicide that I've been but I had one saving grace. I was good at something. I was top at chemistry. Even if I had a miserable life, I was going to achieve something worthwhile. So I organised this major project as a school charity and I started my first bit of public speaking about it. I put all my strength into it and it was something to live for and I did live for it.

The other thing to live for was Sue. When I was 17 we went to the pub for a meal and we talked – it was quite stilted and after this she agreed to be friends but nothing else. So that went on for a year and I started growing up during that year. When I was 18 I kissed Sue; while I was kissing her, (she was wearing a skimpy black top), I had an instant 'flashback' of my sister during one of our encounters. This was disconcerting, and I had to make a conscious effort to ignore it. I can still remember the smell of my sister's fingers and often, as a young child, sniffed her underwear (when she wasn't wearing it), especially when it was soiled. I was really puzzled when I found out that girls smelt nice! Then the relationship went wrong – I stopped seeing her when I felt strong enough. I just got on with my life without her although I was still obsessed with her well into the first year at university. I was still doing everything to make myself into what I should be for her instead of what I wanted to be.

My self-image started improving while I was still in the sixth form. There were a couple of important changes. On this project I got to know a couple of girls and had a really good laugh. It was the first time I had really socialised since I was 12. The girls became good friends. I couldn't ask them out because I had this ridiculous sort of loyalty to Sue, even though she didn't want it. I was basically a very submissive wreck in her presence; I would do anything to please her and she would play on it.

I found the first term at university difficult. By the beginning of the third year I'd got more friends including some females. I hadn't had any – still haven't had a meaningful emotional or physical relationship. I've had female admirers; I've been called the life and soul of the party. I've got this sense of humour. In the second year I met a girl called Joan and we got on very well but I ran away from her – I wasn't ready for it at that point. The other world hadn't gone away;

I'd shut it away but it was still there. Until recently I just tried to shut the whole thing out and behave as though nothing sordid ever happened. Consequently I was always trying to be something I wasn't and was in danger of 'caving in', which I have done on occasions and made a fool of myself.

Up until recently I've always looked for girls who have something slightly wrong with them. I didn't see myself as being whole so I needed somebody with a slight deformity. Joan wasn't one of those girls – she was extremely confident and attractive and represents the only strong emotional attachment I have formed apart from that with Sue.

When I was about 15, and also when I was abusing myself in the final fling last year, sometimes I made myself into a surrogate woman. At 15, I was dressing up completely in women's clothes, including a wig. More recently I assumed the missionary position of a woman and used my own anus as a vagina. This reflects, more my separateness from sex with women than my effeminate nature. However, some months later, I was staying with an effeminate male friend (nothing has ever, or ever will, happen between us) and I pictured myself as an active homosexual partner for the first time ever. Even with women, I usually had fantasised being the passive partner, especially in my teens. More recently I have seen myself as the active partner, usually heterosexual. In reality, I would find sex with men repulsive, and I really do like women.

I've had fantasies about males raping me; they were dirty and arousing. My dad can't stand homosexuals – he can't stand anything that is not in line with Victorian ideals. I was very anti-gay during adolescence. I would bully anyone who was effeminate.

The Easter after my finals I suddenly realised that Sue would be at home. I was genuinely interested to meet up with her. I was hoping that I would look at her and just feel a bit of a fool for having behaved like an idiot, but I didn't know what to expect. Anyway it was like somebody turning on the Blackpool illuminations – she just completely captivated me. At that point I was organising an overseas seminar which I was introducing; she was quite status-orientated and was quite impressed with that. Then we both went back to our homes at opposite ends of the country and I couldn't get her out of my head. I was fighting it but then my friend told me to get on the phone to her to shut me up. So I did.

We agreed that we would just be friends and nothing else. So we both went off to Cornwall for a weekend and it was incredible. Up to then I'd always had some inhibition, but there were no inhibitions with her at all. It was almost as if I was allowed to feel completely natural with her but that I wasn't allowed to feel that with anybody else. But that didn't work. I went to the States for six months. We had agreed that we would meet up in a year; couldn't stop thinking about her without contacting her. And things crept back, so by the time I was seeing her again it was an obsession again. It was bizarre. It fluctuated between me not being able to get her out of my mind and the next minute I wouldn't feel anything. I told her about how I felt when I was in the 'couldn't get her out of my mind' phase and she reacted very patronisingly; basically gave me the impression that she had just been using me as an ego trip all the way along. I didn't feel angry but I thought I should, so I pretended I was. I slammed the phone down, ended the conversation in a very hurtful way. Six months later I still hadn't forgotten about her and I wrote down everything I ever wanted to say and sent it to her. I was living back home again from university – back in the isolated environment – my sister was at home. I found to my horror that the horrible little world was still there – I started abusing myself again; fantasising that I was being raped by men. I beat it by writing everything down and when I got the dodgy urge I would read it through and it would kill the urge dead.

I sent this letter to Sue but she didn't write back so I thought it was the end of it. Then completely out of the blue she wrote one back to me. I had told her that something wasn't right with me but I hadn't told her the full story; just that my sister was a bit dotty. I got this most recent letter four months ago saying she didn't want to see me again, she didn't trust me, that I'd hurt her again; saying what a terrible time she had been having. I wrote one back telling her the whole story – not going into graphic detail but enough so that she could understand the whole thing. Saying that I thought it was my obsession and not genuine, being really honest.

When I saw Sue the last time, it was real and unreal at the same time. I was sitting next to her on the bus feeling very strongly for her and a flash came into my mind, of all the things I would have to deal with if we could ever work out properly.

Every year since I've been in the sixth form, I've been able to make a connection but in this last year or so it's been like a realisation every ten minutes or so. It has made me see things more clearly. When I was writing my last letter back to Sue, I had to re-write it about five times because what I believed changed with the connections I made during the writing of the first letter, then I'd write another and another one. Connections came thick and fast. That letter was the first time I told anybody how badly it had affected me and that had an amazing effect. My writing changed half way through the letter and the acne on my back disappeared after that.

I had difficulty defining what happened to me as abuse because I wasn't touched – I wasn't 'interfered with', which is what most people would call sexual abuse. Up until recently that is what I would have said. It's probably a male thing – a female doing things that weren't physically damaging – is that abuse? I never considered it as abuse until about a year ago. The obsession with Sue and the filthy little world I inhabit sometimes counterbalanced each other; they are very linked. As one goes the obsession goes and I think that the Sue I created was the nice thing that balanced out the horrible thing. It really got inside me in a big way; a lot of boys have romantic dreams during adolescence. Mine were dodgy in the extreme – I was having sex with cows, I was abusing myself, a lot of them had my sister in and she had male genitals in the dreams. I always felt until recently that I was the submissive partner.

I wouldn't consider talking to my parents about it because I've got a good relationship with them now and I don't want to mess that up. They must have known something was going on when I was abusing myself; it went on for years and you can't hide everything – but they never said anything. My mum was very depressed at that time – it's a bit of a coincidence. At one point I was wearing one of my sister's swim suits and hiding in the bathroom and my mum walked into my room and said 'Oh God it gets worse'- so what did she know? When my sister was about 14 she had awful nightmares. She used to walk about the bedroom on all fours and bang her head on the table – so what was she doing? She's got this thing about children – she doesn't ever want to have any – I've always assumed she doesn't trust herself.

My sister is a nightmare – she's overweight; she's married and lives with her husband at home with my father, mother and aunt. My father is the best thing ever in her eyes. She is a complete obsessive; she can't handle things she doesn't like. She still puts me down all the time. Recently I exploded at her – I've never been violent towards people – I've smashed up furniture. She ran upstairs in tears and later I went to try to talk to her and she refused to talk about anything that happened before I had left home. My sister is somebody you don't mess with – it's obviously at the forefront of her mind even now and if I ever catch her out in an argument she resorts to throwing things at me. Her whole life would completely fall apart if anything was exposed so it is better to leave things the way they are.

I sometimes wondered if my sister did it because she hated me – and she wanted to hurt me. If she had been abused, she knew how it had screwed her up and maybe she wanted me to be screwed up too. I looked forward to the episodes when I was abused because she was nice to me. Now I associate it with this horrible world that repulses me and sometimes I direct it towards her but if she has been abused then I can't really bear a grudge.

Kids get on with me really great; I communicate at their level. I really like children and I feel at ease with them. I go round schools and talk with them in my professional role. Children just wouldn't turn me on and besides that I wouldn't ruin a life like that. I don't think there's any excuse for it. But what if a 5- or 6-year-old child is abused and passes it on to a younger sibling at the same time and they grow up with this double think of not seeing it as wrong, having had it done to them all their lives? I was abused by someone in their early to mid-teens, which is precisely the age when the worst consequences manifested themselves in me. What if I'd been abused by an adult?

What helped me to deal with the abuse was my obsession with Sue; it took my mind off it. The biggest help for me was chemistry. If you feel slightly inhuman it can be positive as well as negative; you can do these things better than anybody else because you are slightly inhuman.

I can read through a pile of incoherent data, order it, analyse it and draw conclusions with about as much effort as most people can write their name. Is that a consequence of having continually tried to model reality since I was very young and having a lot of time alone to do it? I have completed one novel, as yet unpublished. Most of my friends think it's great, but I've been told that it's a complete reflection of my own life. Basically, it's a very humorous story with different, erratic, irrational characters interacting (with two or three parallel plots) in ridiculous situations, but still managing to hold together somehow and all tie up at the end. In hindsight, the characters are nearly all different facets of my own (complicated) personality.

In addition to this I have a very singular outlook on life that enables me to see things differently to other people, which is often a great advantage. Most of all, I have a widely acknowledged sense of humour; I can make virtually anyone laugh! How much of this is a consequence of being abused and how I dealt with it? These things are what I most admire in myself, and without them I'd be a completely different person whom I'm not entirely sure I'd like. If that's the case, I wouldn't change a thing that has happened to me. I am much stronger because of it.

Admitting to myself that I was in a bad way (just over a year ago) when I really didn't want to, was the big jump in dealing with this thing. Using, rather than hiding the past, including sexual deviations, was the other big jump. Past experience is past experience, however bad, and it must be embraced – at least in my case.

Until recently I could not understand why a girl would want to enter into a relationship with me, and saw a relationship as something in which only I gained. Obviously, this was a good way of avoiding getting a relationship off the ground. Now I see myself as someone with a lot to give, especially strength.

I had somewhat of an obsession that I only wanted a relationship with a girl if she was 'innocent'. I twisted things all ways to avoid facing up to the fact that Sue (who has had several boyfriends, not all happy relationships) had probably lost her virginity and that was a major inhibition to losing mine – misguided loyalty and maintaining a false image of her.
Footnote: After giving the interview I had a bad case of insomnia and a very unfamiliar, disconcerting feeling that I could not identify. I talked to my best friend (who doesn't know about my past), about whether I ever wanted to have children and I got this very strange 'spinny', light-headed feeling, that I remembered from my very early years with my mum. I now feel that I have come to the end of the 'fence' that I was on the wrong side of, and that I can now walk freely to the other side, and I'm a bit apprehensive. But I'm not going to run away from it!

Sam's story

Sam is 22. He is in prison serving a sentence for burgling offices. This is his thirteenth conviction for burglary. He has passed some computer exams since being in prison this time and hopes to get a job in that field on release. He is single and has no children. His mother has been married three times; she had two girls by her first husband; two further daughters were born to the second marriage and then Sam; three years later another son was born by her third husband. Sam's father left home when he was about 2-years-old and he saw him a few times until he was 4. Sam met up with his father again two years ago and is normally in touch but he does not know Sam is in prison.

Sam told me:

I remember arguments between my mum and stepdad (he wasn't a nice person) and my mum always threatening to pack her bags and us crying and begging her to stay. I was often starving as I was growing up. I nicked a packet of biscuits once when I was 8 and my sister got the blame; then I tried to commit suicide. I'm not sure if it was suicide or if I was just trying to copy my sister who had tried it the night before. I went downstairs to the medicine cabinet, saw all these funny coloured tablets, started taking them, fell off the fridge and the next thing I remember is waking up in the ambulance on the way to the hospital. So I don't know if it was to get attention or what.

I still hate my stepdad for the way he treated me. He didn't show any love but then again neither did mum so I kind of got used to it. My mum was happy to go along with whatever my stepdad did. I can't remember any warmth or comfort from her.

The abuse started off with my 13-year-old sister when I was about 6, before I took the pills. I can't really remember much about it but she was trying to get me to have sex with her and it wasn't working too well; after a while I got up and put on my Y-fronts. That only happened once with her. I don't remember any feelings about that. I can picture it in my mind.

After I had taken the tablets they were asked to keep an eye on me and I had to sleep in their room. My mum was away, either for the day or for a couple of days, and I went home for some food and my sister said, 'you can't have food until you do some things' and I said, 'What?' and she made me get down on her – she said something like 'lick me where I pretend I'm having a baby'. I was revolted as far as I remember. I had to do it to get some grub. I was about 7 or 8 and she would have been 13 or 14. The next time was a couple of nights later when she climbed in bed with me and started kissing me and doing things. I can't remember many details except that it was like before, with me getting down on her again. Then it stopped with her. I don't know if she lost interest or what. It was only two or three times, not much really.

The next time was with my real sister. She used to make me kiss her between the legs – even when she was 10 or 11 and she had nothing there. It disgusts me and I feel embarrassed talking about it now, but with her later on, it did excite me. I think by then I was getting my hormones together. It used to happen to me and my brother at the same time – he was three years younger than me. It used to happen when Susan was babysitting or in some situation where she had complete charge of us. It went on until I was 12 or 13. It included me penetrating her and doing oral sex. When my mum and dad used to go out I was petrified because it would happen then; there did come a point when, in some ways I got enjoyment out of it. There was a time when it really grossed me out; my sister was having a period and she made me penetrate her. It was after that time that I kept away from her. Anyway just a couple of months after that I moved into the children's home.

My brother stayed at home – poor kid. He's the only one I love out of my family still. He goes into prison non-stop. I tried to talk to him about it once when I was at a stage in my life when I had admitted the abuse but I hadn't really faced up to it. He had broken into my mum's bedroom – we weren't living at home at the time. I said, 'Look – what you've done to your mum is wrong – she's only got me and you left, so let's support her. We know what happened when we were small; you got abused and I got abused'. He just turned away.

One night my mum started slapping me and accusing me of breaking into a car – my brother had done it and she wouldn't believe that I had been at my mate's house all evening. I brought my feet and arms up to protect myself and as I brought up my foot it hit her; she took off a Scholl's sandal and started hitting me round the head with it. I jumped out of a second storey window and ran back up to a mate's house and the police got involved. I had already been on voluntary weekend care at the children's home because I'd been in trouble. I loved being in the home. Some of the staff showed you love and it was nice. I'd never known that before; I was there for four years.

I went to court for a Care Order – that was on an arson charge. I went past a garage and dropped a lighted match through the window thinking the drop would make the match go out but it didn't – not realising the garage was full. It was just a childish prank. So I went to court and it was the only time I saw my mum really crying; the judge said 'it's a charge of arson and we are going to give a Criminal Care Order'. When I got back to the kid's home I jumped into the staff's arms and said, 'Yes, I got it'. That was how much I needed it. I was happy as hell.

Then a couple of years later, when I was 14, I tried to get back with my mum and I went home for Christmas. On Christmas Day my aunt had bought me a toy for a 6-year-old. I asked my mum if I could take this back and change it for something else. She said 'No'. So I said 'I'm not having a very happy Christmas – I'm going to go upstairs and pack my bag and go back to the children's home because I'll have a better Christmas there!' And I did and to be honest I had a 100 per cent better Christmas there. I got an electronic lab. – it helped my intellect quite a lot. I was fascinated by it. You could actually choose what you wanted in the kid's home and they would get it for you. When I went to the kid's home they really fed you, you could have a shower every day – it was like being a king. It was really enjoyable.

Also I got my first impressions of proper sex, (by proper I mean not with your sister), with the girls in the home. So at the age of 13 I was having sex with the girls in the home. I think the staff were aware of it but they couldn't do anything about it. Staff slept upstairs and the girls' room were facing the boys room and you just had to walk across the corridor on the same landing. I got caught once and they threw me out. I was 16 then but they let me back in when I explained that it was with one girl the same age as me and not six girls as they had said. I think it was more out of needing love and attention and needing to feel wanted by each other. It was plain sex. A couple of nights you'd have sex with one girl and then you'd go for another one. I have actually been done for 'gross indecency' with a girl of 14 when I was 15.

I've only ever had one homosexual experience and I didn't like it. That was when I was in prison. My cell mate and I tried it out a couple of times. It wasn't full blown sex – just blow jobs. I'm quite clear that I'm heterosexual! I don't want to do it myself but I've got nothing against homosexuals.

One of the reasons I committed crime is that I was thinking that society can't really care too much – I don't see why I am the only one who has to be punished because I wasn't the only one who has committed a crime – my family have as well and they are not being prosecuted. At the time it was happening I wouldn't have liked to see them being punished but now I would, to teach them a lesson. I hated my mum – no question of that. I used to call her names to her face – I lost all respect for her. I suppose I was trying to hurt her back for all the hurt she had caused me; I think she knew the abuse was happening. About a year and a half ago my girl friend and I tried to talk to her about it and she said 'It was half your fault'. Since then I haven't been in contact – I think I can do better without her.

I started to realise I'd been abused about the age of 14. I tried to tell my social worker and she said she didn't believe me. She said, 'It doesn't happen; women don't abuse blokes'. That reaction hurt. By that age I had begun to read in the newspapers about kids being abused by their parents and it came up when I was talking to a probation officer. The social worker didn't want to know about it. It made it hard to tell someone else about it; I thought 'if you don't believe me then who is going to?' So I kept it inside myself. I think by the age of 16 I realised social workers were a load of crap. I had been beaten up by my stepdad a few times and been placed in care overnight, but the social workers believed my stepdad and mum – that it hadn't happened – they tried to put the family back together and a few weeks later it would happen all over again. My stepdad threw me down the stairs once when I was 10 and I ran away and they put me into care overnight and the next day the social worker took me home. I think that was wrong.

Also, at that age I was getting bullied at school. I think it was the reaction from what was happening with my sisters. It made me meek; I was someone people picked on – even people younger than me. I used to let them get away with it until I went to prison for the first time and I shot up to 5′8″ and then people started treating me a lot better.

Sex was just ignored in our house. I think my mum knew that my sister was having sex with her boy friends. I was aware of it at the time. I suppose as it went on I learned the facts of life by myself. Up until the age of 16 I was just purely interested in my own sexual pleasure. I wasn't interested in the woman's. When I was having sex with the girls in the home it was exactly the same for them. They were using me as I was using them. I'd say at least half of them had been abused. They were about as experienced as me.

The abuse has always made me shy with women – if I want to talk to a woman I always get a friend to ask her if she wants a drink because I haven't got the bottle just in case I get rejected. My mum's rejection of me has made me fear rejection.

Maybe my sisters were getting abused by my stepdad. Who knows? It could have quite easily happened. They never spoke about it. I didn't tell anybody when it was happening because I was embarrassed and scared. Scared of what it would do to my family at the time. When I was 11 I got hit by a lorry and my mum always blamed my criminal behaviour on the lorry. She didn't actually look into it to see what was making me commit crimes. I think the main reason I started committing crimes was to get away from home. I wished you could have divorced your parents at that age.

My stepdad had the power. They had power over me and I was too small and too scared to do anything about it. I think if I'd approached anyone at the age of 9 and said I was being abused by my sisters they would have laughed in my face; I've been told (by my counsellor) it wasn't accepted that females abused at that time.

As a little boy I was scared and meek, mild – right at the opposite end from macho. I did well at my exams the first year at the comprehensive school, then it started going downhill. I used to get picked on in the playground and I was scared. I was always being told that I should stick up for myself. My sister used to beat me up and say, 'Look – you are meant to hit me back – you're not meant to just stand there and take it;' it was the same with my brother at times. He would say 'you're a wimp'. My parents weren't really interested – they let me get on with it. I thought being a 'real man' meant being like a policeman. I think maybe that was because I wanted to make some things right in my life instead of it all going wrong. Being a man meant to face up to things in a macho man kind of way – to say 'that doesn't really bother me too much', and just get on with my life; to turn a blind eye and not to accept other people's feelings.

Later I was 'Jack-the-lad' because I'd been to prison; I'd grown up a lot. I wouldn't let people take liberties with me. At the end of the day I became the hardest kid in the school. It made me proud in a way; I didn't bully anyone – I put a stop to the cigarette extortion racket that was going on at the time. I would have been 13 or 14. I was truanting from school even before I went into care so I was sent to this boarding school. It would have been in my second year there that I became the hard guy.

A few times in my life I have had the chance to be loved by people; social services helped to muck it up in a way. I was going to be fostered by a couple and I really loved them. I was at the boarding school at the time during the week and I went back to live with them at the weekends. Then one day I got called into the office and

I was told that they had failed the medical test. I cried and felt I had been rejected again and I started getting into trouble again. I was 14 then.

My little brother and I loved each other. We spent most of our childhood together in the same room. He used to be able to beat me up as well. This is the first time I've ever said this – it did happen between my brother and me but I think that was out of comfort more than anything. It was masturbating each other. I was 10 and he would have been 7. We understand each other – even though he's a ponce. I went down to London last year to see my girl friend and I arranged with my sister Chloe (the only one who didn't abuse me) to stay at her house. I was a heavy dope smoker at that time and I took at least half an ounce down with me and my brother tried to ponce off me – smokes, money, cigarettes. He never had anything of his own. He'd go out and commit crime to get them and I'd rather give him a tenner to tide him over than see him get into trouble.

I've been in trouble with the law about thirteen times. Burglary of offices. In a way I did it for the dope. I just wanted to smoke and be in oblivion all the time – to get away from every day hassles; just to hide it all away – just to be 'Jack-the-Lad'. But my attitude has changed a lot since coming in here; since I've faced up to a lot of things. I used the dope to try to blot out the pain of everything. It's a buzz to live life now. To enjoy life for what I can get out it. Passing exams, using my brains which I've never done before; being in love helps a lot.

The girl friend has made the difference by teaching me how to love. I have had lots of other girl friends but not like this one. Its never been love – its been like three month relationships since the age of 16 and then finish. The longest I've had is nine months. The person I'm going out with now is the one I intend to marry. She loves me as much as I love her. She has supported me through this – I know she's not one who will go out and ruin this relationship by sleeping with anyone else while I'm in here. There's a lot of trust between us and she knows within herself that I've changed a lot since I've come in here. She's the first person I talked to about the abuse. At the time I thought I had come to terms with it but I hadn't accepted it. But since I've talked about the details with her she has helped me to accept it. She understands – she thinks my family are all mad. She's a medical student. I met her in prison; her brother was doing three years for armed robbery on his dad's Post Office. I saw his picture of her in the cell and we started writing as friends and about four months later we got together. Her mum and dad are divorced and she hates her dad for some reason. She says when you come out we'll talk you about it. I don't want to pressure her. But her mum treats me really nicely, she's accepted me.

I think I coped with the abuse by shutting it off, building up barriers against it. It just took the right person to break down those barriers and to bring the person inside me out. The person who doesn't want to get into trouble; the person who doesn't want to smoke drugs; the person who is sick of hiding and running away from life. I've never actually faced up to problems but now I do. There's one bloke in here, he's an ex-policeman and we are good friends. We play backgammon every night. He's the only one I talk with. I get sick of the others who talk about nothing but prison and violence. I'm not like that. I've definitely made up my mind that I'm leaving prison out of my life.

13 Men raped as adults

Until a recent amendment (July 1994) in the Criminal Justice Bill made in the wake of Parliament's decision to lower the age of consent for homosexual men to 18, the term 'rape' in English law was restricted to forced penile penetration of the vagina and so could not be applied to sexual assaults made upon men. Forced anal penetration of a man was considered within the Sexual Offences (Amendment) Act of 1976 as non-consensual buggery and carried a lesser penalty. The change in the law will mean that the maximum sentence for male rape will now be increased from ten years to a life sentence. It will also confer on male victims protection from cross-examination on their sexual history.

Even when the definition of rape is widened to include any gender, male rape is usually considered to be an assault by homosexuals against heterosexual men and boys. This is based on the assumption that rape is a sexually motivated crime, and that if men are the targets then it must be homosexually orientated men who are the perpetrators. McMullen (1990b) reports evidence that indicates that the reverse might be true, with male rape being more likely to be committed by heterosexual men against homosexual victims; an abuse of power rather than a sexual crime.

However, thirteen of the twenty-five men I interviewed were sexually abused during childhood or adolescence by females, so the presumption that it is only males that sexually assault males may be emerging as a myth. In three of these cases penetration of the female was involved. When a male child is abused by an older or more powerful female, then the one who penetrates is the victim not the aggressor.

Eleven men in the study had been penetrated by males, orally, anally, with objects or with the penis. Many of the men assumed that their abuser had been homosexual in orientation; thus causing them to wonder if they had attracted these men who had in some magical way recognised that they would welcome these approaches because they too were homosexual.

The two case I have presented below are those of James and Matthew, men who were anally penetrated by males during childhood or adolescence. James, who was one of the first people I interviewed, told me at that time, that he remembered clearly being anally penetrated at the age of 12 by a stranger. He also intimated that he was beginning to reclaim memories of being abused as a much younger child and wondered if this earlier abuse might have in some way contributed to the second abuse. Recently he told me that he has now remembered that he was anally penetrated as a 3–5-year-old child and he believes this abuser may have been his father and/or his grandfather. His mother tells him that he was not left alone with his father so there would have been no opportunity and that he was left with his grandparents regularly and frequently. James also thinks that his mother's physical abuse of him as a young child might have had a sexual element.

The memories of his early abuse seem to have been stimulated through it's re-enactment during his two rapes as an adult. He experienced his 12-year-old abuse in a dissociated way; he was 'numb', his body carried none of the feelings but he clearly remembered the event – this coping mechanism is dealt with in more depth in the analysis of Harry's story. When a child is abused at a very young age he may cope with this by repression and dissociation, splitting off the feelings and/or the memory of the event in order to survive it. James recognised the similarity between his response to rape as an adult and when he was raped as a 12-year-old boy. This connection opened the door to the memories of his very early abuse. It is almost as though he had to be raped twice as an adult before he could reconnect with his split-off trauma in his very early life.

Matthew was anally raped by a peer during adolescence. During adulthood he has also been raped – something he now sees has a positive aspect in that it helped him to face-up to and deal with his earlier rape. James also commented on the fact that his later rape had helped him to deal with other parts of his life. This leads me to wonder if, unconsciously, the men had re-enacted their childhood victimisation through their rape in adulthood. I do not wish to imply by this that they had in some way 'made this happen' or to deny the rapists full responsibility for the rape; rather that it may be that there was a certain inevitability about it as a part of the way to healing. Both men struggle with a sense of being responsible in some way for their abuse. James, in that he allowed himself to be coerced and Matthew in that he was not 'macho' enough to fight back or resist during his adolescent rape and that he had allowed himself to become drunk and unable to defend himself when he was raped as an adult. It may be that this sense of being responsible might stem from a partly conscious belief that in some way the healthy part of their mind did allow the rape.

Both men blame themselves for not being strong or macho enough to prevent their abuses; they see themselves as 'effeminate' and Matthew's story particularly demonstrates the powerful impact of the socialisation messages from his father, his schoolteachers and the male dominated environment of his secondary school. Whereas a female victim might focus on her feelings of exploitation and of being 'damaged goods', a male victim seems to focus more on feelings related to having been unable to protect himself. This failure to protect himself is often seen as a reflection on his lack of masculinity. Matthew responded to this feeling by attempting to confirm his adequacy as a male by entering into frequent relationships with females, each relationship confirming his heterosexuality in his eyes. For some men their need to re-assert themselves as masculine can lead to extreme macho behaviour which they perceive as 'normal' for a 'real man'. This response has been described by other men I interviewed (Mike, Tim and Robert).

A healthy male is usually physically aroused by genital stimulation and may also be aroused by fear and when these two phenomena come together during a rape, the man can confuse arousal with consent; erection with pleasure and ejaculation with orgasm. Sarrel and Masters (1982) show evidence that a male can respond sexually to abuse even though his emotional state at the time is negative (terror, humiliation or embarassment). The victim will often feel unable to perceive what happened as rape and feel responsible because of their interpretation of their physiological response. This sense of responsibility can prevent the victim from feeling anger towards the rapist; this might be explained in terms of attribution theory, which allows the victim to gain a sense of control over the future and an illusion of safety by attributing what has happened to himself rather than the perpetrator. Matthew's story demonstrates how he has coped by blaming himself for getting drunk and therefore attributing the rape experience to something that in future he has some mastery over. He also draws attention to the need for the right kind of support following rape and raises some questions about the gender of the helper.

These stories also demonstrate the difference between a man who has worked in therapy for several years and a man who has had very brief counselling.

James's story

James is 24 years old; he is single, unemployed and has no children. He had an older brother and younger sister. He described his home as 'emotionally cold'. His father left home when James was 17 and it was at that time he discovered that his father had been in prison for the twelve months after his birth, having been caught embezzling money at work. James had never felt connected with his father whom he remembered as devious, self-centred and violently abusive to James, his mother and his brothers.

His parents in their earlier lives had been radicals and James was taught a form of equality. Although never overtly socialised in extreme gender roles the covert messages he received from his father's demonstration of violence must have been concerned with male power and inequality. He had been taught ballroom dancing rather than how to play football as a child. He learned ballet when he was 15-years-old and never identified with what he called 'the rugby playing shit heads' at school. His best friends at school were girls or the more 'effeminate' boys.

He told of his abuse:

I was abused when I was 12 for definite – (long pause) I'm beginning to believe that I was abused when I was 5 or 6 by my mum; it's something I am working on in therapy at the moment (see footnote) and I had dreams about nine months ago about my father anally abusing me. In the dream I am very small and totally helpless. I have difficult connecting with that emotionally – I go numb – it's really very difficult but I'm starting to work on that in therapy as well – so I don't actually know. I've never lost the memory of the episode when I was 12; it is really clear. That was a stranger; he took us into this tunnel at a disused railway where we used to play and he removed my clothing and did things to my friend and me.

While he was sucking me he put his finger up my anus. At the time I shut off – I dissociated – my body went totally numb. I didn't tell anybody; I had massive guilt for years and years. I'd done something wrong; I'd made this happen – I felt dirty. I think he said that we shouldn't tell anybody because between us we'd broken the law and I took that as I'd broken the law. On a physical level I wasn't aware of anything going on for me during the abuse; I hadn't reached puberty then.

I felt dirty and ashamed; that there was something wrong with me, that I got myself into that situation – it was my responsibility. I didn't recognise at all that I'd been manipulated or coerced. I felt as if there was something inherently wrong with me that made him do it to me. A couple of years later my pal and me were in a youth club and he said 'if any man ever did that to me again I'd kick him in the bollocks'. I told him I was dealing with this stuff and he said, 'oh, I couldn't tell anybody, there's too much shame there'.

I'm not sure how it has affected me. When I went to college I was very political within the student movement. There were all sorts of issues being debated and when it came to rape I seemed to have some level of understanding that male friends and colleagues didn't seem to have. They were repeating something they had heard not something they'd experienced. I remember getting into a serious argument with a couple of women about whether men could be raped or not. I came very close to disclosing then. I wanted to say 'It is possible'.

For a 16-year-old I was very political. I was in CND, a labour party member at 15, involved in anti-apartheid; a member of the Trade Union as well as the Student Union; on the management committee of the local Labour Party; an activist. It was my anger that motivated me. I was angry about this, angry about that. I felt angry about any injustice I saw – it was a good survival mechanism.

Because of peer pressure, I had a girl friend when I was 15; we used to walk home together and hold hands; we might have kissed each other on the cheek a couple of times, but it went no further than that. It was only because it was the done thing (having a girl friend). She was really more interested in studying and I had just realised for the first time that I'd better do some school work – it was in the fourth or fifth year. A couple of friends and I would get a bottle of cider and we'd sit down by the river and get drunk every weekend; it didn't take an awful lot of alcohol to get us pissed – we'd be sick.

I spent a year at College. I didn't really have any particular interest in girls or anybody; then I moved College because the course wasn't what I wanted and I had a girl friend; we used to give each other massages and we went out for a couple of months – for me there was never any sexual feeling in the relationship at all.

I used to masturbate – it was a release that was all. It was very much 'I don't want these feelings, I'll get rid of them.' It was an addiction really – quite compulsive. Quite often it would be when I was supposed to be doing something and I'd get these sexual feelings and masturbate and I wouldn't be doing what I was supposed to be doing. I was always ashamed of my sexuality. The only way I used to gain sexual release was by imagining people hurting me. It is still a problem now.

I think I would say I am bi-sexual but there is massive confusion about that. I know I'm attracted to women. I have slept with men. Until very recently all of my sexual relationships were very abusive. It's only in the past two years that I've started to choose healthy sexuality for myself; to make a conscious choice. I have an attraction to men and at the moment I'm also extremely scared of men. I get close to a man and I get panic attacks. It's the same with women but not to the same intensity. I recognise that my earlier abuse caused a destruction of my boundaries and because my healing has started from the rapes and without consciously working on it, things started to connect together and then a few months later, after meeting another survivor and hearing part of her story, I actually realised. I just cried and cried and cried – it was the pain in me that had finally found some release.

I've actually been raped twice as an adult and that's partly because of me not having boundaries and not being able to detect when something is wrong. Both times I was raped by people I knew; one person I'd known for a couple of years, one I'd met and known for a couple of days. The second time I was extremely stoned on drugs. This was about seven days after my Nan had died (I had been her carer for a period before she died of cancer). There was a festival going on and this guy seemed really nice and I was just hanging around with him. We went off to this secluded place to talk. He kept on propositioning me and I said 'no – I don't want this'; he said 'yes, you do' and then he started removing my clothing and I just went … again, I went numb. I couldn't do anything and it ended up with him touching me and crouching over me and masturbating over me.

I do connect those events with the abuse as a child. I think about how I am now; I'm in a very different place now than I was eighteen months ago.

The person who did this to me was another man; he is part of me, part of a collectiveness. I ask myself 'Is this part within me as well?' I know this is an issue for me and for other survivors I've talked to. I don't have a very strong sense of my masculinity. It's not a problem now for me to see that I was victim. I know how I feel and I've learned to connect with my anger. Two years ago I didn't see that I was a victim; it was something that could happen but it wasn't something that did happen. Before that I had felt as if it was my fault. I knew I didn't encourage him but I thought I had allowed myself to be coerced. He offered us several hundreds of pounds. It was more subtle than that though – sort of hinting at what he might want or what he wanted us to do and what he was going to do but not being explicit or direct about it. Saying things like 'this is something we all do – all your friends are doing this'. Persuading us it was totally natural; that it was right, or it wasn't wrong.

The first person I told was my dad. I told him over a beer and a game of pool one Sunday afternoon when I was 18 or 19. He told me to stop being silly and making a fuss about nothing. I felt angry and pissed off with his response but I couldn't tell him that. I shut up and immediately took on 'it's not important, it's irrelevant' and I ignored it for the next few years. The first time I disclosed after that I was in a gathering of forty anarchists, activists who had come together one evening; they had a 'go round' of feelings. It started with the woman who was upset talking about how it was to be a survivor – how it had affected her life and from that I had the courage to disclose; it was actually a very safe space.

By the time I had told my father I was beginning to think it might have been abuse. I wasn't totally sure; I'd started to hear things in the media about sexual abuse in children's homes and I had started to think about it and I was really asking a question; I asked my dad.

I was 16 when I first began to feel confused or unsure about my gender. I think it was when I first started seeing myself as an individual and not just as my parent's child and I started getting a sense of my own identity. Sometimes I wish I wasn't a sexual being. I very rarely obtain sexual satisfaction. I have body memories of pain during sexual activity. I know that my body feels pain in different parts when I have sexual responses.

From my early teens homosexuality wasn't frowned upon in my home; my mum worked in a pub where they had a gay night – it wasn't something that we explicitly talked about but I knew it existed and that people were like that and that you accepted them for how they were, be that black, white, gays, straight.

About a year before I realised about the abuse, when I was about 17, I tried to commit suicide by taking an overdose but I got the drugs all mixed up and one lot counteracted another lot and it didn't work.

I am on Income Support with a disability premium. I went on working for two months after disclosure; then I realised I couldn't work. I was a care assistant at an elderly person's home. I would get up in the morning and sit on the side of my bed and sit for five hours or more staring into space. I was spaced out – no connection with anything – no connection between my mind and my body at all.

I've been in prison twice – nothing particularly major – attempted burglary and deception. I use drugs; I'm a lot more controlled now – I have more knowledge. Drugs can be very useful at times. I've tried most things apart from coke but mainly its cannabis. I was very easily manipulated – I always went along with things other people said; I put that down in part to the destruction of my boundaries. I had a very unclear sense of what my values and standards were. My anti-social behaviour was almost like me saying, 'I don't care, I'm in pain and I need help.' I needed things to help me feel better and because I live in a society where you have to achieve to get these things, I find myself in need of money. (I've never particularly succeeded in terms of a paid job.) When I was 19 I was unemployed and on reduced Income Support. I needed money to live on. I was living with a woman fourteen years older than me and she wanted me to give her £30 per week, I was only getting £17 – then there was food. It was one of the longest relationships I had. It lasted three years. It was a sexual relationship and it was very abusive.

I'm not clear about when I was first sexually abused. I have suspicions that I was ripe for it when I was 12 because I'd been abused before. I have very strong suspicions... there are all these different things angles that point to it like huge arrows and I'm working towards getting to see the total picture. I'm very certain, but not 100 per cent certain, that I was abused much earlier.

I saw a psychoanalyst, who called himself a therapist at a NHS hospital; he denied my reality and told me I was fantasising, that I was imagining things. That's where psychoanalysis goes wrong because it's based on a theory that things have to fit; instead of 'here's my story, what can I learn about myself'. If it doesn't fit the model then it can't be true. That process devalues the survivor's reality and truth; it can be used as a form of denial – used to suppress memories.The most important person within the therapeutic situation is the client and the person's reality is the most important thing. That has to be valued and often it is not. I feel strongly about that.

Footnote: Six months after this interview James told me that he now remembers that he was anally abused around the ages of 3–5 years – he is fairly sure it was his father and maybe also his grandfather. His father was in prison during the first year of James's life and his mother says he was never left alone with his father as a young child – so this confuses him. He was frequently left in the care of his paternal grandparents.

Matthew's story

Matthew was born in 1960; he has no children and is in a settled homosexual relationship which he regards 'as good as being married'; he is a business man. He has an older brother and sister. His father had been a publican and was then studying to become a psychiatric nurse. His mother had been a music teacher prior to his birth. She had been seriously ill a year before his birth when she had fallen off her bicycle and fractured her skull. This developed into epilepsy and ultimately led to her death when she was 52 and Matthew was 22. One of the side effects was that she was severely ill during most of Matthew's life.

Matthew remembers being very much loved and cared for as a child. His earliest memories were of him not understanding why his mother was sitting at the table crying and of his presence being ignored – something that he felt was quite common during his early life. At the same time he spoke of having a happy childhood with a lot of attention, love and care – he believed he was 'very lucky'. He saw that his brother and sister had a much stricter upbringing and that they were unhappy children; they do not share his own view of his life as 'happy'.

He knew his mother had fought against other people's wish for her to have aborted him because of her illness; he saw himself as 'prized and precious' which made it very nice for him but very unpleasant for his sister who had been sexually abused by an uncle when she was 6 and again at 14 and became a desperately unhappy, very unstable child. He saw his older brother as a bully, his sister as the one who was blamed when things went wrong and himself as a contented child who used to play brother and sister off against one another.

When his mother was not depressed she became alive and vivacious. She filled the house with music, games and books and gave him a lot of attention; but when she came off the tablets or when they were reduced or changed, she was depressed and would often sit and cry for no apparent reason. As she got better she would cry with frustration.

His brother and sister left home when they were 17 and his father, like a lot of fathers, would come home late or he would want to go out for a drink to unwind; he was a weekend father. His mother therefore was left very much on her own; she was bored, she was unhappy, and he felt that was 'dumped' on him because there was nobody else there.

He went on to say:

She was powerfully affectionate; she would touch you; say she loved you, do things for you, she tried to be a good mother, she would listen when you came home from school, she was a caring woman; but when she was in the depths of depression, it was as if someone had pulled the shutters down and she was looking through them. When I was about 10 she had a *grand mal* epileptic fit. It was quite funny, I was only in the room above her and I came down and saw my mother being carried out of the house on a stretcher (laughs); nobody would tell me what was going on. My father's attitude was always that if you didn't need to know you didn't get told.

I know he loves me very dearly but he never showed his affection; he's a bit of a cold fish. He'll tell me he loves my brother and sister and he'll tell them he loves me but he'll never tell any of us directly. There wasn't any real need for discipline because I was one of those nauseatingly good children who could be described as 'professionally cute'; I was fairly placid and easy going and it meant I enjoyed things.

As a little boy I don't think I was as soft or as effeminate as some of my relatives say I was. It was difficult for me to have good masculine examples because all I had was my brother and I loathed the way he was such a bully. My father who was this austere, kindly but distant and unemotional man who you saw at weekends and bedtime, was obsessed with things like shutting the door properly and table manners; all the minutiae of being a proper middle-class person rather than anything macho – he never took me to a football match or played cricket with me – just as well because I hate them.

I was fortunate to have a grandmother two streets away who lived with a maiden aunt and I was more or less brought up by them. I played with a mixed group of boys and girls at school and at home I played with my little girl friend; we used to like dressing up games and because her mother was a widow, there were only female clothes in her house, so we used to end up with me in dresses. People would laugh and say 'isn't that sweet'. It did change when I was 9 and we moved; I was suddenly surrounded by boys, and I didn't like any of them – they were quite rough and they didn't like me. Looking back they probably thought I was a bit of a wimp. I had the misfortune to wear National Health glasses and it was a source of misery for me because I did look funny.

I think my mother was determined to treat me differently from the way my brother was brought up; he had a much more conventional upbringing. She taught me how to knit a jumper for my teddy bear. I used to make that awful grey pastry that children make. I think boys do this sort of thing quite happily but they don't usually get much opportunity.

When my sister was about 14 and I was about 10, she suddenly opened her dressing gown and showed me her newly developing breasts and made me touch her; as soon as I put my finger on it she told me I musn't. Very contradictory; I thought nothing of it but I haven't forgotten. My parents didn't discuss sex with us but my mother was usually open to discussing things. We had basic sex lessons at junior school and I remember asking the teacher embarrassing questions which she didn't know the answers to.

I hadn't been bullied at primary school except by the headmaster. I wouldn't play football and I played with girls. I think I was what he would have called 'effeminate' – he was an old fashioned rugby playing Welsh man. He used to tell me I should be a man! He called my parents in and my father told him to 'mind his own bloody business' and if his son wanted to play with the girls it was nice to know his son had a healthy interest in the opposite sex! In a boys secondary school you can't go around behaving like that if you don't want to be picked on and I didn't. I played the part of being the 'aloof intellectual'. I was sailing along at the top of my stream, winning school prizes, and spent all my time trying to get out of playing rugby.

I was at an all-boys' secondary school and it was when I was in the third year aged 14, that I was assaulted by a kid in my class, Christopher – looking back he was very much a homosexual – certainly he was distinctly odd and very disturbed. Suddenly in the end of the second year, he started showing rather an undue interest in the other boys' genitals – much to everybody's fury. He would flick people's genitals with towels when we had showers. He started to show a lot of interest in me which I didn't particularly like and, with typical ambiguity, I also found it exciting – so I gave him 'go away' and 'come here' messages.

I used to find all sorts of excuses to get out of metalwork and it was a noted habit of mine to go to the loo. He followed me there and grabbed my genitals; I got an erection and, having thoroughly enjoyed getting the erection, I then told him to get lost and then went back to the lesson having re-arranged myself. After that he pestered me. I was getting bullied a lot at school until, ironically, about two weeks before I got attacked by Christopher. A kid from another class hit me in the head quite sharply and, after two years of being bullied, I lost control and smashed him into the ground – which made my reputation.

In the classroom Christopher manoeuvred himself to sit next to me and he continually groped me. I didn't know what to do. I used to get so embarrassed and frustrated and wish that the teacher would do something to stop it. The English master did see it and did nothing. I didn't have any strategy for dealing with most crises that involved anything physical. Dealing with somebody being upset was one thing but dealing with somebody threatening you or embarrassing you physically – I didn't have a clue.

When he finally assaulted me fully, I had done my usual trick at half past three and went off to the loo for twenty minutes. Within a minute, I saw Christopher following me so I immediately went into a cubicle; the cubicles usually had locks on them but they had had a spate of vandalism and they had taken the locks off and I didn't know that. I went in, shut the door and the damn thing didn't lock. There I was, sitting on the loo pretending I wanted to go and he just walked in and I was trapped. Considering I had beaten the living daylights out of a kid just a few weeks before you'd think I'd have had the gumption to have thumped him, but I didn't. Normally when I was cornered I used to talk my way out or run away – I wasn't used to hitting. I'd hit the other kid two weeks before because I'd lost control which was the only time since very early childhood. He grabbed my genitals and I got an erection immediately and he was pressing me, rubbing and I was trying to push him away, rather feebly; I was scared because kids go the loo and the last thing you want is to be caught or your reputation would be ruined – I was having a bad enough time as it was, so I was anxious to just get out of there but I was wedged down the bottom of the bloody wall. If I'd been a macho kid, I'd have punched him on the nose and got the cane for that and he'd have let me alone; it wouldn't have been such a problem, but I wasn't macho.

It was a very good position to put someone at a disadvantage because with trousers round the bottom of the loo and the rest of you over the top you are trapped by you own clothing. I was forcibly buggered – if I had fought harder, I could probably fought him off but I didn't fight hard enough; I was scared and once I felt the shock of the pain of him going in, I just wanted it over with. The effect was pretty awful; at the time I was a bit shaky but I went back to the metalwork class with about one minute to go and he walked in thirty seconds later with a grin from ear to ear. I did what I was very good at – I put on a face as if nothing had ever happened.

It was a one-off – it didn't happen again. I didn't tell anyone until I was 23. Who do you say it to? You don't want anybody to know. What does a boy of 14 say – I had a pretty good guess what my father would say. In fact, years later my sister was raped pretty horrifically and she told my father and he turned round and said 'what did you do to cause that', which wasn't the greatest thing for a psychiatric nurse or any father to say. I had predicted he would say that to her and he said exactly the same to me when I told him when I was 28. I'm a clever plonker – I've been raped twice, I got raped again at 27.

After that episode at school my confidence collapsed. There I was, supposedly suddenly redeemed in the eyes of my colleagues because of beating up the bully, but I had no confidence at all. I became very careful. I only went to the toilet at play times. He didn't get another opportunity. Christopher suddenly backed off – maybe he realised he had gone too far but he also became the victim of bullying himself not long after that – it was nothing to do with me.

If I had been caught with a woman, my kudos would have been through the roof at a boys' school – there would have been ribald humour, everyone would have been grinning about it – you'd have been proud. I don't think I would have seen it as abuse – whether one should or not is another matter. But you don't do it with other men do you? It's not done – it's just a taboo.

What on earth would I say to my mother? In practical terms there was the surety that my mother would do something about it and because she was the sort to complain, that meant it would all come out. She would have been very good I suspect. She would have done what you want someone to do; she would have cried, she would have cared, she'd have made me a cup of tea and listened. She was good like that.

If you keep your mouth shut then nobody is going to accuse you of wanting it; nobody is going to accuse you of causing it, encouraging it. As I was a bit of a wimp, I was a prime candidate for that accusation. In a very aggressively masculine boys' school, you had to be very careful about your behaviour and reputation. Where you've got mainly male teachers, setting a very aggressive male standard, you can't risk it coming out. Three months after that we moved and I went to a mixed school, and along with any other boy who wasn't a macho shit-head, I was called a poof.

As a teenager I didn't trust my father not to turn round and blame me – as an adult he turned round and blamed me. I think I was wrong to think that at 14; I think, looking back that he would have seen me as his little boy. When I told him about my rape when I was 28 I threw the whole lot at him in one go. I was driving his car and when he asked me what I had done to cause it, I swerved right across the road, through the hedge and back again – I think this gave him an accidental demonstration that this wasn't the thing to say. He did have the good grace, for the first time in his life, to apologise.

How on earth do you tell your mother that this has happened? It took me weeks to get round to telling my father and then I only told him because it was turning into a race between me and my brother and sister, who I had just told, and I couldn't rely on them to keep their gobs shut; childishly perhaps, I wanted to say it first. My mum knew something was up because when we moved from Devon she became very, very concerned and very, very gentle – she would talk to me and she would make a thing of touching me because I couldn't bring myself to touch anybody. It might sound a cliché but I felt soiled. I felt like that for years and if someone touched me, male or female, I would shiver, freeze. My mother always touched me and refused to let me get away from it, not aggressively. She was good like that.

We had a tremendous clash when the 'Naked Civil Servant' came on TV in 1976 or so. My father had gone to the pub and my mother and I sat and watched it. She was sitting there saying 'isn't he nice, isn't he wonderful' and I said 'I think he's ghastly, he's revolting' and she looked at me most surprised; we didn't pursue it although we discussed it intellectually. My father's best friend was an effeminate grand dame of an old queen, and he used to come and stay. He was very sweet. I was frightened of homosexuality. I didn't like it and it was also because there had been abiguity in what had happened; it hadn't been as if I'd fought manfully to the last or been taken against every last drop of my will – I'd caved in. I didn't want to deal with that, I didn't want to believe it. That was something that happened when you were a teenager – when you grew up you had girl friends and I had a long series of girl-friends.

I've been in a homosexual relationship for the last five-and-a-half-years. That started immediately after the second rape. There was nothing between what happened at 14 until I had my first sexual relationship with a girl at 18. I was between girl friends when my mother died at 22 and you don't really feel like having a relationship – so there was gap there until I was nearly 24 and then I'd split up with Pam when I was about 27 and about five months later I was raped by my hairdresser's boyfriend.

I was trying to be a terribly broad-minded adult and accept the sexuality of other people and to ignore the fact that this might have some rub off effect on my reputation. I thought it was time I put that sort of behaviour behind me. It was also a way of finally overcoming and putting to rest what had happened to me when I was 14. When I was 14 I don't think I had any thought about my sexual orientation – I thought I was like anybody else until Christopher assaulted me. My confidence went and because I wasn't a macho kid people called me a poof and I took it to heart; whereas before I had a fair amount of bravado and refused to take it to heart. I think I used to wonder all the time and then when I got a girl friend, that was proof to me that I wasn't gay – although my very first girl friend and I didn't do anything. But it didn't stop the taunts until we got to the sixth form; then it was grown up to ignore anybody like that because they were being childish, but my confidence on sexual matters ran down. Each girl friend was proof that it wasn't true; I had a very satisfying sexual relationship with women that I thoroughly enjoyed and I responded perfectly normally; in some ways I was right to destroy the doubts.

I decided at 27 that it was about time that I dealt with all that. My hairdresser and I became good friends; I knew he was gay and I thought I would dispel some of these prejudices. He wanted to bring his boy friend to dinner and I was very much into cooking and I said 'fine'. The boy friend arrived but the hairdresser didn't (he'd fallen asleep on his own bed). I'd already had a couple of pints of Guinness while I'd been cooking something in wine and we had a bottle of red wine and a bottle of Port with the meal (and I'm allergic to Port so I shouldn't have drunk it). Then we had something else and then we went to the pub and eventually I had to be carried to my bed. I wasn't in a position to say yes, no or anything. I don't remember being asked but I don't remember saying no. I did think he should have known better than to go to bed with someone who is leglessly drunk. It wasn't my own fault but I didn't help matters by being blind drunk. It was pretty traumatic and it was very violent. Because I was so drunk it wasn't altogether clear. I must have put up some fight because I was covered in bruises the next day. I didn't have a single bruise in a place that showed. He'd certainly been very clever. I couldn't sit still and I couldn't stand up.

Ironically the man I now live with is an outrageous 'fairy'; he was incredibly camp the first time I met him at a party; he was wearing dungarees with no socks on and pink ribbon sandals and a pink bandanna round his head. I didn't like him – I hated him – he used to make me cringe.

I think it would be technically correct to say I'm ambi-sexual (as my uncle put it). That means that I enjoy sexual relations and it is not so important to me what sex the other person is. I don't know if it's anything to do with being abused. My partner knew he was different as a small boy and as soon as he reached puberty he knew he liked boys.

I'm in a relationship which I regard as good as a marriage; sex with somebody else outside our relationship is not breaking the rules between us, as long as it is not in my bed. As things stand I wouldn't have a relationship with a woman because I don't think it would be fair to her because there are so many more emotions usually tied up with sex with a woman; she would be worrying, fretting – wondering 'did he lie to me, has he got AIDS , will he give me a disease?'

I've just taken a blood test for AIDS and I'm negative and I'm immunised against hepatitis B just in case my partner ever gets it. Another reason for the test was that last year I was asked to father a child by a lesbian couple – the woman turned out to be sub-fertile so it was all a bit of a wasted effort but it is something I'd like to have another go at. I can't have children and that for me is quite a tragedy in my life. I find that I talk about my sexuality an awful lot because other people want to talk about it and that's a bit of a drag. I would love to be Mr Macho man but I'm not. Life's a lot easier for Mr Macho man.

My father finds it very hard to accept my homosexuality. When I first told him about my rape and that I was living with a man, he said I could come for dinner but I couldn't stay – not even on my own and certainly not with my partner, even in separate rooms.

My sister was abused as a child by my mother's brother-in-law. In fact all my female cousins in my mother's family were, nobody has ever dared asked his two daughters if he did it to them. She says now as an adult she can look back and say 'I've recovered and it doesn't matter but as a child it was bloody awful'. My sister was also raped as an adult. If you are brought up with parents who love you and care, you are inclined to be trusting. We were brought up in a very moral, Christian family – we were innocents abroad. My brother seems to have picked up a bit of street nous which we didn't.

I don't know how many problems the abuse has caused me. I don't have any sexual difficulties now but I did have difficulties with my last girl-friend. She kept raising about my abuse and seemed to use it as an excuse for me being too tired for sex even when I had been working late. I once had a dream about making love to mother. I had a hit and run conviction once for failing to report an accident to the police.

I coped when I was 14 by closing down. My academic standards fell through the floor initially and then I hauled them back up. Time doesn't heal but I'm a great one for putting things I don't want to deal with on the shelf and then taking them off again later and thinking why on earth did I worry about that? The 14-year-old rape did a lot of harm because it stopped me being able to enjoy simple things like touching people or being able to joke about anything sexual – I used to die a death when people talked about sex. It stopped me being able to enjoy the rough and tumble, to play rugby without fearing that people would turn round and accuse me of touching them. I'm terrified of that sort of thing; I used to get terrible nightmares about it. My behaviour was withdrawn and I didn't really care and I think it did spoil for me my relationships with girls because I was always trying to prove to myself that this hadn't happened and that it hadn't had any affects, instead of just accepting that it had happened and that I needed some help.

Ironically when it happened at 27 my reactions were better because I knew what not to do. It took me a while to get over the shock; I lost a stone and a half in weight in six weeks. Again I was traumatised and I went onto auto-pilot. When I wasn't working I just used to sit looking out of the window and then after six weeks I finally went to see the GP who asked me why I hadn't been to the police – I told him he must be barmy. I said 'do you really think I'm going to go to the police and admit I've done this?' He said 'you haven't done anything' and I said 'I don't know if that is how the defence would see it'.

I decided the one thing I wanted to do was to meet the man who had done it – and I did. I could have done without meeting him in a pub completely unexpectedly. I bought him a drink and felt really proud of myself. He didn't notice but I was gripping the bar and my knuckles were white 'cos if I took my hand off the bar they would have been shaking. I didn't accuse him because I don't think he would have understood. To be fair he has got an argument; as an adult you are responsible for your own actions to some extent. It was up to me to make sure that I didn't make myself so vulnerable especially as I'm the sort of person who doesn't look after myself.

He was entirely responsible for raping me and I was entirely to blame for getting drunk so that I couldn't do something about it. It was important for me to be able to forgive him. I didn't forgive Christopher. To not forgive is to twist yourself up with hate and I don't think it does you any good; it might for a while, but forgiveness is part of having compassion and letting go and forgiveness isn't words, it's doing something. Bruises don't hurt me. I've been beaten up before. I think most men have been as a teenager or as an adult.

I've felt suicidal and even attempted to do it in a way. I'd been brought up in the Plymouth Brethren and suicide was a mortal sin so you didn't do it; so you had to get someone else to do it for you – in a sense. So my technique wasn't to take pills or anything – it was to step out in front of traffic and if you are going to do it you might as well do it properly – the last thing you wanted was to step out in front of a car and get badly injured – you want to get out in front of a truck and get smashed. I got clipped once. I was ambiguous about what I was doing and I would step out too early or too late. I would shut my eyes. I did that for a while and I didn't tell anybody – I did tell my brother but he didn't take me very seriously. I'm not certain if I really wanted to die. I wanted to put my life in the hands of chance. I didn't want to make the decision because it would have been a mortal sin. I think I wanted someone to ask me what the matter was but nobody ever did. Nobody ever asked me about anything. It used to be a bugbear of mine. Part of this was that my sister was seriously mentally disturbed throughout our teen years. She had a complete depressive breakdown. She made some major suicide attempts with pills and was found at the last minute; I was completely overshadowed by that. This went on all the way into my adult life right up to three months before my mother died.

Now when I look back on what happened at 14, I was upset but in physical terms far worse things could happen; a one-off incident is less than a long sequence of events. The consequences for me were far longer. I see it has had a negative impact on my life. I can see positive aspects of the second one because I then dealt with the first one.

I had counselling very briefly from the CPNs. They sent some chap and a female student with him. She did most of the talking. I responded very well to her but I loathed the chap – I thought he was awful. I did not want a man there. She had that natural ability and human warmth; he was very analytical and probing, very good – he probably would have made me tackle things but what I needed was some human kindness. On the last meeting she said to me 'the first time I saw you I thought you were going to cry and I could have hugged you' and I thought 'Oh God, I wish you had – that was what I needed' because nobody hugged me and let me cry in their arms. That's what I needed. I saw them for three sessions. It took six weeks from when the doctor referred me – so that was twelve weeks after it had happened that they saw me.

14 Men abused by people known to them who were not family members

In this chapter we meet two men who were abused by people known to them who were not members of their family. According to statistics drawn up by the NSPCC, in only 14 per cent of cases is the abuser a stranger to the child: 86 per cent of these crimes are perpetrated by relatives or people known to the child. Children who are identified by abusers as emotionally deprived or in need of adult attention and care are most likely to be singled out for such attention. For the child any attention is better than none. Children have a right to expect love and attention from the adults who care for them and when these needs are not met the child will seek it from whatever source is available. This might put the child at risk of abuse from teachers, sports coaches, scout masters, clergy or any adult normally entrusted with the care of a child.

In this chapter we meet Jeremy who was born to a 17-year-old girl, and although he was loved by his mother, he was deprived of the security of a family in which he could feel safely contained. His father was absent for most of his early life and his mother was caught up with the need to earn enough money to keep them both and the struggles of her own incomplete life. His early abuse by male babysitters, his later abuse by two adolescent girls and his inappropriate exposure to sexuality in general, has left him confused and angry. Although his mother validated him as a person, his father's socialisation messages were that he should keep any pain he felt to himself; as a male he should not be 'a loser' and a loser was someone who was emotionally needy. When a person is not able to acknowledge deep emotional pain in a healthy way, they may go though life trying to find ways of avoiding it, anaesthetising themselves from it or acting it out. Jeremy used drugs and sex as his way of coping; even up to recent times he is still trying to work out his abuse in relationships with men and women. His abuse began so early in his life that he is still confused about his sexual identity. Same-sex abuse contradicts the 'normal' sexual behaviours of the majority of society. As his father was absent during the stage at which he would normally pass through the Oedipal phase and the men who were around were identified by him as 'prats', he may have found it difficult to form a sense of gender identity.

The second story is that of Justin whose home life was dominated by his warring parents. He sought comfort during their rows with his neighbour who betrayed his trust and vulnerability and abused his sexuality. Justin describes the process that many other subjects have identified – the recognition of the experience as 'abuse' during early adolescence. The pre-pubescent child may have accepted what was happening as 'normal', even if it was not experienced as pleasant – he has no way of naming his experience because sexual matters are not openly discussed in most families. As the realisation dawns, so the distress is felt, sometimes coinciding with the powerful upsurge in hormonal changes which accompanies puberty. Justin told his parents what had happened to him but they did not realise the damage it had done. Society denies the damage such experiences could cause a child. After all, the belief until recently has been that abuse doesn't really happen to boys and if it does, because they are males, they probably enjoyed it or at least didn't mind it. Or maybe it was too shameful for them to acknowledge that something has happened to their child whilst they have not been paying attention; perhaps they feared their son was homosexual or would become homosexual. Maybe it seemed better to ignore it and hope it would go away!

Another point raised in this and Jeremy's case, is that the parents have chosen not to report their knowledge of the abuse to the statutory agencies because they fear the extra exposure of their child and have negative expectations of the outcome; the child may not be believed or he may have to appear in court and eventually gain nothing. Sadly this is a reality when many such cases come to the attention of the courts.

The Committee on Video Evidence, chaired by Judge Pigot, recommended in 1989 that a child witness should not have to attend court. An attempt to amend the Criminal Justice and Public Order

Bill to this effect failed in the House of Commons in April 1994. Thus the plight of child witnesses, recognised five years ago, still goes unremedied. In an article for the *Guardian* newspaper (Levy, 16 April 1994) the case of an 11-year-old girl who spent a period of six months awaiting the trial of a man convicted of assaulting her is described. Her parents requested that the Crown Prosecution Service allow her to testify by live video link from a nearby room and the court refused on the grounds that she was too old. She was assurred that screens would be in place so that her attacker would not see her and that he would not be allowed to shout at her. In spite of all these assurances, having waited six hours to be called, she was told that the defendant would be allowed to see her as he said he did not remember her. The man did shout at her in the court and she was requested to tell the court her name and address in the presence of her attacker who was convicted. She lives in fear that he will know where to find her when he is released.

The Pigot Committee recommended that child witnesses would not have to attend court. It recommended instead an initial videotaped interview, which the police would show the suspect. Later there would be a preliminary hearing before a judge in chambers, which would also be videotaped, when the defence would be allowed to cross-examine the child. These two tapes would thereby replace the child's appearance in the court. This proposal was supported by the NSPCC, the Law Society, Criminal Bar Association and the Council of Circuit Judges, among others. The Government however rejected it and instead the Criminal Justice Act 1991 allowed the initial videotaped interview to be used as the child's prosecution evidence as long as the child attended the trial to be cross-examined by the defence. This reflected the concern of the Home Office for the accused whose position, in their opinion, might otherwise be undermined.

Wattam (1989), however describes her research into the relationship between the legal and the therapeutic aims of the initial 'formal' interview which is videoed and used as evidence in allegations of sexual abuse. She expresses a concern that the way the video is used for legal proceedings means that the therapeutic value of such interviews might become an 'incidental by-product' and may indeed act against the best interests of the child.

In many countries including the US, Denmark, and even in limited circumstances in Scotland, children need not attend the court. In England and Wales the abused child is still expected to go through this additional ordeal. Even then, having gone through these procedures, the need for therapy is often overlooked and if the need is acknowledged, it may not be an available option, even in cases where the perpetrator has been convicted and punished.

Resources are not sufficient to meet the needs of all children and often social service resources are spent on uncovering abuse, bringing the perpetrator to justice and removing children to a safe environment rather than on healing the damaged child and family.

In both the case of Jeremy and Justin, the parent's decision deprived the child of the possibility of adequate care, protection and treatment. Jeremy went on to be abused by others over a long period of time and Justin received no help for his serious depression and sexual compulsivity. Both men express a degree of resentment towards their parents for this, whilst acknowledging that they understood their reasons. Justin acted out his aggression sexually and verbally and was seen as a nuisance to society. His behaviour was responded to in a punitive way, no-one sought to understand it. This, in turn, compounded his anger, resentment and sense of isolation. Another important issue raised by these cases, and also found in others in this study, is the sexual acting out of these boys. Jeremy admits that his main reason for giving the interview was his burning need to unburden his guilt about what he now saw as the abuse he perpetrated on a younger boy. He has carried the guilt of that alone for a long time.

One of the ways of coping with unconscious, severe emotional pain is to seek for external comfort through drugs, alcohol and sex. This is particularly true for those people who have a poor sense of 'self-intimacy' and an inability to soothe themselves from within. This ability is normally developed through the introjection of a 'good parent' when a child has been able to internalise the experience of having had its needs met during early childhood.

Jeremy's story

Jeremy is 19. He is at college and living at home with his mother who is expecting a baby. She was 17 when he was born and his father was 21. They weren't married. He lived with his father and mother for the first six months of his life at which time his mother left to find a place for her to take her baby; she came back and took him to live with her when he was 12-months-old. He saw his father once in a while after that but had little real contact until he went to live with him for a period when he was 12-years-old. His mother had boyfriends who lived with them from time to time – he referred to these men as 'prats'. He sees fathers as a 'let down because they have other things to do and they don't really care'.

He described his mother as 'a kind, considerate person who has the time of day for anyone; a bit dotty and a nice person' who has been good to him. He finds it difficult to live with her now but, as she is pregnant, he 'just has to bear with her', as his father taught him he should show respect. He recognises that he has behaved badly towards his mother in the past.

He said:

My mum was a bit lax but when I was 15 she kicked me out because she couldn't control me. She was affectionate towards me; she made sure I was fed and clothed reasonably. My dad is a hard and fair man. I didn't really like him until about a year ago and then I realised he had my best interests at heart. I work for him sometimes. He likes me to work very hard for my money and he doesn't pay good wages but it's 'cash in hand'. He has taught me the value of money. I've made a lot and I've lost a lot of money in the past one way and another. I could spend £100 so quick but now that I have to work for it, I see the value of money. I was earning £2.50 an hour for him and I would be drinking a pint or smoking a whiff – you see it going away right before your eyes and I'd think 'oh my God I've just worked a week for that'.

I can't really remember which abuse started first. There was this Asian kid when I was 4 and he used to get me to perform oral sex on him; he would promise me that I could touch his girl friend up if I did that to him but it never happened. That went on for a year or two. My mum used to work nights a lot and she was in this Healing Group and she would get babysitters. There was this other guy who used to abuse me about twice a week regularly for about two years. Then it happened again when I was about 9 with the Asian guy again. I used to hang about with an older crowd than me and he did it then. It was all happening at the same time. When I was about 7, I used to do it with my friends. You don't see it as sex – you see it as fun. But because I'd been interfered with, I was doing it to them.

Then there was an episode about a year ago; it was me with a 40-year-old man. I was skint at the time – he never gave me money but I lived with him. He wasn't really an abuser because I knew what I was doing. That stopped six months ago. My friends found out and made me see what it for what it was and it made me feel sordid and disgusting, 'cos it was really. Some women stay with a man because they've got money and that is what it was like for me really I'm sorry to say.

As a child I was abused by oral sex; one abuser used to play with my willy a lot and one night he tried to fuck me (anal sex) and I got really scared because I was only young. I see him about now and I gob on him. Next time I'm going to mug him and take his money. Well I won't, but I will beat him up first and when the police turn up I'll say 'this bloke's a paedophile' and they will give him a kicking in the cells as well. I have confronted that guy. I saw the other one about a year ago and I looked at him and he knew that I remembered.

I haven't actually told the police about them.

About six months ago I would have said that I was bi-sexual, because I do like being with women as well as men, and I do fancy men but not as much as I do women. I'm more heterosexual now than homosexual but I suppose you would say I'm bi-sexual. I think my abuse has corrupted me – it stays in your mind and lingers. I find men physically attractive but going to bed is a different matter.

When people touched me when I was little, I used to think it was alright because I didn't know it was wrong. What messed me up in the recent case was that I started thinking that maybe it wasn't wrong when I was a kid after all; but it was wrong because I was too young then. When it happened last year I was making my own choice; I didn't have to be there. When I was little I did have to be there – they were looking after me.

I told my mum when I was about 7 – only about one of the abusers. It just slipped out in conversation; it wasn't because I wanted to tell her. I felt really pissed off with myself and her for telling. She freaked out and went round and had a serious go at him. I would have done the same if it had been my child – I'd have hurt them pretty badly. She didn't report him. I don't know why she didn't. I don't mind about that now – a couple of years ago I did. No, no – I've never cared about the police because at the end of the day, the chances of the kid getting it through the courts, it's hard. It would have been hard for me to deal with it. If the roles had been reversed, I would have just got my mates to have battered him to hell, then taken all his money and burnt his house down. When I see him next time I'll follow him back to his house and take all his money. I don't care if I go to prison for it. It would give me the satisfaction of really hurting him. Maybe I'll do something really horrible to him like cutting his knob off and chuck it in his mouth and say 'Suck that! Look what you made me do – you can do it yourself now'. There's no point in going to the law about it. They'd say it's his word against yours; it's more trouble than it's worth. It has happened – it has gone. I won't get compensation – it would satisfy me more to physically kill him.

After I told my mum about the one abuser she wouldn't let him within a 100 yards of me. She told me that when she found out about him I had a lot of resentment towards her because he used to tell me that it was our secret and I blamed her a lot for breaking the secret. She never knew about the other abuser. After that it was more me doing it with other kids. I don't think anyone, even me, realises the psychological damage it does. If I have children and anyone did it to my children, I'd kill them.

I think being abused has built up a lot of anger inside me. When I go to bed I think about it a lot and I think I'm a piece of shit and I shouldn't be here. Sometimes I worry about what my family thinks. When my dad first found out, he thought I might have been damaged in the head and that just did my head in; people knowing does my head in. It does my head in more when I think about the thing that happened recently than the thing in the past, because I feel guilty about living with that older man. I feel I have an equal responsibility and that it was wrong. In the normal straight world young kids don't sleep with an older man do they?

The fact that it was males who abused me made me think afterwards 'dirty bastards'. I used to say 'oh queers, stay away from me' but then I found out that two of my step-uncles are gay. It made me feel a bit uneasy. If you are homosexual, black, one-legged – everyone is equal. It's the person underneath that really counts. I didn't like gay people when I was a kid. When I first started remembering things (when I was about 13), I used to get really depressed about it and bottle it up inside. I didn't respect myself or other people. I think that had a quite a lot to do with why my mum kicked me out – because I didn't care.

I hadn't really forgotten, it was more that I made myself forget. You just block it out. It's not a thing you want brought up in your mind. Well actually, it's more a case of me finding out when I was 13 that it was wrong. Today I wholly resent those two people – not the more recent bloke. I just think he's a prat – he's gay. He's had charges brought against him for having sex with 13–14 year old kids but they were dropped. A lot of people have taken advantage of him, like I have. A lot of people used to rob him and then, when he said something to them, they came up with all these charges. He's not a paedophile – he's just a gay person who likes boys between 17 and 21. And that, officially, according to the law at the moment is illegal but he's not wrong. People are still biased – they are out of order to gay people. I am the one who defends him. I used him for money and he used me for sex. I didn't like having sex with him. I used to have several girl friends at the same time. I did a lot of drugs, amphetamines and acid so I didn't know what I was doing. I knew as I was walking up to his house that I would end up having sex with him; so it was my fault as much as his really. He's just a dirty old man – he's not an abuser. I had a choice. It used to bring back memories of when I was little – it was almost bad, that's what I got off on sometimes – the sordidness of it was a turn on. He used to say some dodgy things about kids if he was no abuser. You wouldn't know whether he was joking or not.

When I was living with him I was very 'camp'. After it finished I tried to be more macho to prove to myself that I'm not a poof because it started to interfere with my life. The real me is the camp one; I feel feminine a lot. When I see these macho blokes being like that for women I think 'you prats' – women think they are idiots and prefer to be with me rather than a macho man because I can relate to them. I can see the way men come onto women because it has happened to me. Like having sex when I really didn't want to with that bloke. I can see what they are at when they say 'no' and then they say 'oh fuck' – its easier just to do it.

The part I feel really weird and guilty about is what happened when I was about 9; there were three or four kids but the 7-year-old is the one I feel really guilty about. I hang about with the kid now and I can see it in his eyes sometimes when he looks at me – I feel I have corrupted him. Maybe I was his abuser. This is the bit I find hard to tell; I've never told anyone about it. We had anal sex – he did it to me. He was smaller than me so he couldn't take it. The one thing I don't feel so bad about is that it was him doing it to me. Maybe in a couple of years when he is older I can talk to him about it. I couldn't now because it might bring up a lot of shit for him and for me.

I don't know how he knew about how to do anal sex. I think maybe we were always brought up in an open world. Our eyes were open to everything at a young age. I remember hearing my mum having sex and seeing what they were doing. I didn't see it going in and out but I saw a man on top of a woman. I used to do it a lot with girls from about 6 or 7. One time when I was 8 – three girls of 11 and 12 did it to me. It wasn't really abusing because I liked it; they tried to make me penetrate them. I wasn't unwilling but they initiated it. I tried penetrating for the first time when I was about 10 and I succeeded. We just used to kiss and play mummies and daddies in the Wendy house but it was definitely more sexual than just playing games. I've always been very sexual. I feel as if I missed a lot of my childhood because of this. I grew up incredibly quickly. From about 10 upwards, I've always been the age I am now – 19. I've cut out a lot of my childhood. I can't really remember much.

The only thing that would make me feel better towards the ones who abused me is to have their bollocks chopped off … no. I don't feel that bad towards them really – only when I see them. I think 'you bastards you fucked me up' – because they did. I get severely depressed about it. I would never talk about how I feel; I never cry in front of anyone. I'd rather not burden them with my problems, they don't need it as much as I don't need it.

I've felt like committing suicide loads of times. My friend found me once when I'd taken some paracetamol. It was only after an hour and I drank a lot of water and puked them up so no one knew about it. I have fantasies about killing myself and I get rid of the pain. I suffer from a lot of internal pain, in my mind and in my heart, about men and about women and about my life. I feel as if I might be a loser. No-one knows the way I feel. I tried to tell a girl friend once and she just said 'don't be so stupid, pick yourself up and get on with it'. And that's when I started thinking I was damaged goods; I still feel it now when I go to sleep crying sometimes and I wake up crying and people say 'are you alright' and I say 'yes it's just the morning blues'. There's some sort of connection with women and my depression. When we've had sex and they go to sleep I get depressed. It's just some sort of weirdness in me. I just feel really lonely when they go to sleep.

I don't tell people how I really feel; I want them to see me as a normal person. I don't want it to affect their judgement of me. This is what messed me up about my dad for a long time – he said he doesn't like losers, he wants to be on the winning team. I will say I'm depressed but I don't say I feel suicidal because there's no point. I've dealt with it for so long. It's just good to get it out now.

I was a very mixed up little boy. I didn't know my sexuality; boys, girls, men – its all the same really. I have a good time when I have sex now because I gained experienced through the abuse. I'm told that I'm a good lover. It doesn't make up for it though – not at all. I didn't used to like people touching me – I wouldn't let people touch my willy. I couldn't take anyone coming close to me with their face; it reminded me of the abuse. I've never really masturbated. I don't really like it, it doesn't do anything for me. I've never been out of a relationship since I was 14, so I've always had someone to have sex with.

I have had anal sex when I was on acid and it sounds quite bad but I quite enjoyed it. I needed to be on acid to cut out the pain. I didn't really like it before. The bloke that I used to live with would try it quite a lot but I couldn't take it – it was really, really painful. I just liked being touched by a man. When I was having anal sex I felt like a woman, very feminine. I cover it up a lot now because I've started a new thing with the college and I don't want people to see what I am. In the straight society we live in, women, black people and homosexuals are still counted as second rate. All this equal opportunities stuff is a load of bollocks really – and if anyone says it isn't, they are either blind or ignorant.

I used to be very pale and I dropped from 10 stone to 9 stone and I was out of my head all day, everyday, but I don't do hard core drugs now. At weekends now I do ecstasy, I binge on cocaine maybe once every two months. I take quite a large quantity. I used to smoke quite a lot of dope but when I was working at my dad's for about four months and I used to have to get up quite early, I would have a dope hang-over and in the end I just stopped smoking except at the weekend. That was my carrot – at the weekend getting off my head.

I'm a free soul really – if I like something then I get it, so long as it isn't a kid. I used to look after children quite a lot and sometimes I had to do things that meant I had to touch their private parts – I used to have to put cream on this boy's willy and I hated doing it and this little girl's bum hurt and so I put some cream on it to calm it down and as soon as the woman came back I told her exactly what had happened. I didn't want the kid to say 'Mummy that Jeremy touched my bum'. If I found out someone was doing it to a kid then I would kill him – even it was my dad, I'd kill him because there is no justification for that. A child has no control over what is happening, they are too young to know what is happening – they've got no chance.

I was a nutter when I was a kid. I was seriously off my head. I was arrested for shop-lifting as a kid. I did engage in other illegal activities later that I don't want to mention. I didn't care – I was a drug addict at the time.

My mum used to hit me once in a while if I was a little prat. She just used to let me get on with my life which is bad because I just ruined it. The age gap between me and my mum – we were more like friends than she is my mother. You definitely need a guiding hand when you're a kid. When I bring up kids I'm going to be fair and strict – nine o'clock in bed. When I went to live with my dad it was a real shock and he was just being normal. I've always had a good life. You grow up in this world of fantasy and fiction and then you hit the outside world; it was hunger and poverty that made me see why you have to conform and why you have to go to work.

I've slept with between twenty and thirty females – if you count males it's more. The girls I've been with always want sex as much as I do. When I was with my first long-term girl friend she slept with about ten other people in the two years I was with her; it really messed me up for a long time. I thought it was alright to do that. I thought – who cares? I've been in my present relationship for two months and I don't want to go with anyone else. We used to go out with each other before but it didn't work; now we are both a bit more mature. Next time I don't have a boy friend or girl friend I want to try being single for a little while because I think I need it. I've always gone from one to the next. I think I am addicted to sex; I like it more than any drug. When I haven't got a girl friend I crave being with a girl but I won't masturbate. Maybe I'm not addicted because I don't masturbate. I don't like it. This bloke used to masturbate in front of me and I thought it was disgusting. I never said it to him because I wouldn't want to hurt his feelings.

I know exactly what I want in sex. I know how to be a lover. I know what they want 'cos I've had a man do it to me so I know what it must feel like for a woman to be touched, so I try and touch her in a way that she would want to be touched not in the way a man would want to touch a woman.

I might have contradicted myself in some things some of it's like two sides of me. It's like a straight side and a fucked up side. On the one hand I'm trying to be a normal person and on the other hand I want to be my real self.

People do need to know what people go through. I've been through a lot of mental shit. This is the stuff I can't get out to talk to you about. I can talk about some bloke making me suck his prick quite easily – it's not that, it's what it makes me feel in my heart that is hard to get out.

Justin's story

Justin is 26. He is single, unemployed and childless. He has one brother younger than him. His mother and father rowed about something every week until he was 13 or 14. The rows were quite frightening for him with a lot of screaming and shouting on both sides, slamming doors and banging things. Usually the row ended with his mother saying she was going to leave but she never did. Normally his mother was very loving and kind but after one of the rows she was remote and distant. Sometimes she would sit him on her lap and cuddle him; he remembers this as warm and safe.

His father was also loving and kind but after a row, he would sometimes cry and blame his wife, trying to get Justin and his brother to side with him. Justin has difficulty recalling his childhood but remembers going to the beach, walks in the woods and visits to relatives.

He described himself as an outgoing, friendly, popular, balanced and happy little boy. He was inquisitive and intelligent. He thinks the adults around perceived him as being differen from many other children. The only times he felt bad were when his parents rowed.

He had a love/hate relationship with his brother with a lot of rivalry between them and frequent fights. He remembers trying to persuade his brother to play sexual games with him; sometimes without success. Sex wasn't something that was discussed in his house.

He described his abuse:

I was 4 or 5 when I was abused by a next door neighbour who befriended me. It used to happen a lot in school holidays, weekends and half-terms. It went on for about five years. It was mainly masturbation, fondling and kissing. He used to get me to masturbate him but I'm not absolutely sure if he masturbated me. I know there was no anal or oral abuse. It mainly occurred at his parents' house when they were out, in the surrounding woods and forests and in the barn and sheds in the back garden. I went round to the house one day when his mum and dad had gone out and he asked me to come into the living room and help fix his bike. The look on his face frightened me and I really felt that if I had gone into that room with him on that particular day he would have done something really serious. I was very frightened and I ran away and I never went back to see him again.

I don't know why I didn't disclose at the time it was happening. I feel pretty sure he would have told me not to say anything but I can't remember. I was about 13 when I told my mother and father about it; they believed me and comforted me but the abuse was never reported to the police because the person who abused me became mentally ill and was institutionalised. He sometimes came back to visit his parents next door and he was on heavy sedation. My mother and father didn't think it would be worth raking it up because it would be his word against mine and it would be more likely that he would not be prosecuted. I think they thought it would do more harm to me than good.

He would have been about 28 when the abuse began and he committed suicide when he was 43. What led up to me disclosing was that I had just begun to realise that what went on between me and him was very wrong. I had started to realise this because of my growing awareness of adult sexuality through films, books, media and sex education at school. As I became aware of what was right and wrong, I gradually realised it should never have been happening, whereas before I just accepted it as normal. I was used, abused, manipulated by someone who was my friend, who I used to talk to when I couldn't talk to my parents because they may have been rowing.

I am not confused about my gender but I think most of my gender are arse-holes anyway. My mother did not like homosexuals and was intolerant towards them; my father was more open minded although he did make a lot of corny jokes about homosexuals. I don't know any homosexuals myself but I wouldn't feel hostility towards them if I met one.

I do remember thinking in my early teens that a lot of grown up men I knew were false and incomplete. I didn't like them very much and whatever it meant to be a real man I didn't want and couldn't be one. The fact that it was a man who abused me taught me that men oppress other men to a great extent, almost to the extent that they oppress other women.

I feel negative about my sexuality because all it consists of is masturbation; I have been doing this for years and I'm fed up with it but I still have to do it because I get so frustrated, angry with everything. I think this is because I have never had a relationship. It isn't enough; I want something more.

I used to have sexual fantasies about my mother when I was a teenager – that is difficult to admit. I don't ever have sexual fantasies about children and I don't feel tempted to engage in sexual activities with them.

About a month and a half ago I was arrested in a park for shouting and screaming obscenities at my abuser who is now dead. I was freed after three hours in a cell when a social services psychiatrist and a social worker said they were of the opinion that they did not need to sign me away. I was quite frightened that I could just be signed away on the decision of two people on one incident of shouting and screaming in a park. I think the law is an ass in this respect. The psychiatrist pissed me off a lot because he said at the end 'I guess the moral of this is 'don't scream in public places'. I thought that was very unsympathetic to my feelings; it was as if he was just there to do a job and he didn't really care whether he signed me away or not.

I have behaved in anti-social ways on a few other occasions – on a mild scale where people have annoyed me and I have just let rip and shouted obscenities at them or people in cars when they have nearly knocked me over.

When I started my last school at the age of 12 I retreated into a shell. I found it very hard to make friends; I thought that most of the kids were very silly and immature and I didn't like them. I found it very hard to concentrate on anything for any length of time and when exams came up I didn't bother with revision. I got four 'O' levels so I thought that was quite good. After that I left school and I dossed around for two years; I didn't want to work and I wasn't forced into anything. I bummed around, riding my bike around where I used to live; then my sexuality became distorted and I engaged in a lot of 'flashing'; very often I would do it when the person was unaware – they might have been near me on horseback or walking in the woods; I would usually masturbate to orgasm; I did that hundreds of times. It was all I could think about; that was all I lived for. I used to feel very guilty about it afterwards and I was very frightened about getting caught and being locked up but I never was.

Following on from that, from the ages of roughly 18–22, I had very bad depressions; these would last for about a week or for three or four days practically every month. I was like being in hell; I used to have what I now know is 'death anxiety' – this was central to my life at that time. I had lots of very weird thoughts about people. I felt like an outsider, that people were happy, enjoying themselves, engaging in normal sexual activity and I wasn't. I felt very angry and hateful towards people. It was very hard to live. I suppose it impeded my growth; I have only started recently growing into a normal person – whatever that is.

The four sessions of psychotherapy that I had at the beginning of this year helped me to bring all these feelings and the reasons why I had them into my conscious mind but I wasn't given any more sessions and I was left with a lot of bad, angry hateful feeling towards people and I felt very mixed up for about another nine months or so. So basically I've had to help myself; but it has taken me a hell of a long time.

I think I'm only just beginning to realise how oppressed I have been by society; by the stigmatisation of sexual abuse survivors, especially male survivors. There are very few people or places where I could go to talk about my problems and even if I do talk to someone who is sympathetic, because they haven't been through those experiences themselves, I often find they wind me up even more by saying things that are a load of bullshit – or I think they are bullshit – I'm not quite sure and it confuses me even more. I have to say that most people who I come into contact with, including my parents, have hindered me to quite a great extent. They didn't know they hindered me and they haven't wanted to hinder me but they have; they could see that I was very ill and very depressed for a hell of a long time and they just thought it would go away; my mum said 'I thought you'd grow out of it'. I have to admit, I felt very angry towards her for not actually getting me some help.

The one thing that has helped me is the independent support group which is run by 'Kidsline' for male sexual abuse survivors. That is the only thing, (apart from the four sessions of psychotherapy) that has really helped me. At times I have seen people from the NHS for pills and short interviews but I have always felt that I have been in court; I've been interrogated, as if it has been my fault that I have felt this way and done these things. Just thinking about it is making me feel angry.

I think the abuse has affected my whole life in almost every aspect. Especially in relating to people both on a superficial level and on a deep level. Most people think it has probably affected my ability to trust but I seem to go the other way; I probably trust people too much and tell them things I shouldn't really tell them. It really annoys me when I am talking to people and they say 'do you have a problem with trust' and the answer is 'no'.

It has distorted my sexuality in that I used to do a lot of flashing and masturbation in public places. I just felt so inadequate that I would say to myself, 'who the fuck would be interested in you?' It affected me in other ways in that I find it very hard to get a job. In these times, which are bad anyway, people like me who have big gaps in their CV go to an employer and they ask you what you were doing or why you were unemployed and you can't tell them the reason which was basically because you were fucked up inside your head.

In a positive way it has made me think about things on a deeper level than most other people; the problem with that is that it tends to increase my alienation and isolation from others. I think they are boring, full of bullshit, banalities; not everybody is like that but it seems to me that a lot of people are and I'm very intolerant of that. I think it has made me look at life in black and white terms; I used to be very judgemental, which is another way of increasing my isolation.

It has really affected my whole life and I feel very angry, not only at my abuser, but at society too because I feel that they have played quite a large part in the pain and depression that I've been through. It has dramatically affected the whole of my life and I think that if it hadn't happened to me, I would probably be in a stable job and I'd be happy.

There have been so many times (we are talking three figures here I think) when I have felt there is no point to going on living. I can't say I have ever attempted suicide; I have sometimes slashed my wrists, tentatively; not to commit suicide (I think) but to show to the world I've got some pain. I think it was anger, turned inwards. Sometimes I would bang my hands up against the wall or stub cigarettes out against my wrist. I have felt suicidal many times but I suppose it's a good thing on those occasions I haven't done anything; God knows why not.

I can't remember a lot about the abuse – I can only remember when it started and when it finished. I think I viewed it neutrally at the time it was happening. I knew something was going on that never happened with other people, but I didn't know what it was.

There are quite some positive things that have come from being sexually abused. I do now know five other abuse survivors and it seems to me that we all think about things very deeply. We tend to reflect; we are much more open minded about things. I do think when you have been sexually abused (I think this is going to sound a bit weird) but when you have been able to work it out, it does actually make you into a better lover. I think it can make you more sensuous, more in touch with the earth; maybe it's because you've had so much pain you are prepared to give more. I think it tends to make you think about things more deeply.

There are a lot of negative things about it as well but for myself I don't view it so negatively now; I view it as my little secret. It has made me into an unconventional person; a person who breaks rules and takes more risks with their lives – which I have now started to do.

15 Abuse and patriarchal institutions

Introduction

This chapter presents Tony and Len's story which I have linked because I see them as a useful example of how a male dominated institution within a patriarchal society may contribute and sustain some of the 'norms' that underpin the sexual abuse of children (I have expanded on these 'norms' earlier). Lerner (1986) includes in the wider definition of 'patriarchy'

> It implies that men hold power in all the important institutions of society and that women (and children) are deprived of access to such power.

The male dominated institution with which all these men have links is the Catholic Church and I have used this as a focus for my discussion, not because the Catholic Church is unique in needing to deal with issues connected with male sexual abuse, but rather because the subjects of my interviews presented their story within the context of this church. As a society we all share the responsibility to protect children and our more vulnerable members and it is important that we do not scapegoat any one body or organisation. As a member of the Catholic Church I have a part of the collective responsibility involved in that membership and I have struggled with my decision to present this material and risk playing into the hands of those who are only too ready to point the finger of blame at particular groups without accepting any part of it, and my need to be truthful in what I have found through these interviews. My own experience as a woman within the Catholic Church inevitably colours my view.

Other male dominated institutions such as the armed forces might have served an equal purpose had the necessary material been presented by those interviewed. King (1992) states that there is evidence that the sexual assault of males occurs in institutional setting such as military establishments and that male-on-male sexual activity is more likely to occur in setting in which men are deprived of their usual heterosexual outlets. However, assaults within these institutions are usually on adult males and it may be that all male boarding schools, whether or not they are church institutions might be usefully examined for a clearer picture. Mike's story, (previously told), gives us some insight into how the all-male environment of the Borstal institution within which he was held, offered opportunities for same-sex sexual activity and denied him the opportunity for developing opposite-sex relationships. It will only be when the problem is acknowledged by those in authority that these organisations might allow research into these matters.

I believe the Church, like other male dominated institutions, has been in danger of attempting to maintain power and authority at the expense of truth; the suppression of truth can be seen as necessary to preserving order but without truth we become helpless to change anything in our lives, in our world or in our Church. Churches rarely make public the information about sexual misconduct of some of their members for fear that the reputation of all their members will be damaged. Instead I believe such institutions might enhance their stature by demonstrating their concern for the public by openness about the activities of unethical members, as is being demonstrated by some diocesan policies which put victims and parishes before the abusers and will allow the process of law to continue whatever the consequences for the reputation of some members of the Church or the organisation itself. Until recently many religious organisations simply transferred sexually abusive clergy to another locale with no public admission of misconduct. Tabloid exploitation of some such cases can make it difficult for those abusers who are genuinely seeking help and create a 'witch hunt' environment in which it is easy to lose sight of the need to provide help for abusers as well as their victims. If we are to believe the results of research which indicates that the majority of abusers are themselves victims of abuse in their own childhood, then a punitive approach alone is clearly unhelpful and will not in the long term protect children. Men in leadership positions set the ethical tone for society through the messages they pass on to each other. Suppression of truth is harmful in itself, but because it keeps men away from their own inner worlds, it may reinforce the cultural dynamics of sexual exploitation.

It is not entirely coincidental that I have interviewed members of this church; I placed one of the advertisements for subjects for interview in a magazine aimed at this group because I knew the topic of sexual abuse by clergy was a subject for debate on its letter page following a TV documentary which highlighted the issue. This church is now taking responsibility by actively examining its role in response to the growing awareness of the sexual abuse of children; guidelines have been issued in July 1994 in response to the findings of a two-year working party which insist that priests under investigation should be suspended from duty and not moved on and that convicted priests should not be returned to parish work. A priest is being appointed to each diocese to deal with priests and lay workers who sexually abuse children. All candidates for the priesthood will be vetted for any tendency to abuse and the church will co-operate with the police and other churches to deal with what they have described as 'a very powerful evil'.

However, Tony and Len did not come forward as a result of that advertisement, so the additional input from them, relating to the Catholicism, is coincidental. Although issues related to abuse by clergy are probably just as relevant to members of other churches, I believe the issue of celibacy is unique to Catholicism among Christian churches.

The issues I shall focus on are those of the development of homosexual orientation, its relationship to the clergy and the issue of abuse by clergy. I do not wish to imply by this any connection between homosexual orientation and paedophilia, rather that these are separate and unrelated issues. Tony describes himself as 70 per cent homosexual and 30 per cent heterosexual in orientation. Len as heterosexual but could be bi-sexual if he found himself stranded on a desert island with a man and became bored with his fantasies! Tony has been a priest and a monk and Len has spent some years in a junior seminary from which he says he was expelled 'for being a leader'! Tony and Len were sexually and physically abused by priests/monks, although both found it hard to identify their experiences as 'abuse' and Martin, whose story is told in Chapter 16 of the book, was abused on two separate occasions by two non-clergy males and later became a priest; he is homosexually orientated. None of these men are abusers although all three in retrospect identified ways in which they might have re-enacted their own abuse by initiating sexual activity with other children. Another man I interviewed was abused by a priest/monk, but was too distressed to give a clear account of this; I have therefore not included his interview. Another, who was sexually abused by his sister around the age of 7 years and is now homosexual, spent some years in a seminary but did not complete his training; he spoke of the anguish of confession, 'difficulties with communion' and a history of 'lying at school, fear and imagined illnesses'. I have not used his interview in this section as it was incomplete. These discussions will include observations from psychological and social perspectives and the theory of patriarchy.

Introduction to Len's story

Len offered to tell his story because he overheard me saying that I thought sexual abuse of males was probably always damaging and he disagreed. He joined in a lively conversation telling his story in an entertaining way; how he had attended a junior seminary and had sexual encounters both with boys and with adult men who were priests and how he felt that he had not been adversely affected by these encounters. I will leave you to judge for yourself as his story unfolds. I have discussed Len's story in conjunction with Tony's at the end of this section as there are similarities and differences which can be drawn upon in the understanding of their stories.

Len's story

Len was born in 1945, with an older sister and two younger brothers. He is married without children and he is in advertising.

He remembered the atmosphere in his home:

It was terrific in our house when I was little; very social, very touchy, feely, a kissing and cuddling family, always playing, sometimes volatile. My mother was strong, loving, comforting, loyal, playful. I don't remember my dad ever being cross with us. He used to get cross with my Mum – he would 'tut'. My mother used to threaten us with my father. I guess we never quite knew what would happen if she did tell our father. He bought us sweets every Friday night with his 'paltry pay packet' (as my mother used to call it). I guess he provided the finance for the comics; he would take us to football matches. That was a great adventurous walk for a couple of miles. He would cuddle, kiss and hold you and grizzle you with his beard. He encouraged us with everything to do with sport.

Latterly, since my father died, I have thought it was he who really had the power. Since he died my mother has been a shell. We always thought of her as Dominatrix; the total wild Irishwoman, unreliable, who never told the truth and didn't know she was lying; she was an intelligent under-achiever; she spent far more years at the cooker than in the classroom. She was a teacher and she had her own nursery for a few years.

Father moved with his work, so we all moved. Until I came to live on the Yorkshire moors I had never lived anywhere longer than 4 years. I think we had 9 moves before I was 9-years-old. The first four years of our life until we moved (although I have no memory of them) were, I feel, fairly halcyon. The thing that I always remember in the years from 0–9 was moving around all the time. We were middle-class gypsies; we moved from house to house instead of moving from caravan to caravan.

I was an adventurous, cautious, rumbly tumbly little boy. I'd play football but my knees would be clean at the end of the game whereas the others would have mud on their kit. I was probably male with a good streak of the feminine. I was a gregarious loner. I didn't incur the wrath of any of the established gangs – I was never in them – I never led anything.

I went to school at 4 and then changed schools at 6 and then 7 then 9, and then at 11 I went to prep boarding school, a Cathedral Choir School – the first time I'd been away from my parents. I had been a totally angelic altar boy from the age of 8–11. There was this lovely Irish priest and I wanted to be a priest like him. So it grew as an idea in the family and I seemed to be getting so much kudos, they all thought it was a good idea, so off I went. This was the first step to Junior Seminary.

My first memory involving my sexuality was at prep. boarding school when I was 12. We had single beds in a dormitory and I must have been playing with myself and I had 'come'. I went to see my confidant who was six months older and I asked him what had happened and he said 'Oh that's no problem. Just go back to bed and go asleep – just go to confession in the morning.' I didn't know what I was going to confession for, so I must have gone and described what had happened.

I don't think I was sexually abused as a child. Now in my adult life I think that the spanking and leatherings we got at prep school were a kind of abuse but they were the standard punishment of the school of the day, so you accepted it. I think it was always 'in the air' at prep school from 11–13. Then I went to Junior Seminary when I was 13 and I guess it was in my second year there when I approached the guy in the next bed to me – on the basis of, 'I'll show you mine if you'll show me yours.' (He thinks for a while) I'm thinking I must have been approached before that – I'm feeling that there was a sexual experience before that. I can't quite engage with that. The guy I approached in the dormitory, I think we must have masturbated each other and then he split on us the next day to a group of friends and I felt angry, shamed and embarrassed. At the time I had no sense of him being unwilling but I think he might have been because I've had enough feedback as an adult about the power of my personality. Looking back I think I saw him as one of the weaklings in the dormitory so it was safe to approach. I was perceiving myself as an equal to him but I think he would have perceived me as quite persuasive. I could imagine he might have gone along with it because he would have looked sissy if he hadn't. I suppose that would have been a good reason that he told people – I'd never thought of that before now.

When I was 15 or 16 I had some fairly mild sexual encounters with priests. One who took me out in his car asked me things like 'which way does your penis lie in your trousers when it is down and which way does it lie when it sticks up?' and 'do you want to show me?' and I said, 'No.' He still remained a family friend.

Nothing happened then until I was a fifth former; an older boy had taken me away in his parents' car for a holiday; we had gone off and slept together the whole way round and masturbated each other. He was at least 17, a driver and a prefect in the sixth form, really sophisticated. I think he must have initiated the sexual activity between us. You see he was paying for everything. My parents were delighted to see their son going off on holiday with this well-heeled young man. We were away for six or seven days and I remember being in bed with him on the first night. I don't remember feeling worried. I imagine it was a holding exercise – filling in time until we discovered women. Of course I'd two or three 'homosexual affairs' with boys at school by then – just mutual masturbation. So I knew about males .... I was going to say 'loving each other'; there was affection there but it was more like riding each other's motor bikes, at that level; it was 'using' rather than 'loving'.

The next incident was when I was at the university chaplaincy helping out in the holidays and the priest, a lovely guy who had been a family friend for a long time, came into my bed when I was half asleep at three o'clock in the morning. I'd had a relationship with him very much like the relationship I had with my father in that he was touchy, feely, intimate and he cuddled all the family including my mother and everybody cuddled him and he was a family hero; he was well on the way to becoming Archbishop or Cardinal. There had never been anything before like that with him, and never since. I'm still a friend of his and he's now quite elderly. I see in his eyes a doubt that I might raise it. We have never discussed it. He's always pretended that I must have been asleep and I've always played along with it.

I guess I knew he wanted a wank. I would have known from Catholicism that it wasn't right. I think I was fascinated and impressed by the size of his plonker – it was just incredible. I felt it – he must have put my hand on him. I don't think I would have thought I had done something wrong; I would have seen it as me performing a service for him and as long as everybody kept quiet about it, then it wasn't going to be a problem. I must have wondered whether he would come back other nights but I don't think he did. If he had I would probably have done the same but starting to get nervous, uneasy that it was going to get into something I couldn't handle. I don't think I felt uneasy as long as it stayed at the level of 'let's all pretend to be asleep, let's all pretend this is happening in the middle of the night, in the dark and it's an accident and nobody's responsible'.

I don't know when I got hold of 'homosexuality' as a concept. I think phrases like 'queer bashing' came later. I went with a friend to the cinema (although we were banned in case it would seduce us) and he told me a story about when he had gone to the pictures before and someone had attempted to pick him up. So I must have been aware of homosexuality. I think someone once attempted to pick me up too. I don't think I felt negative about homosexuality but I knew it was a sin. Well masturbation was – so if you did it with somebody else it must be mustn't it? My school friend had told me to go to confession for masturbating and I had been given three Hail Marys for my penance so I knew it was a sin and I knew what size of a sin by the size of the penance.

We had two priests – one of them was a very masculine male and he was fine; there was no question of him being a woose or a wimp (he played cricket and did all the right things). Then there was the other one who was the headteacher and he used to put his hand down your trousers when he was spanking you to 'hold your tummy in position' and I think we all had doubts about him. If he was going to cane you or tolley you he used to go into a very wimpy voice and say, 'well this is very bad isn't it. Oh dear!' in a kind of sado-masochistic way; then you knew you were for it. He would send you through a different door into his bedroom to lie over the end of the bed and he would come in and whack you with this whale bone in leather. I don't remember getting it on the bare bottom but I'm sure we had to take our trousers off after we had it a few times. He would put his hand on your tummy or do something with his hands. Whether or not he rubbed your bottom for you after he'd smacked it I don't know. I didn't sense it as sexual then. Not then – it was too fearful, too terrifying. You were being punished. I remember it as a very small room.

I didn't see this stuff as sexual abuse then but it's what I am identifying now that suggests it might have been. I think if I felt abused at all in childhood it was moving around so much. If I felt abused in adolescence it was incidents like the one at break time when I was chased by a prefect into the loo because he thought I was smoking. That all felt abusive in the sense of 'unfair'.

How I feel about it now is that (long pause) – it seems fair enough – you know. I feel sorry for the guy. I have quite a few homosexual friends and they always seem to be at one end of the spectrum or the other – they don't seem to find a balance for very long. I feel that this guy (the Chaplain) probably wasn't homosexual; he had a good war record and came from a landed family; he'd espoused celibacy for Christ. I feel that with a plonker like that it seems a bit of a shame really. He should have been making himself and some partner happy. I liked him, I loved him and I still do. So it was kind of 'out of the way' but as long as it doesn't become 'dirty' it was no problem.

If he'd done it with a girl that would have felt quite naughty, quite bad. That would have been abuse – taking advantage of a weaker person. If a man in his mid-thirties, had done that with a girl of whatever I was (I imagine myself as 15 but I can't have been), I must have been 16 or 17. Well, if it had been with a young girl of 14 or 15, my morality says it wouldn't have been right for him to have slipped in during the night with somebody who was staying in his house, he ought to have negotiated it. It's like playing rugby – in male company its all right.

If that boy had been my son or daughter and he was staying in our house and he did that, I'd have quite a different attitude; that is something I haven't confronted before – that quite surprises me. If it was my son at 15, I would have used it as an opportunity to talk – I'd probably have talked it through with him. I would probably have told the priest it was a bit naughty and not to do that again. I might have looked quite firmly at him just to make it perfectly clear that he was getting close to violent territory. If he did that again I might bop him one; I'd raise that spectre just to get him to keep his distance. Then I'd have a problem of course if I had spoken to my son and found that he'd enjoyed it and wanted to carry it on. Then I would have been in difficulty about telling the priest to lay off.

If it had been a daughter it would be completely unacceptable. Not that girls can't look after themselves or should be more protected than boys. I suppose it's the spectre of pregnancy or unwanted pregnancy. It would be up to her – if she had seduced him then it would be fine; but if a man of that age had made approaches – girls should have the chance to relate to their peers. In the end my common sense would say that I would have to talk to her about it, to see how she felt about it and agree some course of action between her and me. It wouldn't be that different an outcome to talking to a son of the same age. I was just thinking it would be more participative, more understanding and insightful with a son and more protective, more defensive with the daughter.

I wouldn't mind being a woman at these times. I have tried on women's clothes to see what it felt like – just for fun. I would classify myself as heterosexual but I could be bisexual if I was stuck on a desert island with a man I liked and I had got bored with masturbating to my fantasies. It's just that men's bodies don't appeal to me like women's do; the curves aren't right.

I don't think what happened has affected me. I have intermittent impotence and the ongoing problem of female monogamy as against arrant male polygamy. I think the whole Catholic business of ritual and the boarding school thing of spanking and caning – they've affected me. If I have a sexual fantasy it will be built around some situation of equality – headmaster and headmistress of a school or both company directors – it will be a fairly ritualised fantasy and sometimes involves caning or spanking and I will actually climax in that fantasy before there's any pain involved; it's the ritual that counts. I also suspect it's about making some aspects of sexuality remote so there isn't too much intimacy – like rear entry heterosexual sex.

I have thought about suicide but never attempted it. It was a kind of sexual frustration after a rather beautiful kind of affair which was untenable with my marriage because I loved my wife. I don't think I've ever had my sexuality in balance. The feedback I get from my loved ones is that I want to have my cake and eat it. By most of my friends' tokens I have it all; I have a kind of lifestyle that looks to them very enviable and I don't actually feel I have a right to it.

The whole celibacy thing at the seminary always struck me as weird even when I was young. I didn't think of my parents as not celibate and priests as celibate and then I began to realise that there was a distinction and I thought the priests were mad. In fact most of them weren't celibate.

I was expelled from junior seminary at the age of 16. The official report was that I was a leader. I think I was suspected of all kinds of mischief but most of the time I wasn't even there. But that's what they said – that I was a leader. Weird isn't it – it sounds like a qualification to me. I still don't really understand it. I've had that experience in my adult life that I don't understand why I am perceived the way I am by others. Although I might go out of my way to do unusual things because I want to find new ways of doing things – especially where I see disease – I don't think of myself as unusual or abnormal; just prepared to do some things that other people only think about.

Tony's story

Tony is an ex-priest and religious who describes his sexual orientation as 70 per cent homosexual and 30 per cent heterosexual although he is trying to live a celibate life at present. He is single, professional man with no children. He was an only child, born in 1937. His parents divorced in 1941 but had been separated two years before that. When he was a year old he was left with his grandmother whilst his parents were abroad. He has no early memories of his father at all although he recalled his father thinking he was a 'wimp' and a 'mummy's boy'.

Tony recalled his early years:

We had no home until I was 9-years-old. We moved around, staying in boarding houses; we frequently went to my uncle and aunt's farm. There was just my mother and me – just the two of us and we were very close. I think my mother felt inadequate about bringing me up alone as a male and that is why she sent me to boarding school. My grandfather, her father, was held up as a model for me. He was a very sociable man and my mother obviously adored him; he was quite a 'woman's man'. My mother only married after he died.

My childhood wasn't a peaceful time because we seemed to be always on the move because of the war and I was separated from my mother at times and I didn't understand why we were moving all the time. I do have a sense of a very close relationship with my mother and depending entirely on her and, in that sense, I was happy.

When I was 5- or 6-years-old there was a period when my mother was working as a personal assistant to a head mistress; I think she was fairly indispensable. My mother and I shared a room at the school. I can remember her lying naked and me lying on top of her. A few years ago I made some reference to some people who were around at that time and she said 'I wonder what else you remember about that time'? I said nothing but I knew exactly what she was referring to. My mother was very old then and I wouldn't have wanted to upset her. Anyway we didn't talk very intimately about that sort of thing and one thing might have led to another; I never admitted to my mother that I was homosexual and it might have got into that sort of area.

I don't remember that episode as being a highly erotic, exciting or attractive experience. I remember it as being just something that happened. It was just an event – but I was very close to my mother in other respects so I suppose it didn't seem surprising. My mother was physically very affectionate, lots of kisses and cuddles. I would guess that I had a separate bed in the same room. My mother had a double bed.

I suspect that my mother had a relationship with a woman called Violet who I think was employed as cook at the same hostel where my mother was warden but it's only conjecture that they had a relationship at that time. My mother was the warden of a hostel for civil servants. I was taken by the maid to school every morning by the Underground – we used to walk through the streets and see blocks of flats that had been demolished by bombs. There were air raids and I used to go down into the basement.

Overnight I was suddenly whipped away back to where we had lived previously to stay with my mother's friends. The V1s had started and my school had closed down again; it was thought to be dangerous for me to stay in London. I remember feeling desperately bereft, really dreadful. I must have been very angry about that because I can remember playing with a younger boy and we clubbed to death a young duckling; we were poking it around and it started gasping so we decided to finish it off. We were caught and told off about it. I remember feeling bereft and crying all the time and then my mother coming down at the weekend and coming to my room at night after hearing about the duckling saying 'How could you?' There was once a row when I was sent to be looked after by this family. I remember this woman bathing me and spending a lot of time washing my private parts. I mentioned this to my mother and she was very interested and concerned about this.

I think this feeling of being 'banished' has affected me even up to now. I still get feelings about it. It's only now that I begin to wonder if there was some sort of relationship between my mother and Violet and if she was responsible for me being banished – she had great anger and aggression towards me that went on for years.

Then my mother and Violet and I moved up to the Midlands. We didn't stay there long. Then we went further North where I remember my mother and Violet sunbathing in the nude; my mother would normally never be seen naked – I don't think I was meant to be there.

I have another frightening memory of rows between my mother and Violet and of going for a walk with them along a canal and Violet pushing or threatening to push my mother into the canal – having a physical fight with my mother. That is the reason why I have thought that they were having a relationship. Just prior to that, at the age of 7, I was taken by my mother to boarding school and once again I was bereft; left alone just after my seventh birthday. We stayed living at that place for another year and then we went to another hostel where we stayed for a year or so. I had a big room and my mother and Violet shared the room next door; it was smaller and had a double bed. I was coming and going to boarding school during this period. A year later we moved to London because my mother got a job and we lived in a little flat where I'm sure they shared a bedroom.

I remember masturbating at boarding school when I was 7 – perhaps I'd learned to do it before that. I can remember having a room at school with two or three other people. I can remember enticing the boy who was in the room with me to have a sort of sexual rub-up naked against me behind the door. It only happened once. It was my initiative. There was no more until later on which was not my initiative. I used to masturbate a great deal when I was about 12–14. I think it was a sort of compulsion. It was pleasurable but it was considered to be a mortal sin. We confessed it – there was a queue for confession every morning – all the people who had masturbated the night before (laughs).

I can remember having a passionate crush on my housemaster who was a priest; when I was 9, I fell in love or had a passionate attachment to another priest. I think to some extent it was reciprocated. I used to sit on his knee and cuddle and kiss him. When I was 10 or 11 we went outside and he put up a tent; we lay down together in there and he cuddled me. We both had our clothes on. I didn't feel excited by it – rather like with my mother. It was just a fact. We didn't sleep in the tent – it was just put up so that we could have a cuddle, we didn't spend the night in there. I didn't talk about it to anybody but I didn't have a sense of it having to be kept a secret. I do remember him hugging me very tightly. I wouldn't be surprised if he'd been masturbating but he never did anything more than that. I remember I was going to go over to Ireland to stay with a friend when I would have been 11 and this same priest suggested that he and I share a sleeper. I felt uneasy about it.

I missed a term because I had broken my leg. I was in a dormitory with about 6 people and in that last summer term when I was 12, I can remember one night being invited into bed by one of the people in the dormitory and quite enjoying it; and in the same term I can also remember being told by this same priest (who was then acting headmaster), that when I had been away, there had been a bit of sexual behaviour among the people in that dormitory and they had been had up in front of the headmaster; they had told the headmaster, in mitigation, that I had said it was alright; I seem to have been seen as an authority on this matter. I know I wasn't there when they were caught. Curiously enough, this was the same priest who had taken me into the tent and now he was saying 'it is wrong'.

Nothing happened in my first year in my next school except that

I fell passionately in love with an older boy and I was ostracised by my friends. The following year I think in all three cases in which I had sexual mucking around with three separate people, (I was capable of ejaculation by that stage), in all three cases, in the first instance they enticed me; afterwards I probably attempted to entice them. They were all in my year – two were older and one was younger but he was tougher and bigger. I think I felt they had more power than me. Somebody reported us to the headmaster. I was had up, thrashed and threatened with expulsion. I suspect I was regarded as the villain and they weren't; one of them became Head Boy a few years later. I think I was seen as the dangerous one. They both came from good respectable homes. I was probably the misfit, because of my dubious background; not having a family, not having parents. This is something I have always felt angry with my school about 'To him who has will more be given; from him who hasn't, even that little he has will be taken away'. That could have been my school motto.

I think I was physically abused by an abnormal amount of beatings at school. We were beaten by the headmaster, for example, just for leaving books lying around in the school. It was either a painful beating with a cane with trousers on or, on other occasions, when I had a bad work report or was caught smoking, with a leather tolley; that was up to 14 strokes. You had your trousers down and I'm not sure that there wasn't something sexual about that. There was a convention that after the thrashing, you would shake hands to show there was no hard feelings – but he would hug us before we pulled our trousers up again. There was nothing overt. At the time, you just wanted to get out of there as quickly as possible; it was so painful. You just wanted to rub your bum; you were screaming to get out (not literally).

I just wanted him to die because I was so ashamed of the sexual episode and I didn't want anybody else to know about that; I thought if he died then nobody else would know about it. He was actually very good with confidentiality. I was scared of him; he was a big man, but I didn't have the guts to have it out with him. I had great resentment towards him.

When I went to take a university entrance examination I seduced the fellow who shared the room with me. There was never any emotional attachment; no romantic attraction. It was purely physical – I wouldn't dignify it with the name 'relationship' – we had physical sex from time to time. After the year was over we remained in the same circle, but there was quite an awkwardness between us.

During the school holidays parties were being replaced by country dances, square dances and I started going to them. There was one girl who I professed to have some interest in – one had to keep up certain appearances. There was a Norwegian boy who came to stay with us one summer to learn English whom I was passionately in love with – he was a very feminine boy.

At university we didn't meet girls. We did come across a few at classes but I was terrified of them. There were girls at home. I became a frequent party-goer and I used to love dancing. I have to say I was more interested in some of the men, but the women became good friends. I had a girl friend; I think she was quite keen on me and we used to see a lot of each other but she was too like my mother to be somebody I could really get close to. She was a beautiful English Rose kind of girl, tall, keen on riding.

I'm not sure if I thought I was 'a homosexual'. I did know what the word meant; I learnt that at school quite early on but I didn't connect my feelings for this boy when I was first at school with homosexuality at all. I didn't connect my feelings with *sex* actually. There was a whole spate of homosexual prosecutions while I was at school; many of them were famous people; one or two had been friendly with my mother in her younger days. I was very fascinated by all that. Certainly when I was at university and I was thinking about becoming a priest I put it to myself that there was good chance that I may be homosexual. I don't think I put it more strongly than that. I was very interested in anything that appeared in the newspapers about homosexuality and I would read the sexual details and find them quite titillating. I didn't like homosexual people generally. I don't think there was a lot of homophobia about actually. Yes, there was homophobia but for instance – being beaten by the headmaster would have been the same if it had been with a girl. It was sex that was wrong not just homosexuality.

I thought it was a good reason for becoming a priest; in that I couldn't marry, I couldn't make a woman happy or be happy living with a woman. I suppose I thought that I could sublimate my sexuality and make it a positive thing by being a priest and teaching in a school run by my congregation. I certainly didn't become a priest thinking 'oh good, I'll go and get some homosexual sex'. Sex was suppressed quite consciously by joining a religious congregation. That was because I felt that homosexual sex was wrong. It wasn't just a way of controlling it. It was a way of finding a positive sublimation of it – something that would be creative. So I think my sexuality was something I felt guilty or bad about. Religion was a substitute. I was very religious at university.

I was 20 when I joined the congregation. My sexuality went completely into limbo. The first time I masturbated after joining was after my final vows. There must have been some significance in that. That was after four years. I certainly had sexual feelings coming to the surface although nothing happened. I was aware that there were male friends who were attracted to me and that I was attracted to them, but nothing happened.

When I became a teacher I suppose my sexuality definitely gave me energy for relating to boys. The relationships I had were not paternal; they were more equal than that – don't forget I was only ten years older than the boys. They became more paternal when I became a Formmaster later on. I can remember being very attracted to boys in the classes I had at first. I'm sure the boys felt it too. I had a sort of reputation. I think some of the more observant boys would have said 'Oh yes, Anthony is queer.' There was a rather unpleasant episode when I was called up before the Superior on one occasion who said that one of the boys had reported to his parents that I was queer. You can imagine the feelings there were. The whole thing was shrouded in potential scandal, shock horror and guilt. I never did get to the bottom of it – the boy subsequently said that he had made it up. I imagine I had that vague sort of aura about me but I was popular and I got on well with certain boys; no doubt there were jealousies but in the first five years I was teaching there, we had a very screwed up headmaster. I think he was convinced that I was having sex with loads of boys – he was very suspicious because I did have some very close friendships with one or two boys who were both heterosexual; they were both probably more mature than I was. Some people said the headmaster was jealous of my closeness with the boys and I happen to know that he went in for some strange behaviours with some boys himself – he used to have this boy in and hug and kiss him. So you can imagine the atmosphere with a headmaster like that. It was partly to get away from all that I went abroad – that and other things. A lot of people were leaving the Church at that time in the '60s. I wasn't so aware of the suspicion about me until people told me about it.

When I went abroad I had a sexual relationship with a woman but it wasn't an emotional relationship. It was purely physical – well 90 per cent physical. Even at that stage, in my early 30s, I still thought I might be capable of marrying because people were leaving the Church at that time to get married. I came back and I was left high and dry because so many of them had left and I was still there.

I went to see a psychiatrist before I went abroad because when the Superior said, 'well there is this allegation about you being queer', I said, 'well I am queer, it's quite true and so I should do something about it'. He was very nice; I guess he was homosexually orientated himself. He said, 'well, if you suffer from a gammy leg (a wonderful Freudian image isn't it) there are two courses of action: You can go from one specialist to another spending your whole life and your money trying to put it right or you can learn to live with it and I recommend the latter!' But I went to see a psychiatrist. I remember him telling me there wasn't much chance of getting married; he said he thought I had a bit of residual heterosexuality, but not enough to carry me through a lifetime and I think that's right.

I consciously went to see him because I was worried about the effect I might have on boys at school. I wasn't worried about having sex with them. I was worried about possible emotional entanglements – doing some damage to them. I didn't want to do it to them. I don't think I really connected it to the relationships I had with monks and certainly not with what happened with my mother. In fact I have had some difficulty with this whole idea of having been 'sexually abused'; I think it's difficult just linguistically. I'm very suspicious of this word 'abuse'. Abuse is a word used both for beating and physical assault and for sexual activity. I know the two can be combined in rape or violent physical sexual assault – and in my case there is no question of assault of any kind. So that makes it difficult for me to see it as abuse. What would apply to me is when it is part of a close loving relationship. Sexual abuse carries overtones of wickedness and prison and I don't like to apply that, for example, to my mother. Again with my mother it was not just sexually or emotionally when I was very young, but when I was about 12 she would confide in me about her worries about money and things. I feel compassionate towards my mother. I don't feel angry with her. I think of it as some sort of weakness on her part. I think its unfortunate, like the war, but I can't blame her. I think that it could be responsible for my homosexuality. I don't subscribe to the view that we (homosexuals) are genetically different. I am prepared to bet quite a lot of money that it is either caused by lack of a father or too intrusive a mother and I think it may well be the latter. I think my mother may well have put me off women at some level which I am not aware of. I think I couldn't cope with my girl friend who was too like my mother I suspect ... but then that might be true of a lot of people.

A frequent criticism of me as a teacher was that I didn't observe the boundaries too well between adults and children. I tended to be on the side of the boy who was in trouble. I certainly wasn't very aware of the adult/child barrier.

I feel quite grateful for the opportunity to tell my story; it – it may have highlighted a few things for me. Because of the overtones of guilt, scandal etc. it's probably a good thing for all that to be aired.

Discussion

These stories raise several overlapping issues; it is interesting to note that both Tony and Len felt very disturbed by the disruption caused in their early life by the sense of homelessness they experienced. In both cases that was the most painful childhood memory which caused other experiences to become less significant. Both men expressed painful feelings of abandonment and emotional insecurity; Len by the constant moving from one house to another and his frequent changes of school which did not seem to be sufficiently compensated for by his 'halycon' early days of which he has no actual memory, and Tony by never having a home of his own, his early separation from his father and later from his mother. Both children would fit the picture of the emotionally needy child who is often singled out by paedophiles who recognise the child's need for an adult's approval, attention and company. Len however, describes himself as being 'a rumbly tumbly sort of little boy' and 'masculine with a good streak of the feminine'. He was 'a totally angelic altar boy' – a bit of an adventurer and 'a dreamer' – he does not remember any abuse occurring before early adolescence although he seems to be searching his memory at one point for something that had occurred earlier.

Tony received messages from his fathers that he was not sufficiently masculine; probably leaving him seeking approval from other adult males, especially with the memory of his father accusing him of being 'a mummy's boy'. His unorthodox home environment caused him to feel inferior and disapproved of within the culture of his school.

Tony acknowledges his homosexual aspect as well as his 30 per cent heterosexual inclination; he believes his mother's behaviour may have contributed to the development of his homosexuality. Len believes he is heterosexual but also acknowledges that he could engage in homosexual sexual activity if no females were available.

Homosexuality

I shall link Martin's story (presented in Chapter 16) here with that of Tony and Len. Martin was sexually abused during childhood by men known to him but not family members. He is a Catholic priest and a homosexual. These three men seem to represent the three types of people described by Freud in his theory of homosexuality as a developmental process which he described in his *Three Essays on Sexuality* (1905). He distinguished three types of people having what he called 'contrary sexual feelings'; the first type he described as 'obligatory' (Martin) which refers to those who feel there is no other option for them; the second 'amphigenic' (Tony) or those who have an attraction to both sexes (bisexual) and the third 'contingent' (Len) or those who may become homosexually active when in the situation which influences that activity (situational). Freud also dealt with the questions of innate predisposition versus acquired character of the sexual instinct, and degeneracy.

The development of homosexual orientation may depend on several factors. Tony points out a theory he does not subscribe to; that homosexuality arises because of a genetic predisposition. He believes that homosexual orientation is more likely to be the outcome of a too intrusive mother–son relationship or the absence of a father. All of these are ideas that have been put forward to explain the 'abnormality' of homosexual behaviour.

The fact that homosexual behaviour is seen in the animal kingdom among the more intelligent primates e.g. baboons and monkeys, as an alternative to heterosexual behaviour, supports the idea that genetic factors may be involved.

Some sociologists accept homosexuality as entirely normal in a biological sense and believe that it has always existed in well-adapted populations because they are the carriers of rare altruistic propensities which are important to the survival of the group.

Psychoanalytic theory suggests that homosexuality might be the outcome of an incomplete separation at the Oedipal stage between the mother and her son, compounded by an ineffectual, absent or distant father or one who is harsh and unloving (Skynner and Cleese 1983). Skynner suggests that a boy who has not had a 'same-sex' warm, loving relationship with his father goes through life seeking both the warmth of that relationship and the authority and strength of the 'masculine', symbolised by the penis. However, as the penis is only a symbol of that love and authority and not actually *what* it symbolises, then the man is never satisfied and often goes from one partner to another.

Kinsey (1948, 1953) reports that a high proportion of men (as well as a substantial proportion of women) have taken part in homosexual acts at some time in their lives. Kinsey found that about 50 per cent of American men were, in his terms 'exclusively heterosexual', i.e. they had neither participated in homosexual activities nor felt homosexual desires; 18 per cent were exclusively homosexual or persistently bisexual.

Single sex boarding schools, such as that which Tony and Len attended, may be 'hot beds' of homosexuality, but they probably do not create the condition. At school, homosexuality among peers may be part of adolescent curiosity; it may bring out natural homosexuality but it is unlikely to implant it.

Examining Tony's life within the understanding offered by psychoanalytical theory, it might be seen that the early sexual contact with his mother would have created an erotic bonding between them which remained unbroken perhaps until his first separation which he describes as causing him great emotional pain and a sense of abandonment. He also describes the sense of 'homelessness', something that caused him evident pain when he spoke of it during the interview. Len also describes this aspect of his life as being what he felt most abused by. He refers to his family as 'middle class gypsies', constantly moving from home to home.

Tony's father had been absent since his early childhood and when he was sent to live in the all-male environment of his preparatory school he would have undoubtedly been very susceptible to any perceived offer of affection or attachment to an adult male. The physical separation from his mother left him feeling 'bereft'; a sense of loss that must have been evident to the men who were entrusted with his care.

The Catholic Church with its lack of openness about sexuality and its requirement for celibacy among its clergy, reflects attitudes to sexuality found in the wider society in general and in the homes of most of the men in my study in particular. Many of the men who commenced their seminary training before the 1960s would have been around the age of 14 years. At this stage in their sexual development many young men are concerned with homosexual feeling towards their peer group; this could be seen to be part of normal development and has been likened to the strong sexual feelings the child experiences during the Oedipal stage towards the same sex parent which are resurrected during early adolescence.

From both Tony and Len's story we hear the messages they were given – that masturbation is a sin and should be confessed. This attitude was one that probably engendered strong feelings of guilt and may have caused them to suppress their normal sexual feelings. The suppression of sexuality, at a time when normal adolescence permits an exploration of these feelings through the formation of same and cross gender behaviour, may cause young men to remain fixated until such time as they leave the confines of the seminary and go out into a world in which sexuality is part of most people's experience. It may be that the seemingly higher proportion of homosexuals within the clergy group is explained in some degree by this. This view is shared by Sipe (1990) whose study highlighted the number of adult priests who seemed to be fixated at a homosexual level of 'normal development' and because of their commitment to celibacy, were never able to move to opposite sex relationships and thereby move to mature adult sexuality.

The fact that Tony managed to control his normal sexual urges during his training for the priesthood and before ordination and gives in to them afterwards, ties in with Sipe's findings (1990). For those seminarians whose urges are more problematical, such as those who engage sexually with children – this is the time they begin to act out those urges. Sipe found that very few priests in his study acted on their paedophilic urges whilst in the seminary.

Tony recognises that he is unlikely to form a sexual relationship with a woman and decides that he might usefully sublimate his sexuality (which he perceives as unfortunate or wrong) in a way that feels congruent with his spirituality.

Martin, on the other hand, sees no connection between his homosexuality and his childhood sexual abuse. He remembers what he calls '(homo)sexual memories from the age of 6', four years before being abused. He believes the abuse educated him as to the mechanics of same sex genital behaviours, but did not cause, evoke or awaken his homosexuality. Unlike Tony, he subscribes to the 'genetic' argument as a basis for his homosexuality. He likens homosexuality to: 'our DNA, like our fingerprints, examples of the uniqueness of our creaturehood'.

Tony indicates that part of his thinking about becoming a priest was that he would not be able to have a sexually fulfilling heterosexual relationship with a woman and, therefore, he saw the priesthood as way of sublimating, in a wholesome way, his sexuality. Martin sees a very strong and intimate relationship between his homosexuality and his response to his vocation. He feels that he can only be called to God as he is, with his particular, unique and complex personhood. This dynamic unravelling of ideas was coloured by his family's non-acceptance of his homosexuality, which meant he could never have an open sexual relationship with a man and be accepted by them, and by his need to live in harmony with his authentic self.

Len sees his 'homosexual' behaviour as a phase through which boys pass on the way to developing heterosexual relationships. Several men refer to this as a period of preparation for opposite sex relationships, a practice for the 'real thing'. Interestingly this argument is also used by some of the abusers of the men in this study as a way of normalising the abuse and thereby making it acceptable to their victims.

Abuse by clergy

The men who abused Tony and Len (and another man in my study) were members of a Church which requires its priests to be celibate. Celibacy is generally thought to be synonymous with sexual abstinence and restraint, so when priests are unable to live their lives in accordance with the demands of the church their sexual activity may be shrouded in secrecy and shame.

Parents who send their children to schools run by religious organisations have the expectation that they will be safe physically, sexually and morally; a sacred trust that they expect will foster good character, growth in self-confidence, moral values, spiritual and mental health. This attitude of concern and sexual protection is particularly expected from the clergy. Some priests use this position of trust and the presumption of moral integrity as a cover for their sexual activity. The majority, of course, do not.

When the abuser is a priest this creates an additional problem for those who are abused. Generally, victims express the fear that they would not be believed as a contributory factor to non-disclosure, both at the time of the abuse and afterwards; this fear is greatly exacerbated when the abuser is seen as someone who is meant to be a representative of Christ on earth, a 'man of God'. These are powerful people within a powerful organisation and hardly to be reckoned with by a nameless, powerless victim. How does a child deal with the confusion created by a priest who preaches of God's love and administers the sacraments to the same child he is molesting? What is the effect on the child's spiritual and moral development? An added confusion may be created by the fact that sometimes these particular priests are close family friends; men who may have developed relationships, particularly with the mother of the child they are molesting, which is condoned and even welcomed by the father of the child as it provides a good religious mentor for his family; someone his wife can relate to on a deep level without the threat or concern of 'sex' becoming involved in a way that is threatening to his own relationship with her. Len describes how his family had welcomed and befriended the priest who abused him.

In his study of the secret world of sexuality and celibacy, Sipe (1990), who himself had spent many years as a priest before leaving and marrying, interviewed 1500 people with first-hand knowledge of the sexual/celibacy adjustments of priests. Sipe estimated that 48 per cent of the clergy in his study were not celibate; 20 per cent had a homosexual orientation and 4 per cent of these have more or less consistent relationships with little or no guilt attached to their behaviour (or at least not sufficient to change). Approximately half the priests who described themselves as 'homosexual', either practice celibacy or have consolidated or achieved celibacy and generally have done so in the same proportions as heterosexually orientated priests.

Of clergy in his study 6 per cent were sexually involved with minors and 4 per cent of these had a homosexual orientation but '3 per cent are so clearly dominated by their paraphilias that the sexual orientation is secondary'. Bearing in mind that abusers rarely admit to their behaviour and that this behaviour would probably be even harder to admit to as a member of the clergy, this figure is disturbingly high, although because we shall never know the percentage of abusers among the general population, it is not possible to know for certain that this is higher than average. Sipe says:

> The clergy paedophiles probably enter seminary training with a strong sexual attraction towards prepubescent children. Because their training is protective and does not challenge their psychosexual development, many of these men are unaware of the extent of their developmental deficits and sexual tendencies until after ordination. Few act out before that.

Some of these men are developmentally fixated sexually on children because of their own childhood abuse (sometimes by priests) and it may be that their early decision to remain celibate is an attempt to avoid the confusion and distress connected (maybe unconsciously) with their early sexual experiences. Celibacy is not a running away from sex and Sipe acknowledges that anyone who has been subjected to any compulsive sexual behaviour, without regard for real relationship, will have a hard time choosing celibacy freely. Those who may be developmentally fixated may be 40-year-old men who are psychosexually the same age as their adolescent victims.

The argument that celibacy is to blame for somehow bottling up a priest's healthy sexual feelings is dismissed by the church, not least because the overwhelming majority of known abusers are married heterosexual men. But it has been accepted by some that Catholicism may have added its own peculiar 'twist' to the phenomenon when it condemned the sexual urges of its priest in training just at the time they were first fully experiencing them. Some paedophilic priests twist this to the extent that they feel they are 'serving God by steering clear of sexual contact with adult females, whom they have always been taught to avoid' (Freedland 1993).

For many priests, work with children and young people is a healthy and productive sublimation of their generational drive which Erikson (1968) sees as a necessary stage in healthy psychosocial development. They perform a parental function and become like the 'father' in the very best spiritual sense. Monastic schools have had centuries of experience in the schooling of young boys. The Jesuits, founded in the sixteenth century, took upon themselves the mission of educating boys among the general population, not only the sons of the wealthy. As a result they had a profound influence on society's attitudes towards children. Schetky and Green (1988) say:

> The Jesuits began to view children with compassion, urged speaking decently to them, ended the practice of children and adults sleeping together and prohibited familiarity between servants and children (p.25).

In a recent report on the 'epidemic' proportions of allegations of sexual abuse, the Catholic Church has been forced to face up to the fact that in the USA during the last eight years 400 priests have been convicted of sexual assaults on children (McHardy and Schwartz

1994). In Great Britain similar stories are emerging but figures are not available. The Church up to now has stuck its head in the sand over sexual matters; a system of secrecy about sexuality, one of the underlying norms for sexual abuse, has run throughout the Catholic Church when faced with the choices of either recognising or confronting sexuality of the clergy or ignoring it and hoping it will go away. A priest I questioned about these matters recently said that he thought things were changing for the better and that his own renewal course, in which the integration of one's sexuality formed an important part, would be one example of bringing about healing at a personal level (personal communication). Martin's story describes the workshop at which his own realisation of childhood abuse occurred and was a provision for the clergy by the Church to enable the development of self-awareness and personal growth. The treatment centre at which he had a four month rehabilitation programme was also a resource provided by the Church which indicates a changing attitude and a willingness to deal with these matters.

The Church reflects the wider patriarchal society in that it is not well informed on these issues; scandal is an anathema to the Church which needs to be respected and wants to be an example of moral leadership. Celibacy may also be linked with the view of the Church as patriarchal society within itself. Celibacy is based on the assumption that a man who is free of the ties to a woman within marriage will be more available to his 'flock' both practically and spiritually; something which may well be true in terms of time and commitment. Freely chosen celibacy, which implies an understanding and maturity about the nature of the choice, may however only develop over time and once attained may indeed enhance the quality of the priesthood. A priest who was sexually abused by a priest during his adolescence, writing anonymously (Didaskalos 1994), identifies himself as homosexual and sees that the confusion between the charisma and the discipline of celibacy has resulted in priests shouldering the burden of the discipline as the cost of serving the people of God. He comments on the lack of spiritual discussion about celibacy during a seminarian's training.

However, it may be naïve to ignore the suggestion that celibacy may be more about the church's attitudes to women. Sipe says in his study of celibacy he found the attitude to be one of,

> Women cannot have power. Women are equal, necessary, one in Christ, if they keep their place. The idea that the place of women is subordinate to men runs deep, not only in the history and culture of the Church, but in the conscious filter of many men and women who justify this bias as natural (sanctioned by grace) (p.29).

He adds that according to Church tradition, although not an official church teaching, the only good woman is 'silent, sexless and subservient'. Sipe's study of celibacy has left him with 'no doubt that this attitude is alive and well in the Church of today', a reflection of views expressed in a recent survey of women in my own Diocese. The vote by the Church of England to allow the ordination of women has in some measure shown a movement away from this attitude. No such attitude change is seen in the Catholic Church which offers a haven for those disaffected Church of England clergy who remain adamant in that view.

Another type of abuse found among the men in my study and in that of Sipe, involved severe physical punishments of boys by priests – usually with a leather tolley (a whale bone covered in leather), and perhaps masking the sexual excitement of the perpetrator. Sipe reported that following this abuse the perpetrator would often masturbate and would sometimes experience ejaculation during the beating of the boy without the boy being aware of it.

In my interviews these incidents were reported by the recipients of this abuse. Often the covert sexuality of this type of abuse leaves the boy sensing something amiss, but because the priest did not expose his genitals or touch the child in an overtly sexual way, (although putting the hand down inside the front of the trousers to hold the stomach came close to it), the child is left with the conviction that any inappropriate thoughts or feeling were his fault and not the priest's.

In this way sex becomes depersonalised and is referred to as 'what was' by Len. This young man had the experience of a priest involving him in masturbation after getting into his bed in the middle of the night; 'it' was never referred to again, and as long as both parties assumed that the boy was asleep then the activity was depersonalised. Len says that he suspects one of the effects of his early sexual experiences is 'about making some aspects of sexuality remote, so there is not too much intimacy – like rear entry heterosexual sex'. Tony experienced a similar situation with the monk who erected a tent where they lay down together and hugged. Looking back on that with an adult's understanding, Tony imagines that the young monk was masturbating or obtaining some sexual satisfaction from the contact; the child was being used for the adult's satisfaction without any sense of being personally involved in it as a sexual act.

All of these men have been abused by other men – Tony was also abused by his mother at an earlier stage in his development. None of them ever reported their abuse so they would not have been included in the reported statistics about prevalence. One reason Tony and Len did not report their abuse was that they did not define what happened to them as abuse and in Martin's case he repressed the memory through fear, guilt and shame; Tony experienced his mother's abuse as 'love' and later sexual activity with priests and boys as 'normal', if sometimes worrying; to do otherwise he might have to acknowledge his mother as an abuser, something that is against all his deepest instincts and all the socialisation messages he has received about women, sexuality and the role of the mother. Even now as an adult Len still does not experience emotionally (although he does intellectually) what happened to him as sexual abuse. To do so would be acknowledge that he was a victim and that is antithetical to his view of maleness.

I believe much of this is due to the socialisation they have received as males in a patriarchal and homophobic society which views male sexual behaviour as 'normal' when it is used as a demonstration of power over someone who is in some way perceived as 'inferior'. It is also obvious that none of these men would have been happy to talk of their sexual contact with another male because of the implications that this may have in terms of being viewed as homosexual which is universally perceived as 'wrong'. Martin says 'who does this say I am?' as though his admission of such sexual contact defines him as a person.

The additional difficulty, in being believed, in defining what happened as abuse and in daring to name a priest (God's representative) as an abuser, speaks for itself.

Part 3

Part 3 consists of three chapters concerned with issues related to the recovery process after childhood sexual abuse. In Chapter 16 the main discussion points from Martin's story are those of repression and disclosure. Martin had repressed his memory of his sexual abuse for nineteen years. As previously stated repression is only one of the reasons for non-disclosure but it is a relevant and necessary one to describe, especially in the face of claims made by supporters of the 'False Memory Syndrome' lobby.

As well as the main issue of disclosure, Martin's case will also raise our awareness of such issues as: effects of abuse, treatment of survivors, homosexuality, celibacy and the concept of 'the wounded healer'.

16 Martin's story

Martin is a priest and a homosexual. He has no children. He was born in 1961 and has two older sisters and two younger brothers.

He began by recalling his first abuse:

One day when I was 10-years-old my father took me fishing and in the afternoon I went looking for him along the river bank; I didn't find him but I found his friend, a single man in his forties, and I asked him where my father was; he said he didn't know but told me to come and sit down and wait for him. He helped me down the river bank and placed me between his legs (I was wearing shorts) and he began to fondle me genitally. That was a one-off event and of course I never went fishing again. I felt that somehow my father was responsible since this man was my father's friend; I told no one at the time.

Just after that I was abused by John, the 17-year-old brother of my friend. On this occasion I went to my friend's house to see if he was coming out to play and he wasn't in. His older brother told me to come into the house and wait. When I got into the house he told me to sit on the settee and he put his arms around me and began to rock to and fro. He then made me perform fellatio on him and basically held me in what felt like hostage circumstances for the next hour or so until Paul returned from church.

Over the next few months it seemed wherever I was, John was also there; when I went swimming or playing in the fields near my home he would turn up, and on each occasion he forced me into masturbation and oral sex with him. This went on for a period of about three months; it happened almost once a week during that time. It stopped because the family moved away from the area when their father got a new job.

I thought I must be a bad person who caused these good people to do these things to me, particularly when it happened the second time; there was definitely something strange about me. I was responsible, I was to blame. I couldn't disclose because I was too scared. I have no recollection of my father's friend suggesting that this was our secret but John said I was to tell no-one. I have a vague recollection of a threat that if I did tell he would get me.

I felt guilty, partly because there was a certain attraction and interest in it, a sexual excitement which, I have to say, I enjoyed. That was a very confused feeling alongside the childhood feelings of having nowhere to place this experience; it was outside my understanding. It was a whole new world of playing that I did not know. Being a serious child, I appreciated adult company and this new thing was a way of being with adults; but I was scared stiff. What did it say about me; who did it say I was; would my parents believe me; what would happen to the people who had abused me? I couldn't face the publicity and being at the centre of something so awful. I wanted to live on the edge; life was so precarious as it was, I couldn't bear any further exposure.

I was a 29-year-old novice when I eventually told someone. I was taking part in an intensive journaling workshop led by a member of my religious order. On day four of this workshop we were asked to journal under the headings 'Happenings in my life'. My mind was quite blank and I began to 'blitz' write on the page. The first word I wrote was 'abuse' and I was stunned. Until that moment, nineteen years later, I had buried this information so deeply within myself that I just could not remember; I had no access to this crucial information about my life.

I didn't know why my behaviour, my feelings, my patterns of thought, my patterns of relationships, had been tarnished. That day was the beginning of the unlocking of these secrets even to myself and, bit by bit, it started to come back. Yes, I had been abused; yes, I had been sexually abused; yes, it had been more than once; and yes I had enjoyed, to a certain extent, something of it. But yes too, it filled me with fear. It left me with a pool of heaviness, just ever so close by, that the slightest thing provoked me falling into. I wouldn't have used the word 'depression', but I would have said that I was permanently heavy or that heaviness was always just around the corner. The slightest thing, the look, or the lack of the look; something that somebody said or didn't say; waking up in the morning, was always experienced as falling into this heaviness which could, in turn, sometimes take me into depression.

So that day I went to the man in charge of my formation and told him. He panicked; he didn't know what to say or do; he said that he would get me help. This felt quite devastating. It felt like he was saying 'don't bring it to me; I can't cope, take it somewhere else, go away!' I understood that the man was acting correctly in not pretending to be able to deal with something so professionally demanding, but my emotional reaction was stronger than my intellectual understanding.

Before I told him I had bumped into a friend on the stairs and in a very flippant way, which when I look back actually disturbs me, I said: 'you'd never believe what I wrote today. I discovered today I was sexually abused as a child'. I told this person on the stairs, in a public setting in which other people could have overheard and I think my flippancy was all part of my attempt to conceal the devastating importance of the discovery. I didn't really want it to be as big as it was.

What is very interesting is that from that day onwards and certainly for the first three months, there were different moments of deeper disclosure to myself, even before I got to other people. Having allowed this to surface, I refused to bury it again and further incidents began to re-emerge; the effect began to dawn on me more and more.

At first I spoke of it as 'that unfortunate incident' and then later as 'that awful thing that happened to me'; until at its full height when I couldn't think, breathe or dream anything other than these memories, I was referring to it as 'the day I was murdered'. That was something of the journey I had to go on; acknowledging, disclosing to myself, allowing myself to feel the extent of the issue and gradually being able to tell others. But it is very significant to me that the first disclosure that I made was the flippant one, as if I had just bought a new record or a new T- shirt: 'I was abused you know'; to go from that right through to 'I was murdered'. That was the truth of the matter and that was the journey of disclosure. As I was able to embrace the truth of my experience, I also began to recognise so many other things that were part of the package. Things like very low self-esteem; always discrediting my own experience; a sense of permanently missing the point; the experience of desperately and frantically searching for approval; of always feeling let down by authority figures; of being scared of men as a group and yet as a homosexual, attracted to men; of being vulnerable; of having enormous compassion and sympathy and energy for any person or group of people which suffers exploitation. The experience of living in a world where laws made no sense – a sort of antinomian tendency within myself – nothing made sense from the age of 10, so who can prescribe law now and what validity does it have? A sense of boundaries constantly flipping and flopping, ebbing and flowing.

Who was I? Did others determine my identity or did my identity come from within. Do I always just respond to what happened or could I be an actor? These were some of the things that began to emerge but more than anything, beyond the level of articulation, was a gut feeling that the bastards who murdered me had ruled my life for twenty years, it was now my turn to live. I would call the shots; I would live life my way. And so first thing in the morning when I would wake up, I would refuse to live out of that sense of heaviness, that sense of alienation, of meaninglessness. There was a conscious: 'I will live today in light, in freedom, in joy. I will live today free from the negative influence of the past.' That was the beginning, the conscious beginning of my recovery of which there have been many stages.

There has also been physical abuse. I remember as a child of 6 or 7 my father trying desperately to teach me to play football and I couldn't manage it. Emotional abuse is involved here too because he began to refer to me as a poof, a pansy, a jessie, a queer because I couldn't play football and began to ridicule me and one day, when it all got too much, he physically beat me to the point where I had concussion. Being a 'real man' in my family was someone who played football very well. It meant no affection with other men. It definitely meant a hardness.

There was also psychological abuse from my mother. At the age of about 6 I remember a recurring threat 'if you are bad I'll take you to the home for bad children'. One particular evening she said to me that I was going to the 'bad home' tomorrow. She took me upstairs, brought out an old suitcase and made me watch while she packed some of my clothes into a suitcase which was left at the bottom of my bed. Needless to say I didn't sleep that night and when morning came, I'll never forget the experience of walking to school with mum holding my left hand, my right hand carrying that suitcase. There, in that little caricature, on the one hand was the experience of being bonded, wanted and united to my mother, to love, to family, to relationship and in the other hand the suitcase symbolising that I wasn't wanted, that I could be discarded. In many ways that little cameo is indicative of my childhood with my parents.

I remember being very aware from very early on, that there was very little money around, that there was tension between my mother and father. And I was very, very sensitive to this tension particularly around the age of 6; my father constantly told me about his father dying in the war. In response to any negative criticism which he perceived to be coming from me, he would often say 'at least you have a father'; so I was supposed to feel gratitude for him, for his role, for his presence in my life and yet the real truth was that I couldn't relate to this man who rejected me as a poof, a pansy, a queer, simply on the basis that I couldn't play football. My mother, on the other hand, tried to stand up for me and that caused further tension within the family.

Also my father drank heavily at the weekends from when I was 6–12 years old. I remember many a tense afternoon waiting to hear if his team had been beaten or had won. If they had been beaten we lived in fear of him coming home, because when he did, he would shout or withdraw into silence. Whatever way he came home my mother would fight with him; sometimes she would be slapped by him and week after week for a few years, I would sit in our front room crying my eyes out while I listened to them screaming at each other upstairs; my mother screaming because he was hitting her. Sometimes I intervened, always I was rejected, with yet more verbal abuse. My mother would storm out of the house and it always felt like she would never come back. My experience of childhood is one of enormous tension and sadness.

My mother was a strong character, she had to keep the thing going but she was also a manipulator. My father was so pathetic; he was weak; he was vulnerable; he was very, very needy, very lonely and very insecure. My mother always seemed to be on the verge of a nervous breakdown. Even though I didn't know what this meant, she would say to us from when I was 5 or 6, ' you'll cause me to have a breakdown'. There was always this threat that something dramatic and drastic was going to happen. I think it was my mother who had the power in our house; the power exercised by walking out, through withdrawal, through threats.

My parents were sometimes affectionate towards each other. They would kiss and tease each other in public. They definitely looked like they loved each other. There was always a goodnight kiss for us children. My father would play with us sometimes; he would give us rides on his back as if he was a horse.

Sex was not discussed except that I remember once telling my mother a joke about a woman with pubic hair, I was only about 7 and I didn't understand it myself – she led me to believe that all that sort of thing was naughty, disgusting and I wasn't to talk about it. I learned about sexual matters at school; the way that kids tell each other what they'd seen and heard or they'd brag about thing that they are supposed to have done, but of course they hadn't.

I was a very, very sensitive young boy. I was very aware of sadness, people's pain; I was very serious, frightened. I constantly craved the approval and affection of my parents. I thought if I ran home from school on a Friday and cleaned the house, then my mother would love me and that if I washed the car for my dad, then he would love me. I was desperately trying to cull that love and affection. I was lonely; I tended to only have one friend at a time and then people would get fed up with me. I wasn't sporty; I didn't take part in competitive things.

It definitely wasn't OK for me to be that kind of little boy. My father had been a P.E. instructor in the army. My mother had played professional hockey for her country – sport was everything in our house and to have one child out of five who was not participating, to have a boy who was sensitive, who preferred to play with girls, and who preferred knitting and music (piano lessons were something I had to fight for in my family because it wasn't the done thing), all these thing meant it wasn't OK to be me in my family. And yet to be fair to them at one level they did try to comply, but always leaving me with a sense of their enormous tolerance of this dreadful behaviour that they had to put up with.

My father didn't work for me as a role model; it was such a set of confused ideas; if this is what a man was like I didn't want to be a man and to be abused by other men meant, more than anything, that I didn't know what men were like and if my father and the two abusers were indicative of the adult male, then I did not want to be a man.

I felt confused about my gender identity between the ages of 14 and 18. During this time I was a heterosexual with masturbatory fantasies of a homosexual nature resulting always in feelings of self-disgust, horror, self-hatred and rejection. I finally came to terms with my homosexuality when I realised it was not a phase I was going through; that there was not a tablet I could take that would ensure that tomorrow I would wake up as a heterosexual. I am definitely homosexual and I am very comfortable with that now. My family's attitude to homosexuality was completely and utterly dismissive. When I told my parents I was homosexual, my mother screamed repetitively 'I wanted a boy'. To this day she refers to the make-up of our family being two girls, Martin, and two boys.

I am open with discretion about my homosexuality and it's very much a part of me. I am not of the opinion that being gay *gives* me my identity but that being gay is *fundamental* to my identity; that is no less so as a priest as it was in the past when I was sexually active and had a partner. It may sound pious, but the 'cause' of my homosexuality lies within the gracious providence of God; He chose to love me into being by giving this shape to my life – it is therefore the locus of His grace towards me – a blessing for me to unravel in my life but, like all blessings, it carries responsibilities with it and must be returned to the 'Good Giver' with gratitude.

I see no connection whatsoever between my abuse and my homosexuality. I have (homo)sexual memories from the age of 6, four years before being abused. What the abuse did perhaps was to educate me as to the mechanics of same sex genital behaviours, but not to cause, evoke, awaken ... I subscribe to the view that homosexuality has a genetic basis. Our DNA, like our fingerprints, are examples of the uniqueness of our creaturehood.

Motivation to take up the 'vocation' to the priesthood and/or religious life is always murky and lacking in purity of intention (the negative view) or put positively, it's another outworking of the 'grace builds on nature' argument, that I can only be called by God as I am, with this particular psyche, temperament, set of feelings, personal history. On this view of course there is a very strong and intimate relationship between my homosexuality and my response to vocation. I tend to this latter view.

I suspect there is another question lurking behind that one – 'did you decide to become a priest as a way of dealing with your homosexuality, either as an escape, or as a silencing-off of this part of your life?' The answer to that is that it has been quite a dynamic unravelling. I've journeyed through earlier stages of 'I couldn't possibly live with another man since my family couldn't cope and I couldn't bear their rejection – therefore, since I'm going to be single, I might as well stay in the Church'; right through to the present which is, 'I am in ministry in the Church because it is where I feel most authentically me, alive and empowered'. My decision is an ever-reviewed and daily one, based on listening to my inner moods, my consolations, my desolations, my body (fatigue and energy levels); the focus here is not primarily on sexuality at all but on the harmony of my whole personal identity.

I would have to say that, even in the earliest stages, at no time was priesthood as an option, ever considered *because* I was homosexual. The two discoveries of 'vocation' and of sexual orientation were parallel journeys from around the age of 8. I have committed myself to celibacy in my present life. At the period prior to taking on the obligations of celibacy I began to be concerned that I was seeking casual sexual encounters not for sexual arousal but for seeking power; the sort of situation which would send me looking for casual encounters would be when I would come across a person in authority, (always a male of roughly the age of my father), with whom dialogue was impossible and who I experienced as autocratic, dogmatic or just pig-headed, and wherever stalemate situations arose, I would go in search of sex; first of all because, in the moment of being desired by another person, I felt empowered, and partly, bringing another person to orgasm was the ultimate moment of power over that person. In these situations I would not allow this other person to bring me to orgasm. Perhaps that would have equalled out the relationship which was not what I was about at that time. Conversely when I have been in a 'relationship' with a person, the motivation would have been affection between myself and my partner; power would have nothing to do with it.

In casual sex I would feel guilty of having abused people; I have used people for my emotional, psychological and occasionally sexual needs. When that had been the case, I had been left with very negative feelings after sexual activity.

When I was 12, I engaged in oral sex and mutual masturbation with my brother who was then 11. This took place over a period of about four weeks.

On a couple of occasions when I was alone with a child I have become very conscious of the possible power I could have over this child; it has brought home to me just how vulnerable the child is. That realisation has filled me with horror to think that someone could abuse that position. I distinguish this very clearly from a temptation, a fantasy about children. I had no idea at all of exploiting this situation.

I was arrested and charged with gross indecency in a public lavatory in a city in this country some years back. I was there explicitly looking for casual sexual encounters. I was looking to masturbate with or in the presence of another adult male without any social involvement, without knowing the other person's name or anything about them; that sort of silent sexual encounter. Two policemen in plain clothes came in, stood on either side of me as if they were looking for sex and then proceeded to arrest me. I was charged and put on two years' bail with an adult caution.

My first way of coping with the abuse was by telling the person who was responsible for my formation; then I used my journal and then after a month or so I went to see a friend who was a psychologist – to check out with him that I wasn't going off the rails. A few months later I began to feel that I wasn't coping at all and needed to see a therapist. So I went for three months to a psychotherapist and told this person in the first session that I had recently re-remembered, that I had been abused and wanted to deal with all the debris. Although I went for twelve sessions, abuse was never mentioned! The therapy was client-centred in its approach, so it was for me to give the agenda for each session. It's fair to say that at the half-way point the therapist did say that we only had so many sessions left and that I hadn't mentioned it and asked if I wanted to; I declined. Four sessions from the end the therapist once again offered me the opportunity and once again I declined. Looking back I realise that I wasn't comfortable enough to access such painful memories at that point.

At the beginning of this year I began to experience the whole of my life collapsing around me. I was back into casual sexual experiences; I felt my integrity completely dissolving; I was living in a very tight situation with a member of my community whom I experienced as a very autocratic, angry, aggressive, abusive man. I became so frightened of him and especially of his anger that I began to live my life such that it would placate him; everything was geared around saving him from getting angry because on the one occasion that I had seen his anger I had suffered too much. This placating took the form of staying out of his way, staying out of the house until I began to feel that there was no safety anywhere for me. I also felt back in the world of secrets where I cannot speak; where I cannot tell; 'who can I turn to; who will believe me; who will understand?'

I began to have nightmares in which I was abused again; this time by a woman. It was in this situation that I realised that I was in a very sorry state and something drastic had to happen. All my confidence and self-esteem had gone again; I was unable to work; I wanted to stay in my room and never leave it. At this point I was able to secure a four month intensive therapeutic experience in a residential treatment centre for clergy, to deal with the debris of being an adult child of a dysfunctional family, to deal with the sexual acting out of all this with casual sexual behaviour.

What helped me was to be listened to, to be able to speak freely, openly, in an unedited way. What helped me more than anything, when I consider what I've been through in individual therapy and group therapy, was the power of peer group; meeting with other people who had been through the same experiences. It was hearing their stories that helped me to unlock further recesses; it was through group therapy that information which was hidden from me began to emerge.

What hindered me was my own fear of unlocking even more. It was bad enough having unlocked twenty years' worth, but then in group therapy to hear someone else's story and to think 'yes that's me too. My God when will this stop, when will this ever end?' Feeling the fear of being rejected, the fear of feeling that my acting out sexually was much worse than anybody else's; that they just drank or withdrew but look what I was doing.

I think the abuse has affected my life profoundly. It has made me incredibly vulnerable, it has made me, on the other hand, very sensitive to people; it's an enormous gift for the ministry now. It sends me straight into a whole world of compassion where I can reach people who haven't necessarily had my experience but have suffered some other major trauma in their life. I can reach them with an openness, with a familiarity, a level of empathy that I myself would never have had if I had not been through this awful business.

It's left me though, very much a victim; it's left me angry and although I've worked a lot with anger, anger like heaviness is never too far away; it is something that I can touch into quite easily. Anger is something I have to watch. It's left me constantly struggling with feeling that I'm not quite up to the mark; that I'm not quite the real thing. It's left me very definitely in the pattern of workaholism where I measure my worth, my sense of self by my productivity, constantly producing new work, new documents, new packaging, new ideas, constantly proving myself. It's left me guilty about taking days off, about being good to myself. It's left me having to watch boundaries. It still leaves me with a difficulty of knowing what is right and what is wrong; a sense of 'anything goes'. It has left me with a struggle to establish boundaries to protect myself, in some ways to protect myself against myself. My seeking approval or affection will take me into all sorts of difficult situations. If there were ten people in a room and nine of them liked me and one didn't, I would pursue that one. I would only feel secure if everyone liked me.

I have felt suicidal – not immediately connected with the experience of abuse. It was the day after I had told my parents that I was gay and they had reacted so badly. I relived in those few hours all the pain of my childhood, of being and feeling unwanted, of not being what they had hoped me to be. I relived also my own trauma and pain of coming to terms with my homosexuality and I was back again into the 'Yes society is right; you are a pervert. Yes, the Church is right; you are a sinner and you are damned.' And it was very much in those feelings that I walked in front of a double decker bus, the bus swerved and I was untouched; I lived.

I viewed the abuse by my father's friend very definitely negatively at the time. I viewed the abuse by my friend's older brother negatively in the first few instances, moving towards neutrally, if not positively, as a sense of excitement developed over time, especially when he performed fellatio on me.

When I look back now, I view my abuse entirely negatively. It was a total infringement, a total denial of my human rights and my rights as a child. Nobody should have to undergo that. It has damaged my life, I would not like to say 'irreparably' because I believe in the resurrection, but it has left a mark that will always be there, even if redeemed.

But then, if it's not a contradiction, I can say that I have learned so much about life, so quickly. It has given me so much to bring to my life and other people's lives by way of compassion, by way of empathy, by way of energy against any form of abuse or exploitation.

Discussion

Repression

Freud first used the term repression in a paper he wrote which was later to form the first chapter in *Studies on Hysteria* (1896) although the term had been used earlier by Herbart, a psychologist whose work had influenced Freud's thinking. Freud used the term to describe a phenomenon whereby feelings that are unacceptable or overwhelming are repressed from conscious thought. As a concept it contributed to an understanding of the origin of the symptoms of 'hysterical conversion'. Feelings which were stimulated in an initial situation but were experienced as unacceptable before even emerging into consciousness, were held back in the unconscious mind by the force of repression. However, this was not always fully successful and some of these feelings found unconscious expression as a physical symptom in such cases as 'hysterical paralysis'. The damming up of these feelings uses a considerable amount of psychic energy over long periods of time. The feelings defended against in this way often are associated with pain or fear.

When a child is sexually abused, the feelings attached to the event may be repressed into the unconscious as a way of coping with what otherwise might be intolerable. It may be that the whole event is repressed, including memories of whole portions of the child's life around the time when the abuse occurred. This phenomenon has been particularly well described by Janov (1990). However because these memories are sometimes not remembered until the person becomes psychologically sufficiently mature to allow them into consciousness in adulthood, some people doubt their validity.

False memory syndrome

The first meeting of the False Memory Syndrome Foundation (FMSF) was held in the USA in March 1992. This is a support and advocacy organisation composed of parents who say they have been falsely accused by their adult children of having sexually abused them during childhood. Many of these parents now find themselves involved in court cases for abuses committed two or three decades ago which their adult sons and daughters have recently remembered. That these parents can be sued at all reflects the powerful impact that the incest-recovery movement has had on the law in the USA. During the 1980s in the USA, twenty-one states altered the legislation to allow an extension of the statute of limitations, which normally sets the time limit – usually seven years – following an alleged offence, after which the lawsuit or criminal charges cannot be brought. Now a movement, which seems to be spreading to other states, allows a person to bring legal action against alleged sexual abuse perpetrators up to two or three years after he or she recovers the memory of that abuse, which may be decades after the event.

These parents have formed a volunteer advocacy organisation to lobby public opinion on behalf of their cause. They seek as much media attention as possible; more than thirty members of the press were invited to the first meeting in 1992. Everybody is anxious to tell as many people who are willing to listen, the outrageous story of these misplaced accusations.

In Britain there is now a similar organisation, The British False Memory Society (BFMS), which models itself on the FMSF. As in the USA many of the parents of adult children who are disclosing their childhood abuse are finding comfort in the sharing of their grievances. In Britain the number of adults claiming compensation through the Criminal Compensation Scheme is dramatically rising and is set to rise even further. In Britain there is a three year limit for bringing a personal injury claim (if the victim is a child three years from the time they reach 18). There have been cases to test this time limit in the face of the fact that there is often a much greater passage of time before people remember their abuse due to repression. It is argued that it should be three years from the time that the victim has the 'requisite knowledge' of the abuse and its effects.

A Court of Appeal ruling in April 1991 marked a breakthrough. The judges decided that a woman could bring charges against her stepfather and adoptive brother whom she alleged had sexually abused her as a child – even though she had not issued the writ until she was 30. She argued that it was not until receiving professional help that she realised the psychological damage the abuse had caused her and therefore the writ was served within the three year limit of her having the 'requisite knowledge'. However, the Law Lords ruled in December 1992 that too much time had passed. She then lodged a petition (along with two other women in the same situation) with the European Commission of Human Rights in Strasbourg, claiming her rights had been violated under the European Convention for Human Rights. In Britain, a 1980 Act states that to file a personal injury claim, an individual has three years from the time he or she realises the injuries are the result of the event, although the court has the power to allow claims later but the Lords ruled that this does not apply to sexual abuse. The complaint would need to be filed within six years of the date of the alleged offence or within six years of the person's eighteenth birthday.

Unlike Canada and certain states in the U.S. which have changed their laws to allow greater time limits, the British ruling eliminated any hope of redress after the age of 24. The awareness of the damage caused by sexual abuse and the retrieval of repressed memories frequently occurs after the age of 30 – it often requires enough time for adults to separate from their family of origin and begin to develop a life of their own before this process can begin.

Organisations such as FSMF and BFMS say they do not doubt the reality of child abuse, or its power to damage victims, and the need to bring the perpetrators to justice, but they attack the recently increased figures as evidence to support their claims that the 'child abuse industry' is cashing in on situations that are invalid and that it is this fact that explains the swelling numbers of alleged cases of child abuse. This sweeping allegation dismisses the research data that professionals have spent the last ten years carefully accumulating in the new and healthier climate of openness surrounding such matters.

The founder of the British society, declares that 'true victims do not forget their abuse' (Scotford 1993), nor he says, do they feel anger towards their parents and want to pursue them through the courts. This unsupported statement is the basis upon which he argues that adult children accusing their parents are the victims of therapists and others who are causing distress to countless families. The FMSF argue that the fact that their children are normal, bright, accomplished and successful is added proof that these allegations are untrue; that children who had really been abused would show none of these signs of healthy development; that they would be impoverished creatures living in some sort of twilight state – a far cry from how they and others see their own accusing offspring. FSMF presents a self-administered questionnaire which identifies that, on the whole, these families are models of wholesome family life; middle to upper class, educated, active in their churches and staunch advocates of family values. Implicit in this statement is the outdated view that child abusers are never respectable members of society and can in some way be identified as a group. The reality is that abusers come from all classes and backgrounds and are as frequently found among church members, professionals and those in caring roles as well as many other positions of trust and authority and are often perceived as models of correctness and moral responsibility.

In an article in the *Guardian* (25 April 1994) Linda Grant announced a new organisation which aims to counter the claims made by False Memory Syndrome theorists which is called Accuracy About Abuse and is founded by Marjorie Orr, a psychotherapist, with the support of Helena Kennedy, Professor Anthony Clare, Dr Gillian Mezey, forensic scientist at St George's Hospital, Tooting, Liz Sayce, director of MIND and Michele Elliott, child psychologist and director of KIDSCAPE. The founder members of the

FMSF in the US who coined the name for the 'syndrome' were both highly qualified academics. Their eldest daughter is a psychology professor at an American university and their younger daughter is also an academic. Like most members of their organisation, the founder members claimed that their's was a happy home that was wrecked by the intervention of a therapist who had implanted in their daughter's mind the fact that she had been sexually abused in childhood. Their daughter has now publicly spoken out about her father's alcoholism and that he was sexually abused by a male artist with whom he lived when he was 9-years-old. Her father admits that this man was a paedophile and that he was a 'kept boy'. She describes how sexual boundaries were frequently blurred in the home. In the early 80s Peter had been admitted for treatment for chronic alcoholism, something that was totally denied until after his daughter had left the house.

The organisation has been further undermined by the recent forced resignation of an executive director, Dr Ralph Underwager who has appeared as a defence witness in more than 200 cases of alleged child abuse in the US, Canada, Australia, New Zealand and Britain. At the end of 1993 an interview with Underwager appeared in a Dutch paedophile magazine in which he supported the activities of paedophiles. He was then asked to resign from the board of FSMF.

Mary Sykes Wylie in her report (1993) relates one of FSMF's pet theories as:

> The very stability and closeness of the families, the apparent happiness, good behaviour and high performance of the children were themselves somehow perversely related to the sudden explosion of bizarre accusations. These children were so used to living up to and beyond expectations, that when they did seek out therapy for current difficulties in their lives, they carried that drive to achieve within them and became the 'best' patients the therapist ever had – the ones most likely to produce what was wanted (p.23).

This argument rests upon the assumption that what the therapists 'want' is for the client to believe that they have been sexually abused in childhood, whether in fact they have or not.

Psychoanalytical theorists explain these accusations as a manifestation that these adult children (normally daughters) have never managed to separate themselves from their family emotionally and are finally getting round to a long delayed adolescent rebellion in order to achieve that separation. The daughter's early dependency on her family of origin has left her with feelings of hostility towards her parents which she is unable to express because of her love–hate relationship with them. She displaces her dependency on to the therapist who becomes the 'ideal' mother-substitute figure, who is all accepting and believing and approving, and who will offer her client the mechanism whereby she can separate from her parents. The therapist then, instead of working through the underlying real conflict, offers symptomatic relief by providing a new symptom to explain the previously unreasonable anger and hostility the client felt towards the parents – she then has an excuse to cut the umbilical cord! The therapist provides a reason for making separation and individuation that the client could not have otherwise made.

This theory provides a face-saving rationalisation which neatly avoids the need for accused parents to feel the dissonance created by the accusations. It offers parents the answers to the unanswerable question of 'how can I have been a good parent and still have such a child? How can I believe in my own innocence without having to hate my child?'

Other theorists see the accusing women as angry paranoids, as are their therapists, who are also incompetent fanatics. However, most of these parents do not wish to blame their daughters for these allegations any more than they wish to blame themselves. Doubts expressed seem to centre around the presumption that it is the therapist who in some subversive way 'implants' these memories into their clients minds. In the USA in May 1994 a therapist was successfully sued for $500,000 by a father whose daughter had accused him of sexually abusing her during childhood. However, Martin's story demonstrates this same process of recovering memories of childhood sexual abuse after nineteen years during which he has been unconscious of these events. These memories have emerged without the input or company of a therapist. It is frequently the case that such memories are also disbelieved – something that leads me to wonder if the therapist has become the handy scapegoat of those who would prefer to deny the reality of child abuse, especially when the alleged perpetrator is themselves or a member of their own family.

Displacement of guilt is often seen in incestuous families where the child who has been abused is blamed for the disruption to the family once they have disclosed the abuse. It seems that the family is now putting the guilt onto the therapist, perhaps as a way of avoiding any responsibility themselves. It is interesting to note that it is families of victims which have started this protest group, rather than people who are not family members and have been accused of abusing children. Does this mean that when retrieved memories pertain to non-family abusers they are not so often disputed? Is it only when family members are involved that there is a need to deny?

Martin's case, which does not concern abuse by a family

member, clearly demonstrates how a child who is traumatised by sexual abuse copes with this by repressing all memory of the events until such time as he is able to cope with reclaiming the memory. There is research evidence (Finkelhor and Brown 1986) that indicates that a child is even further traumatised when the abuser is a close family member and this would seem to indicate that in such cases the need to cope by repressing the memory would be even more powerful. Children who are abused by a parent are more likely to have been abused at a younger age; the child's fragile and undeveloped ego would need to use the most powerful form of self-protection psychologiclly available to him. Martin also demonstrates how the person lives his life in reaction to, and in the grip of those feelings which are outside conscious awareness.

> Until that moment, nineteen years later, I had no memory of having been abused. I had buried this information so deeply within myself that I just could not remember – I had no access to this crucial information about my life. So for nineteen years I didn't know why my behaviour, my thinking, my feelings, my patterns of thought, my patterns of relationships had been tarnished. That day was the beginning of the unlocking of these secrets even to myself and, bit by bit, it started to come back.

His process of recovering memories of repressed experiences outside a therapeutic relationship, cannot be seen as a product of implantation by any third party and parallels the process as it occurs within a therapeutic relationship.

For the person who has used the powerful defence of repression as a protection against his traumatic childhood experiences, usually the first requirement is that he has left the unsafe environment (often the family) which has been replaced by one which feels more secure. Many survivors begin the process of recovery of memories once they have left their family home to go to College or when they have created their own families (which may in Martin's case be seen as the family of the church or his religious community). This safer environment may never be experienced by some people until they establish a trusting therapeutic relationship with a counsellor or psychotherapist. They may come into counselling for any of the reasons Martin describes – lack of self-esteem, depression, sexual difficulties or relationship problems.

Martin describes the suddenness with which this process of memory recovery sometimes occurs, although it is not always so sudden or dramatic. Others have told of their first realisation which has started whilst driving along a motorway; or when a certain smell has triggered off the first memory and opened the 'door' to other memories; sometimes memories emerge whilst watching one's own child at the stage of development that the abuse happened. There are many life events that might trigger the start of this process and many instances of this process beginning outside the formal therapeutic situation. For some men the disclosure by another family member permits the emergence of their own abuse by the same person (see Tim's story in Chapter 11); something that seems more frequently to be the case in male abuse.

Sometimes the picture emerges much more slowly with a greater degree of fuzziness and lack of clarity. This is why many people who experience this process question the veracity of their own memories and are usually reluctant to accept the notion of their abuse (see Wayne's story in Chapter 11). The undoing of denial is a gradual and painful process – no-one wants to believe in such a deep and personal betrayal; the stigma of being abused is not one that people normally enjoy or want for themselves.

The denial of the reality of the abuse is, in my view, one reason why family members may have difficulty believing the accusations that come 'out of the blue'. For the survivor the process may have been lengthy, slow and tortuous; they may have gone in and out of varying levels of minimisation or denial over a period of time. For the relatives there is no time for such a process. The victim may have decided to confront the abuser who, along with the rest of the family, is not prepared. One of our most natural psychological defence mechanisms is denial. When we hear sudden bad news our normal reaction is to deny it, 'oh, no!' When we hear of a sudden death or tragedy, the mind immediately repels the information with such statements as 'I was only speaking to him yesterday'. We grasp at the old reality and deny the new, as a necessary part of adjustment. Some people, of course, remain pathologically stuck when the cost of undoing the denial is greater than maintaining it. Work undertaken by the NSPCC (1989) with mothers who refuse to believe their child's abuse, indicates that they are often in a state of arrested grief and need help and support to come to terms with the facts. There is no reason why this should be easier when the disclosure is made by an adult son or daughter. The shock and need for denial may indeed be all the greater when the secret has been maintained for so long. Craig et al (NSPCC, 1989) say:

> It is our contention that learning to work effectively with mothers who do not, or cannot, believe that their children have been sexually abused, is the biggest and most critical challenge facing workers (p.72).

They recognise the mother's response at the point of disclosure is crucial to the prognosis of the victim's recovery.

Research has shown that many perpetrators of child abuse have themselves been victims of childhood abuse. Their own abuse might be re-enacted when it remains outside conscious knowledge and control. It seems reasonable therefore to suggest that maybe those who are accused of perpetrating the unthinkable crime of sexually abusing their own child, cope with this by denial and repression. Of course the other members of the family are shocked. Sexual abuse is a crime usually committed within the confines of a two-person relationship – there are no observers and therefore no corroborating evidence. The family rarely know about this abuse unless they themselves are involved in it.

It has been argued that people claim to have been abused in order to gain attention. For anyone who has been part of this process, as a therapist, counsellor or survivor, it can only seem a ludicrous suggestion that anyone would want to put themselves through such pain when attention can be gained in much less costly ways. I know of no therapist who enjoys listening to the stories of childhood sexual abuse. As a Supervisor I know of many counsellors/therapists who need support through supervision to deal with their own pain and horror at the unfolding revelations of people they have come to respect and care for.

Clem's story in Chapter 9, demonstrates how it was necessary for the social worker who was helping him to heal from his depression and suicidal feelings to 'reframe his experience' in order for him to recognise his abuse for what it was. False Memory lobbyists might call this 'implanting ideas' and condemn her for opening up his mind to the possibility that he had been abused when a 21-year-old woman engaged with him sexually from the age of 11–17. Many of the men in my study had needed an external view of their abusive experiences before they were able to understand where the root of so many of their adult problems lay. Society has indoctrinated males in ways that have added to the problems of male children who are sexually abused.

The families of survivors who contribute to the false memory syndrome theory tell of the painful disruption these accusations cause in their lives; therapists hear of the pain of the survivor who sometimes lose their whole family because they face up to the perpetrator and are disbelieved by the rest of the family – they lose the support of brothers, sisters and non-abusing parent; the pain on both sides is caused by the perpetrator. The greatest fear of any survivor, even those who have not repressed their memory, is that they will not be believed and sadly that is frequently the case for adult survivors (although this seems to be changing for children who disclose abuse at the time or shortly after it has happened). The cost of this disbelief is considerable to the injured party and the non-abusing members of their family; another level of abuse perpetrated by the original abuser. The isolation they have imposed on their victim in childhood is further compounded for them as adults. One of the arguments used by those who disbelieve recovered memories is that victims often recant – is it any wonder? This is a phenomenon which has been seen among children who have disclosed their abuse; once they realise what they have forfeited by their disclosure, they have recanted their stories. Children may not realise the full cost of that disclosure if their abuser denies the abuse. The child might be removed from his home, he is stigmatised by society, he may be pathologised and disbelieved; he is re-victimised by the denial of the perpetrator. Is it any wonder that adults who find themselves in the same situation sometimes withdraw into the response of the hurt, betrayed child they once were, and recant?

In Martin's case it is easy to see the cost to him of recovering his memories. He felt he was 'bad' because of the degree of sexual arousal he experienced during the abuse which made him feel that he must, therefore, have been in someway responsible; he had to acknowledge the fear, hurt and anger surrounding the whole of his childhood. He had to accept the possibility that he was not acceptable or loved enough by either of his parents and that they had not protected him from harm; he had to feel his pain. His graphic story shows us the severity of that pain and how he would have needed to 'anaesthetise' himself from it. It is a measure of the healthy psyche's drive for wholeness that once the memories began to surface, no matter what the cost, they had to be allowed:

> Somehow because I had said 'yes' and 'having allowed this to surface I will allow it to stay; I refuse to bury this again', further incidents began to re-emerge and the effect began to dawn on me more and more.

There are undoubtedly some untrained, badly trained, defensive and maybe even unscrupulous workers who may have asked their clients leading questions and thereby create situations that will cause suffering and harm to clients and their families. There is evidence to show that people are sometimes abused/re-abused within the therapeutic relationship (Russell 1993). There is a training video for hypnotherapists in circulation in the USA which clearly shows methods that should not be used by therapists. There are undoubtedly people working in the field who have not dealt with their own childhood abuse and may be vicariously 'dealing' with it or responding to it unconsciously through working with clients. Professional organisations are aware that steps must be taken to safeguard clients and the British Association for Counselling has a code of ethics for its members and an accreditation process in place; further discussions are in hand that will hopefully lead to ensuring that people seeking help can be guided into working with therapists who will not abuse them. Many workers in the field are calling for registration to be set up at the level of government to ensure that workers who are well-trained and responsible should be recognisable by those seeking help. However, as within every professional body, even registration will not guarantee against the fact that there will inevitably always be a few members who abuse their position of trust.

Sometimes details of memories are confused and unclear and people can mistake the identity of their abusers, especially where there are family resemblances (e.g. grandfather mistaken for father). However, to negate the reality of the process of repression and the reclaiming of buried memories, something that is well understood and supported by research and to ignore the fact that one of the most common defences used by abusers is denial and scapegoating, is to attempt to recreate the climate in which survivors remained silent in their suffering; in which abuse is perpetuated because abusers are not brought to justice; and in which the cycle continues ad infinitum. In my view this is too great a cost to protect the few families who might be wrongly accused by attempting to go back into the 'dark ages' and try to halt the progress of the march of the survivors who are fighting back.

17 Therapeutic journal: Kevin's story

Kevin was born in 1964 and he has a younger brother. He is married and has no children; he is employed in the creative arts. He has been in therapy for three years and only remembered that he had been sexually abused by his mother five months ago. He remembered this through physical work in therapy which he started because of severe depression and despair. As a young boy he was timid. As an adolescent he had one furtive sexual relationship with a girl about which he felt very guilty. He was heavily into pornography which he used for masturbation every day; a habit which he only dropped a few months ago.

He loved his father and felt as though they were one person. He has no memory of ever receiving any affection from his mother, in fact he remembers virtually nothing at all before the age of 5 years. He experienced his mother as a very cold person; he felt unsafe with her when they were alone together. He has always regarded his adult sexual behaviour as problematic and finds it difficult to initiate sex; he always feels the victim of his partner and orgasm brings feelings of guilt. He has spent his life believing that he is a natural victim and that suffering is an unavoidable human condition. He now wants to blow these myths apart by uncovering the abuse which he believes lies at the heart of these feelings.

Kevin has permitted me to reproduce some of his poems and

diary extracts which he used as a therapeutic vehicle on his journey towards healing. The following two poems were written by Kevin two years before he remembered his abuse. The memories of early traumas can be buried in the unconscious where they are stored and reacted to until such time as they can be dealt with consciously. Kevin did not understand his poems at the time he wrote them but reading them now, with the knowledge of his mother's abusive sexual behaviour, he sees them as 'slippages' from his previously repressed memories and the beginning of his process of reclaiming them. The unconscious 'speaks' to us through dreams, art, poetry and in many other ways when we are ready to hear.

The issue of confronting the abuser is discussed following Kevin's story.

STONE ROWS IN DEEPENING NIGHT

Stone rows in deepening night
Dark circles reflecting light
of golden chains, wrists afire,
dark mystery, entombed desire.
Regal passion – asking, pleading,
Sobbing, legs asunder, apart,
Heaven's stone shadows piercing her heart.

Old slippery granite
In hard enthroning stances,
Withered the belly's pulse.
Music! Music!
Around the stones a Princess dances,
Crying, laughing, shouting,
Head flung heedless as seeds,
Her feet sing on cobbled grasses.

Stone rows in deepening night,
The embers red.
Come squirming Queen,
Let your wet clay
Eclipse those rigid, mortal shafts.

ROEBURN WOODS July 1991

As the roots of a forked tree
As her light falls into darkness

I make no sound.
Surrendering in mortal fear, I yield,
Opening legs to the Goddess
As She sweeps in from all around
Gathered together
Deeper and deeper
To fuck my heart.

Her pumps subside
Exhausted I sleep.
Awake, my neck aches cold
And light's noises
Wings in the shadows
Mix with low moans

Ferns turn from black to green
I fling away sticky slugs,
Stretch, and walk,
Quick, open, panting,
Her footsteps soft behind

Some Excerpts From *A diary of therapy* by Kevin

15/5/93

More memories returning. I regress into a dark and cold room – the adult looks on in full awareness. SHE comes and goes. When SHE comes my teeth chatter, I am cold and afraid. I feel the sexual arousal, the physical pleasure and the psychological shame; the child reacting to stimulus and the adult full of guilt. SHE leaves again and calm returns. It is a cycle of coming and going, of arousal and release. I have a taste in my mouth; I hate to think what it is. SHE is rubbing against me; she rubs my groin and on my mouth. The adult is disgusted, the child is aroused and afraid. I am hyperventilating and my therapist, Ann, asks me to breathe more slowly. I breathe more slowly and SHE comes back again. SHE rubs herself on me, and I need rescuing – I reach out in the dark for Ann, I call her name, I cry for her. She takes my hand and leads me out of it. 'It will never happen again' she says. We hold hands for a long time.

What is it that the Bible says? 'Once I was a child, but now I am an adult I put away childish things'. Once I was a child, but now I carry the child in my heart, and cannot put him away because he lost so much.

24/5/93

This word despair; it comes like a rapier, gnawing into my brain. I take it to therapy with me; I take the words 'I feel like dying'. Then I just sit with these words, and I sit, and I sit, until the words become a physical sensation and the gnawing at the brain becomes a gnawing at the very quick of me, the very core of me. At this moment I start to feel very calm, very relieved.

Do you understand why I don't kill myself? First perhaps you need to understand why I do sometimes feel like killing myself. This is because I feel despair and I want it to go away, but it never does; *never*. The harder I try to make it go away the more it attacks me, and the more I want to die. This is because I am an incest survivor, and consequently, near the core of me, there is despair. Hardly surprising really, given the circumstances.

But I don't kill myself; I've never even tried, because, although the despair is very near the core of me, it is not actually at the core. There is something else there, though it takes patience to feel it. That something else is me, but it is also bigger than me. It's a lovely place, effortless, full of beauty. When I go there I am really me and everybody else is really everybody else, though we are also connected.

7/6/93

A dream – I am making love to D's mother – I detest the feelings, hate myself for it.
I take fake forgiveness to therapy and within minutes I am just boiling with revenge.
I found a picture of my mother and father together when they were children.
I told N about me. Abuse bubbles away everywhere. It is in the air. It is just everywhere.

8/6/93

Idea for ritualistic and symbolic revenge. I build an effigy, and I take it to the water, and I hold it under the water by the neck until it drowns. Then I release it and it floats downstream away for ever. My father is with me and witnesses my actions.

I might need another ally, a man, to represent my father. First he sits with the effigy at his side as my parents, and I tell him what happened to me. Then I take the effigy from him and drown it. He watches me, and then leaves.

The design of the effigy must be absolutely right symbolically and I will make it myself. It is a human form but shrouded in a blanket or sheet. Only when I take it to the river do I remove the sheet.

Ophelia's Daughter

Daddy Come see
me drown the faceless effigy,
Witness the revenge so sweet,
A drowning where two rivers meet
and flow, forever, hand in hand,
Their manly waters o'er the sand.

●

Daddy, Come see
the body float towards the sea,
The seaweed that we glued for hair,
The carcass of that lifeless mare
floating, half immersed,
As I have many times rehearsed.

●

Daddy Come see
the way she bobs around so free,
Sack legs twisting in the breeze,
Faster as the current caught her
sodden, like Ophelia's daughter,
Sinking slowly in the water.

●

Daddy, Come see
she's gone, she's disappeared from me,
Her feet are dragging on the bed,
The angry tears I start to shed
from where the rivers are both fed,
They swell the banks where she is dead.

●

15/6/93

Thinking that I know how I feel 'underneath', I dash off to therapy. But I find after some minutes that actually I am not full of anger but full of grief, and once I rid myself of something intellectual, something controlling, the grief pours out and I once again touch the me that is contented and full, and is able to let go.

What is this mechanism that makes me wonder how I feel, rather than just feeling? Often it is proved wrong. It takes so long to stop thinking and wondering before the feeling comes in its real form. Beware the man who, in his vanity and superiority, says 'what are feelings anyway?' How many times that has been said to me! Are we to accept all the parts of ourselves – are we to experience the joy of being alive or just sit there and wonder what it feels like to be OK.

It's the same with the abuse. The more I think about it the more it hurts. The more I feel it, live it in all its parts, the despair, the anger and the grief, the more I am liberated from it. I *was abused*, and this is a part of me that will never disappear, so either I live it or I run from it. A simple choice. I either think about it from dawn to dusk, or I integrate it and 'become it'. In fact I don't even need to 'become it', as I am 'it' already.

It's a paradox, but the more I take and own the pain, the more liberated I am. These 'what are feelings anyway?' people – say that enlightenment is about letting go of the self, letting go of the feelings, but how can you let go of what you don't own? To let go of something, you have to hold it first. Letting go means completely knowing and owning. You can't think letting go, you can't do letting go and you can't fake letting go.

And so the terrible events of our childhoods are inflicted upon us, and we suffer, and we can't let go of suffering because we can't accept those terrible events. They are just too painful. So we wonder how to let go of all the pain. But to let go of it we must remember it all first, and for some people there is only one way to do that, and that is to regress and re-experience. Then when we know, we can start to feel and understand and let go.

21/6/93

All I have worked on in therapy really is allowing myself to experience how I really feel. The only reason it has taken me so long is that those feelings were so deep and so terrifying. The symbolic revenge, though not acted out, has served its purpose.

28/6/93

Absolutely terrifying session today – the most awful so far. I am feeling 'pissed off': Ann confronts me really hard – says I am pissing about, that I need to own my anger. But that just feels impossible because I feel it will destroy me, and I hate her for saying it. I try with the cushions, but it's no good, and I know I need to try with HER – with my mother, with Ann.

I can't look at her; I try to find any way I can to avoid this confrontation, but she goads me, and finally I flip into rage and attack her with vitriolic words and gestures. I know all the time that I won't hurt her physically. Then I almost faint. I put my head between my legs and my whole body has pins and needles – I can't feel my legs at all. Gradually I surface and sit on the sofa. 'How do I look now?' she says. She looks like a beautiful face, but I still feel the vestiges of rage, and I still can't look at her with complete ease.

This confrontation feels like the beginning of the forthcoming real thing with my mother.

August 1993
No therapy this month and soon I want to stop completely. We talked about the unhealthy support that victim receives if I stay too long in therapy. It's been three years now. Really I manage my life pretty well so long as I allow myself the space for an hour's mediation every day. I still look into Ann's eyes and feel hatred, and that is just the way it is.

Confronting the abuser

One of the issued raised by Kevin's story is confrontation of the abuser. At some point in their journey to recovery many people express a desire to confront their abuser. Some therapists encourage this in order to break the silence and provide the survivor with a sense of power and control. However, confrontations may not always produce positive results. Poorly planned and executed confrontations may cause the survivor additional trauma. Whilst confrontation might be useful and necessary for some people, it may not be for all and recovery can occur without it. However, when a survivor has planned and examined all aspects of the possible outcomes, as well as their goals for such confrontations, there are several factors that must be taken into consideration.

Confrontation should not be for the purposes of expressing anger or convincing the perpetrator that their actions were harmful. Such goals are seldom achieved by any means because most perpetrators are neither willing nor able to feel the way the survivor wants them to feel. To encourage survivors to confront for those reasons exposes them to the risk of further harm.

Confrontation needs to occur from a position of emotional strength and the survivor will normally have successfully undertaken most of the steps towards recovery before confronting the abuser. He should require nothing from the abuser in order to complete his recovery; he should have already gained strength far beyond that used by his abuser. Confrontation then becomes a stage upon which he can demonstrate his emotional health, power and control rather than an expression of angry feelings based upon the need for an apology or admission of guilt. Once the survivor and therapist have agreed that a confrontation is appropriate, the type of confrontation should be addressed.

Some survivors express the wish for face-to-face confrontation with their abuser but for others a more comfortable way is by using a less direct method. Direct confrontation might not be possible because of the death of the abuser. All the costs and risks of the various methods should be discussed and understood and can be role-played in advance of the actual event. Bolton et al. (1989) highlight several useful methods of confrontation in their chapter on building a new life. These include preparing the agenda, selecting the setting and establishing realistic expectations regarding the perpetrators response. Most frequently the response will be one of denial, usually ranging from denial that anything happened to acknowledging that something happened but it must have been somebody else who did it. Denial is one of the most potent weapons against the survivor's attack on the secret.

Most survivors dream of a response in which the abuser admits the offence, acknowledges the harm and sincerely apologises and expresses a wish to make amends. Sadly this is rarely, if ever, the reality. If it does happen the survivor might be thrown off track; it would be a mistake to rush into an alliance with the abuser in which the need for pacing and time to process the event is overlooked. He will need time in which to evaluate if the response is genuine or manipulative. He must remember that the next step must be in his own best interest and not that of the abuser.

Other responses may be admission without remorse by a perpetrator incapable of empathy; admission with accusation when the blame is placed on the survivor; admission accompanied by an attempt to resume the abusive relationship; abusers may admit whilst at the same time attempting to manipulate the survivor into feeling sorry for them or they might minimize the abuse.

Symbolic confrontation such as that described by Kevin can offer the client an opportunity to express pent-up feelings and may satisfy the need to confront directly. It may serve as a practice for a direct confrontation and ensure that the survivor is better prepared for the encounter.

Sometimes confrontation may occur through letter writing – whether or not the letter is actually sent or presented to the perpetrator may be decided after the role-playing in a group or individual therapy setting. These letters can also be used as a preparation for direct confrontation and give the survivor a chance to explore and express verbally their feelings about the abuse, the perpetrator and themselves as a survivor. Other forms of symbolic confrontation such as visiting the dead abuser's grave and talking to them or the place where the abuse occurred, may enable the process of healing and empower the client to say the words to the abuser that they were unable to say as a child. He can place the reponsibility for the abuse where it belongs.

Legal confrontation carries with it some considerable risk for the survivor. The system can become another form of abuse and rarely meets the full expectations of the survivor. Childhood sexual abuse is a criminal act and perpetrators can be prosecuted and punished. Some survivors have been successful in gaining restitution through the legal process. However, any survivor who is considering such action must be realistically prepared for the possibility of a costly (in terms of time and emotions), frequently abusive and seldom satisfying outcome. In the court situation not only might the abuser attempt to re-abuse by denial but so also might the defence lawyer. This is not to say that this system should not be challenged and used when appropriate to do so, but the survivor must be prepared for the potentially damaging costs of such action.

18 Therapeutic work for sexually abused adult males

Recovery from childhood sexual abuse for males is in many respects the same as that for females although there are some essential differences. As there are already many very good books written on the subject for females which describe treatment issues, (Hall and Lloyd 1989; Bass and Davis 1988; Sanderson 1990; Briere 1992; Elliot 1993) I will limit myself in this chapter to issues that are particularly pertinent for males.

Difficulties in identification with the victim role

Gender specific presentations of symptoms and behaviours following childhood sexual abuse among males can be seen as a part of their response to socialisation. From a very early age boys are taught to become separate and responsible; messages such as 'big boys don't cry', 'look after mummy while I'm gone' and 'mummy's little man', (see George and Len's stories), serve to reinforce the idea that being male invests the child with power over and responsibility for females as the 'weaker sex'. This false sense of power disallows the male child the right to feel vulnerable and powerless or to be a victim. These messages are strengthened by films, TV, toys and books. The dolls provided for male children (if at all), are usually adult soldiers or action men of some kind, whereas females are given baby dolls, encouraging the girl to learn to dress, feed and nurture a small and helpless replica of a human child. The male counterparts do not need such care as they are usually armed with weapons. Sexist attitudes continue throughout the development of the child, creating an environment in which the idea of male vulnerability to sexual assault become antithetical to maleness. All of this has led to the invisibility of male sexual abuse victims among the population until recently.

Socialisation messages about the nature of females (sugar and spice and all things nice) have contributed to the ignorance about the reality that females abuse as well as males. Females are identified as carers and much of the abuse perpetrated against males by females has been disguised as 'caring' or is of a covert nature. When females abuse the behaviour is more frequently coercive and seductive rather than aggressive and forceful, although force and aggression has been used by some female abusers; the men I have interviewed more frequently experienced coercion than force with perpetrators of either gender. The use of language that focuses on assault and violence may create barriers for males who have been abused in non-violent ways. Assault can easily be identified as a physical act but coercion or seduction is of a more cognitive, covert nature. Several men in my study had difficulty defining what happened to them as abuse simply because of their understanding of what the word meant and its associations with force. Perhaps such phrases as 'the abuse of sexuality' (Bolton et al. 1989) or 'sexual misuse' could more usefully be included at the early stages of therapy to allow the reframing of the experience to develop in a way that allows the client to face up to his victimisation.

The images conjured up by the word 'victim' are usually of a small, female, helpless, passive powerless creature who is trapped by dominant male oppression into a role of submission. This image has been rejected by most adult females who have been sexually abused who prefer to identify themselves with the word 'survivor' which is more acceptable as a positive and powerful image. If this is how women, having been socialised to accept themselves as the passive recipient of male sexuality, react against the word 'victim' – it is likely that males will have an even stronger reaction. This may be very detrimental to a male's recovery from a sexual abuse experience; recovery cannot begin until they are able to acknowledge the word 'victim' as a human condition which has resulted from a traumatic occurrence and one with which they can identify. Whereas it may be therapeutically advisable to encourage a woman to move from the view of herself as 'victim' to 'survivor' – it might be equally important to allow and encourage a man to accept his victimisation as an early part of his healing process. Later in the process, he can be encouraged to follow the same route as the female and identify himself as a survivor. If a man cannot identify with the term 'victim', he might then extrapolate from that to the idea that if there is no victim, then there are no adverse effects. Many men who have been abused in childhood avoid their feelings of victimisation in this way – they might say 'oh yes, I was abused but it didn't do me any harm' (see Len and Paul). This phrase can be heard on the lips of men who physically punish their children as a justification for and recommendation of physical abuse as part of the process of disciplining them; 'my father gave me a good hiding when I was child if I misbehaved and it hasn't done me any harm!'

Men need to learn that their abuse is something that was done to them and that it was not their fault. When they permit this idea, it can arouse strong feelings of shame, hurt, anger, fear and grief. It may only be possible to access these feelings when the person recognises and accepts that they have indeed been victimised. Because men have not usually been encouraged to express such feelings, they might not have developed a language of feelings or a healthy behavioural response to them and they might fear becoming overwhelmed. Male role models in the home have rarely demonstrated a healthy expression of feeling from which their male child can learn; the child may have observed females expressing feelings through language and behaviour and may have come to identify this as 'effeminate' and therefore behaviour that is not valued by the male dominated society which often denigrate the male expression of painful emotions as 'sissy'. At the other extreme, acceptable 'masculine' feelings, such as anger, may be expressed when other feelings might be more appropriate (such as sadness or hurt). Part of the recovery process for males may involve learning to recognise and name feelings and to identify when they might be confusing or substituting one for another. For instance when anger is expressed instead of hurt, the underlying feeling is not dealt with and will therefore not change; thus preventing the man from moving forward.

Identification with the aggressor

The impact of socialisation messages can contribute to the man's chosen defence mechanism which may contribute to his denial of victimisation. One of the gender specific psychological coping mechanisms that has been identified among males who have been abused is 'identification with the aggressor'. When a boy has been socialised to believe that 'real men are powerful', the degree of dissonance created by being overpowered during a sexual assault may force the boy to tell himself that he is the one in control and not the victim. This can be the case when a young male is abused by an older or more powerful female and is reinforced by societal messages about sex and gender roles in which the male is always seen as the sexually active person and the female as passive.

For men who have coped in this way, the idea that they have been abused at all may be impossible for them to accept; thus blocking them from working through the issues that have arisen in response to the abuse. They might acknowledge symptoms but deny their basis in the sexual abusive situation in which they were involved. Paul's story demonstrates this mechanism when he accepts that his serious medical condition is stress-related but he cannot connect the stress with his abuse by both his parents during childhood. He cannot afford to see his mother as his main abuser and because he was actively involved during penetrating her, he interpreted that as 'behaving like a man should'. Clem also shows how a young male might need to see himself as the person in charge of the sexual activity in order to defend himself from the pain of recognising that he has been abused.

Identification with the aggressor might also be seen when the abuser is male; the child shares his gender with the abuser and identifies with that part. This might be most likely when the child is abused by a same-sex parent. George says how he felt that 'it was almost as if I was in control of it' when he was molested in the cinema at the age of 10. When a boy identifies with the aggressor it is then possible for him to see his own child/victim as having the responsibility for the sexual activity; the child perceives himself as the seducer. George, who became a paedophile, attributes to his child victims equal status with adults when he says of his child neighbours, 'I think she has fallen in love with me.' He goes on to say that he tells the child that 'we can't do this; we just cannot have relationship'. His use of the word 'we' indicates that he sees the child as having equal responsibility for this decision. By identifying with the aggressor George defends himself from the need to contact his unconscious feelings associated with being a victim – something that is an anathema to his self-concept as a male.

Robert speaks of the girls he abused as 'precocious' and that he had told himself that it was OK to touch them because of that. In Robert's case his identification with the aggressor meant that, not only was he unable to perceive these girls as victims, neither was he able to perceive himself as a victim of his mother's abuse. In order to ensure that he took full responsibility for his own abusing behaviour, it was essential for him to identify with his own victimisation. Both George and Robert went on to abuse as adults and had not seen themselves as victims of their own childhood abuse which preceded their abusing behaviour. Both had molested their own child.

Men who experience pain or force during their molestation seem to be more likely to identify themselves as victims thereby making it less likely that they go on to aggress others. When the abuse is responded to with arousal or is part of a 'loving' relationship, this mitigates against the recognition of the person as a victim. Arousal can be wrongly interpreted as consent; an erection as pleasure, and ejaculation as orgasm. This is a particularly gender specific response; females are less visibly aroused during sexual stimulation. However, females can and do become aroused during sexual abuse and the same feeling of responsibility for the abuse can be seen in those cases. However, arousal can be the outcome of a healthy body's response to an unhealthy and inappropriate set of circumstances. For males the response is more obvious, more immediate and therefore the feeling of involvement may create a greater sense of guilt and responsibility, which in turn leads to the denial of the victim role. During the recovery process men need education to separate out their normal physiological response from the abnormal circumstances. They need to learn that a child who enjoys sexual stimulation and seeks it out in his relationships with adults, is no more responsible for the abuse than a child who felt no arousal. It is always the adult's responsibility to hold the taboo.

Men who are socialised to equate sexual activity with masculinity may become further confused, especially when the abuser is a female; Robert said of his mother's abuse of him;

> At the same time I felt as if my manhood had been inflated. It wasn't just genital; I felt big and strong. I felt as if I could take on the world.'

It would appear that a male usually identifies his sexuality as central to his self-concept ('a man is his prick'). When his self-concept excludes the possibility of a view of himself as a victim, the work required is usually at a very deep and fundamental level. The pain and fear of disintegration that might be aroused by the challenge to his self-concept, is likely to create an existential anxiety and a crisis of identity.

Crisis can be seen as an opportunity for growth or a danger; if the man can be sufficiently contained at this time he may be able to risk using it as an opportunity for personal growth and change; if he is not contained he may withdraw in fear. This requires the therapist's full understanding of the many levels of work with which the man is coping. Support must be well in place through an established relationship of trust before any challenge to his self-concept is made either by himself or the therapist.

Powerlessness is an anathema to maleness within a patriarchal society which equates the concept of 'man' with the concept of power. Victimisation means powerlessness; another reason for identifying with the aggressor as a way of avoiding identification with the victim. When a child has been subjected to an event in which they have felt without power or the ability to control, he may re-enact this event through play as part of his normal way of dealing with it. A child who has been scolded by a parent may be found, a while later, scolding his younger sibling with the same words and expression as the parent used. The child seeks a sense of mastery through becoming the powerful one; this is often a greater need for a male child who is socialised to equate masculinity with power and control. A male who has been abused may re-enact his own abuse in a similar way in response to his unconscious feelings (see Jeremy and Tony's stories). This behaviour is reported by men who realised, in retrospect, that they had abused other children during their early lives in response to their own victimisation which had not been acknowledged at the time.

Males who equate the word 'victim' with 'passive', may react against that aspect of themselves by becoming sexually and physically aggressive or promiscuous. In order to prove their masculinity and in response to their unacknowledged victimisation, they may behave in ways that are at the extreme end of the spectrum from behaviour they identify as victim behaviour. This has been described as 'reaction formation' when a person acts out in ways that deny his deep seated feelings. Lance describes how at the age of 13 he became a tyrant and in his twenties he engaged in frequent and promiscuous behaviour:

> I had a little black book of conquests – that was how I viewed it – it was a sexual pursuit … My wife was the sixty-third woman I had slept with. It was how I measured my manhood; notches on my gun.

The recovery process

Once the man has contacted at least the possibility that he has been a victim of childhood sexual abuse, recovery has begun. This realisation may create a period of crisis during which there may be intrusive images, thoughts and feelings which need to be 'contained' until this stage has passed. The person may fear that he is out of control and 'going mad' and reassurance may be required and a recognition of this as part of a process of healing that has now commenced.

Recovery requires that the man is open to change and this will entail the development of a cognitive frame of reference in which the memory of the abusive incident/s can be processed, focusing on identifying and changing unhelpful beliefs and attitudes related to responsibility for the abuse, trust, and self-concept; recognition and discharge of feelings associated with the abuse; and identification of necessary behavioural changes and the provision of a safe environment in which these changes can be supported and rehearsed.

Therapeutic relationship

A safe environment can be created within the therapeutic relationship where issues of trust will be paramount. Trust needs to be earned by the therapist and develops with time; for many victims this relationship will provide a testing ground for building future relationships and will hopefully ameliorate some of the damage created by the betrayal of trust in the relationship in which the abuse occurred. If the abuser was the same sex as the therapist, this will need to be acknowledged early in the relationship if it is not to become a barrier. It may be that a therapist of the opposite gender to the abuser should be available for the client. This seems to be more often an issue when the therapist is male – it may be easier for a client to allow themselves to be vulnerable with a female who they perceive as being more comfortable with emotions and less likely to criticise them as unmasculine than the males they may have encountered. This question was raised with subjects of the interviews upon which this book was based and many of them felt they would not be able to work with a male therapist. This was true for those whose abusers were both male and female. Matthew describes his feelings when both a male and female psychiatric nurse was sent to his home following his rape experience:

> I had counselling very briefly from the CPNs. They sent me some chap and a female student with him. She did most of the talking. I responded very well to her but I loathed the chap – I thought he was awful. I did not want a man there. She had that natural ability and human warmth; he was very analytical and probing, very good – he probably would have made me tackle things but what I needed was some human kindness. On the last meeting she said to me 'the first time I saw you I thought you were going to cry and I could have hugged you' and I thought 'Oh God, I wish you had – that was what I needed' because nobody hugged me and let me cry in their arms.

Matthew had been raped twice by males so it is perhaps understandable that he would not want to expose his vulnerability again to a male for fear of re-abuse. It may be that working with a male might be most useful for survivors at a later stage in their work – this could be true for both male and female survivors.

During recovery, issues of power and control will need to be addressed both within the therapeutic relationship and in the person's life. In the contracting period and in the session, the client should be given as much control and choice as possible. This should include a choice of therapist or at the very least, an acknowledgement that the gender of the therapist may be an issue for discussion. However, if the therapeutic environment is to avoid becoming another potentially abusive situation, the client should ideally be given a choice.

However, limits about safety need to be clear and enforced, as healing can only take place in a safe environment. The therapist is also modelling for the client how to set personal boundaries and rules in other areas and relationship in their lives. Boundaries such as confidentiality, time, frequency, payment and holidays should be clear before work begins. The client should be informed of the counsellor's use of supervision and that although his issues will not be discussed outside supervision, there will be a need for the counsellor to have permission to consult the supervisor whenever the need is felt. This will help the client to avoid thinking of the relationship between himself and the helper as 'a secret' relationship such as the one in which the abuse might have occurred. Clients who have held secrets as a necessity during abusive relationships may find this prospect a difficult one to come to terms with as there will be a powerful need to feel in control of the material he shares with the helper. It may be very useful for the helper and the client if the issues taken to supervision were discussed once the helper has become clear about them.

Externalised responses

Externalised responses seem to be more common in males than females generally, and therefore are more likely among men who have been abused. Men in my study have described these as drug and alcohol abuse, sexual addiction, aggressive and anti-social behaviour, and becoming the abuser. It is important that the contract for therapy includes a statement about the unacceptability of the continuation of this behaviour and a commitment to change. It will not be possible to work usefully in therapy with a person who is continuing to act out in self- or other, destructive ways. Acting out behaviour is a way of coping with unexpressed feelings and until it is eliminated as an option, the person may continue to use it as a way of avoiding facing up to the issues that are a necessary part of their healing. A client needs to be prepared to commit himself to the healing process before it can commence.

Controlling behaviour can be explored both within the therapeutic relationship, such as the client coming late or staying away; they might pick fights or attempt to bully the therapist as a representative of a figure of authority; all these issues can be made conscious within the therapeutic setting which can become a 'laboratory' for experimenting with new ways of dealing with these feelings.

New ways of re-asserting masculinity might include the use of sport or involvement in martial arts which focus on the development of self-esteem and internal feelings of power; thereby dispensing with the need to act out in what they might perceive as 'macho' ways.

The working alliance is a necessary part of the shared process of therapy. For this reason de-toxification may need to precede work on abuse issues if the person is dependent on drugs or alcohol. A contract will need to include an agreement that no sexual acting out will be acceptable during therapy. This must be disclosed and resolved in a healthy and useful way that is in line with the values of the client. It may be that someone who engages in compulsive masturbation will need a behaviourist approach – perhaps setting aside a time that is masturbation free which might be increased as tolerance develops as the feelings underlying the behaviour are expressed and explored in a healthy way. Self-harming behaviour can be dealt with in the same way. Old habits are notoriously hard to break and will take time.

Work with survivors of childhood sexual abuse is likely to be long-term and unless the therapist is able to commit themselves to such work, it would be disrespectful to the client to begin; referral to another therapist might be more appropriate. This is particularly the case when sexual abuse is uncovered in another setting such as during detoxification, attendance at a VD clinic or other medical settings, or during marital therapy. If this situation arises it may be that the worker feels that the client might interpret a referral as a rejection. For this reason such a situation must be handled with care and the client included in the decision making process. If the worker suggests to the client that it may be in their best interest to see another person who is able to offer them a weekly session over an extended period against the possibility of occasional visits for a shorter period of time – it may be that the client can be helped to make the decision for himself. The timing of such suggestions about referral are crucial. It might be damaging for a therapist to make this suggestion immediately following disclosure when the client might be most vulnerable to feelings of rejection. (See Martin's experience in Chapter 16.) It is tempting when a client has opened up about the issue for the first time, for the worker to want to continue with the work and not make a referral. The best interest of the client must be paramount at this time. The work requires great patience and a deep understanding of the relevant issues.

Homophobic concerns

Homophobic concerns can be dealt with by exploring the feeling connected with the issue and may involve education for males about physiological responses of a healthy male body to sexual stimulation and a clarification that this response is likely to be the same if the abuser is male or female and may not indicate sexual orientation. Confusion around sexual identity may be clarified through the process of developing an understanding of the effects of sexual abuse on male children – both of these issues have been highlighted in earlier parts of this book and in others (Sgroi, 1989; Hunter 1990a, 1990b). Family, personal and societal values need to be explored with the client in order to help them to accept their sexual identity and any dissonance around that which may have been created by introjected heterosexist messages about acceptable and unacceptable sexual behaviour.The pain of Martin's mother's rejection was evident when he told me:

> When I told my parents I was homosexual, my mother screamed repetitively 'I wanted a boy.' To this day she refers to the make-up of our family being two girls, Martin, and two boys.

He described a particularly painful part of the process of recovery when the rejection was reinforced by the messages he received within his Church:

> I relived also my own trauma and pain of coming to terms with my homosexuality and I was back again into the 'Yes society is right; you are a pervert. Yes, the Church is right; you are a sinner and you are damned.' And it was very much in those feelings that I walked in front of a double decker bus, the bus swerved and I was untouched; I lived.

The therapist needs to accept whatever preference the client might demonstrate. This will require therapists to have dealt with their own attitudes and responses to their own and other people's sexuality.

Inner child work

Denial of victimisation can be dealt with by helping the client to connect with the hurt child within. They might be helped to re-connect with this part of themselves by visualisation, drawing, working with dolls, or with photographs of themselves around the time the abuse occurred. This work might be helped by enabling the client to connect themselves at that age with another child with whom they have a close relationship (perhaps their son or daughter) and who is around the same age.

Bradshaw (1988) and Whitfield (1989) have developed the concept of the inner child and see that part of the requirement for the adult client is to work through the disconnected feelings of the child. Some tools for this way of working have been described by Abrams (1991) and Parkes (1990). The unconscious anger of the child might cause depression, suicidal feelings and self-destructive behaviours. These behaviours might stem from the need to punish themselves and may arise from feelings of guilt, responsibility, and badness. This 'badness' might be connected with body concerns; self-hatred and dislike of the genitalia. Self-image might be distorted, the person might perceive themselves to be ugly, deformed, damaged, powerless and unable to defend themselves; feeling which lead to shame, fear and avoidance behaviour. When the client is helped to express these feelings and to 'normalise' these responses, this may lead to the creation of a different cognitive framework which allows them to see their responses as acceptable coping mechanisms during childhood which no longer serve a useful purpose in adulthood and are no longer required by the adult.

Working with feelings

Many men have never been taught the language in which they could express their feelings. Their male role models may more frequently have 'acted out' feelings rather than found healthy ways of expressing them. Fear, anger and anxiety is sometimes expressed through dreams which can be externalised and made concrete through gestalt work, drawing or clay work in order to gain a sense of mastery over the childhood feelings.

Sadness and loss of family and normal childhood experiences need to be worked through as part of the grieving process if the person is to let go and move on. This process will usually follow the five stages identified by Kubler-Ross (1969); denial, bargaining, anger, sadness and acceptance and Hunter and Gerber (1990) have outlined the five stages in terms of the work the client might need to undertake at each one:

First stage: denial

This involves the therapists helping the client to tell the story without interpretation; the therapist helps to clarify details, reframe the experiences by pointing out cognitive distortions. This must not happen too early or clients will feel that they have not been listened to. It may be that Justin had experienced just that when he said:

> I have seen people from the NHS for pills and short interviews but I have always felt that I have been in Court; I've been interrogated, as if it has been my fault that I have felt this way and done these things. Just thinking about it is making me feel angry.

It would appear that the best help is given by those working in a humanistic way – a way that demonstrates respect for the client as a unique individual and as a person with the potential to find and use their own resources for healing. At this stage it might be useful for the therapist to use term 'victim', even if client is still demonstrating intermittent denial.

Second stage: bargaining

At this stage the client may be saying 'It did happen but it didn't have any effect' – or 'I asked for it' – or 'I'm over it'. The client may feel affection for abuser and the therapist should not push him into the position of having to choose between the therapist and abuser. Positive feelings towards the abuser need to be acknowledged, especially when the abuser has been a close family member such as the mother. This stage is one where people may become stuck if they loved the abuser – the therapist should avoid labelling the perpetrator as such, but should label the behaviour as abusive.

As this bargaining lessens the client may feel fear. The client may need to be helped to recognise this as an appropriate response to being violated; if he has been socialised not to acknowledge fear it might feel overwhelming. This is a time when client might respond by self-mutilation, alcohol or other drug usage, compulsive eating or sexual acting out. Without unduly focusing on it, this behaviour needs to be identified as an unhealthy way of responding to or avoiding an underlying feeling which the behaviour is attempting to defend the client against. However, inappropriate confrontation can reflect the original abuse of power. The right to confront or challenge needs to be earned by the therapist by the creation of adequate support within the therapeutic relationship and an openness to being challenged herself. Validation of fear is important as it contributes to the understanding of the event as abuse. If the abuser used coercion this might deny the victim the possibility of it being abuse; he may see himself as a willing participant, so he discounts his fear.

During this stage the client might prematurely wish to forgive or reconcile themselves with the abuser to avoid the need to feel the discomfort they are experiencing or the pressure from family who tell them to put it all behind them or may come from their religious indoctrination. Matthew describes how his religious beliefs influenced his need to forgive his rapist:

> It was important for me to be able to forgive him. I didn't forgive Christopher (his earlier rapist). To not forgive is to twist yourself up with hate and I don't think it does you any good; it might for a while, but forgiveness is part of having compassion and letting go and forgiveness isn't words, it's doing something.

His need to 'do something' was satisfied when he unexpectedly met up with his rapist one night in a pub:

> I decided the one thing I wanted to do was to meet the man who had done it – and I did. I could have done without meeting him in a pub completely unexpectedly. I bought him a drink and felt really proud of myself. He didn't notice but I was gripping the bar and my knuckles were white 'cos if I took my hand off the bar they would have been shaking. I didn't accuse him because I don't think he would have understood. To be fair he has got an argument; as an adult you are responsible for your own actions to some extent. It was up to me to make sure that I didn't make myself so vulnerable especially as I'm the sort of person who doesn't look after myself.

Matthew was still stuck at the stage of avoiding his fear and anger and was caught up with a sense of having some responsibility for his rape because he had drunk too much.

Third stage: anger

Anger may trigger fear and shame. The client may fantasise violent revenge. Jeremy lets himself get in touch with his revenge fantasy when he says:

> I would have just got my mates to have battered him to hell, then taken all his money and burnt his house down. When I see him next time I'll follow him back to his house and take all his money, I'll take everything. I shouldn't be saying these sort of things on tape – I don't care if I go to prison for it – I wouldn't care about doing time for it. It would give me the satisfaction of really hurting him. Maybe I'll do something really horrible to him like cutting his knob off and chuck it in his mouth and say

> 'Suck that! Look what you made me do – you can do it yourself now'.

Such strong feelings might frighten the client who thinks he might be just as bad as the abuser, triggering shame and self-loathing. He might deal with these feeling by the over-use of drugs, food or alcohol to numb the feelings. As a child he may have been told he had no right to be angry or was punished for anger. He might also feel anger towards others who did not protect him, not only the abuser. He may have been neglected or emotionally abused within the family even if the abuse occurred outside the home. His parents might have been preoccupied and not noticed what happened to him as a child. He might have been driven to seek attention from the person who abused him; exploitative attention being better than no attention at all (see Justin's story). If the abuse had been disclosed the parents may have been more concerned about the family image than the harm to child – they might have thought the child was abnormal and added to the child's negative experience of himself. Jeremy says:

> I think being abused has built up a lot of anger inside me. When I go to bed I think about it a lot and I think I'm a piece of shit – I shouldn't be here. Sometimes I worry about what my family thinks. When my dad first found out, he thought I might have been damaged in the head and that just did my head in; people knowing does my head in.

Stage four: sadness

The client grieves for the irredeemable loss of childhood. Jeremy recognises this when he says:

> I feel as if I missed a lot of my childhood because of this. I grew up incredibly quickly. From about 10 upwards, I've always been the age I am now – 19. I've cut out a lot of my childhood. I can't really remember much.

Sadness is not a feeling that is normally encouraged in males – 'boys don't cry'; this attitude is still alive in homes and institutions today; it may be seen as self-pity. Jeremy seems to have internalised these messages from what he says:

> I would never talk about how I feel; I never cry in front of anyone. I'd rather not burden them with my problems, they don't need it as much as I don't need it. I've felt like committing suicide loads of times. My friend found me once

> when I'd taken some paracetamol. It was only after an hour and I drank a lot of water and puked them up so no one knew about it. I have fantasies about killing myself and I get rid of the pain. I suffer from a lot of internal pain, in my mind and in my heart, about men and about women and about my life. I feel as if I might be a loser. No one knows the way I feel. I tried to tell a girl friend once and she just said 'don't be so stupid, pick yourself up and get on with it'. And that's when I started thinking I was damaged goods; I still feel it now when I go to sleep crying sometimes and I wake up crying and I make it change very quickly and people say 'are you alright' and I say 'yes it's just the morning blues'.

At this stage the client might become more comfortable with the use of the term 'survivor'.

Stage five: acceptance

This stage may be identified when the client begins to reorganise his life so that he shifts attention from the abuse to ways he can live an enjoyable life. The focus at this stage can be on healthy behaviours rather than on the 'label'. The survivor becomes comfortable with this concept as he integrates the abuse as only one part of himself; and the event takes its rightful place in the memory store as an experience that has affected his life but no longer dominates it. The client may find some meaning in the experience that he can identify has strengthened him as a person. Having spoken about the negative impact the abuse had on his life Martin went on to say:

> But then, if it's not a contradiction, I can say that I have learned so much about life, so quickly. It has given me so much to bring to my life and other people's lives by way of compassion, by way of empathy, by way of energy against any form of abuse or exploitation.

For some people this stage requires that they forgive their abuser. This must be something that comes from the client and not something that is imposed as a condition of healing from outside. The need to forgive is often part of the socialisation requirements for those who have been a member of a church and this might create problems for the client who is not willing or able to forgive.

Presenting these stages in the above way may seem to oversimplify what is a complex, lengthy, painful and usually non-linear process of healing. The client may go in and out of stages and return at times to previous ones. I do not wish to underestimate the difficulties of the work but recognising the process as one of 'stages' might enable the helper to stay with the client without feeling overwhelmed. Knowledge of the process can be shared with the client as a tool for self-empowerment, particularly when the going seems rough and clients want to retreat from the work.

Therapeutic stance

Person-centred therapists who require that it is always the client who sets the agenda during sessions might consider that any reference to the abuse by them is interference and disrespectful of the client; they may see this as a way of re-victimising the client. This is a view I would have taken before working with and studying male victims of childhood sexual abuse. However, I believe that male clients may not be helped by this approach; the client may perceive this as the therapist's discomfort or lack of concern for him, and in some cases I believe that they may be correct to assume this. A therapist who has not been adequately trained or has not worked on their own sexuality may become too uncomfortable and avoid the issue of sexual abuse; this can reinforce feelings of shame or the message that the abuse does not matter. I believe the therapist has a responsibility to indicate a willingness to talk about it and to provide information clients may lack when appropriate. The therapist must never impose the agenda but neither must she collude with the avoidance of the issue because of her own discomfort or inability. If the therapist becomes aware of these feelings within herself then it would be more appropriate to refer the client than to continue to work with him. Competent and ethical workers will be in supervision (BAC code of ethics) and it may be that when this issue is worked through in supervision they can offer more effective help. Respect for the client's pace of work must be an integral part of this approach and a tentative offering to work with the issue may avoid colluding with the client's denial or evasion. Martin described this when he spoke of his own unreadiness to deal with his work. His case highlights how difficult it is to work with a client who has a time-limit on the number of sessions; a trusting relationship requires time to establish itself and no work can commence until it is in place. This problem will be compounded if the client needs time to reclaim the memory of his abuse – something that Martin had already begun before his therapy started:

> I went for three months to a psychotherapist and told this person in the first session that I had recently discovered, re-remembered that I had been abused and wanted to deal with all the debris. Although I went to this person for twelve sessions,

> the abuse was never mentioned. The therapy was client-centred in its approach so it was for me to give the agenda for each session. It's fair to say that at half way point the therapist did say that we only had so many sessions left and that I hadn't mentioned it and asked if I wanted to; I declined. Four sessions from the end the therapist once again offered me the opportunity and once again I declined. Looking back I realise that I wasn't able at that point; I wasn't comfortable enough to access such painful memories.

Some therapists have become anxious about the accusations levelled by those who propound the False Memory Syndrome theory and this may create an atmosphere in which both therapist and client avoid working with dreams and flashbacks for fear of being seen to falsify or 'implant' memory. A therapist who avoids leading questions, interpretation and remains tentative has little to fear. Staying with the client in a spirit of shared and supportive exploration will enable clients to discover from within themselves the truth about their past lives.

It is important that the therapist believes the client's 'truth' which might sometimes change over time as it becomes clearer. Psychoanalysis when rigidly adhered to as a theory can feel like a re-abuse to the client whose experience is interpreted as fantasy. James describes how he felt disbelieved in his experience of formal psychoanalysis:

> I saw a psychoanalyst, who called himself a therapist at a NHS hospital; he denied my reality and told me I was fantasising, that I was imagining things. That's where psychoanalysis goes wrong because it's based on a theory that things have to fit; instead of 'here's my story, what can I learn about myself'. If it doesn't fit the model then it can't be true. That process devalues the survivors reality and truth; it can be used as a form of denial – used to suppress memories. The most important person within the therapeutic situation is the client and the person's reality is the most important thing. That has to be valued and often it is not. I feel strongly about that.

Clients sometimes fear being disbelieved almost more than the abuse; they think they might be judged as 'going mad' because, at the time the abuse was happening, people around them might have given them the message that everything was alright. William described how at the age of 11:

> I had 'controlled breakdowns' lasting about an hour during which I would hysterically cry and laugh alternately. One happened spontaneously during a lesson at school and the

> teacher asked me if I was OK (obviously aware that I wasn't) and I broke off manic crying, looked up and said in a coherent, calm voice that I was fine and then burst out laughing again. The teacher asked me if there was anything wrong at home. I replied (in a coherent pause), that everything was fine at home. At that point I honestly believed what my Dad continually told me – that I was very lucky indeed, very privileged and happy.

Others may have invalidated the client's reality by telling them such things did not happen. Sam tells how his anger at society was fuelled when he realised that even those he turned to for help were unwilling to believe what he was saying:

> I started to realise I'd been abused about the age of 14. I tried to tell my social worker and she said she didn't believe me. She said, 'It doesn't happen; women don't abuse blokes.' That reaction hurt. By that age I had begun to read in the newspapers about kids being abused by their parents and it came up when I was talking to a probation officer. The social worker didn't want to know about it. It made it hard to tell someone else about it; I thought 'if you don't believe me then who is going to?' So I kept it inside myself.

Body work

In Chapter 11 I have looked at ways that men might be helped through massage and other forms of body work to access their feelings and memories. Counselling and psychotherapy are not the only ways to heal from childhood abuse. Men and women have been helped by many of the alternative therapies such as acupuncture (see Robert's story), shiatsu, art therapy, music therapy, dance and dramatherapy.

Groups as treatment

Group work can seem far too threatening for the person who has only recently contacted their abuse memories but for others it may feel far less threatening than the intimacy of the one-to-one relationship in individual therapy. Ideally clients could be offered a choice although the reality is that often these choices are simply not available. Therapists working in private practice often identify some of their clients who may be ready to move into group treatment but lack the knowledge of availability of such groups. Issues related to whether the group should be same gender or mixed, fixed term or open ended, closed or open need to be thought through carefully and clients should be assessed for readiness for working in this setting; these issues are usefully discussed in other books (Elliot 1993; Sgroi 1989). A client who has never disclosed their abuse outside the client/therapist relationship is probably not ready for group work.

However, for some men groupwork might be preferred when the pressure of working in individual therapy seems overwhelming. In a group a man can work at a pace that he might more easily tolerate – staying in the observer role until he feels able to contribute to the work in hand; learning from others how to express and cope with feelings and gaining reassurrance about feelings of isolation and stigmatisation. Being in a group might enable the building of trust and the sense of sharing a problem with others instead of feeling alone.

A group might provide a man with his first experience of non-abusive, non-sexual touch or his first chance to make contact with men who allow themselves to express their vulnerability. It may provide a resocialisation in which the 'norm' is very different from the more familiar patriarchal culture. A new member might resist this and become disorientated initially but as time passes and he observes a male nurturing environment he may be enabled to risk contacting his own vulnerability and sense of victimisation without the fear of rejection or derision. Martin describes his powerful mixture of feelings during group therapy and compares this with his experience of individual therapy:

> What helped me more than anything was the power of the peer group. To meet other people who had been through the same experiences and to hear their stories helped me to unlock further recesses, dark corners of my own story which I had long forgotten. What hindered me was the fear of unlocking even more. It was bad enough having unlocked twenty years' worth, but then in group therapy to hear someone else's story and to think 'yes, that's me too! My God when will this stop, when will this end?'. To feel the fear of being rejected, the fear of feeling that I was the worst, that my acting out sexually was much worse than anybody else's, that they just drank or withdrew but look what I was doing.

Groupwork can be in a formal or informal therapeutic environment; what seems to matter is that it is a safe place. James first disclosed in a group of anarchists during a camp when he heard a woman disclose the effects of her own abuse on her life. What matters it seems is that the person is heard, believed and validated. He had previously experienced his father's dismissal of his story and a psychoanalyst's interpretation of his experience as fantasy – neither of which was helpful.

> The first person I told was dad. He told me to stop being silly and making a fuss about nothing. I told him over a beer and a game of pool one Sunday afternoon when I was 18 or 19. I felt angry and pissed off with his response but I couldn't tell him that. I shut up and immediately took on 'Oh, it's not important, it's irrelevant.' I ignored it for the next few years. The first time I disclosed after that was to a group of forty people! I was in a gathering of anarchists, activists who had come together one evening; they had a 'go round' of feelings. It started with the woman who was upset talking about how it was to be a survivor – how it had affected her life and from that I had the courage to disclose; it was actually a very safe space.

Towards a healing society

Male childhood sexual abuse emanates not only from the relative powerlessness of children and the way adults misuse them; it also emanates from patriarchy, the norms that underlie that and the socialisation processes which stem from those norms and make lasting impressions on boys who, as adults, maintain and pass on those unhelpful norms to future generations of males.

Macho ethos is not going to emasculate itself voluntarily; few men write on the subject of patriarchy. Most men think they have too much to lose and they will not willingly relinquish what they and society value most highly. It is at a fundamental level that this attitude must change if we are to achieve a well-balanced society which permits every person to be valued equally. This can only happen when feminine and masculine qualities are valued equally. The majority of the men I interviewed did not perceive themselves as typically macho little boys – many saw themselves as 'effeminate' and that they were not valued on that account. This is one of the outcomes of devaluing the 'feminine' in our society. There needs to be a view of maleness that is not necessarily 'macho' into which male children can comfortably fit. I do not advocate a reversal of values – this would lead to a mirror image of what we now have and an equivalent problem; the masculine would be driven into the unconscious thereby becoming voracious or demonic. Rather than a suppression of one by the other, what we need is a marriage between the masculine and the feminine. What I have heard from the men in this study is a kind of revulsion, even a hatred of the masculine. Masculine values cannot be abandoned; anyone who attempts to do that will become their victim, just as many people today are the victims of the repressed feminine.

Roger Horrocks (1991) says that there is no doubt that the whole earth and its people are crying out for the restoration of the feminine:

> Men are terrified of it and internally possessed by it; women are unsure what it means to be a woman, and what the feminine is concretely, and how to live it. There is an enormous amount of confusion ...

Exploring sex-role stereotypes and attitudes towards children is one way to challenge our cultural values. Whilst this might initially cause shock or discomfort to men, the ultimate rewards can be a profound change in the relationships between men and women and a reduction in child sexual abuse. Boys need to be taught from an early age how to look after and bond with children. This starts with the choices of play activities, toys, dolls, and attitudes in the home modelled by their same sex parent. When men learn to feel competent in handling children and comfortable around them, they are more likely to enjoy them in an appropriate way – not as possessions. One result of this is that men might be more likely to take a stand in creating safety, care, good education and protection for children. Men within institutions, such as government and the church, might then become more concerned with matters that are more traditionally seen to be the concern of women, such as the provision of creches within the workplace, the acceptance of the need for fathers to have 'paternity leave' on the birth of their child and equal opportunities for women to obtain senior positions in previously male dominated institutions, with all that means in terms of career development and equal pay.

However, we also need to acknowledge that women have abused just over half the men I interviewed and if we do not face up to the fact that women can and do sexually invade, abuse and exploit male and female children, then we deny women the right to acknowledge that they may feel lost, overwhelmed, ashamed and confused about their sexuality and their behaviour towards children. This exploration too must be done within the understanding of the inequities that patriarchy has imposed on women. We must face what we may not want to see in the spirit of openness and wish for healing that will allow for the development of a more humane society within which there lies the possibility of the growth of a deeper human understanding for all.

References

Abel, G.E. and N. Harlow (1987). The child abuser. *Redbook Magazine*, 98–100, 138–139, August.
Abrams, J. ed. (1991) *Reclaiming the inner child*. London: Mandala.
Allen, C.M. (1990) Women as perpetrators of child sexual abuse: recognition barriers. Ch. 8 in *The Incest Perpetrator* ed. A. Horton et al. London: Sage Publications.
Allers, C.T., K. Benjack, J. White and J. Rousey (1993) HIV vulnerability and the adult survivor of childhood sexual abuse. *Child Abuse and Neglect*, **17**, 291– 298.
Allport, G.W. (1937) *Personality: a psychological interpretation*. NY: Holt.
Anthony, E.J. and B.J. Cohler (1987) *The invulnerable child*. New York: Guilford.
Bagley, C. and R. Ramsay (1991) Disrupted childhood and vulnerability to sexual assault: long-term sequals with implications for counselling. *Journal of Social Work and Human Sexuality*.
Bancroft (1980) Psychophysiology of sexual dysfunction in *Handbook of Biological Psychiatry*. New York: Marcel Dekker, 359–392.
Bandura, A. (1969) *Principles of behaviour modification*. New York: Holt, Rinehart and Winston.
Bandura, A (1977) *Social learning theory*. Englewood Cliffs, New Jersey: Prentice-Hall.
Bass, E. and L. Davis (1988) *The courage to heal: a guide for women survivors of child sexual Abuse*. New York: Harper and Row.
Beck, A.T. (1967) *Depression: clinical, experimental and theoretical aspects*. New York: Harper & Row.
Bennetts, C., M. Brown and J. Sloan (1992) *AIDS: The hidden agenda in child sexual abuse*. Harlow: Longman.
Bentovim, A., A. Elton, J. Hildebrand, M. Tranter and E. Vizard (1988) *Child sexual abuse within the family: assessment and treatment*. London: Butterworth.
Bentovim, A., P. Boston and A. Van Elburg (1987) Child sexual abuse – children and

families referred to a treatment project and the effects of intervention. *British Medical Journal*, **295**, 1453–7.

Berlin, F.S. (1983) Sex offenders: a biomedical perspective and a status report on biomedical treatment, in Joanne Greer and Irving Stuart (eds.) *The Sexual Aggressor: Current Perspectives on Treatment*, 83–123. New York: Van Nostrand Reinhold.

Berne, E. (1961) *Transactional analysis in psychotherapy*. New York: Grove Press.

Berne, E. (1964) *Games people play*. New York: Grove Press.

Bolton, F.G., L. Morris and A. MacEachron (1989) *Males at risk: the other side of sexual Abuse*. Newbury Park, Calif: Sage Pubs.

Bowlby, J. (1973) Attachment and loss: Separation, anxiety and anger. Vol.2. New York: Basic Books.

Bradshaw, J. (1988) *Healing the shame that binds you*. Deerfield Beach, Fla: Health Communications.

Braun, B.G. (1986) *Treatment of multiple personality disorder*. Washington. American Psychiatric Press.

Braun, B.G. (1988a) The BASK model of dissociation. Part 1. Dissociation 1 (1): 4–23.

Braun, B.G. (1988b) The BASK model of dissociation. Part 2: Clinical Applications. Dissociation 1 (2) : 16–23.

Briere, J.(1992) *Child abuse trauma: theory and treatment of the lasting effects*. NY.: Sage.

British Association for Counselling (1990) *Code of Ethics and Practice for Counsellors*. Rugby: BAC.

Bruckner, D. and P. Johnson (1987) Treatment for adult male victims of childhood sexual abuse. *Social Casework*: 81–87.

Burgess, A., R. Hazelwood, F. Rokous, C. Hartmen and A. Burgess (1987) Serial rapists and their victims: Re-enactment and repetition. Presented at the New York Academy of Sciences Conference on Human Sexual Aggression: Current Perspectives, New York City.

Burke, M. (1993) *Coming out of the blue*. London: Cassell.

Butler-Sloss, E. (1988) *Report of the enquiry into child abuse Cleveland 1987*. London: HMSO.

Calderone, M.S. (1985) Adolescent sexuality: elements and genesis. *Pediatrics*, **76** (4) 699–703.

Cantwell, H.B. (1988) Child sexual abuse: very young perpetrators. *Child Abuse and Neglect*, **12**, 579–82.

Carey, J. (1993) The age of innocents. *Sunday Times book critics report*. Section 7, p.8. 7 March.

Carnes, P. (1983) *Out of the shadows: understanding sexual addiction*. Minneapolis: Compcare.

Carlson, S. (1990) The victim/perpetrator: Turning points in therapy, in *The sexually abused male* (vol.2) M. Hunter(ed) Lexington: Lexington Books.

Chasnoff, M.D., W.J. Burns, S.H. Schnoll, K. Burns, G. Chisnum and L. Kylespore (1986) Maternal-neonatal incest. *American Journal of Orthopsychiatry*, **56**: 577–80.

Children's Society Report (1993) *Hidden truths*. Margery St.; London. WC1X 0JL.

Christopherson, J. (1990) Sex rings in *Working with sexually abused boys: an introduction for practitioners*, eds. A. Hollows and H. Armstrong. London: TAGOSAC.

Cicchetti, D. (1987) Developmental psychopathology in infancy: Illustrations from the study of maltreated youngsters. *Journal of Consulting and Clinical Psychology*, **55**: 837–845.

Coleman, E. (1987) Assessment of sexual orientation. *Journal of Homosexuality*, **13**: 9–24.

Conte, J.R. (1985) The effects of sexual abuse on children: A critique and suggestions for future research. *Victimology: An International Journal*, **10**, 110–130.

Conte, J.R. and J.R. Schuerman (1987) Factors associated with an increased impact of child sexual abuse. *Child Abuse and Neglect*, **11**, 201–211.

Craig, E., Erooga, M., Morrison, T. and Shearer, E. (1989) Making sense of sexual abuse – charting the shifting sands in NSPCC: Child Sexual Abuse: listening, hearing and validating the experiences of children, Ch. 4, ed. by Wattam, C., Hughes, J. and Blagg, H., Harlow: Longman.

CROSS (Campaign for rights for survivors of sexual abuse). c/o 76a Southbridge Road, Croydon, London. CR0 1AE

De Jong, A.R., G.A. Emmett, and A.A. Hervada (1982) Epidemiologic factors in sexual abuse of boys. *American Journal of the Diseased Child*, **136**, 990–3.

De Jong, A.R. (1989) Sexual interactions among siblings and cousins; experimentation or exploitation? *Child Abuse and Neglect*, **13**, 271–9.

Department of Health and Social Security (1986) *Child Abuse – Working Together*, HMSO.

Didaskalos (1994) Charism of celibacy. Article in *The Tablet* 9 July. 856–857.

Dimock, P. (1988) Adult males sexually abused as children. *Journal of Interpersonal Violence*, **3**: 203–221.

Doll, L.S., D. Joy, B.N. Bartholow, J.S. Harrison, G. Bolan and J.M. Douglas (1992) Self-reported childhood and adolescent sexual abuse among adult homosexual and bi-sexual men. *Child Abuse and Neglect*, **16**.

Draucker, C.B. (1992) Counselling survivors of sexual abuse. London: Sage.

Durden-Smith and de Simone (1983) Birth of your sexual identity. *Service Digest*, Vol **9**, pp. 86–8.

Eaton, L. (1993) Child abuse ... who's counting? *The Guardian*, Tuesday, 31 March.

Edwards, S. (1988) Neither mad nor bad: The female violent offender reassessed. *Women's Studies International Forum*, **9**(1), 79–87.

Egan, G. (1986) *The skilled helper* (3rd ed) Monterey, Calif: Brooks/Cole.

Egeland, B., D. Jacobvitz and A.L. Sroufe. (1988) Breaking the cycle of abuse. *Child Development*, **59**: 1080–1088.

Eisenberg, N., R. Owens and M. Dewey (1987) Attitudes of health professionals to child sexual abuse and incest. *Child Abuse and Neglect*, **11**, 109–116.

Ellerstein, N.S. and J.W. Canavan (1980) Sexual abuse of boys. *American Journal of Diseased Child*, **134**, 255–7.

Elliott, M. ed. (1993) *Female sexual abuse of children; the ultimate taboo*. Harlow: Longman.

Erikson, E. (1959) Identity and the life cycle. *Psychological Issues*, **1** (19), 1–171. 35, 83.

Erikson, E. (1963) *Childhood and society*. New York: W.W.Norton.

Erikson, E.H. (1968) *Identity, use and crisis*. New York: Norton.

Erikson, M.R. and B. Egeland (1987) A developmental view of the psychological consequences of maltreatment. *School Psychology Review*, **16**: 156–168.

Faller, K. (1987) Women who sexually abuse children. *Violence and Victims*, **2** (4), 263–276.

Faller, K. (1989) Characteristics of a clinical sample of sexually abused children: how boy and girl victims differ. *Child Abuse and Neglect*, **13**, 281–91.

Festinger, L. (1957) *A theory of cognitive dissonance*. Evanston, Illinois: Row Peterson.

Fingleton, K. (1989) The attitudes and approaches of school psychologists and child guidance services to sexually abused children. *Educational and Child Psychology*, **6**, 15–21.

Finkelhor, D. (1979) *Sexually victimised children*. New York: Free Press.

Finkelhor, D. (1984) *Child sexual abuse: New theory and research*. New York: Free Press.

Finkelhor, D. (1986) *A sourcebook on child sexual abuse*. Newbury Park, California: Sage Pubs.

Finkelhor, D. and D. Russell (1984) Women as perpetrators: Review of the evidence, in *Child sexual Abuse: new theory and research*, ed. by D. Finkelhor, 171–187. New York: Free Press.

Finkelhor, D. and A. Browne (1986). Initial and long-term effects: A conceptual framework, in D. Finkelhor *A sourcebook on child sexual abuse* (180–198). Beverly Hills, CA: Sage Publications.

Fraiberg. S., E. Adelson and V. Shapiro (1975) Ghosts in the nursery: a psycho-analytical approach to the problems of impaired mother-child relationships. *Journal of the American Assoc. of Child Psychiatry*, **14**: 387–421.

Freedland, J. (1993) Sins of the fathers. Article in *The Guardian: Inside Story*. Tuesday, 21 December.

Freud, A. (1946) *Ego and the mechanisms of defence*, Vol. 2 (revised) Madison, Connecticut: International Universities Press.

Freud, S. (1896) Studies in hysteria, in the Standard Edition of the *Complete Psychological Works of Sigmund Freud*. Hogarth Press and the Institute of Psycho-analysis, London.

Freud, S. (1905) Three essays on sexuality, in the Standard Edition of the *Complete Psychological Works of Sigmund Freud*. Hogarth Press and the Institute of Psycho-analysis, London.

Freud, S. (1910) Three contributions to the sexual theory. *Journal of Nervous and Mental Disease*. New York.

Freud, S (1912/3) *Totem and taboo*. London: Routledge.

Freud, S. (1920) *Beyond the pleasure principle*. New York: Bantam Books.

Freud, S. (1924) *The dissolution of the Oedipal complex*. S.E., Vol. XIX.

Freund, K., G. Heasman, I. Racansky and G. Glancy (1984) Pedophilia and heterosexuality *v.* homosexuality. *Journal of Sex and Marital Therapy*, **10** (3), 193–200.

Freund, K., R. Watson and R. Dickey (1988) Does sexual abuse in childhood cause pedophilia? Joint Study of the Department of Behavioural Sexology and the Forensic Division, Clarke Institute of Psychiatry, Toronto, Ontario, Canada.

Friedrich, W.N. (1988) Behaviour problems in sexually abused children. Ch. 10 in *Lasting Effects of Child Sexual Abuse* ed. by G.E. Wyatt and G.J. Powell. London: Sage Publications.

Friedrich, W.N., R. L. Beilke and A.J. Urquiza (1988) Behaviour problems in young sexually abused boys. *Journal of Interpersonal Violence* **3**: 1–12.

Friedrich, W.N. and W.J. Leucke (1988) Young school-age sexually aggressive children. *Professional Psychology: Research and practice* **19** (2) 155–164.

Fritz, G.S., K. Stoll, and N. Wagner (1981) A comparison of males and females who were sexually molested as children. *Journal of Sex and Marital Therapy*, **7**, 54–59.

Fromuth, M.E. and B.R. Burkhart (1989) Long term psychological correlates of child sexual abuse in two samples of college men. *Child Abuse and Neglect*, **13**: 533–542.

Gay, P. (1989) *Freud: a life for our time*. London: Macmillan.

Gerber, P.N. (1990) Victims becoming offenders: a study of ambiguities, in *The sexually abused male*, Vol.1 ed. by M.Hunter. Lexington MA: Lexington Books.

Gilgun, J.F. (1990) Factors mediating the effects of childhood maltreatment, in *The sexually abused male*, Vol. 1 by M. Hunter (ed). Lexington, MA.: Lexington Books.

Goldstein, S. (1987) *The sexual exploitation of children*. New York: Elsevier.

Goldwert, M. (1986) Childhood seduction and the spiritualization of psychology: The case of Jung and Rank. *Child Abuse and Neglect*. **10,** 555–557.

Grant, L. (1994) Tricks of memory. Article in *The Guardian* 25 April.

Green, R. (1987) *The sissy boy syndrome and the development of homosexuality*. Newhaven, CT: Yale University Press.

Groddeck, G. (1923) *The book of the It*. New York: Basic Books.

Groth, A.N. and H.J.Birnbaum (1979) *Men who rape: the psychology of the offender*. New York: Plenum Press.

Groth, A.N. and H.J. Birnbaum (1987) *Men who rape: The psychology of the offender*. New York : Plenum Press.

Groth, A.N. and A.W. Burgess (1979) Sexual trauma in the life histories of rapists and child molesters. *Victimology: An International Journal*, **4**, 10–16.

Groth, A.N., Hobson, W.F. and Gary, T. (1982) The child molester: Clinical observation, in J. Conte and D. Shore)eds) *Social work and child abuse*, NY: Haworth, 129–144.

Groth, A.N. and F.J. Olivera (1989) Understanding sexual offence behaviour and differentiating among sexual abusers: basic conceptual issues. Ch. 12 in *Vulnerable Populations*, Vol 2. ed. Suzanne M. Sgroi, Lexington MA. Lexington Books.

Hall, E. and S. Lloyd (1989) *Surviving child sexual abuse: a handbook for helping women challenge their past*. London: The Falmer Press.

Hartley, R.E. (1959) Sex-role pressures in the socialisation of the male child. *Psychological Reports*, **5**, 459–468.

Haynes-Seman, C. and R.D. Krugman (1989) Sexualised attention: normal interaction or precursor to sexual abuse? *American Journal of Orthopsychiatry*, **59**: 238–45.

Hewitt, S. (1990) The treatment of sexually abused preschool boys, in *The Sexually Abused Male*, Vol.2 ed. by M. Hunter.

Hindman, J. (1988) New insight into adult and juvenile sex offenders *Community Safety Quarterly* **1** (4): 1.

Holder, D. (1993) Why young abusers are victims too. Article in *The Guardian*; Tuesday, December 14.

Home Office (1993) The offender's tale: Janus studies. Summary details of the new Offender's Index system. Version 3.

Horrocks, R. (1991) The divine woman in Christianity, in *The Absent Mother* ed. by Alix Pirani. London: Mandala.

Hunter, J. (1991) A comparison of the psychosocial maladjustment of adult males and females sexually molested as children. *Journal of Interpersonal Violence*, **6**, (2), 205–217, June.

Hunter, M. (1990a) *The sexually abused male*. Vol.1. Lexington, MA: Lexington Books.

Hunter, M (1990b) *The sexually abused male*. Vol. 2. Lexington MA. Lexington Books.

Hunter, M, (1990c) *Abused boys: the neglected victims of sexual abuse*. Lexington MA; Lexington Books.

Hunter, M and P.N. Gerber (1990) Use of the terms Victim and Survivor in the grief stages commonly seen during recovery from sexual abuse. Ch. 3 in *The sexually abused male* Vol.2. ed. Mic Hunter. Lexington MA: Lexington Books.

Janov, A. (1990) *The new primal scream*.

Johnson, R. and D. Shrier (1987) Past sexual victimisation by females of male patients in an adolescent medicine clinic population. Am. *Journal of Psychiatry*, **144**, 5: 650–652.

Johnson, T.C. (1988) Child perpetrators – children who molest other children: preliminary findings. *Child Abuse and Neglect*, **12**, 219–29.

Johnson, T.C. (1989) Female child perpetrators: children who molest other children. *Child Abuse and Neglect*, **13**, 571–85.

Kaplan, B. (1983) A trio of trials, in Lerner, R.M. (ed.) *Developmental Psychology: Historical and Philosophical Perspectives*, Hillsdale, N.J. Lawrence-Erlbaum, **2**, 27–9, 38.

Kasl, C. (1990) Female perpetrators of sexual abuse: a feminist view, in *The Sexually Abused Male*, Vol.1 M. Hunter (ed) Lexington: Lexington Books.

Kempe, R.S. and C.H. Kempe (1984) *The common secret: Sexual abuse of children and adolescents*. New York: Freeman.

King, M.B (1992) Male sexual assault in the community. Ch.1 in *Male Victims of Sexual Assault*, eds G.C. Mezey and M.B.King. Oxford: Oxford Medical Publications.

Kinread, J.R. (1993) *Child-loving*. London: Routledge.

Kinsey, A.C., W.B. Pomeroy and C.E. Martin (1948) *Sexual behaviour in the human male*. Philadelphia and London: W.B. Saunders Co.

Kinsey, A.C., W.B. Pomeroy, C.E. Martin, and P.H. Gebhard (1953) *Sexual behaviour in the human female*. Philadelphia: W.B. Saunders.

Knopp, F. and L. Lackey (1987) *Female sexual abusers: a summary of data from 44 treatment providers*. Orwell, VT: Safer Society Program.

Krug, R. (1989) Adult male reports of child sexual abuse by mothers: case descriptions, motivations and long-term consequences. *Child Abuse and Neglect*, **13**: 111–119.

Kubler-Ross, E. (1969) *On death and dying*. New York: Macmillan.

Lamb, S. and M. Coakley (1993) 'Normal' childhood sexual play and games: Differentiating play from abuse. *Child Abuse and Neglect*, **17**: 515–526.

Lawson, C. (1993) Mother-son sexual abuse: rare or underreported? A critique of the research. *Child Abuse and Neglect*. **17**, 261–269.

Leonard, L. S. (1982) *The wounded woman*. Athens, Ohio, Chicago: Swallow Press.

Lerner, G. (1986) *The creation of patriarchy*. New York: Oxford Univ. Press.

Levy, A. (1994) Witness to cruelty. Article in *The Guardian*. 26 April.

Lew, M. (1988) *Victims no longer: men recovering from incest and other sexual abuse*. New York: Nevraumont.

Logan, R. (1980) Differential attitudes toward adult behaviours as they relate to child abuse. *Dissertation Abstracts International*. **41** (4–A), 1388.

Maccoby, E.E. and C.N. Jacklin (1974) *The psychology of sex differences*. Stanford: Stanford Univ. Press.

MacFarlane, K. and J. Waterman (1986) eds. *Sexual abuse of young children*. London: Holt, Rinehart & Winston.

Marshall, J. (1981) Making sense of a personal process, in *Human Inquiry* eds. P. Reason and J.Rowan, New York: Wiley & Sons.

Marvasti, J. (1986) Incestuous mothers. *Am. Journal of Forensic Psychiatry*, 7 (4), 63–69.

Masson, J.M. (1984) *The assault on truth: Freud's suppression of the seduction theory*. New York: Farrar, Straus and Giroux.

Masten, A.S. and N.Garmezy (1985) Risk, vulnerability, and protective factors in developmental psychopathology, in *Advances in Clinical Child Psychology*, Vol.8, ed. by B.V. Lahey and A.E. Kazdin, 1–52. New York: Guilford.

Masters W.H. and V.E. Johnson (1982) *Sex and human loving*. Boston: Little Brown.

Masters, W.H., V.E. Johnson and R.C. Kolodny (1985) *Human sexuality* (2nd edn.) Boston: Little Brown.

Mathis, J.L. (1972) *Clear thinking about sexual deviation*. Chicago: Nelson-Hall.

Matthews, R., J.Matthews and K. Speltz (1990) Female sexual offenders. Ch. 13 in *The Sexually Abused Male*, Vol.1, M. Hunter (ed) Lexington MA: Lexington Books.

McCann, I.L., D.K. Sakheim and D.J. Abrahamsom (1988) Trauma and victimisation: a model of psychological adaptation, in *Counseling Psychologist*, Vol. 16 no. 4. October 1988. 531–594.

McCarty, L. (1986) Mother-child incest: Characteristics of the offender. *Child Welfare*, **65**, 5, 447–458.

McHardy, A. and W.Schwartz. (1994) Article in *The Guardian* 6 July, p.3.

McMullen, R.J. (1990) *Enchanted youth*. London: GMP Pubs.

McMullen, R.J. (1990b) *Male rape: breaking the silence on the last taboo*. London: GMP Pubs.

Metcalfe, A. and M. Humphries (eds.) (1985) *The sexuality of men*. London: Pluto Press.

Miller, A. (1983) *For your own good: the roots of violence in childrearing*. New York: Farrar, Straus & Giroux.

Miller, A (1984) *Thou shalt not be aware*. London: Pluto Press.

Moir, A. and D. Jessel (1989) *Brain sex: the real difference between men and women*. London: Michael Joseph.

Money, J. and A.A. Ehrhardt (1972) *Man and woman, boy and girl*. Baltimore: Johns Hopkins University Press.

Myers, M. (1989) Men sexually assaulted as adults and sexually abused as boys. *Archives of Sexual Behaviour*, 18: 203–215.

NSPCC (1989) *Child sexual abuse: listening, hearing and validating the experiences of children*. Ed. by Wattam, C., Hughes, J. and Blagg, H., Harolow: Longman.

NSPCC (1990a) *Listening to children: the professional response to hearing the abused child*. Ed. by Bannister, A., Barrett, K. and Shearer, E., Harlow: Longman.

NSPCC (1990b) *Research Briefing No. 11*. London: NSPCC.

Wattam, C. in Ch. 7. The interface between assessment and therapy, NSPCC (1992) *From hearing to healing: working with the aftermath of child sexual abuse*. Ed. Bannister, A., Harlow: Longman.

O'Brien, M.J. (1989) *Characteristics of male adolescent sibling incest offenders: Preliminary findings*. Orwell, Vermont: Safer Society Press.

O'Hagan, K. (1989) *Working with child sexual abuse*. Milton Keynes: Open Univ.

OPCS/GRO(S) (1991) *Census topic monitor: sex, age and marital status, Great Britain*. OPCS, 1993. ISBN 1 85774 058 0. £2.00.

Osborne, J. (1990) The psychological effects of childhood sexual abuse on women. Social Work Monograph. Norwich: Univ. of East Anglia.

Parkes, P. (1990) *Rescuing the inner child*. London: Souvenir Press (E&A) Ltd.

Peters, S.D., G.E.Wyatt and D. Finkelhor (1986) Prevalence, in *A sourcebook on child sexual abuse* (ed.) D. Finkelhor. Beverly Hills: Sage Publications.

Peterson, C. and M.E.P. Seligman (1983) Learned helplessness and victimisation, *Journal of Social Issues*, **39**: 2, 103–116.

Petrovich, M. and D. Templer (1984) Heterosexual molestation of children who later became rapists. *Psychological Reports*, **54**, 810.

Phillips, A. (1993) *The trouble with boys*. London: Pandora.

Piaget, J. (1929) *The child's conception of the world*. New York: Harcourt, Brace.

Piaget, J. (1952) *The origins of intelligence in children*. New York: Norton.

Pierce, R. and L.H. Pierce (1985) The sexually abused child: A comparison of male and female victims. *Child Abuse and Neglect*, **9**. 191–199.

Pierce, L.H. (1987) Father-son incest: using the literature to guide practice. *Social Casework*, **68**, 67–74.

Pirani, A. (1988) *The absent father*. England: Routledge.

Porter, E. (1986) Treating the young male victim of sexual assault: Issues and intervention strategies. *Syracuse*, New York: Safer Society Press.

Rascovsky, M. and Rascovsky, A. (1950) On consummated incest. *International Journal of Psychoanalysis*, **31**, 42–47.

Reich, W. (1972) *Character analysis*. 3rd edn. New York: Farrar, Straus and Giroux.

Reinhart, M.A. (1987) Sexually abused boys. *Child Abuse and Neglect*, **11**: 229–235.

Reinisch, J. and R. Beasley (1990) *The Kinsey Institute New Report on Sex*. New York: Penguin.

Risin, L.I. and M.P.Koss (1987) The sexual abuse of boys: Prevalence, descriptive characteristics of childhood victimisation. *Journal of Interpersonal Violence*, **2** (3) 309–323.

Rogers, C.M. and T. Terry (1984) Clinical interventions with boy victims of sexual abuse, in *Victims of Sexual Aggression*, edited by I.R. Stuart and J.G, Greer, 91–104. New York: Academic Press.

Russell, D.E.H. (1984) *Sexual exploitation: Rape, child sexual abuse and workplace harassment*. Beverly Hills, CA: Sage.

Russell, J. (1993) *Out of bounds: Sexual exploitation in counselling and therapy*. London: Sage Pubs.

Rutter, P (1990) *Sex in the forbidden zone*. Mandala.

Sanderson, C. (1990) *Counselling adult survivors of child sexual abuse*. London: Jessica Kingsley.

Sansonnet-Hayden, H., G. Haley, C. Marriage and S. Fine (1987) Sexual abuse and psychopathology in hospitalised adolescents. *Journal of the American Academy of*

Child and Adolescent Psychiatry, **26**, 753–757.
Sarles, R.M. (1975) Incest. *Pediatric Clinics of North America*, **21** (3), 633–642.
Sarrel, P. and W. Masters (1982) Sexual molestation of men by women, in *Archives of Sexual Behaviour* **11**:2: 117–31.
Schecter, M.D. and L. Roberge (1976) Sexual exploitation, in *Child Abuse and Neglect: the family in the community*, (ed. R.Helfer and C.H. Kempe) Cambridge, MA: Ballinger.
Schetcky, D.H. and A.H. Green (1988) *Child sexual abuse: A handbook for health care and legal professionals*. New York; Brunner/Mazel.
Scotford, R. (1993) *Newsletter for False Memory Society*, Bradford-on-Avon. U.K.
Seligman, M.E.P.(1975) *Helplessness: on depression, development and death*. San Fransisco: Freeman.
Sepler, F. (1990) Victim advocacy and young male victims of sexual abuse: an evolutionary model. Ch. 3 in *The Sexually Abused Male* Vol.1. Lexington MA: Lexington Books.
Sgroi, S.M. (1975) Child sexual molestation: The last frontier in child abuse. *Children Today*, 44, 18–21.
Sgroi, S.M. (1988) *Vulnerable Populations*, Vol.1. New York: Lexington Books.
Sgroi, S. (1989) *Vulnerable Populations*, Vol. 2. Lexington: Lexington Books.
Sgroi, S.M. and Sargent, N.M. (1993) Impact and treatment issues for victims of child sexual abuse by female perpetrators. Ch.2 in *Female sexual abuse of children: the ultimate taboo*. Ed. by Michele Elliott. Harlow: Longman.
Singer, K.I. (1989) Groupwork with men who experienced incest in childhood. *Am. Journal of Orthopsychiatry*, **59**: 468–72.
Singer, M., D. Hussey and K. Strom (1992) Grooming the victim. *Child Abuse and Neglect*, **16**: 877–886.
Sipe, A.W.R. (1990) *The secret world: Sexuality and the search for celibacy*. New York: Brunner/Mazel Pubs.
Skynner, R. and Cleese, J. (1983) *Families and how to survive them*. London: Methuen.
Sroufe, L.A. and M.J. Ward (1980) Seductive behaviour of mothers and toddlers; Occurrence, Correlates and families of origin. *Child Development*, 51: 1222–1229.
Sroufe, L.A. and M. Rutter (1984) The emergence of developmental psychopathology. *Child Development* **55**: 17–29.
Stevens, A. (1990) *On Jung*. London: Penguin
Storms, M.D. (1981) A theory of erotic orientation development. *Psychological Review*, **85**. 340–353.
Struve, J. (1990) Dancing with patriarchy: The politics of sexual abuse, in *The Sexually Abused Male, Vol. 1* ed. by M. Hunter. New York: Lexington Books.
Summit, R.C. (1983) The child sexual abuse accommodation syndrome. *Child Abuse and Neglect*, **7**, 177–93.
Sykes Wylie, Mary (1993) The False Memory Debate: The Shadow of Doubt in *Networker*. Sept/October issue.
Taylor, D. (1994) The school for unlearning. Article in *The Guardian*: 24 April.
Timms, R. and P. Connors (1990) Integrating psychotherapy and body work for abuse survivors: a psychological model, in *The Sexually Abused Male, Vol. 2*, ed. Mic Hunter. N.Y. Lexington Books.
Urquiza, A.J. (1988) The effects of childhood sexual abuse in an adult male population. Unpublished Doctoral Dissertation, University of Washington, Seattle.
Urquiza, A.J. and L.M. Keating (1990) The impact of sexual abuse:Initial and long-term effects. Ch. 5 in *The Sexually Abused Male* Vol. 1, ed. by M. Hunter, Lexington MA: Lexington Books.
Vander Mey, B.J. (1988) The sexual victimisation of male children: A review of previous research. *Child Abuse and Neglect*, **12**: 61–72.
Walker, L. (1970) *The battered woman*. New York: Harper and Row.

Waterman, J. (1986) Developmental considerations. Ch. 2 in *Sexual abuse in young children*. F. MacFarlane and J. Waterman (eds.) London: Holt, Reinhart and Winston.

Watkins, W. and A. Bentovim (1992) Male children and adolescents as victims: a review of current knowledge, in *Male victims of sexual assault* ed. by G.C. Mezey and M.B. King. London: Oxford University Press.

West, D.J. (1992) Homophobia: covert and overt. Ch. 2 in *Male victims of sexual assault* ed. by G.C. Mezey and M.B. King. London: Oxford University Press.

Whitfield C. (1989) *A gift to myself: a workbook and guide to healing my child within*. Deerfield Beach, Fla: Health Communications.

Woollett. E. (1993) Report to the Annual General Meeting of 'Survivors'. January.

Wyatt, G. (1987) Maximising appropriate populations and responses for sex research. Paper presented at a conference entitled 'Sex and Aids' at the Kinsey Institute, Bloomington, Indiana, December.

Wyatt, G.E. and M.R. Mickey (1987) Ameliorating the effects of child sexual abuse. *Journal of Interpersonal Violence*, 2: 403–414.

Wyatt, G.E. and G. Powell (1988) *Lasting effects of child sexual abuse*. Newbury Park: Calif. Sage Pubs.

Wyre, R. and A. Swift (1990) *Women, men and rape*. London: Hodder and Stoughton.